The Cambridge Companion to the Singer-Songwriter

Most often associated with modern artists such as Bob Dylan, Elton John, Don McLean, Neil Diamond, and Carole King, the singer-songwriter tradition in fact has a long and complex history dating back to the Medieval troubadour and earlier. This *Companion* explains the historical contexts, musical analyses, and theoretical frameworks of what it means to be a singer-songwriter. Divided into five parts, the book explores the singer-songwriter tradition in the context of issues including authenticity, gender, queer studies, musical analysis, and performance. The contributors reveal how the tradition has been expressed around the world and throughout its history to the present day. Essential reading for enthusiasts, practitioners, students, and scholars, this book features case studies of a wide range of both well and lesser-known singer-songwriters, from Thomas d'Urfey through to Carole King and Kanye West.

KATHERINE WILLIAMS is Lecturer in Music at the University of Plymouth. Her monograph *Rufus Wainwright* is forthcoming in 2016 and she has published in *Jazz Perspectives*, *Jazz Research Journal* and *Journal of Music History Pedagogy*. She was awarded the Ella Fitzgerald Charitable Foundation/Jazz Education Network Research Fellowship 2015 to conduct research on Duke Ellington. She is active as a saxophonist, and regularly works with contemporary composers to create and perform new music for saxophone and electronics.

JUSTIN A. WILLIAMS is Lecturer in Music at the University of Bristol, and the author of *Rhymin and Stealin: Musical Borrowing in Hip-Hop* (2013) and editor of *The Cambridge Companion to Hip-Hop* (Cambridge, 2015). As a professional trumpet and piano player in California, he ran a successful jazz piano trio and played with the band Bucho!, which won a number of Sacramento Area Music Awards and were signed to two record labels.

The Cambridge Companion to

THE SINGER-
SONGWRITER

. . . .

EDITED BY
Katherine Williams and
Justin A. Williams

CAMBRIDGE
UNIVERSITY PRESS

CAMBRIDGE
UNIVERSITY PRESS

University Printing House, Cambridge CB2 8BS, United Kingdom

Cambridge University Press is part of the University of Cambridge.

It furthers the University's mission by disseminating knowledge in the pursuit of education, learning and research at the highest international levels of excellence.

www.cambridge.org
Information on this title: www.cambridge.org/9781107680913

First published 2016

Printed in the United Kingdom by TJ International Ltd. Padstow Cornwall

A catalogue record for this publication is available from the British Library

Library of Congress Cataloguing in Publication data

Names: Williams, Katherine (Katherine Ann) | Williams, Justin A.
Title: The Cambridge companion to the singer-songwriter / edited by Katherine Williams and Justin A. Williams.
Description: Cambridge : Cambridge University Press, 2016. | Includes
   bibliographical references and index.
Identifiers: LCCN 2015029103| ISBN 9781107063648 (hardback) | ISBN
   9781107680913 (pbk.)
Subjects: LCSH: Popular music—History and criticism. | Popular
   music—Writing and publishing. | Songs—History and criticism.
Classification: LCC ML3470 .C364 2016 | DDC 782.4209—dc23 LC record
available at http://lccn.loc.gov/2015029103

ISBN 978-1-107-06364-8 Hardback
ISBN 978-1-107-68091-3 Paperback

Dedicated to our parents: Michael and Valerie Lewis, Vicki Corda and Richard Williams.

Contents

Figures

Music examples

Contributors

Marcus Aldredge is Associate Professor of Sociology at Iona College, New York. His areas of scholarly interest include culture, interactionism and deviance. His book *Singer-Songwriters and Musical Open Mics* was published in 2013 and the co-edited anthology *David Riesman's Unpublished Writings and Continuing Legacy* is due in 2015.

Phil Allcock is a PhD candidate at the University of Huddersfield whose research interests include topics such as stardom and celebrity, gender and identity, and computer-aided methods of analysis. Central to his work is the way in which humans create, interact with, and interpret music.

Simon Barber is a Researcher in the Birmingham Centre for Media and Cultural Research at Birmingham City University. He has published work in *The European Journal of Cultural Studies*, *The Radio Journal*, *The Journal on the Art of Record Production*, and the *Jazz Research Journal* among others.

Lucy Bennett completed her PhD in online fandom at the Cardiff School of Journalism, Media and Cultural Studies (JOMEC), Cardiff University. Her work appears in journals such as *New Media & Society*, *Journal of Fandom Studies*, *Transformative Works and Cultures*, *Social Semiotics*, *Continuum*, *Cinema Journal*, *Celebrity Studies*, and *Participations*. She is also the co-founder of the Fan Studies Network.

Christa Anne Bentley is a PhD candidate in musicology at the University of North Carolina at Chapel Hill. Her research focuses on the politics of popular music at the intersections of folk and commercial styles. Her dissertation considers elements of the local scene as well as national social movements that shape the development and reception of the 1970s singer-songwriter movement in Los Angeles.

Megan Berry teaches Ear Training, Harmony and Media Theory in the School of Media Arts at the Waikato Institute of Technology in Hamilton, New Zealand. She is a singer-songwriter who gigs locally with her band, The Heartbreak Kids. Her research interests include gender and popular music, and creativity and play.

Sarah Boak is a Teaching Fellow in Twentieth-Century Music at the University of Southampton, where she is also writing up her PhD. Her thesis examines 'phono-somatics' – the relationship between embodiment and voice in recorded music – in the work of female singer-songwriters debuting in the 1990s.

Michael Borshuk is the author of *Swinging the Vernacular: Jazz and African American Modernist Literature* (Routledge, 2006), and numerous essays and book chapters on African American literature, American modernism, and music. From 1999 to 2009, he wrote on jazz for the magazine *Coda*. He teaches at Texas Tech University.

Nick Braae is a doctoral student in the Conservatorium of Music at the University of Waikato, New Zealand, where he is writing a thesis on the music of British rock band Queen. Other research interests include New Zealand popular music and issues of cultural identity.

Lori Burns is Professor of Music at the University of Ottawa. Her work on gender and popular music has been published in leading journals, edited collections, and in monograph form (*Disruptive Divas: Feminism, Identity and Popular Music*). Her research on gender and popular music is supported by the Social Sciences and Humanities Research Council of Canada (2013–18).

Jo Collinson Scott holds an AHRC-funded PhD in musicological 'schizoanalysis' and is a Lecturer in Music at the University of the West of Scotland. She writes, records and performs as a singer-songwriter under the name Jo Mango and has toured internationally, playing in the backing band of Vashti Bunyan.

Joshua S. Duchan researches American popular music. His first book, *Powerful Voices* (2012), examined collegiate a cappella groups. He is currently writing a book about Billy Joel's music. He is Assistant Professor of Music at Wayne State University, where he teaches music history and ethnomusicology.

Franco Fabbri is a musician and musicologist, and teaches popular music and sound studies at the University of Turin. His main interests are in the fields of genre theories and music typologies, the impact of media and technology across genres and musical cultures, and the history of popular music.

Kevin Fellezs is an Assistant Professor of Music at Columbia University with a joint appointment in the Institute for Research in African American Studies. His book, *Birds of Fire: Jazz, Rock, Funk and the Creation of Fusion* (2011), is a study of fusion (jazz–rock–funk) music of the 1970s.

Mark Finch is a PhD candidate in ethnomusicology at Memorial University of Newfoundland. His research interests include urban development, music scenes and networks, and alternative histories of popular music. Portions of his research have appeared in *Popular Music and Society*, *MUSICultures*, and *Canadian Folk Music*.

Katy Hamilton is a freelance researcher, writer and presenter on music. She has taught at the Royal College of Music, the University of Nottingham, and Middlesex University. Her research specialisms include the music of Johannes Brahms and his contemporaries, and early twentieth-century British concert life.

Timothy Koozin is Professor and Division Chair of Music Theory at the Moores School of Music, University of Houston. His research interests include music and meaning, popular music, film music, and music instructional technology. He is co-author of two textbooks for theory and aural skills.

Marc Lafrance is Associate Professor of Sociology at Concordia University. His research relates to representations of gender, sexuality, and the body in popular media culture and has been published in a variety of refereed journals and edited collections. His current research project on gender and popular music (with Lori Burns) is supported by the Social Sciences and Humanities Research Council of Canada (2013–18).

Natasha Loges is co-editor of *Brahms in the Home and the Concert Hall* (Cambridge, 2014) and has published in various journals including *Music & Letters*. She oversees the postgraduate programmes at the Royal College of Music, London.

Mark Marrington is an academic specialising in a number of music-related areas including popular musicology and creative uses of music technology. He currently holds positions at York St John University and the University of Leeds, teaching in subjects ranging from the musicology of record production to computer-based music composition.

Chris McDonald is Assistant Professor of Music at Cape Breton University. He is the author of *Rush, Rock Music, and the Middle Class: Dreaming in Middletown* (2009), and is currently researching singer-songwriters as well as the Celtic fiddle tradition of Cape Breton.

Tōru Mitsui is Professor Emeritus at Kanazawa University, where he taught English and musicology. His chapter in the present volume is a shortened and revised version of 'Thomas D'Urfey' originally written in Japanese in 1968 without using the embryonic term singer-songwriter.

Allan F. Moore writes mainly about popular song in its various guises. Recent books include the monograph *Song Means*, and the co-edited collections *Legacies of Ewan MacColl* and *Song Interpretation in 21st-century Pop Music*.

madison moore is a Research Associate in 'Modern Moves' in the Department of English at King's College London. His writing on performance, popular culture, and music has appeared in *Vice*, *Interview* magazine, *Art in America*, the *Journal of Popular Music Studies*, and *Theater* magazine. His first book, *The Theory of the Fabulous Class*, is forthcoming.

Josep Pedro is a pre-doctoral researcher at Complutense University of Madrid, Department of Journalism III. He has published articles in the International Association for the Study of Popular Music Journal, *Cuadernos de Información y Comunicación*, *Revista de Estudios Norteamericanos* and in collective books like *The Handbook of Texas Music* (2012), and has written chapters in the volumes *Jazz and Totalitarianism* (forthcoming) and *Talking Back to Globalization: Texts and Practices* (forthcoming).

Sarah Suhadolnik is a PhD candidate in historical musicology at the University of Michigan, interested in jazz, popular music, and the music of the United States. She has presented her work at a number of national and international conferences, and has contributed to the New Grove Dictionary of American Music.

David R. Shumway is Professor of English and Literary and Cultural Studies, and the founding Director of the Humanities Center at Carnegie Mellon University. He is the author most recently of *Rock Star: The Making of Musical Icons from Elvis to Springsteen*.

Jennifer Taylor holds a PhD in Music from York University (Canada), where she is a Sessional Lecturer. Her research and teaching interests are in the areas of popular music, ethnomusicology, gender, music education, and female youth culture.

Rupert Till is Reader in Music at the University of Huddersfield. His research covers popular music composition and performance; the art of record production; prehistoric music and archaeoacoustics; electronic dance music cultures; popular icons and stardom; and religion and popular music. He is currently Chair of the International Association for the Study of Popular Music UK and Ireland Branch, and Director of the University of Huddersfield's Popular Music Studies Research Group.

Ioannis Tsioulakis is a Lecturer in Anthropology and Ethnomusicology at Queen's University Belfast. His research focuses on markets of musical labour and discourses of value in Greek popular music. Ioannis is also a professional pianist, composer, and arranger.

Jada Watson is a PhD candidate in Musicology at Université Laval; her research interests include geography, environment, politics, and identity in country music. She has contributed to *The Grove Dictionary of American Music*, and her work on the Dixie Chicks appears in the *Journal of the Society for American Music* and *Popular Music*.

Justin A. Williams is Lecturer in Music at Bristol University (UK). He is the author of *Rhymin and Stealin: Musical Borrowing in Hip-hop* (2013) and is editor of *The Cambridge Companion to Hip-hop* (2015). He is co-editor of this volume and co-editor (with Katherine Williams) of *The Singer-Songwriter Handbook* (forthcoming).

Katherine Williams is Lecturer in Music at Plymouth University (UK). In addition to co-editing and contributing to this volume, she is co-editing and contributing to *The Singer-Songwriter Handbook* (forthcoming, also with Justin Williams). Her first monograph, *Rufus Wainwright*, will be published in Spring 2016.

Alyssa Woods holds a PhD in Music Theory from the University of Michigan and teaches at University of Ottawa as well as Carleton University. Her dissertation examined race and gender in rap and hip-hop and she has published articles in this domain in a number of journals and edited volumes.

Acknowledgements

Many of the ideas in this volume have been prompted or investigated organically in the many higher education courses we have taught on popular music and production. In particular, Katherine's Music Production students at Leeds College of Music (cohorts of 2011–13), and Justin's Popular Music students at Anglia Ruskin University (2010–12), deserve thanks for the initial exploration of ideas. Education is a two-way process: you all, in your own way, helped to develop this concept.

Our thanks go to all scholars and acquaintances who have tolerated discussions about the themes and issues surrounding the figure of the singer-songwriter. Katherine is particularly grateful to Stan Hawkins and her colleague Bethany Lowe, both of whom who offered prompt and helpful comments on a late draft of her own contribution to this *Companion*.

We both would like to thank all the contributors to this volume. They were all prompt and professional, and also easy to work with. Many more individuals wanted to contribute to this than we could include, and we also thank them for their interest and for contributing to academic singer-songwriter studies in various arenas. Special thanks to Marcus Aldredge, Simon Barber and Jo Collinson Scott who participated in a special panel on the singer-songwriter at the International Association for Popular Music in University College, Cork in September 2014. And thanks to Lori Burns, Marc Lafrance and Alyssa Woods for letting Justin read their Kanye West paper at the conference. We would like to thank our current institutions, the University of Bristol and Plymouth University, for providing research support for the volume.

We especially want to thank Victoria Cooper at Cambridge University Press for being open-minded enough to listen and discuss the importance of the singer-songwriter to music history and music education. We would also like to thank Fleur Jones, Emma Collison and Kate Brett, the last-named of whom has taken over from Vicki as music editor and has done a fantastic job. The music department at the University of Bristol were generous in helping provide some additional subvention funds for permission costs, and we would like to thank Professor Katharine Ellis for her support in this endeavour. Thanks also to Benedict Todd for helping with some musical examples towards the end of the project.

At the risk of sounding self-congratulatory, we would like to thank each other for a productive and pleasant collaboration. Many colleagues and peers warned about the potential stress and dangers of collaborating with your spouse, but the process has been nothing but a pleasure.

This book is dedicated to our parents, who have been constant sources of encouragement and enthusiasm. Justin: Thanks to my mom, Vicki Corda, who taught me about 1970s singer-songwriters like Carole King and Carly Simon, and my dad, Richard Williams, who taught me about singer-songwriters such as Jim Croce and Roy Orbison. Katherine: Michael and Valerie are enthusiasts of the singer-songwriter idiom, and although they are not musicians by trade they keep the tradition alive. In my youth, they sang Peter, Paul and Mary songs, and two years ago (2013) they attended a Nick Cave performance. Since my childhood passions emerged, they nurtured and supported my loves of music and reading, and have always allowed me the time and space to develop these interests. So this is for you, Mum and Dad: a book, about music.

Introduction

KATHERINE WILLIAMS AND JUSTIN A. WILLIAMS

The year 2014 was a good year for singer-songwriters past and present. The most visible in 2014 was Ed Sheeran, whose album *X* spent a non-consecutive twelve weeks at number 1 (the longest run since Adele's *21*), and, perhaps an even better indicator of success in this digital age, was the most streamed album on Spotify in 2014. In fact, 2014 was a good year for British artists in general as it was the only year that the top-10 UK albums chart was entirely dominated by British artists, and the top four (Sheeran, Sam Smith, George Ezra, Paolo Nutini) are often defined as singer-songwriters.[1] The year 2014 also saw two Tony Awards go to the new musical *Beautiful* about the life and work of the singer-songwriter Carole King. King, one of the defining artists of the genre, is becoming part of a history of singer-songwriters as musical genre that arguably lives on with newer artists like Sheeran.

If BBC documentaries are anything to go by, the figure of the singer-songwriter has been firmly planted into cultural consciousness in recent years. In 2011 Morgan Neville's documentary *Troubadours: The Rise of the Singer-Songwriter* aired in England on BBC4 alongside compilation footage entitled 'Singer-Songwriters at the BBC' that featured Elton John's 'Your Song' and other artists such as James Taylor, Cat Stevens, Harry Nilsson, Sandy Denny, Steve Goodman, Joni Mitchell, Neil Young, Judee Sill, Jackson Browne, Neil Diamond, Tim Hardin, Joan Armatrading, Tom Waits, and many others. The documentary chronicles the Los Angeles scene in the 1970s and features iconic figures such as King and James Taylor.[2]

Hundreds of higher education institutions in the UK and America feature songwriting and performance, essentially teaching today's music students to be singer-songwriters as well as to hone and refine existing techniques and abilities. There is a keen enthusiasm for the idiom amongst these students, who often perceive it as a natural and unmediated expression of their emotions through music. Yet despite the four decades of chart success, documentary coverage, biographies, and autobiographies, and the desirability of the idiom to music students, the academic literature on singer-songwriters has been sparse. We hope that this volume begins a wider academic conversation about the phenomenon, genre, performance traditions, and geographical spaces of the singer-songwriter.

But what does it mean to be a singer-songwriter? Tim Wise poses a useful definition: 'Singer-songwriter is a term used since the 1960s to describe a category of popular musician who composes and performs his or her own songs, typically to acoustic guitar or piano accompaniment, most often as a solo act but also with backing musicians, especially in recordings.'[3] Yet he is also right to note the difficulty in considering 'singer-songwriter' as a stylistic genre since singer-songwriters draw from a wide variety of styles (for example, Joni Mitchell) and lyrical themes. It is for this reason that artists such as Hoagy Carmichael, Leadbelly (see Chapter 9), Chuck Berry, Barry Manilow, Bob Marley, Dolly Parton (see Chapter 10), Brian Wilson, Paul McCartney, Paul Anka, or Kanye West (see Chapter 14) will not be generically defined as 'singer-songwriter' in the media any time soon even though they fit Wise's (and our wider) definition.

This volume embraces the complexities of such a condition, and in most cases we have been able to look at artists who perform their own material as the starting point. In some cases (as with Adele, or Elton John), the material written is part of a collaborative process, yet audiences associate authorship with the star performer/persona. In Chapter 1, David Shumway sets the scene with the conventional notion of singer-songwriters that rose out of the late 1960s contexts and into the 1970s before moving on to more historical and varied perspectives. As he notes: '"singer-songwriter" is not anyone who sings his or her own songs, but a performer whose self-presentation and musical form fit a certain model'. He proceeds to point out that the future of singer-songwriters was not necessarily bound by the confessionalism of the early examples, but that it most certainly retained the expectation for 'authentic individual expression'. The collection of chapters that follows embraces stylistic variety, musically speaking, and also embraces both the 'professional' singer-songwriter (King, Joel, Newman) and those who emerged from less formal training and vocational practice (Mitchell, Dylan, Newsom, and many of the yet-to-be-discovered performers at open mic nights). Although the book takes the UK and the USA as its starting point, many chapters explore perspectives further afield: we offer a snapshot of global practices such as New Zealand (Nick Braae, Chapter 27), Italy, and Greece (Franco Fabbri and Ioannis Tsioulakis, Chapter 28).

A tension emerges with the widening definition of 'singer-songwriter' that we have encouraged. We have intentionally kept the definition flexible in order to fully investigate the ideological threads around such a categorisation. First of all, some of the artists within this volume will meet with resistance in terms of their categorisation as 'singer-songwriter'. The *Companion* is not an attempt at a comprehensive history of the singer-songwriter, nor a list of great men and women who have contributed to the genre. Although many of the case studies command the label of singer-songwriters (Joni Mitchell, Billy Joel, Elton John, Tori Amos), they often have a purpose of highlighting wider issues in popular music and its surrounding themes.

The book is not necessarily intended to be read from start to finish (though one could do this and the trajectory is logical). The reader can dip in at any point and work through chapters in any order. We intend to host a companion website which should direct readers to further reading, discographies, and music videos to supplement the journey.

The authors in this collection offer many widely varied analytical frameworks to consider the music and sociological themes surrounding the singer-songwriter tradition. There is a recurring theme of performer persona of the singer-songwriter as unmediated, and a number of chapters discuss the tension between the individualised persona and the (often) highly constructive and collaborative process of creating that persona (with figures like Adele, Elton John, and Bill Monroe). Another theme is the ability of singer-songwriters to defy stereotypes, either in terms of their own gendered identities, or stereotypes associated with their genre (for example, the 'female singer-songwriter' categorisation as 'women's music' and stereotypes attached to such a label). Artists such as k.d. lang, Rufus Wainwright, and Joni Mitchell subvert traditional notions of genre, gender and sexuality through both music and extra-musical factors (see Williams, Chapter 20). Joni Mitchell, though marketed as expressing 'female perspectives' (Fellezs, Chapter 18), tried to complicate female stereotypes of the singer-songwriter which arguably go back into the nineteenth century, as shown to us by Hamilton and Loges in Chapter 2. As they tell us, most singers of German Lied were female: 'the Lied evolved from a technically undemanding type of music largely aimed at amateur (often female) singers', as well as Lieder being appropriate for women in ways that opera was not perceived to be. And yet while physically confined to the salon, the Lied was also a space of freedom, a safe space for women to explore creative, compositional ideas, and as such represented one of the few spaces in nineteenth-century Europe that this had been accepted. In pop today, male producers and engineers grossly outnumber women, and it seems that the singer-songwriter genre is still an (unfortunately) rare space for women to explore their creativity.

The relationship between the old and new singer-songwriter can also be seen in newer artist James Blake performing Joni Mitchell's 'A Case of You' at his 2011 debut performance at the historic *Troubadour* club in Los Angeles (recounted in Bentley, Chapter 6). Mitchell was in the VIP section that night, and despite Blake's stylistic differences to Mitchell, it was clear they were part of a lineage of stylistically eclectic singer-songwriters. Both have an interesting relationship to race, Blake being part of the 'blue-eyed

soul' British interest in black music seen in a number of white British artists, and Mitchell's interest in black music as well as black identity (even
becoming a black man named 'Claude' for a party, as well as on the cover
of her *Don Juan's Reckless Daughter* from 1977).

Furthermore, the theoretical frames used in the book will be applicable
to cases beyond the singer-songwriters in this book, and beyond the genre
as a whole. From the use of Deleuze and Guattari's 'becoming other' (in
Chapter 17), gender theories (Chapter 22), geographies of the Troubadour
(Chapter 6), the Brill Building (Chapter 5) and English localisms in folk
(Chapter 4), Allan Moore's distinction between first-, second-, and third-
person authenticity (Chapters 16, 20 and 26), Schechner's theories of
performance (Chapter 21), liminality and *communitas* (Chapter 25), or
Moore's persona–environment model (Chapter 27), the book provides
not only historical snapshots but models for analysis and theorisation.

The volume is divided into thematically related sections. Part I
explores the birth and establishing of the tradition, beginning with
Shumway's exploration of the etymology of the term 'singer-songwriter'.
In Chapter 2, Loges and Hamilton return to the German Lied composer-
performers of the eighteenth century, demonstrating a way in which the
tradition developed outside typically expected norms. In Chapter 3, Mark
Finch discusses Bill Monroe as part of the post-war subgenre of country
music known as bluegrass. Finch uses Monroe's 'Uncle Pen' (1949–50) as
an example of collaborative songwriting in a system that valued (financially and ideologically) individual authorship. What this chapter shows,
as does Till's case study of Adele, that 'song authorship is not only determined by creative practice, but is influenced by the mechanisms of the
commercial music realm' (Finch, p. 44). Chapter 4 looks at another post-
war phenomenon, this time across the pond, of the singer-songwriters of
the English folk revival. Allan F. Moore examines themes such as politics,
regionality, humour, emotion, the supernatural and the tradition to reveal
a diverse group of British artists that fall squarely within a broad notion
of folk and singer-songwriter traditions. In Chapter 5, Simon Barber
considers the Brill Building and Aldon Music, explaining the practices
of songwriting teams and individuals that operated from this important New York centre in the 1960s. Some of the artists that were associated with the New York City scene just discussed, including King, would
find their artistry recognised through performances at the Los Angeles
Troubadour, and Christa Anne Bentley discusses the origins, geography,
and success of the venue in Chapter 6. She shows how the Troubadour
'became the premiere establishment for singer-songwriters', a venue that
still has a great deal of importance for up-and-coming acts wishing to add
their names to the great canon of King, John, Mitchell, Taylor, and others. In Chapter 7, Michael Borshuk outlines three case studies that help

debunk the common myth that the professionalised singer-songwriter had gone away by the 1970s. He looks at the stylistic eclecticism of Randy Newman, Billy Joel, and Walter Becker and Donald Fagen of Steely Dan as a cross-fertilisation across ethnic lines. Borshuk notes the importance of professional craftsmanship in their work, while additionally promoting a 'personal' style that fit within the ethos of the singer-songwriter.

Stepping outside a conventional chronological narrative, Part II considers individuals that could be broadly defined as singer-songwriters, covering a range of genres and eras. In Chapter 8, Tōru Mitsui investigates the English singer-songwriter, poet, satirist, and playwright Thomas D'Urfey, whose style divided opinion under the reign of Charles II. In Chapter 9, Josep Pedro considers the outlaw bluesman archetype in the blues musician Leadbelly, and the mutually beneficial relationship he had with John and Alan Lomax in the 1930s and 40s. Place-based narratives in Dolly Parton's concept album *My Tennessee Mountain Home* (1973) form the basis of the analysis in Chapter 10 by Jada Watson. The autobiographical tone of the album emphasised her poor, rural roots and was a crossroads in her career, taking it in a different and more successful direction. Chapter 11 looks at Elton John as author and brand, his performance persona adding to the notion of singer-songwriter although he is only one half of a songwriting collaboration. Joshua S. Duchan analyses three songs by Billy Joel that depict working-class life in Chapter 12. In Chapter 13, Timothy Koozin looks at the body and gesture in the creative process through the guitar tuning and gestural movement of the music of Nick Drake. Lori Burns, Alyssa Woods, and Marc Lafrance step into the digital realm in Chapter 14, investigating the art of storytelling in hip-hop, fitting Kanye West into a broad categorisation of singer-songwriter, connecting closely and intimately with his instrument: the sampler. A multi-media analysis of three West videos demonstrates complex critiques of fame, consumer culture, race, and class. In Chapter 15 madison moore investigates how post-dubstep sounds embrace digital technologies and club culture while fitting into singer-songwriter tropes in the music of London-based artist James Blake. Sarah Suhadolnik (Chapter 16) looks at the confessional songwriting from the 'Queen of Heartbreak' Adele, the 'anti-Gaga', with stripped-down performances such as her appearance at the Royal Albert Hall that reflect a specific artistic persona within the broader landscape of mainstream pop. Chapter 17 looks at the artist Joanna Newsom, including a close reading of her song 'Only Skin'. Jo Collinson Scott reclaims the oft-used concept of authenticity by reframing it within the concept of Deleuze and Guattari's 'becoming other', to paint a more nuanced picture than the usual reception of Newsom as part of 'New Weird America' in folk.

Part III shifts focus to further theoretical avenues in terms of gender and sexuality in particular. Like Newsom's work that arguably works against stereotypical 'female' singer-songwriter categorisation, Chapter 18 looks at issues of gender and race in Joni Mitchell's work in the 1970s. Mitchell was not willing to be defined as a 'female singer-songwriter', and interviews and early marketing demonstrate these tensions. According to Fellezs, her 'performance alterity' was to explore possibilities as well as testing the limits of identity claims. In Chapter 19, Jennifer Taylor discusses the all-female music festival Lilith Fair in the late 1990s. While Taylor argues that the festival did not revolutionise the music industry, it did help female community formation, and the chapter is an interesting investigation of the layout and demographics of the various stages that comprised the festival. Katherine Williams' Chapter 20 involves three case studies over the past half-century that demonstrate an increase in openness and tolerance of LGBTQ singer-songwriters: Elton John, k.d. lang, and Rufus Wainwright all complicate the heteronormative pop mainstream, and their own openness about their sexuality (in different eras) paralleled increasing visibility in both mainstream popular culture and in musicology as an academic discipline. Tori Amos is the sole subject of Chapter 21, where Chris McDonald discusses her as a shaman figure. Known as a confessional and intimate performer, Amos also draws from mythology and religious symbolism, and is a performer of 'healing songs'. In this way she mediates between a spirit and material world to a wide and loyal fan base. This extended metaphor and all it entails, as McDonald argues, is a main factor in what gives Amos such legitimacy in the singer-songwriter realm. Chapter 22 discusses gender, identity, and the queer gaze (adapting Mulvey's concept of the 'male gaze') with three artists who destabilise typical binary notions of gender: KT Tunstall (UK), Missy Higgins (Australia), and Bic Runga (New Zealand). Through an analysis of music videos, Megan Berry shows how these female musicians perform distinctive 'female masculinities' that appeal to a queer gaze. Chapter 23 focuses on a specific moment in the history of singer-songwriters, the early 1990s and the rise of a highly creative and talented 'group' of females, more distinctive than similar yet often treated similarly in the press due to their shared gender. With artists such as PJ Harvey, Björk, Tori Amos and Ani DiFranco, and many others, Sarah Boak explores themes of embodied femininity, sexuality and female power in their work.

Part IV expands the focus and analytical frameworks further to interrogate education, scenes, and emotion. In Chapter 24, Mark Marrington looks at key themes and threads of songwriting pedagogy and the relationship between theory and practice. Marcus Aldredge looks at the 'open mic' night as a liminal and ritualistic space. He looks at the social rituals of performing, the musical pilgrim that becomes part of a community as well as a journey (Chapter 25). Rupert Till suggests that the singer-songwriter is a subset of 'the composer' in Chapter 26, and uses theories from Nattiez,

Attali, and Moore, as well as interviews with songwriters, to investigate the term. The chapter closes with an account of Adele's 'Someone Like You', and how subject matter, music and live performances mediate emotion for both performer and audience.

The final section, Part V, expands the geographies away from England and America, as well as embracing digital fan communities and marketing. Chapter 27 looks at local authenticity in New Zealand singer-songwriter Don McGlashan, while Chapter 28 provides a comparative overview of post-war Greek and Italian traditions. As Fabbri and Tsioulakis note, their singer-songwriter traditions sound little alike but both have parallel histories, and in some cases, similar influences (such as Bob Dylan). In the final chapter (Chapter 29), Lucy Bennett looks at singer-songwriters in the digital age. She argues that the confessional and personal natures of singer-songwriters translate well into social media such as Twitter, Facebook and Instagram. From Tori Amos' posted setlists on Twitter, Imogen Heap's request for sounds to become 'song seeds' in her work, and James Blunt's humorous responses to 'trolls' on Twitter, Bennett outlines an exciting and varied space that can only become more utilised by artists in multifarious ways as we progress further into the twenty-first century.

The personal communicative impulse in music is a highly desirable phenomenon by audiences: we want great composers to communicate their feelings via symphony orchestra and we want Adele to tell us about her break-up with her voice and a piano. Both are arguably intensified from a Romantic-era subjectivity, but have existed much longer than that. For many, it is that search for the 'authentic' performer, unmediated by industry agendas and commercial impulses, a chance to experience humanity through music. We hope that this volume begins an academic conversation about a wide nexus of music that we have broadly termed the singer-songwriter. Read, listen, think, debate and enjoy.

Notes

1 The rest of the list includes Coldplay, Paloma Faith, One Direction, Olly Murs, Pink Floyd, and Take That. Some of these names, and individual performers within the groups, could be interpreted as singer-songwriters in the broader sense of the term.

2 'Singer-Songwriters at the BBC' is just one of a series of compilations created for and aired by the BBC in recent years. Other topics include *Prog at the BBC, Synth Britannia at the BBC,*

Southern Rock at the BBC, Irish Rock, New York Rock, Hip-Hop, Folk, and Reggae.

3 Wise's excellent dictionary article on the singer-songwriter sets up the 1960s music industry context for the rise of the singer-songwriter as genre. See Tim Wise, 'Singer-Songwriter', in John Shepard and David Horn (eds.), *Continuum Encyclopedia of Popular Music of the Worlds,* vol. 8, *Genres* (London: Bloomsbury, 2012), pp. 430–3.

PART I

Establishing a tradition

1 The emergence of the singer-songwriter

DAVID R. SHUMWAY

The category and perception of a class of performers known as singer-songwriters did not emerge into public consciousness until after 1968. Indeed, Google Ngram shows that the term 'singer songwriter' has no usage prior to the early 1970s. It is true that there were individuals referred to as 'singer and songwriter' as early as the 1870s, and earlier in the twentieth century the descriptions 'singer songwriter' and 'songwriter-singer' were used. These terms are rare, however, after World War II.[1] The 'singer-songwriter' is not anyone who sings his or her own songs, but a performer whose self-presentation and musical form fit a certain model. There had been rock singers who wrote their own songs since Chuck Berry, but they were not singer-songwriters. Bob Dylan, who helped create the conditions for their emergence, was not himself called a singer-songwriter in 1968, and he did not produce an album that fit the label until *Blood on the Tracks* in 1974. While the singer-songwriter becomes highly visible in 1970, in retrospect we can see that the movement emerged in 1968, when Leonard Cohen, Joni Mitchell, and Laura Nyro released important early examples. What distinguished the singer-songwriter was both a musical shift away from the more raucous styles of rock and a lyrical shift from the more public concerns that had helped to define the folk revival. By the early 1970s, James Taylor, Mitchell, Carole King, Jackson Browne, Carly Simon, and others created a new niche in the popular music market. These singer-songwriters were not apolitical, but they took a confessional stance in their songs, revealing their interior selves and their private struggles.

The year 1968 was a turning point not only because it was the high-watermark of the New Left, but also because it saw the assassinations of Robert Kennedy and Martin Luther King, the bloody police riot at the Democratic National Convention in Chicago, and the disappointment of Richard Nixon being elected President and the Vietnam War continuing unabated. Up until 1968, youth culture was hopeful about progressive change and about individual opportunities, but the events of that year began to alter the dominant outlook. In the summer of 1969, Woodstock provided a few months of uplift, but the shift was solidified in the reading given to the free concert at Altamont in December. The anti-war movement would continue, of course, and the student strikes of the 1970, which shut down more than 450 campuses in the wake of the Kent State shootings and the US invasion of Cambodia, might be seen as the largest manifestation of the student Left, but also its last gasp. There would be no major campus 'unrest' in the years that followed. In the summer of 1969, Students for a Democratic Society, the leading New Left organisation, disintegrated. One of its fragments, the Weatherman faction, turned to a strategy of violence it hoped would incite the working class to join them. It resulted rather in the opposite reaction, and made the New Left look loony, dangerous, and out of touch. There had been sporadic violence throughout the 1960s, but as *Time* reported in early 1971, even the Weatherman group, by then reduced to a tiny underground contingent, had publicly forsworn violence after an explosion killed three of its own in a Manhattan apartment used for bomb-making. *Time* noted this as part of what it called 'the cooling of America', discussed in a ten-page special section, which observed that 'In rock music … a shift can be perceived from acid rock to the soft ballads of Neil Young, Gordon Lightfoot, and James Taylor'.[2]

Time's 'cooling' thesis is questionable with regard to music. The Rolling Stones, Led Zeppelin, Black Sabbath, and Grand Funk Railroad represented the emergence in the early 1970s of what Steve Waksman has dubbed 'arena rock', the latter three representing the roots of what would by the end of the decade be known as heavy metal. As Waksman's title, *This Ain't No Summer of Love*, suggests, he also sees the 'decline of the sixties', but in favour of 'the growing demand for a heavier brand of rock'.[3] Moreover, while *Time*'s assertion that 'Large numbers are alienated from present political patterns. . . they believe that all the effort and idealism they have expended on such issues as the war and racism have had little impact on Washington'[4] is doubtless correct, that does not mean that one can account for the rise of the singer-songwriter entirely in terms of a retreat from the politics of the New Left. For one thing, even among the young, it is not clear that opposition to the war, much less to racism and other social inequities, was ever a majority view. For another, the student Left was never driven purely by these issues. Nick Bromell argues a 'sense of estrangement from everything that might give life meaning is what the writers of the Port Huron Statement [the founding document of SDS[5]] were trying to articulate as a political problem when they claimed that people are "infinitely precious and possessed of unfulfilled capacities", and when they opposed "the depersonalization that reduces human beings to the status of things"'.[6] The insistence on the personal in the work of the singer-songwriters remains consistent with this position. The rock audience was maturing. While The Beatles had expanded the audience for rock and roll to include college students, a younger cohort, who had been early teens when The Beatles invaded, was now entering college. With The Beatles having broken up, they were looking for something new. But it is also true that new political issues were emerging. One might hazard a guess that female listeners in particular sought not only more mature themes, but also perspectives that matched their own experiences as women, especially in light of the women's movement that was emerging at just this moment.

The key to understanding the changes in popular music in the early 1970s is the realisation that the market was already beginning to fragment. By 1969, the top 40 format, which had long dominated radio, was being challenged. Progressive rock stations were programming album tracks – and sometimes, whole albums – instead of singles. Bands like Grand Funk and Black Sabbath, who appealed to younger listeners, continued to be heard on top-40 stations, while the singer-songwriters clearly benefited from the style and mood of new stations. In place of shouting and hype, the new format featured DJs who spoke, if not quite in hushed tones, more or less conversationally. Their approach was no longer to sell, but to curate. But it was not just changes in rock that mattered. Another condition for the emergence of the singer-songwriter was the decline of folk as a distinct style and scene. The early issues of *Rolling Stone*, a magazine identified strongly with rock, give a good sense of this process. In one of its first issues in 1967, one finds a story about Joan Baez going to jail to protest the draft and a notice of Judy Collins' new album, *Wildflower*, of which is observed, 'for the first time she has written her own material for the record … three of her original songs'.[7] Baez was known as a folk-singer and Collins is identified as such, but their very presence in *Rolling Stone* is evidence that the boundary between rock and folk had already become flexible.

An indication of the way in which the singer-songwriter would be understood is apparent in Jon Landau's positive review of James Taylor's self-titled first album. The review begins,

> James Taylor is the kind of person I always thought the word folksinger
> referred to. He writes and sings songs that are reflections of his own life,
> and performs them in his own style. All of his performances are marked
> by an eloquent simplicity. Mr Taylor is not kicking out any jams. He seems
> to be more interested in soothing his troubled mind. In the process he will
> doubtless soothe a good many heads besides his own.[8]

These remarks reveal the moment of the singer-songwriter's emergence with striking clarity. One key point is the connection Landau makes to folk music, which is utterly inaccurate. The folk revival of the 1950s and early 1960s had little to do with reflections of individual lives. Folk music of this era was a celebration of community. It promised to put the listener in touch with 'the people', and even when its lyrics were not explicitly political, the identification of it with the people made it a political statement. As one of the chief proponents of the revival, Izzy Young put it, 'the minute you leave the people, or folk-based ideas, you get into a rarified area which has no meaning anymore'.[9]

Bob Dylan is, of course, a key figure in the transition from folk to singer-songwriter music even though he was not himself a singer-songwriter until later. Dylan's very early work is folk, and Dylan's songs were heard as public music and not private revelation even though as early as 'It's All Over Now, Baby Blue', he was writing songs that were rooted in his private experience. But this song, along with later expressions of similar emotion, such as 'Maggie's Farm' and 'Like a Rolling Stone', were not heard as particularly personal. And the dominant emotion they seemed to express, anger, is one not typically associated with introspection. Dylan, however, did turn to introspection in 'My Back Pages', a song that was heard as repudiation of his earlier, more political stance.[10] Irwin Silber in 'An Open Letter to Bob Dylan', published in *Sing Out* (November 1964), wrote about songs that would later be released on *Another Side*, 'I saw at Newport how you had lost contact with the people ... [the]new songs seem to be all inner-directed, no, inner-probing, self-conscious.'[11] In 1965 Izzy Young describes Dylan and others going through a 'period of gestation from "protest" to "introspection"'.[12] But Dylan moved away from introspection in his work of the later 1960s, which culminated in *Nashville Skyline* (1969), an album of commercial-sounding country music.

Folk music began 'a sharp commercial decline' in 1965, the year Dylan performed his fabled electric set at the Newport Folk Festival.[13] Almost at the same time, folk rock emerged as a successful commercial genre, but the singer-songwriter movement did not in the main come out of folk rock, which retained folk's public orientation and married it to rock beats and arrangements. The first singer-songwriters were people who came from outside rock. These emerge in 1968, including Randy Newman, who had been writing songs since 1961, releasing his first album (*Randy Newman*) in 1968, Laura Nyro, who had been part of folk scenes in New York and San Francisco, with *Eli and Thirteenth Confession*, and Canadian poet Leonard Cohen releasing his first album (*Songs of Leonard Cohen*). All of these records would be influential, and taken together they are evidence of change in popular music. But these first buds of the singer-songwriter spring are not in the main typical of what the movement in the 1970s would become. Those central to mainstream of the singer-songwriter in 1970s had some connection to the folk movement itself. A key figure in the transition from folk to singer-songwriter was Tom Rush, a folk performer who did not mainly record his own compositions. According to Stephen Holden, Rush 'was the first to popularize songs by Jackson Browne, James Taylor, and Joni Mitchell'[14]. In 1968, Rush released *Circle Game*, which included songs by all three, at a time when only Mitchell had an album of her own. It may be the Tom Rush of *Circle Game* whom Jon Landau was thinking of when he listened to *James Taylor*, especially since Landau was then writing for Boston's *Real Paper* and Rush's home base was the Boston area folk scene. Rush's most famous composition, 'No Regrets', first released on *Circle Game*, is an introspective song that has more in common with the confessional songs Mitchell would later write than with those Rush recorded on this album. 'No Regrets' recounts the narrative of a past relationship in images that belie the chorus' assertion that the singer has no regrets about its ending. While this disjunction makes the song a bit less overtly confessional than, say, 'Fire and Rain', or 'River', it is more personal than Mitchell's contemporary work.

James Taylor was the first of the group to emerge clearly as a new kind of performer. That did not happen with his first album, which despite good notices did not sell many copies. In 1969, he appeared to acclaim at the Newport Folk Festival, where he met Joni Mitchell who would be his girlfriend for the next several years. But it was not until the success of his second album, *Sweet Baby James*, and especially the song 'Fire and Rain', which got wide AM airplay, that Taylor began to be recognised as 'a new troubadour' and 'the first superstar of the seventies'.[15] What distinguished the new singer-songwriters was the confessional mode, and 'Fire and Rain' was the first song in this mode to become a hit.

'Fire and Rain' illustrates the confessional mode perfectly. As I have written elsewhere, 'What is remarkable about "Fire and Rain" is the starkness of the pain and despair it reveals. Pop music had long featured laments about lost love, but being pop they seemed to be conventional rather than personal. "Fire and Rain", however, advertises itself as autobiography.'[16] It does this, however, not by the explicitness of its references – or by their truth or accuracy – but by the language of the lyrics and the style in which the song is performed. That fans heard the song as autobiographical is clear from the press coverage, although while the song was on the charts the references remained obscure. In early 1971, *Rolling Stone* explained the autobiographical background of each verse: a friend's suicide, Taylor's heroin addiction, and the break-up of Taylor's first band, the Flying Machine.[17] *Rolling Stone* and the nearly simultaneous *New York Times Magazine* piece also discuss at some length Taylor's confinement on two occasions in mental hospitals, one of which he sang about in an early song, 'Knockin' Round the Zoo.' Indeed, both of these long articles are more focused on Taylor's personal life than on his music.

As I argued in *Rock Star*, songs like 'Fire and Rain' came to be called 'confessional' because of a perceived similarity to the poetry of what by the late 1960s was being called the confessional school. Robert Lowell's *Life Studies* (1959) was the first book to be discussed as confessional, its poems making explicit use of autobiographical materials presented in a relatively plain style, especially compared to the more elaborate diction and poetic effects of his earlier work. Among the other members of the school were three of Lowell's writing students, W. D. Snodgrass, Sylvia Plath, and Anne Sexton, the latter two embodying for many a connection between confessional poetry and the emerging women's movement. Clearly, one appeal that this poetry had for readers was its sense of authenticity; it seemed to be not only telling the truth, but also telling it about problems that anyone might suffer. Confessional poetry, however, was not defined by its accuracy to the facts of the author's life. For the critic who first named the movement, M. L. Rosenthal, the key issue is the way that the self is presented in the poems, the poet appearing as him or herself and not in the convention of an invented 'speaker'.[18] As Irving Howe explained later, 'The sense of direct speech addressed to an audience is central to confessional writing.'[19] That sense of direct address is present in 'Fire and Rain' and in many other songs of Taylor, Mitchell, and Browne. In other words, what mattered ultimately is not whether the details were true, but that they were presented in a form that made them seem so.

Joni Mitchell's *Blue* (1971) cemented the confessional stance of the singer-songwriter. Mitchell's previous release, *Ladies of the Canyon* (1970) had included a mixture of confessional songs, such as 'Willy' and 'Conversation', with the more folk-like compositions 'Circle Game' and 'Big Yellow Taxi.' *Blue* leaves out the folk sound and lyrics entirely, in favour of a style likened at the time to both 'torch' songs and 'art' songs.[20] Yet neither of these labels is quite right. The lyrics establish a sense of direct address and autobiographical reference by using more or less conversational language, including specific details of time and place. Like 'Fire and Rain' which begins, 'Just yesterday morning', and Mitchell's 'River', opens with 'It's coming on Christmas', Mitchell's 'Carey' is set in a tourist town where she complains of having 'beach tar' on her feet, while 'A Case of You' and 'The Last Time I Saw Richard' include accounts of particular taverns. These latter two songs also include fragments of conversations, giving them a documentary character. There is also often a sense of helplessness that Taylor and Mitchell's songs share with confessional poetry. Taylor cannot remember to whom he should send the song his friend's death has provoked him to write. Mitchell complains that she is 'hard to handle,' 'selfish' and 'sad', a description that sounds strange in the first person. The admission of such failings, along with revelations such as Taylor's stay in a mental hospital, point to another dimension of the term, 'confessional', the sense that secrets are being revealed. Finally, there are musical cues that make us feel that what we are hearing is a direct address to us and not a performance or show meant mainly to entertain. I have already noted that the singer-songwriters moved away from the sing-along style, with its catchy melodies, major chords, and upbeat tempos typical of the folk revival. What we get instead are Mitchell's open tunings or Taylor's

unusual chords presented at a slow tempo in arrangements that distinguish these recordings as something other than folk. The accompaniment,
unlike in much rock, allows the lyrics to take the foreground, but it is
also distinctive, individualising the material rather than making it sound
traditional.

Rosenthal had understood Lowell's confessional poetry as 'self-
therapeutic'.[21] One finds evidence of that in both Taylor and Mitchell as
well. Taylor's songs on first several albums often report on his mental
state, or describe one, such as when he's 'going to Carolina' in his mind.
Mitchell's songs may be less obvious about their therapeutic intent, but it's
hard to read songs like 'River' any other way. Why is the singer telling us
she's selfish and sad? In an interview in 1995, Mitchell said of this song,
'I have, on occasion, sacrificed myself and my own emotional makeup …
singing "I'm selfish and I'm sad" [on "River"], for instance. We all suffer
for our loneliness, but at the time of *Blue*, our pop stars never admitted
these things'.[22] Earlier, she had said she 'became a confessional poet' out
of 'a compulsion to be honest with my audience'.[23] Later, Mitchell herself
would deny that her songs were confessional, rejecting the idea that she
wrote them under 'duress', and describing their motive as 'penitence of
spirit'.[24] It is not clear that confessional poetry directly influenced singer-
songwriters like James Taylor or Joni Mitchell. But whether the singer-
songwriters were reading Plath or Lowell is irrelevant to the fact of the
similarities in the two bodies of work and that the audiences for each
seemed to like them for similar reasons.

One of those reasons has yet to be addressed. Rosenthal does
not value Lowell's poetry merely because of its shift away from high-
modernist norms or its honest expression. He reads these poems as
expressions of social critique that reveal 'the whole maggoty character' of
American culture that the poet 'carries about in his own person'.[25] With
regard to *Life Studies* this may be a strong reading, but Lowell went on,
in the sonnets that would make up the *Notebook* and *History* volumes, to
write poetry that was explicitly critical. And with Plath and Sexton, the
fusion of personal revelation and social critique was much more widely
perceived. These poems were commonly understood as feminist statements by 1970, and this connection leads us to reconsider the question
of whether the emergence of the singer-songwriter represented a retreat
from politics or social concerns. While the new genre clearly represents
a change in focus and in attitude from public confrontation and anger to
personal struggle and a reflective sadness, it does not entail a rejection of
social concerns.

Indeed, feminist issues were often entailed in the concerns of the
singer-songwriters, and this mode was well suited to their expression.
Joni Mitchell became known as a performer who expressed a distinctly

female perspective (see Chapter 18). 'Mitchell's songs illustrate the notion that the personal is the political by the way in which they deal with the power dynamics of intimate relationships.'[26] Feminist organising in the second wave was focused on consciousness raising, that is, helping women understand that what had seemed to be merely private problems were in fact the product of systemic male dominance. Consciousness raising might be seen as a confessional form because it asked women to publicly voice their personal issues. Moreover, the turn away from confrontation and anger, while not entirely reflective of the women's movement, can also be seen as consistent with feminism's goals. Because feminism could not succeed by depicting men and women as inherently opposed camps, its expression needed to offer the possibility of mutual understanding and positive personal transformation for both genders. Mitchell refused to call herself a feminist, saying that the term was 'too divisional', but that very refusal reveals the desire for a different kind of politics. Here songs gave voice to the concerns of many women by using her own life as an example. But one could argue that it was not just female singer-songwriters who raised feminist concerns. While I will not assert that Taylor, Browne, or the Dylan of *Blood on the Tracks* were intending to make feminist statements, by reflecting on their roles in intimate relationships, they were at least beginning to react to a key feminist demand.

By 1972, the phenomenon of the singer-songwriter was already widely recognised, as Meltzer's profile of Jackson Browne from that year reveals:

> for those of who were listening Jackson … was the prototype singer-songwriter years before it had a context. He was ahead of his time so they called him a rock singer, an individual rock singer without a band. The only others at the time were people like say, Donovan and [Tim] Buckley and Tim Hardin – and Donovan was already recording with a group, in fact, they all were. Certainly Jackson was not *folk*, that category had already been erased from the slate.[27]

Browne's confessionalism was less consistent than Taylor's or Mitchell's at this time, but one song on *For Everyman*, his second album, 'Ready or Not', is as clear an example of the mode as one can find. The song is a narrative in which the singer describes how he met a woman in a bar, took her home for the night, and discovers soon after that she is pregnant. As Cameron Crowe describes it, the story is about the origin of Browne's first child, Ethan, and meeting of his mother, Phyllis, 'the model, actress, and star of the bar-fight/knock-up adventure described in Jackson's song'.[28] The song's attitude differs from that of 'Fire and Rain' or 'River' in being someone what distanced and ironic. The singer is not depressed, but bemused. Browne would continue to mix confessional material with more public songs, and he would be associated with environmentalism and the anti-nuclear movement.

Carole King and Carly Simon were also widely understood to be important examples of early 1970s singer-songwriters, and they would both further the mode's association with feminist concerns. While on the whole these artists' work was less confessional than Mitchell's, it was understood as direct address. King had begun writing songs with partner Gerry Goffin in the early 1960s, and the duo penned hits for a long list of artists including The Shirelles, The Drifters, The Animals, The Byrds, and Aretha Franklin. King did not release her first record as a singer, *Writer*, until 1971, but it was her second album of that year, *Tapestry*, that broke through. The album included a version of 'Will You Still Love Me Tomorrow', a song she and Goffin had written for the girl group The Shirelles who made it a hit ten years earlier. Susan Douglas argued that The Shirelles' recording had made female sexual desire explicit, but King's version made the song's question seem personal.[29] But the big hit from *Tapestry* was 'I Feel the Earth Move', a much more explicit celebration of a woman's pleasure in sex. Carly Simon's 'That's the Way I've Always Heard it Should Be', called into question the traditional expectation that marriage was what all women want. As Judy Kutulas described it, 'Simon situated her song within feminism and self-actualising movements with lines such as "soon you'll cage me on your shelf, I'll never learn to be just me first, by myself".' The performance, by contrast, was hesitant and fragile, conveying uncertainty.[30] Her later hit, 'You're So Vain', upped the autobiographical ante, making everyone wonder about whom the song was written. The songs of both King and Simon were perceived as authentic and personal, even if the personalities they expressed seemed more stable than those of Mitchell or Taylor.

As the singer-songwriter genre developed, it did not remain bound by confessionalism per se, though it retained the idea of authentic individual expression. Even in the early 1970s, there were artists associated with the movement, such as Gordon Lightfoot and Cat Stevens, whose work was less explicitly personal. Lightfoot's big hit was 'The Wreck of the Edmund Fitzgerald', a traditional ballad about a Great Lakes shipwreck. But the confessional mode has continued to be used, from Dylan's account of the break-up of his marriage in *Blood on the Tracks* to Richard and Linda Thompson's record of their break-up, *Shoot out the Lights* (1982), on through to Suzanne Vega, Tori Amos, Liz Phair, Alanis Morissette, Juliana Hatfield, Laura Marling, and many others. The emergence of the singer-songwriter was not just a moment in the early 1970s, but the start of a new formation that continues to this day.

Acknowledgements

I want to thank the participants, especially Scott Sandage and Brent Malin, in the Humanities Colloquium at Carnegie Mellon University for their helpful comments and suggestions.

Notes

1 For example, the *Chicago Daily Tribune* (24 September 1876) identifies Mr P. P. Bliss as a 'singer and song writer' and the *Cincinnati Enquirer* (13 October 1895) describes Henry Russell as 'the famous singer and song writer'. In the early 1940s, country star and Louisiana Governor Jimmie Davis was called a Songwriter-Singer (*Lincoln Star*, 19 January 1944). My claim is not that the usage 'singer-songwriter' is novel after 1968, but that what is new is a genre of music and performer with which it then becomes associated.

2 Gregory Wierzynski, 'The Students: All Quiet on the Campus Front', *Time* (22 February 1971), p. 15.

3 Steve Waksman, *This Ain't No Summer of Love: Conflict and Crossover in Heavy Metal and Punk* (Berkeley: University of California Press, 2009), p. 21.

4 Wierzynski, 'The Students', p. 14.

5 Students for a Democratic Society, the leading New Left organization in the US.

6 Nick Bromell, *Tomorrow Never Knows: Rock and Psychedelics in the 1960s* (Chicago: University of Chicago Press, 2000), p. 33.

7 'Wildflower, Judy Collins' New Lp', *Rolling Stone*, 23 November 1967, p. 7; 'Joanie Goes to Jail Again', Ibid., p. 7.

8 Jon Landau, 'Review of James Taylor', *Rolling Stone*, 19 April 1969, p. 28.

9 Scott Barretta, ed. *The Conscience of the Folk Revival: The Writings of Israel 'Izzy' Young, American Folk Music and Musicians* (Lanham: Scarecrow, 2103), p. 178.

10 Mike Marqusee, *Wicked Messenger: Bob Dylan and the 1960s* (New York: Seven Stories, 2005), pp. 111–13.

11 Quoted in Ronald D. Cohen, *Rainbow Quest: The Folk Music Revival and American Society, 1940–1970* (Amherst, MA: University of Massachusetts Press, 2002), p. 222.

12 Barretta, *The Conscience of the Folk Revival*, pp. 196–7.

13 Cohen, *Rainbow Quest*, p. 230.

14 'Tom Rush Does It Himself', *Rolling Stone*, 2 October 1980, p. 22.

15 Susan Braudy, 'James Taylor, a New Troubadour', *New York Times Magazine*, 21 February 1971, p. 28.

16 David R. Shumway, *Rock Star: The Making of Cultural Icons from Elvis to Springsteen* (Baltimore: Johns Hopkins University Press, 2014), pp. 154–5.

17 Timothy Crouse, 'The First Family of the New Rock', *Rolling Stone*, 18 February 1971, p. 35.

18 M. L. Rosenthal, *The Modern Poets: A Critical Introduction* (New York: Oxford University Press, 1960), p. 226.

19 Irving Howe, 'The Plath Celebration: A Partial Dissent', in *The Critical Point: On Literature and Culture* (New York: Dell, 1973), p. 167.

20 Peter Reilly, review of *Blue*, reprinted from *Stereo Review*, October 1971, in *The Joni Mitchell Companion: Four Decades of Commentary*, ed. Stacy Luftig (New York: Schirmer, 2000), p. 41; Dan Heckman, 'Pop: Jim Morrison at the End; Joni Mitchell at a Crossroads', review of *Blue*, by Joni Mitchell, *New York Times*, 8 August 1971, p. D15.

21 Rosenthal, *Modern Poets*, p. 233.

22 Timothy White, 'A Portrait of the Artist', *Billboard*, 9 December 1995, p. 15.

23 Joni Mitchell, 'The Rolling Stone Interview', *Rolling Stone*, 26 July 1979, p. 49.

24 Stephen Holden, 'The Ambivalent Hall of Fame', *New York Times*, 1 December 1996, p. 36.

25 Rosenthal, *Modern Poets*, p. 233.

26 Shumway, *Rock Star*, p. 148.

27 Richard Meltzer, 'Young Jackson Browne's Old Days', *Rolling Stone*, 22 June 1972, p. 14, italics in original.

28 Cameron Crowe, 'A Child's Garden of Jackson Browne', *Rolling Stone*, 23 May 1974, p. 39.

29 Susan J. Douglas, *Where the Girls Are: Growing up Female with the Mass Media* (New York: Times, 1994), pp. 83–98.

30 Judy Kutulas, '"That's the Way I've Always Heard It Should Be": Baby Boomers, 1970s Singer-Songwriters, and Romantic Relationships', *Journal of American History* 97, no. 3 (2010), p. 687.

2 Singer-songwriters of the German Lied

NATASHA LOGES AND KATY HAMILTON

The era of the German Lied stretched approximately from the mid-eighteenth to the early twentieth century. It flowered most richly during the nineteenth century, chiefly in the hands of four leading composers: Franz Schubert (1797–1828), Robert Schumann (1810–1856), Johannes Brahms (1833–1897), and Hugo Wolf (1860–1903). Altogether they produced more than a thousand songs, from which the core Lied repertoire is drawn today.[1] These men were fine pianists although none was a singer of their own material except in the loosest sense.[2] This chapter focuses on figures who were both composers and performers of their own material, in other words, possible precedents for a modern conception of the singer-songwriter. Their activity has often been overlooked because the concept of the public song recital was in its infancy for the greater part of the nineteenth century, so while most singers sang songs within mixed programmes, none could earn a living exclusively in this way and most participated in a thriving salon culture.[3] Many were women, who benefited from the opportunities for musical training which emerged in the late eighteenth century. In comparison, professional pianists or even conductors, as in Schumann's case, had clearer routes to establishing a professional identity. Indeed, from the very outset, the piano was integral to Lied performance. Therefore although the term 'Lied singer-songwriter' is used throughout this chapter, the implication is always, in fact, Lied singer-*pianist*-songwriter. This chapter traces the history of Lied singer-songwriters in three stages: a consideration of Schubert's predecessors and contemporaries (*c.* 1760–1830), Schubert's followers (*c.* 1830–48), and finally, contemporaries of Brahms and Wolf (*c.* 1850–1914).

Broadly speaking, the Lied evolved from a technically undemanding type of music largely aimed at amateur (often female) singers, to a genre which eventually dominated professional recital stages in 1920s Berlin.[4] Various interlinked factors contributed to this shift: the rise of institutionalised musical training; the concomitant emergence of the idea of a 'recital'; and the astronomical growth of the music publishing industry, which made sheet music for every conceivable technical standard available to the public.[5] Songwriters worked in an ever more complex environment which coexisted with (but did not fully supplant) the original, amateur, private nature of the genre.

The years 1820–48 were arguably the golden age of the Lied singer-songwriter, since the genre had matured in Schubert's hands, whilst the keyboard writing was still usually within the reach of a keen amateur. From the mid-century onwards, many instances of the genre were so pianistically demanding that singers without the requisite keyboard skills could only hope to compose simpler, folk song derived types that persisted throughout the century. While Lied singer-songwriters were almost inevitably superb singers themselves, the compositional emphasis upon the accompaniment grew.[6] As musical training grew more specialised, multi-skilled musicians became increasingly rare. Nowadays, there is not a single professional Lieder singer who would consider accompanying themselves onstage, and only a few would have the keyboard skills to accompany themselves in private.

Schubert's predecessors and contemporaries

The work of a number of early Lied singer-songwriters includes examples of two coexisting, but discrete, influences: the virtuosic Italian sacred and stage music which dominated the courts and public performance spaces of the Holy Roman Empire; and the new, transparent, folk-styled German Lied which emerged in response to the literary and philosophical theories of Johann Christoph Gottsched (1700–1766) in the 1730s.[7] Gottsched's contemporary, the tenor Carl Heinrich Graun (1703/4–59), exemplifies this split. A professional tenor at the court of Brunswick-Wolfenbüttel, Graun composed the simplest of Lieder alongside his Italian opera, court and church music. His songs appeared in various compilations from 1737 onwards. The 'Ode' below, drawn from the posthumously published compilation *Auserlesene Oden zum Singen beym Clavier* (1764) is a typical example.

Example 2.1. Graun, *Auserlesene Oden zum Singen beym Clavier* (1764), vol. 1, no. 7, 'Ode', bars 1–6.

The singer and composer Johann Adam Hiller (1728–1804) is now mainly remembered for his operas. Hiller greatly admired his predecessor Graun, and like him, was proficient in the techniques and styles of Italian opera.[8] By his own admission, in the 1750s his tastes drew him increasingly towards the 'light and singable, as opposed to the difficult and laborious'.[9] Hiller's importance in the development of German musical culture lies not only in his composition of songs, but also in his commitment to raising the standard of public concert singing:

> It has always been a concern of mine to improve the state of concert singing. Previously this important task had been regarded too much as a lesser occupation, and there was no other singer except when one of the violists or violinists came forward, and with a screechy falsetto voice … attempted to sing an aria which, for good measure, he could not read properly.[10]

Hiller was involved with the subscription concerts of the Grosse Concert-Gesellschaft in Leipzig, and also founded his own singing school, which embraced general musicianship, choral and solo singing.[11] Crucially, he supported the training of women, and several female singer-songwriters of the next generation studied with him, including Corona Schröter (1751–1802), discussed further below, and Gertrud Elisabeth Schmeling (later Mara) (1749–1833). Hiller drew his pedagogical aims into his songwriting, thus aria-like works sit alongside simple folk-style tunes in his collections. These include the *Lieder mit Melodien* (1759 & 1772), *Lieder für Kinder* (1769), *Sammlung der Lieder aus dem Kinderfreunde* (1782), and 32 songs in the *Melodien zum Mildheimischen Liederbuch* (1799).

The great Lied scholar Max Friedlaender (1852–1934) argued that this was the point at which the German Lied became truly independent of foreign models.[12] Hiller's generation of songwriters consisted of a mixture of amateurs and professionals, singers, composers, poets, collectors and editors. Their activity acquired huge ideological and political significance in Germany following Johann Gottfried von Herder's coining of the term 'folk song' ('*Volkslied*') in the 1770s: this would define the distinct cultural identity of 'Germany', a country which did not yet exist except in the imagination of its peoples.[13] By the early nineteenth century, building on Herder's ideas, writers like the Schlegel and Grimm brothers regarded folk song as a 'spontaneous expression of the collective *Volksseele* (or folk soul)'.[14] This new manifestation of German identity had to be accessible, in keeping with the way that lyric poetry was developing; indeed, poetry and music were so closely wedded that the term *Lied* applied equally to poems as to songs. The poetry often consisted of 'two or four stanzas of identical form, each containing either four lines of alternating rhymes or rhymes at the end of the second and fourth lines only'.[15] The melodies were often short and memorable, supported by the barest of accompaniments. Importantly, the prevailing aesthetic of simplicity meant that the singing and composition of the Lied was not limited to technically skilled professionals as, say, the composition of operas and symphonies might be. This ideology persisted well into the next century, endorsed by influential figures such as the writer Johann Wolfgang von Goethe (1749–1832) and the song composers Johann Friedrich Reichardt (1752–1814) and Carl Friedrich Zelter (1758–1832). Melody remained paramount; the accompaniment would ideally provide just harmonic support, 'so that the melody can stand independently of it'.[16] It is therefore unsurprising that some of Goethe's amateur associates in his home town of Weimar were more prolific Lieder composers than many professional musicians.[17] Alongside its political weight, the Lied was also the symbol of culture in the upper classes, evidence of *Bildung* or self-cultivation.

The Lied was also considered respectable for women in a way that opera could never be. Goethe's friend Corona Schröter was a beneficiary of Hiller's belief that women should have access to musical education. A singer, actress, composer and teacher, Schröter published two Lieder collections in 1786 and 1794, prefacing the first set with an announcement in *Cramer's Magazin der Musik*: 'I have had to overcome much hesitation before I seriously made the decision to publish a collection of short poems that I have provided with melodies … The work of any lady … can indeed arouse a degree of pity in the eyes of some experts.'[18] A sense of her compositional style can be seen in Example 2.2. Schröter was also an important voice and drama teacher. She was awarded a lifelong stipend for her singing by the Duchess Anna Amalia of Weimar and her voice was praised by both Goethe and Reichardt.[19] Despite her close association with Goethe (she acted in and composed incidental music to his play *Die Fischerin* of 1782), her compositions are hardly known.[20]

In an age when the two leading songwriters, Zelter and Reichardt, were not singers of their own songs, it is figures like Schröter who emerge as central. Two other women who, unlike Schröter, had no access to formal musical education but benefited from their cultivated home environments, were Luise Reichardt (1779–1826) and Emilie Zumsteeg (1796–1857). Reichardt was the daughter of Johann Friedrich Reichardt. She gleaned her musical knowledge from the illustrious company which frequently met in her father's home in Giebichenstein near Halle, for whom she regularly sang. These figures included the leading lights of German literary Romanticism such as the Grimm brothers, Ludwig Tieck, Novalis (Friedrich von Hardenberg), Joseph von Eichendorff, Clemens Brentano, and Ludwig Achim von Arnim. Luise Reichardt was a remarkable woman. She moved to Hamburg in 1809 while her father was still alive, supporting herself as a singing teacher and composer. Additionally, she played a central role in bringing Handel's choral works to wider attention, translating texts and preparing

Example 2.2. Schröter, 'Amor und Bacchus' (published 1786), bars 1–12.

Mit Munterkeit, doch nicht zu geschwind

Durch die__ dun-keln Myr-ten-wäl-der   füh - ret   ü - ber   Li - lien- fel- der__

A-mor sei - ne__ Mäd- chen- schaar; Fröh - lich__ schwankt der_ Gott der_ Trau- ben,

aus   den   küh - len   E - pheu- lau-be   her,__ mit__ der be- rausch - ten__ Schaar.

choruses for performances which were then conducted by her male colleagues. Although her compositional achievements were overshadowed
by her father's, she wrote more than seventy-five songs and choruses, many
of which became extremely popular. Some of her songs were published
under her father's name in *12 Deutsche Lieder* (1800). Luise Reichardt's
'Hoffnung' (see Example 2.3) was so popular that it endured well into the
twentieth century in arrangements for small and large vocal ensembles,
particularly in English translation under the title 'When the Roses Bloom'.

Reichardt's contemporary Emilie Zumsteeg was also the daughter of one of the most successful songwriters of the day, Johann Rudolf
Zumsteeg (1760–1802), who lived in Stuttgart. Emilie Zumsteeg had a
fine alto voice and developed a substantial career as a pianist, singer,
composer and teacher.[21] Like Luise Reichardt, Emilie Zumsteeg's social
circle included many leading poets of the day, which stimulated her
interest in the Lied. She wrote around sixty songs, and her Op. 6 Lieder
were praised in the national press. Almost a century later, they were still
singled out for their rejection of Italian vocal style: 'After this modish
Italian entertainment music, it does us much good to get acquainted
with the simple, straightforward and intimately sung German songs of
Emilie Zumsteeg.'[22] The quality of Zumsteeg's voice was reflected in the
relative adventurousness of her compositions; the same reviewer also
observed that the first and third song of the set required a larger vocal
range than usual.

Example 2.3. Luise Reichardt, 'Hoffnung', bars 1–18.

Bettina von Arnim (1785–1859) presents a very different model of Lied singer-songwriter from the professionally independent Reichardt, Schröter, and Zumsteeg. The sister of one great poet, Clemens Brentano, and the wife of another, Ludwig Achim von Arnim, she too existed in a highly cultivated literary circle that encouraged a text-centred conception of the Lied. Although she composed roughly eighty songs, most of these are fragments, since her true strength lay in improvisation. Von Arnim 'constantly struggled to commit her ideas to paper and permanence'.[23] Only nine songs were published in her lifetime.[24]

The Westphalian poetess Annette von Droste-Hülshoff (1797–1848) was one of a significant number of nineteenth-century writers who composed settings of their own and others poets' verses. These settings tended to follow transparent folk song models, reflecting the original ideological underpinning of the Lied as poetry/music for the people. Similar songs by the poets Hoffmann von Fallersleben and Franz Kugler were absorbed into German folk culture and reproduced anonymously in anthologies throughout the century.[25] Von Fallersleben in particular popularised his songs through his own performances. The children's songs he composed remain popular nursery rhymes in Germany today, while his patriotic songs are still sung by male-voice choirs.

Von Droste's musical activity was more in keeping with her cultivated and aristocratic background in Westphalia. Music was practised at a high standard at home and was complemented by frequent visits to the theatre and concerts. Her letters reveal her to have been a great admirer of keyboard improvisation, when it was well done, and this is also evident in her songs.[26] She was a highly competent pianist; one letter to a friend recounts the events of a concert in which she was to participate with another singer: 'Finally, when the concert was about to begin, Herr Becker, who was to accompany us, declared that he couldn't do it and that I, therefore, would have to play the piano myself … well, it went fine and we were greatly applauded.'[27]

Von Droste's composition was further stimulated by her growing interest in collecting folk songs (through the influence of her brother-in-law, the antiquary Johann von Lassberg). As a result, she made an arrangement of the Lochamer Liederbuch, one of the most important surviving collections of fifteenth-century German song, in *c.* 1836. Her uncle, Maximilian Friedrich von Droste-Hülshoff (1764–1840), also gave her a copy of his 1821 guide to thoroughbass, entitled *Eine Erklärung über den Generalbass und die Tonsetzkunst überhaupt*. Drawing together these various influences, she made settings of her own poetry and verses by leading writers such as Goethe, Byron, and Brentano. None were published in her lifetime.

Women singer-songwriters generally came from well-to-do, cultivated families which offered creative stimulus through an educated social circle – essential in the absence of widespread opportunities for formal training. While gifted Italian women could gain an outstanding musical education, this was not the case in Germany.[28] Barred from most public activity, the Lied offered women an arena in which they could be creative without transcending the limitations imposed by societal mores. In other words, women, as well as men, could compose songs, but the professional status of 'composer' was deemed appropriate only for men. The nature of the genre fixed it in the home, a space in which women could perform their own compositions without attracting criticism. Following the work of Hiller, Schröter, Zumsteeg and others, education for women flourished. The idea of the Lied as private entertainment and edification was increasingly embraced by a 'bourgeoisie now prosperous and ambitious enough to want to imitate the sophisticated leisure of the upper classes'.[29]

Most importantly, from the 1810s onwards, Schubert exploded the limits of the genre by revolutionising the piano accompaniments, and fusing a German sensibility with the richness of Italian vocal music (thanks to the influence of his teacher, the distinguished composer Antonio Salieri (1750–1825)). The tenor Johann Michael Vogl (1768–1840) was thirty years older than Schubert, but their collaboration was to bring about the 'professionalisation' of Liedersinging. The 'German bard's' memorable performances of Schubert's songs with the composer himself at the piano were widely celebrated.[30] Like Schubert himself, Vogl initially trained as a chorister.[31] His own compositions included masses, duets, operatic scenes and, of course, Lieder.[32] As an aside, Vogl's two published volumes of songs evince a range of influences from cosmopolitan Vienna: the folk-like German Lied and his professional background as an operatic singer. As a result, while his songs are generally quite straightforward, they are not formulaic (see Example 2.4).

Lied singer-songwriters after Schubert

Despite the transformations effected by Schubert, the political and ideological urge to resist the evolution of the Lied was very much alive. In 1837, long after Schubert's death, the Lied was defined in Ignaz Jeitteles' *Ästhetisches Lexikon* as possessing: 'easily grasped, simple, undemanding melody, singable by the amateur; a short or at least not lengthy lyric poem with serious or comic content; the melody of the Lied should only exceptionally exceed an octave in compass, all difficult intervals, roulades and ornaments be avoided, because simplicity is its main characteristic.'[33] Such a definition could just as easily have been penned half a century earlier. At the same time, public song performance was burgeoning, culminating in the baritone Julius Stockhausen's performances of complete song-cycles by Schubert and Schumann in the mid-1850s and 1860s.[34] Within this maelstrom of influences, the Lied could be anything from the simplest

Example 2.4. Vogl, 'Die Erd' ist, ach! so gross und hehr' (published 1798), bars 1–20.

tonal melody accompanied by a few chords, to vocally and pianistically virtuosic songs for the concert stage. In this context, it is worth turning to two Viennese Lied singer-songwriters: Johann Vesque von Püttlingen and Benedict Randhartinger. Each represented a strand of song-making that has been largely forgotten, but was just as productive and popular as works by the masters of the genre.

The distinguished diplomat, jurist, musician and artist Johann Vesque von Püttlingen (1803–1883) was extremely well-connected. He participated in soirées with Schubert, Vogl, the composer Carl Loewe, and the playwright Franz Grillparzer. However he also socialised with composers of the next generation including Robert Schumann, Otto Nicolai, and Hector Berlioz. He even sang his own settings of the poetry of Heinrich Heine to Schumann, who liked them very much.[35] Vesque exemplifies the thriving and unselfconscious culture of amateur song performance and composition in the nineteenth century. Like many figures of the Biedermeier period, he was astonishingly proficient in many diverse areas. He was skilled enough to take the tenor role in Schumann's oratorio *Das Paradies und die Peri* at the Leipzig Gewandhaus when the singer due to perform had to cancel at short notice – a testament to just how porous the term 'amateur' was.[36] Under the pseudonym 'J. Hoven' (which drew on the last two syllables of Beethoven's revered name), he composed 300 songs, of which no fewer than 120 are settings of Heine. His 1851 song-cycle of Heine settings, *Die Heimkehr*, is, at 88 songs, the longest in musical history. After the revolutions of 1848, which were not only a political but also a cultural watershed in Austro-Germany, Vesque's songs were dismissed as sentimental and old-fashioned. Nevertheless, many have innovative forms, exceptionally well-crafted melodies, and imaginative accompaniments. See, for instance, the rippling, watery texture he devised for the opening of 'Der Seejungfern Gesang' (The Song of the Damselfly) Op. 11 no. 2:

Example 2.5. Vesque, 'Der Seejungfern Gesang' Op. 11 no. 2, bars 1–6.

(Continued)

Example 2.5. (*Continued*)

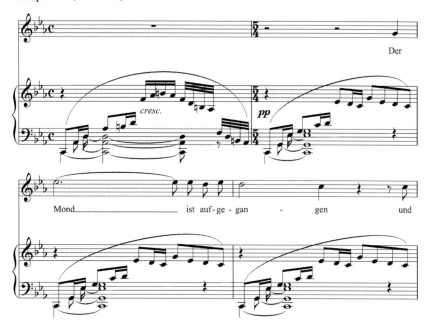

It has also been pointed out that Vesque anticipated some aspects of Wolf's songs, particularly his flexible, speech-like setting of the German language.[37] See, for example, Op. 81 no. 58 'Der deutsche Professor':

Example 2.6. Vesque, 'Der deutsche Professor' Op. 81 no. 58, bars 1–15.

(*Continued*)

Example 2.6. (*Continued*)

set - zen, und er macht ein ver -ständ - lich Sy - stem_____ dar-

aus.   Mit sei - nen Nacht - müt - zen und Schlaf- rock - fet - zen

stopft er die Lük - ken des Wel - ten - baus, mit

sei - nen Nacht - müt - zen und Schlaf - rock - fet - zen

Vesque's songs also testify to the quality of his voice. There is no doubt that he deserves to be better known as an exceptionally successful amateur singer-songwriter.

One further Viennese Lied singer-songwriter is the tenor Benedict Randhartinger (1802–1893). Like Schubert, he studied at the Wiener Stadtkonvikt and also with Salieri, before joining the Wiener Hofmusikkapelle. Alongside many other works, he wrote an astonishing four hundred songs, and was successful as a professional performer of

his own works – a singer-songwriter in the truest sense, and one with
the added lustre of having known Schubert and Beethoven personally.[38]
Indeed, he was so highly regarded that in 1827, he was ranked alongside
Schubert and Franz Lachner as one of the 'most popular Viennese composers'.[39] Clara Schumann and Franz Liszt were among his accompa-
nists.[40] He had particular success with his dramatic ballads, a sub-genre
of German song that gained enormous popularity through the century.

An important influence on Randhartinger was the north German
tenor and composer, Carl Loewe (1796–1869). Loewe's development as a
singer-songwriter was shaped by a promise he made to his devout father,
a Pietist cantor, not to write music for the stage; possibly as a result of this,
he channelled his sense of the dramatic into his songs and ballads, some
of which are nearly half an hour long and show some similarities to dramatic *scena*. He was also a highly successful composer of oratorios. For
most of his life, Loewe was the civic music director in Stettin, the capital of
Pomerania near the Baltic Sea. He taught at the secondary school during
the week and supplied music for the local church on Sundays.[41] However,
during the summer holidays, particularly from 1835–47, he travelled and
built his reputation as a performer of his own ballads. His performances
were enjoyed in Mainz, Cologne, Leipzig, Dresden, Weimar, and Vienna,
and further afield in France and Norway.[42] In 1847 he even performed
for Queen Victoria and Prince Albert in London.[43] Among his fans was
Prussia's crown prince, who later became King Friedrich Wilhelm IV.[44]

Loewe's ballads have remained in the repertoire, but many are unpre-
possessing on the page. Randhartinger apparently preferred Schubert's
songs to Loewe's because he found them more 'singable'; it is possible that
Randhartinger found the demanding vocal range of Loewe's songs not to
his taste.[45] Nevertheless, as with Schubert, Loewe's first opus from 1824
already marked him out as a songwriter of great imagination and distinction, as is seen from the drama of the vocal line and the detail of the shim-
mering, unearthly accompaniment in Example 2.7.

The rapid decline of Loewe's tremendous popularity suggests that his
own interpretation was central to the success of the music. His recitals
had an intimacy that distinguished them from the public world of, say,
the piano recital. There were never more than two hundred people in the
audience. Given the small scale of this musical career, Loewe's fame is
all the more remarkable. For Schumann, Loewe was nothing less than a
national treasure, who embodied a 'German spirit', a 'rare combination of
composer, singer and virtuoso in one person'.[46]

Lied Singer-Songwriters in Brahms' and Wolf's day

By the second half of the century, opportunities for singer-songwriters
were shifting. On one hand, it was increasingly acceptable for women to

have concert careers (if not operatic careers) after marriage. On the other hand, the Lied onstage had evolved well beyond the simple folk song, thereby excluding anyone who was not truly proficient on the piano.

The career of the teacher, composer, singer and pianist Josephine Lang (1815–1880) showed how the possibilities of publication for female Lied

Example 2.7. Loewe, 'Erlkönig' Op. 1 no. 3, bars 1–14.

(Continued)

Example 2.7. (*Continued*)

singer-songwriters had been transformed. The daughter of a noted violinist and an opera singer, Lang was a precociously talented pianist who composed her earliest songs when she was just thirteen years old.[47] At fifteen she met Felix Mendelssohn, who listened to her performing her own Lieder, and he praised her talent warmly, calling her performances 'the most perfect musical pleasure that had yet been granted to him'.[48] Lang was to publish over thirty collections of songs during her lifetime, as well as gaining a considerable reputation as a singer at the Hofkapelle in Munich.[49] Her circle of friends included Ferdinand Hiller, Franz Lachner, and Robert and Clara Schumann. She married the poet Christian Reinhold Köstlin in 1842; when he died in 1856, she supported herself and her six children through teaching. Lang, like Vesque, wrote songs which merit greater attention, as evinced by the opening of 'Schon wieder bin ich fortgerissen', published in 1867 (see Example 2.8).

Pauline Viardot-García (1821–1910) was a tremendously successful singer from a family of celebrated vocal performers. Sister of Maria Malibran and daughter of Manuel García, she enjoyed success on the operatic stage as well as the concert platform, and regularly appeared in London, Berlin, Dresden, Vienna and St Petersburg. A fluent speaker of Spanish, French, Italian, English, German and Russian, she composed vocal works in all of these languages (over a hundred items in all), and also added vocal parts to piano works by Chopin.[50] Her Lieder include settings of poems by Eduard Mörike, Goethe and Ludwig Uhland, including her very first published song: a setting of Uhland's *Die Capelle* which she produced at the request of Robert Schumann for inclusion in his journal,

Example 2.8. Lang, 'Schon wieder bin ich fortgerissen' Op. 38 [39] no. 3, bars 1–18.

(*Continued*)

Example 2.8. (*Continued*)

the *Neue Zeitschrift für Musik*, in 1838.[51] As a cosmopolitan performer and composer, Viardot-Garcia's contribution to the Lied is small but significant, given her close friendships with the Schumanns, Mendelssohn, Brahms and Wagner. She was also an influential vocal teacher.

In the last few decades of the nineteenth century, the Breslau-born George Henschel (1850–1934) emerged as an exceptionally gifted singer, pianist, conductor and composer who did much to promote the Lied in Germany, England and America. Henschel was a member of the Brahms circle and a protégé of the violinist Joseph Joachim and his wife, the contralto Amalie. The Joachims were keen to support Henschel's career as a singer, and he appeared in many concerts alongside Amalie Joachim, who was a great proponent of the Lied in public concerts.[52] Henschel later performed with Brahms in the mid-1870s; but by this stage, he was already accompanying himself in private gatherings.[53] Following a hugely successful debut in London in 1877, he travelled to the United States in 1880 with his Boston-born fiancée, Lilian Bailey (1860–1901), who was also a singer. When the two gave their first Boston recital on 17 January 1881, Henschel took the role of singer and accompanist, playing for both himself and his bride-to-be.[54]

Henschel's importance as a Lied performer was twofold. He was one of the first performers to give regular vocal recitals in which there were almost no non-vocal items – he turned away from the traditional 'miscellany' model of programming in order to put the song centre-stage.[55] He also acted as the sole interpreter of his own compositions on many occasions, and both the accompaniments of his own pieces, and those of other songs he chose to perform, suggest that he was a prodigiously talented pianist. His numerous song compositions include twenty-five numbered opus sets for solo voice, several collections for duet and vocal quartet, choral works and an opera. Since he was popular with both English and German-speaking audiences, many of his Lieder were published with English translations, and he also composed many songs to English poems, such as Tennyson's *Break, Break, Break* and texts from Charles Kingsley's *The Water-Babies*.[56] They range from straightforward parlour pieces, almost certainly intended for an informal setting, to more pianistically and vocally complex items, such as the ballad *Jung Dietrich*, Op. 45, published in *c.* 1890:

Example 2.9. Henschel, 'Jung Dietrich' Op. 45, bars 1–16.

(Continued)

Example 2.9. (*Continued*)

The decline of the Lied is often dated to the outbreak of the First World War, with Richard Strauss' *Vier letzte Lieder* of 1948 as its epilogue. As a result of Germany's defeat, the growing international popularity of the genre was abruptly halted; within the nation, other changes took place which affected its fate. It should be stressed, however, that in the pre-war period, the Lied was more popular than ever.[57] For this reason, it is more accurate to talk of a fragmentation of the Lied than a decline, and this was brought about by a range of social and musical factors. Firstly, the collective political impetus behind the Lied – the establishment of the German nation – was defused through Prussia's victory in the Franco-Prussian War of 1870–1, which led to the establishment of a unified German nation. The narrowing of professional pathways, and the rise in complexity of both vocal and piano parts meant that the likelihood of finding a single performer capable of singing and playing the piano at a professional level had decreased. In connection with this technical elevation, composers sought to lift the 'humble' Lied to the perceived grander status of the symphony and opera, and thus were increasingly attracted by larger-scale, more complex variations of the genre such as the song-cycle and orchestral Lied. A significant aesthetic shift was initiated by Hugo Wolf, who reasserted the centrality of the poem, as Gottsched had proposed a century and a half earlier. It was Wolf's practice to preface the performance of each of his songs with a recitation of the text; although this arguably restored its supremacy, it also put asunder words and music, which in the ablest of hands had fused so seamlessly. Furthermore, in order to give due attention to each inflection of a poem, Wolf's musical realisations were musically and conceptually extremely demanding. Harmony in the age of Modernism – of which Wolf was an important precursor – also altered the relationship between melody and accompaniment, which had hitherto generally been intuitive and supportive.

The rejection of received musical models by the followers of Richard Wagner also led to a diversification of approaches to the Lied. Gustav Mahler integrated his songs into his symphonies; Arnold Schoenberg used his Lieder for small-scale experiments with radical harmony; and his pupil Hanns Eisler rejected this aesthetic entirely to write Hollywood-style songs in an attempt to reclaim the Lied's 'traditional location at the border between the popular and the serious'.[58] The lack of a unified view of what the Lied should be served to render it too esoteric and practically complex to retain a place in live private music-making and contemporary popular culture. As jazz and light music took its place there, the development of recording technology offered the Lied a new home. While the Lied continues to live on the recital stage and in the recording studio, the singer-songwriters of the Lied exist no more.

Notes

1 For general histories of the Lied, see, for example, Walther Dürr, *Das deutsche Sololied im 19. Jahrhundert: Untersuchungen zur Sprache und Musik* (Wilhelmshaven: Heinrichshofen, 1984); Lorraine Gorrell, *The Nineteenth-Century German Lied* (Portland: Amadeus Press, 1993); and Rufus Hallmark (ed.), *German Lieder in the Nineteenth Century*, 2nd edn (New York and London: Routledge, 2010).

2 Various accounts of Schubert singing to and with his friends can be found in Otto Erich Deutsch, *Schubert. A Documentary Biography*, trans. E. Blom (London: J. M. Dent & Sons, 1946), *passim*. Brahms memorably performed his *Vier ernste Gesänge* Op. 121 to friends near the end of his life. See Florence May, *The Life of Johannes Brahms*, 2nd edn, 2 vols. (London: William Reeves, 1948), vol. 2, p. 276. Hugo Wolf sang and played his songs at the private recitals of the Wagner Verein in the late 1880s, but also frequently accompanied singers, as on the occasion of the first public recital of his songs. See Frank Walker, *Hugo Wolf. A Biography*, 2nd edn (London: J. M. Dent, 1868), p. 213–14.

3 The tension between private and public conceptions of the Lied is discussed in Natasha Loges, 'The Limits of the Lied', in Katy Hamilton and Natasha Loges (eds.), *Brahms in the Home and the Concert Hall: Between Private and Public Performance* (Cambridge University Press, 2014), pp. 300–23.

4 See Edward Kravitt, 'The Lied in 19th-Century Concert Life', *Journal of the American Musicological Society* 28 (1965): pp. 207–18.

5 See Natasha Loges and Colin Lawson, 'The Teaching of Performance' in Colin Lawson and Robin Stowell (eds.), *Cambridge History of Musical Performance* (Cambridge University Press, 2012), pp. 135–68.

6 See Leon Botstein, 'Listening Through Reading: Musical Literacy and the Concert Audience', *19th-Century Music* 16 (1992): pp. 129–45, here pp. 135–6. Botstein traces a shift from the voice to the piano as the central instrument through which the majority of people engaged with music.

7 Gottsched was a philosopher and literary critic based in Leipzig, whose numerous treatises, particularly the 1730 *Versuch einer critischen Dichtkunst* (*Critical Essay on the Art of Poetry*), triggered a grand shift in German cultural thought. See Phillip M. Mitchell,

*Johann Christoph Gottsched (1700–1766).
Harbinger of German Classicism* (Columbia:
Camden House, 1995).

8 Johann Adam Hiller, *Lebensbeschreibungen
berühmter Musikgelehrten und Tonkünstler,
neuerer Zeit. Erster Theil* (Leipzig: Dykischen
Buchhandlung, 1784), pp. 294–5.

9 'Leichten und Singbaren, als zum Schweren
und Mühsamen'. Hiller, *Lebensbeschreibungen*,
p. 298.

10 'Dem Gesang beym Concert in eine
bessere Gestalt zu bringen, hatte ich mir bisher
immer angelegen seyn lassen. Man hatte
dies wesentliche Stück ehemals zu sehr als
Nebenfache angesehen, und nie andere Sänger
gehabt, als wenn einer von der Bratsche oder
Violin vortrat, und mit einer kreischenden
Falsetstimme, … eine Arie nachsingen wollte,
die er oben drein nicht recht lesen konnte.'
Hiller, *Lebensbeschreibungen*, p.310.

11 Ibid., pp. 315–7.

12 For a substantial discussion of this, see
Max Friedlaender, *Das deutsche Lied im 18.
Jahrhundert*, 2 vols. (Stuttgart and Berlin:
J. G. Cotta'sche Nachfolger, 1902). Another
important figure in this context is Johann
Valentin Görner (1702–1762), a singer and
composer who published simple, singable songs
in *Oden und Lieder* in 1742, 1744 and 1752.

13 Herder's significance is discussed in
Matthew Gelbart, *The Invention of 'Folk Music'
and 'Art' Music: Emerging Categories from Ossian
to Wagner* (Cambridge University Press, 2007).

14 Harry Seelig, 'The Literary Context: Goethe
as Source and Catalyst' in Hallmark, *German
Lieder in the Nineteenth Century*, pp. 1–34,
here p. 1.

15 Ibid., p. 1.

16 Letter of 10 January 1824, from Zelter
to Carl Loewe, in Max Hecker (ed.), *Der
Briefwechsel zwischen Goethe and Zelter*, 3 vols.
(Leipzig: Insel-Verlag, 1913–18), vol. 2, p. 263.

17 See Seelig, 'The Literary Context', p. 4.
Seelig is quoting from Max Friedländer,
*Gedichte von Goethe in Compositionen seiner
Zeitgenossen* (Weimar: Verlag der Goethe-
Gesellschaft, 1916), reprinted as *Gedichte von
Goethe in Kompositionen* (Hildesheim:
Olms, 1975). See also Lorraine Byrne (ed.),
Goethe: Musical Poet, Musical Catalyst
(Dublin: Carysfort Press, 2004).

18 *Cramer's Magazin der Musik*, 1785,
p. 693, quoted in Marcia J. Citron, 'Women
and the Lied' in Jane Bowers and Judith Tick
(eds.), *Women Making Music: The Western
Art Tradition, 1150–1950* (Urbana & Chicago:
University of Illinois Press, 1986), pp. 224–48,
here p. 230.

19 Ibid., p. 233.

20 See Marcia J. Citron, 'Corona Schröter:
Singer, Composer, Actress', *Music & Letters* 61
(1980), pp. 15–27.

21 See 'Nachrichten. Stuttgard', *Allgemeine
musikalische Zeitung* 23/48 (28 November
1821), col. 816, in which the reviewer mentions
Zumsteeg's 'beautiful alto voice' and her
praiseworthy rendering of various solo and
ensemble numbers.

22 See K. Stein, 'Recensionen', *Allgemeine
musikalische Zeitung* 44/47 (23 November
1842), col. 935.

23 See Briony Williams, 'Maker, Mother,
Muse: Bettina von Arnim, Goethe, and the
Boundaries of Creativity' in Byrne (ed.),
Goethe: Musical Poet, Musical Catalyst,
pp. 185–202, here p. 192.

24 Several complete songs are included in
Williams, 'Maker, Mother, Muse'.

25 For recent studies of these two figures, see
Bernt Ture von zur Mühlen, *Hoffmann von
Fallersleben* (Göttingen: Wallstein, 2010) and
Bénédicte Savoy, Céline Trautmann-Waller and
Michel Espagner (eds.), *Franz Theodor Kugler:
Deutsche Kunsthistoriker und Berliner Dichter*
(Berlin: Akademie, 2010).

26 Karl Fellerer, 'Annette von Droste-Hülshoff
als Musikerin', *Archiv für Musikwissenschaft* 10
(1953), pp. 41–59, here p. 43.

27 Letter of January 1820, from von Droste
to Ludwine von Haxthausen, quoted in ibid.,
p. 44.

28 Citron, 'Women and the Lied', p. 227.

29 Jane K. Brown, 'In the Beginning was
Poetry' in James Parsons (ed.), *The Cambridge
Companion to the Lied* (Cambridge University
Press, 2004), pp.12–32, here p. 17.

30 Andreas Liess, *Johann Michael Vogl:
Hofoperist und Schubertsänger* (Graz &
Cologne: Böhlau, 1954), p. 7.

31 Ibid., p. 30.

32 These are listed in Ibid., pp. 149–51. This
study also contains an analysis and overview of
the two songbooks Vogl composed.

33 This definition was coined by Eduard
Lannoy, Vesque's composition teacher. Quoted
in Wolfgang Suppan, 'Die Dialektlieder von
Benedict Randhartinger im musikalisch-
kulturellen Kontext' in Andrea Harrand
and Erich Wolfgang Partsch (eds.), *Benedict
Randhartinger und seine Zeit. Wissenschaftliche
Tagung 3. bis 6. Oktober 2002, Ruprechtshofen,
N. Ö.* (Tutzing: Hans Schneider, 2004), pp.
61–72, here p. 66.

34 Notably, Stockhausen gave the first
complete performance of *Die schöne Müllerin*
D795 in 1856 at the Musikverein, Vienna,
accompanied by Benedict Randhartinger.
See *Wiener Zeitung* no. 104 (6 May 1856),

pp. 413–14. In the 1860s he sang Schumann's *Dichterliebe* Op. 48 accompanied by Brahms; he later added Schumann's *Frauenliebe und –leben* Op. 42, the *Liederkreis* Op. 39 and Schubert's *Winterreise* D. 911 to his repertoire.

35 Erich Wolfgang Partsch, 'Johann Vesque von Püttlingen als Liedkomponist' in Andrea Harrand and Erich Wolfgang Partsch (eds.), *Vergessene Komponisten des Biedermeier. Wissenschaftliche Tagung 9. bis 11. Oktober1998, Ruprechtshofen, N. Ö.* (Tutzing: Hans Schneider, 2000), pp. 171–80, here p. 172.

36 Ibid., p. 172.

37 Ibid., p.175.

38 Erich Wolfgang Partsch, 'Vergessene Komponisten. Gedanken zu einem rezeptionsgeschichtlichen Phänomen', in Harrand and Partsch, *Vergessene Komponisten des Biedermeier*, pp. 13–30, here p. 26.

39 This description, taken from the *Wiener Allgemeine Theaterzeitung*, is reproduced in Adolfine G. Trimmel, 'Neues zu Benedict Randhartinger (1802–1893). Komponist, Sänger und Hofkapellmeister' in Harrand and Partsch, *Benedict Randhartinger und seine Zeit*, pp. 7–19, here p. 11.

40 Trimmel, 'Neues zu Benedict Randhartinger', p. 11.

41 Jürgen Thym, 'Crosscurrents in Song: Six Distinctive Voices' in Hallmark, *German Lieder in the Nineteenth Century*, pp. 178–238, here p. 180.

42 See ibid., p. 181 and Henry Joachim Kühn, *Johann Gottfried Carl Loewe. Ein Lesebuch und eine Materialsammlung zu seiner Biographie* (Halle an der Saale: Händel-Haus Halle, 1996), p. 142.

43 Loewe was unable to sing on this occasion, but played the piano instead. See Robert Hanzlick, *Carl Loewe – der "norddeutsche Schubert" in Wien* (Frankfurt am Main: Peter Lang, 2002), p. 18.

44 'Während ich vor [Crown Prince Friedrich Wilhelm] sang, pflegte er ganz nahe am Flügel rechts von mir seinen Platz zu nehmen, und zwar so, dass er mir voll in's Gesicht sehen konnte. Das sicherste Wohlgefallen fanden bei ihm stets meine historischen Balladen.' Carl Hermann Bitter (ed.), *Carl Loewe. Selbstbiographie* (Berlin: Verlag von Wilhelm Müller, 1870), p. 98.

45 Richard Hanzlik, 'Benedict Randhartinger und Carl Loewe – Parallel Vertonungen samt Werkvergleich' in Harrand and Partsch, *Benedict Randhartinger und seine Zeit*, pp. 115–22, here p. 122.

46 Quoted in Kühn, *Johann Gottfried Carl Loewe*, p. 134.

47 Harald and Sharon Krebs, *Josephine Lang. Her Life and Songs* (New York: Oxford University Press, 2007), pp. 13–15.

48 Ibid., p. 23. For Mendelssohn's complete letter, see Paul and Carl Mendelssohn Bartholdy (eds.), *Felix Mendelssohn. Briefe aus den Jahren 1830 bis 1847*, 2 vols. (Leipzig: H. Mendelssohn, 1861–3), vol. I, p. 292.

49 Lang was promoted to the official post of 'königliche Hofsängerin' ('royal court singer') in 1840. See Krebs and Krebs, *Josephine Lang*, pp. 43–4.

50 Patrick Waddington, *The Musical Works of Pauline Viardot-Garcia (1821–1910). A Chronological Catalogue with an Index of Titles & a List of Writers Set and Composers Arranged*, 2nd edn (Pinehaven, NZ: Whirinaki Press, 2004).

51 Ibid., p. 8.

52 See, for example, reviews of oratorio performances in which both Henschel and Joachim performed, including Bruch's *Odysseus* (H. G., 'Berichte. Nachrichten und Bemerkungen. Berlin', *Allgemeine Musikalische Zeitung* 9 (1 April 1874), col. 203) and Handel's *Samson* (E. K., 'Das 51. niederrheinische Musikfest im Köln', *Allgemeine Musikalische Zeitung* 9 (30 September 1874), col. 369).

53 See George Henschel, *Musings and Memories of a Musician* (London: Macmillan & Co., 1918), *passim*.

54 A full review of this first performance, including details of the complete programme, is given in *Dwight's Musical Journal* 41/1038 (29 January 1881), p. 20.

55 For a full discussion of the 'miscellany' model and changing approaches to concert programming, see William Weber, *The Great Transformation of Musical Taste. Concert Programming from Haydn to Brahms* (Cambridge University Press, 2009).

56 The Tennyson setting dates from *c.* 1880; Henschel's three settings from *The Water-Babies* were published as his Op. 36 in 1883, and also issued in German translation.

57 James Parsons, 'Introduction: Why the Lied?' in James Parsons (ed.), *The Cambridge Companion to the Lied*, pp. 3–11, here p. 3.

58 David Gramit, 'The Circulation of the Lied' in Parsons, *The Cambridge Companion to the Lied*, pp. 301–14, here p. 312.

3 Bill Monroe, bluegrass music, and the politics of authorship

The early history of bluegrass music provides numerous opportunities to examine the tangly issues of song authorship and ownership. Emerging as a sub-genre of country music in the years immediately following World War II, the bluegrass sound and repertoire are rooted in pre-war 'hillbilly' music, traditional Anglo-Celtic folk song and tunes, as well as African American blues, jazz, and spirituals. The bluegrass sound found an audience and became a 'genre' within the context of a booming post-war commercial country music industry.[1] Indeed, the most highly esteemed bluegrass groups, such as Bill Monroe and the Blue Grass Boys, Flatt and Scruggs, and the Stanley Brothers, were established in the late 1940s and 50s. It is during this period that many bluegrass standards were first composed and recorded for commercial release. Bluegrass, then, reaches back into the tradition of anonymously penned, publicly shared folk song, but evolved in a nascent country music industry that peddled publishing contracts and legally determined composition credits.

Focusing on the early career of bluegrass pioneer Bill Monroe, this chapter explores the tensions that emerge between songwriting practice and conventional views of authorship in the commercial music industry. Monroe, the self-proclaimed and widely acknowledged 'father of bluegrass', began his professional performing career in the 1930s amidst a quickly evolving recording industry. During this period, underdeveloped and vague copyright legislation enabled industry executives and, in some cases, artists to secure copyright in ways that did not necessarily reflect the songwriting process. Authorship claims were even murkier in the country music industry where artists regularly recorded, 'arranged', and/ or asserted ownership of a vast repertoire of 'traditional' material. While most of Monroe's songwriting credits are sound, a number of ambiguous or decidedly misleading authorship claims have surfaced.[2] In some instances, erroneous credits stem from the politics of ensemble composition and Monroe's governing position in his ever-changing group, the Blue Grass Boys. More often, however, it appears he was adopting conventional industry practice (e.g., using pseudonyms, purchasing material, et cetera) and attitudes towards songwriting and ownership.[3]

I begin with a brief biographical profile of Bill Monroe (1911–1996), which is inevitably intertwined with the early histories of both blue-grass and the country music industry. This section provides context for an examination of one of Monroe's most well-known songs, 'Uncle Pen'. Through this case study I consider songwriting as a collaborative pursuit while examining the ensemble politics and industry pressures that perpetuate a rigid view of songwriting concerned with individual composers and their works. In addition to providing a profile of one of the most celebrated songwriters in bluegrass and country music, this chapter aims to broaden our understanding of the songwriting process and demonstrate how song authorship is not only determined by creative practice, but is influenced by the mechanisms of the commercial music realm.

Bill Monroe, bluegrass, and the early country music industry

Bill Monroe's interest in music flourished during his adolescent years. The youngest of eight children, the music he encountered in church, on recordings, and in his small community near Rosine, Kentucky, provided respite from boredom and loneliness.[4] He was encouraged by his mother Malissa Vandiver, a multi-instrumentalist with a vast repertoire of old-time tunes and ballads, and was particularly drawn to the fiddle playing of her brother, Pendleton Vandiver. As a teenager, he experimented with his voice, singing old-time songs or 'hollering' in a bright, high tenor on the vacant fields of his family farm.[5] Monroe was largely a self-taught musician and during these early years he closely observed a number of local musicians, picking up fragments of musical knowledge and sounds that would later form the basis of his own style. Aspiring to perform with his older brothers, Charlie and Birch, he adopted the mandolin as his primary instrument. With a few rudimentary lessons from Hubert Stringfield, one of his father's farmhands,[6] Monroe quickly excelled on the instrument.

Through the 1920s, Bill Monroe began his performance career accompanying, on rhythm guitar, two local musicians who would become major influences on his artistic growth. Shortly after his father died in 1928 (his mother died just six years prior), the teenaged Monroe briefly resided with his Uncle Pendleton (aka Pen), the relative who initially sparked his deep interest in traditional music. Pen, who maintained an extensive repertoire of fiddle tunes, regularly performed at weekend barn dances. Alongside his Uncle Pen, Bill not only acquired paid performance experience, but he also developed a strong sense of rhythm and amassed a collection of tunes that he could transpose to his mandolin.

During these years Monroe also accompanied Arnold Schultz, a local African American blues guitarist and fiddler. Backing Schultz's fiddle, he clocked in more hours playing all-night barn dances and earned respect as a capable performer.[7] Perhaps more valuably, elements of both Schultz's guitar and fiddle playing seeped into Monroe's own style. 'There's things in my music', he states, 'that come from Arnold Schultz – runs that I use a lot in my music'.[8] Schultz also galvanised Monroe's fondness for blues music.[9] Indeed, blues-inflected harmonies, rhythm, and phrasing permeate his music and bluegrass in general.[10]

In 1929 Bill Monroe followed his brothers Charlie and Birch to Chicago where the three found work at an oil refinery.[11] While there, the brothers began to take their music in a more professional direction performing as the Monroe Brothers at Chicago area barn dances and on local radio stations. By 1934 Birch departed for a more stable livelihood just as Charlie and Bill secured a regular radio spot on Iowa's KFNF. Now, sponsored by a patent medicine company called Texas Crystals, the pared-down Monroe Brothers were able to perform music on a full-time basis. Soon after, they would encounter Victor Records Artist and Repertory producer, Eli Oberstein.

In 1933, Oberstein was in charge of relaunching a subsidiary of Victor called Bluebird Records, which specialised in southern blues and country music. Oberstein, like many of his counterparts in the early country music industry, embarked on 'field trips' throughout the rural south with the aim of unearthing marketable songs and unexploited talent. Setting up makeshift recording studios throughout the southern United States, he 'discovered' and established recording deals with a number of notable early country artists including Ernest Tubb and the Carter Family. In February 1936, while on a field trip to Charlotte, North Carolina, he crossed paths with the Monroe Brothers and promptly made plans to record them. Under Oberstein's direction, the Monroe Brothers recorded a total of sixty songs for Bluebird, the majority of which consisted of material from established gospel songbooks, commercial country/hillbilly music, as well as a smattering of traditional folk songs, ballads, and popular songs from the African American tradition.[12]

That the Monroe Brothers' repertoire drew so heavily on popular, religious, and folk music written by other songwriters, both known and anonymous, is not exceptional. Indeed, those on the ground floor of the commercial country music industry in the 1920s and 30s inherited a vast catalogue of unrecorded music that had circulated between amateur and folk musicians for decades prior. This large stock of pre-composed material provided lucrative, and often questionable, opportunities to release a continual flow of music. Eli Oberstein was particularly notorious for his ability to attain legal control of artists and their music, aggressively hunting artists already signed to contracts, establishing dummy publishing houses, and publishing songs using pseudonyms with most of the royalties directed towards himself.[13] Not surprisingly, working with Oberstein, Bill and Charlie did not retain publishing royalties for their Monroe Brothers recordings and made only dismal returns with Bluebird's sales royalty rate (0.125 cents per side sold).[14]

While they were not necessarily profitable for the Brothers, the Bluebird singles were a valuable marketing tool that helped them establish a place within the country music industry. Stylistically, the Monroe Brothers represented the 'brothers duet' trend that surfaced in the 1930s and included such acts as the Delmore Brothers, the Blue Sky Boys, and Karl and Harty. The brothers duet sound is characterised by close harmony singing. In the Monroe Brothers, Bill built on his early experimentation 'hollering' in isolation by harmonising with his brother, working his powerful, high pitches into performance and recording contexts, and incorporating his distinctive voice into the Brothers' interpretations of stock material. In later years, Bill Monroe's singing style, commonly described as the 'high lonesome sound', would become a defining characteristic of bluegrass music.

Like a number of other brother ensembles, the Monroe Brothers backed their vocal harmonies with guitar (Charlie) and mandolin (Bill). However, as Neil Rosenberg observes, their virtuosic musicianship set them apart. They often performed at a much quicker tempo than their counterparts, giving their music a driving sense of urgency. Furthermore, while Charlie ornamented his rhythm guitar playing with melodic bass runs, Bill chopped percussively on his mandolin and burst into explosive leads.[15] In his mandolin solos, Bill aimed to capture all of the nuances of his favourite fiddlers, especially his uncle Pen. He also worked in other influences such as 'accidental notes and half-tone ornamentations taken from blues guitar'.[16] In doing so, he not only developed his own style, but reimagined the mandolin as an exhilarating lead instrument.

The Monroe Brothers recorded their Bluebird singles over the course of six hasty sessions. For the most part, the rapid-fire succession of songs demanded straight reproductions of pre-composed material. At times, however, they used their vigorous and occasionally haunting brothers duet sound to enliven songs they heard in their community, on the radio, or discovered in gospel songbooks. While they did not claim songwriting credits for any of their Bluebird material, the brothers demonstrated compositional skill through their arrangements. For instance, the success of their signature song, 'What Would You Give in Exchange for Your Soul?', spawned three sequels, which included alternate lyrics and made slight melodic deviations from their original source, a gospel songbook called *Millennial Revival*.[17] Meanwhile, Bill's mandolin leads were becoming more exploratory and inventive on songs like 'Nine Pound Hammer is a Little too Heavy' and 'I Am Ready to Go'.[18]

In 1938, after prolonged sibling tensions came to a head, the Monroe Brothers disbanded. Soon after, Bill Monroe established his first band, the Blue Grass Boys. Looking to distance himself from the sound of the Monroe Brothers, he fused instrumental prowess with a range of musical influences in a small ensemble context. This required musicians that were both capable instrumentalists and could follow direction. In addition to Monroe's mandolin, the first Blue Grass Boys line-up[19] consisted of Cleo Davis (guitar), Art Wooten (fiddle), and Amos Garren (upright bass). By including the fiddle, Monroe created opportunities for new melodic possibilities while tying his musical vision to the fiddle-tune traditions he held in such high regard. Amos Garren's bass, on the other hand, encouraged a tight rhythmic discipline, which was lacking in the Monroe Brothers.[20] Monroe coached each musician, imparting specific runs, licks, and textures inspired by his love of folk tunes, old-time string band music, blues, and jazz.

With all four members sharing the vocal duties, Monroe's new band also broadened the harmonic scope beyond that of his previous act. Like his instrumental coaching, Monroe facilitated quartet-singing rehearsals in which the band arranged harmony parts for a number of well-known gospel songs. All-male gospel quartets, which sang in close four-part harmony, were popular during the 1920s and 30s. Appearing as the Blue Grass Quartet, Monroe's group would perform gospel standards, reducing the instrumentation to just guitar and mandolin in order to showcase their vocal harmonies.[21] In later years, quartet singing would have a strong presence in the harmonies of secular bluegrass music.

Through the early 1940s Bill Monroe and his Blue Grass Boys achieved a distinctive sound within the country music field. It wasn't until the second half of that decade, however, that 'bluegrass' was solidified as a genre.[22] Specifically, the 1946–48 roster demonstrated unparalleled virtuosity, released a string of commercially successful singles, and maintained a popularity that yielded dedicated fans, as well as imitators. This 'classic' Blue Grass Boys era included Lester Flatt's smooth lead vocals and rhythm guitar, was pinned down by Cedric Rainwater's walking bass lines, and featured exhilarating instrumental breaks from Monroe (mandolin), Chubby Wise (fiddle), and Earl Scruggs (banjo).

Apart from the band's capability as a cohesive unit, perhaps the most noteworthy contribution during this era was Earl Scruggs' exceptional banjo playing. Employing his thumb, index, and middle fingers, Scruggs was able to produce continuous, rapid arpeggios that contained complex melodies while propelling the music forward. The sound became known as 'Scruggs-style' banjo, and for many fans it is a defining feature of bluegrass music.

By the early 1950s, bluegrass was characterised as a style of music rooted in the ostensible simplicity of folk song and early country, but with a sonic explosiveness and instrumental mastery more reminiscent of bebop. Bluegrass, Alan Lomax famously reported, is 'folk music in overdrive'.[23] While each Blue Grass Boy brought their unquestionable talents to the group, and many contributed to the genre in the decades following, bluegrass is ultimately a realisation of Bill Monroe's musical vision. The Blue Grass Boys became a space where he could creatively assemble his musical influences. What's more, utilising the resources of a highly skilled band, Monroe was able to earnestly demonstrate his proficiency as a songwriter and arranger. Over the course of his career with the Blue Grass Boys, he composed or co-composed a number of bluegrass and country standards such as 'Kentucky Waltz', 'Blue Moon of Kentucky', 'Can't You Hear Me Callin'', and 'Uncle Pen'.

While Monroe's contributions to the popular music canon are now widely recognised,[24] his legacy has been dogged by questions regarding the legitimacy of his songwriting credits. These uncertainties emerged from three main philosophical and ethical discussions surrounding creative influence, the songwriting process within an ensemble setting, and the mechanisms of the early country music industry. The remainder of this chapter explores issues of composition, authorship, and ownership focusing on one of Monroe's most well-known songs, 'Uncle Pen'. The song is noteworthy for how it reflects Monroe's biography and influences, was composed collaboratively, and highlights some of the complexities that emerge when establishing authorship in the commercial music realm.

'Uncle Pen': authorship, ownership, and collaborative composition

While it is difficult to pin down exactly when 'Uncle Pen' was composed, accounts from former Blue Grass Boys indicate that the song emerged around 1949–50.[25] It was first recorded for Decca Records on 15 October 1950. In the decades following, 'Uncle Pen' would become one of Monroe's signature compositions, featured regularly in his live shows, sprinkled throughout his recorded output, and performed innumerable times by both professional and amateur bluegrass groups. What's more, Monroe's Uncle Pendleton Vandiver (d. 1932), for whom the song is a tribute, would emerge as a key presence in the artist's biography and the broader narrative of bluegrass music. Indeed, for fans and followers of Monroe, especially those within the 1960s urban folk revival, Uncle Pen, the person, became something of a mythical figure – a repository of obscure Irish and Scottish fiddle tunes, a catalyst of bluegrass' driving rhythm, an emblem of and musical link to some notion of pre-modern, pre-commercial 'authenticity'.

Meanwhile, 'Uncle Pen', the song, has emerged as an archetypal bluegrass composition. As David Gates observes, recounting the life of 'an old fiddler and the tunes he used to play', the song imparts an anxiety 'that the old ways of life, and the music that went with them, are vanishing'.[26] This is certainly reflected in Monroe's nostalgic lyrics, which offer a bucolic image of Pen's fiddle resounding through the countryside, drawing the townspeople together. In an allegorical move alluding to the anxieties observed by Gates, the final verse laments the death of Uncle Pen and the silence that comes over the community.

Like many bluegrass songs, 'Uncle Pen's' lyrics convey nostalgia for a pre-modern sense of community and a view of traditional music as part of the social fabric of rural America. This is tied to notions of collective music-making, which the bluegrass ensemble epitomises and celebrates. Within bluegrass discourse there is an emphasis on the collective; the constituent parts coming together as one unit, listening and responding to one another in order to create a tight, cohesive musical entity. Indeed, the bluegrass sound relies on interlocking rhythms, vocal blending, and subtle shifts in the instrumental balance.

Within this collective music-making environment, songs are often composed as group members exchange and build upon each other's musical ideas. Such was the case with 'Uncle Pen'. The first recording of the song features, in addition to Monroe, Jimmy Martin (guitar, vocals), Merle 'Red' Taylor (fiddle), Rudy Lyle (banjo), and Joel Price (bass, vocals). There are slightly divergent accounts of who exactly produced the initial spark for the song, though most agree it started with Monroe and Red Taylor.[27] All agree that 'Uncle Pen' was a group effort and, indeed, the first recording bears the stylistic mark of each performer.

Rudy Lyle recalls that Monroe first begin composing the song 'in the back seat of the car … on the way to Rising Sun, Maryland'.[28] This scenario is likely given the numerous accounts of Monroe picking his mandolin and devising lyrical fragments while on the road between performances.[29] Sometimes the musicians surrounding Monroe would latch on to and experiment with one of his musical ideas.[30] Alternatively, he might approach particular Blue Grass Boys with a basic melody or single verse in the hopes that they might help develop it into a complete song. According to Merle 'Red' Taylor, this is precisely how the framework for 'Uncle Pen' was initially sketched out. While resting at a hotel near Danville, Virginia, Monroe came to Taylor's room with a few ideas for a song about his uncle Pendleton Vandiver. Monroe directed his fiddler to come up with a melody that would mimic the 'old-timey sound' of Pen's fiddling. After spending some time working on his own, Taylor emerged with a fiddle melody that pleased Monroe and became the song's primary instrumental hook. 'Bill wrote the lyrics for "Uncle Pen"', Taylor recalls, 'and I wrote the fiddle part of it'.[31]

Two other contributions also stand out in the performance and arrangement of 'Uncle Pen'. Firstly, as Rosenberg and Wolfe note, Monroe, Jimmy Martin, and Joel Price's three-part harmony on the song's chorus was uncommon in the group's Blue Grass Boy repertoire during this time.[32] They were, however, accustomed to singing harmony during their gospel quartet features, and if Monroe did not specifically direct his singers, it is likely that they were experimenting with the stylistic conventions of gospel harmony in arranging the song's chorus. The second contribution is Jimmy Martin's guitar run, which caps off the final a cappella moments of the song's chorus while providing an elasticity that propels the reintroduction of Taylor's fiddle melody. The lick strongly resembles what is now referred to as the '(Lester) Flatt run' and has become a stylistic marker of bluegrass guitar.

In some respects, then, 'Uncle Pen' can be viewed as a collaborative composition that involved the creative work of the entire band. The social context in which the song was composed, however, extends well beyond the immediate ensemble. Richard D. Smith maintains that the concept for 'Uncle Pen' emerged when a Decca Records executive suggested that Monroe record Hugh Ashley's song, 'The Old Fiddler' (113).[33] 'The Old Fiddler' is inspired by and features an old-time fiddler from Arkansas named Frank Watkins. While the song is quite distinguishable from 'Uncle Pen', both incorporate old-time fiddle tunes in their arrangement. One of Watkins' tunes is at the centre of 'The Old Fiddler'. Likewise, during 'Uncle Pen's' instrumental outro, Red Taylor transitions into the fiddle tune 'Jenny Lynn', which Monroe learned from his uncle.

The network of influence surrounding 'Uncle Pen' is expansive, comprising pre-commercial tunes, early country recordings, and input from several artists. In his discussion of the song Richard Smith describes Monroe as 'the synthesizing creator who ... brought it all together' (113).[34] There's no doubt that he was pivotal in composing 'Uncle Pen', and, like most popular music artists, he was a synthesising creator. However, the apparent obligation to elevate Monroe in this role reflects the difficulty of reconciling, on the one hand, Western representations of the songwriting process and, on the other hand, conventional songwriting practice. Western romantic and legal understandings of the songwriting process maintain a rigid emphasis on the 'genius-author' who, working alone, creates static 'works'.[35] A thorough investigation of the narratives surrounding 'Uncle Pen's' composition, however, supports Morey and McIntyre's assertion that 'It is more productive to understand creativity as distributed across the participants in musical practice, while composition itself – often seen as the paradigm of individual creation – is better under-stood in implicitly social terms.'[36]

Removing the emphasis from an individual author demystifies the songwriting process while drawing attention to collaboration and ensem-ble performance as a mode of composition.[37] This is particularly befitting of bluegrass, which, as noted above, celebrates the collective. Within the bluegrass ensemble, musicians carve out a sonic space from which to listen and respond to their peers, all the while attempting to maintain or elevate the performance with their own contributions. This might involve, for instance, subtle dynamic shifts that draw attention to a particular performer. Alternatively, instrumentalists might step out front during improvised solos. Here the artist responds to the overall feel of the song or competes with other soloists. Over the course of a solo the performer draws on his/her own specific influences and instrumental skills. Former Blue Grass Boy fiddler Gordon Terry, for example, describes Merle Taylor's inventive 'slow bow' and 'funny reverse' on 'Uncle Pen'.[38] Like the basic melody, structure, or lyrics, such features of performance shape songs like 'Uncle Pen' in ways that draw attention to the collective as author. This becomes more palpable when we consider that Monroe generally offered little creative direction to his Blue Grass Boys.[39] Indeed, like others in the group, Monroe com-municated with the musicians around him in the moment of performance with subtle bodily or musical gestures. Furthermore, when subsequent Blue Grass Boys approached him for direction on staples like 'Uncle Pen', he would often refer them to the original recording.[40] In this way, the crea-tive exchanges not only occur between contemporaries, but also cut across time as artists engage with and build upon past performances.[41]

With all of this in mind, why has the narrative of 'Uncle Pen' as a musi-cal work composed during a particular time (*c.* 1949–50) by a lone Bill Monroe maintained such authority? For one, it complements the hierar-chical politics of ensemble music-making. In this case, Bill Monroe was the leader of the Blue Grass Boys, and, according to the logic of the early country music industry, he was the central force behind that ensemble's creative output. So, while some viewed the Blue Grass Boys as a largely 'democratic' outfit[42] and were satisfied with their role within the ensem-ble, there was a general understanding that Monroe was the 'bossman' and hence he would receive credit for the group's music. Mark Hembree, who played bass with Monroe from 1979–84, compares the Blue Grass Boys to a corporation, stating 'Any work you did for the corporation belonged to the corporation … I think you had to go a long way before you got any kind of a half credit … on something that you wrote with Bill'.[43]

Hembree's reference to 'half credits' points to another reason why 'Uncle Pen' is viewed as a fixed work composed by an individual author: the 'author→work' model of artistic production underpins copyright law and has a utilitarian value in the mechanisms of the commercial music industry.[44] 'Copyright', Jason Toynbee argues, 'institute[s] a form of property in music … As such it has been central to music industry strategies of profit-making'.[45] While copyright law doesn't necessarily reject the possibility of co-authorship – Monroe's catalogue includes a number of shared composition credits – 'half credits' tend to complicate the simplicity of individual authors and their works in ways that increase the potential for disputes and interfere with gainful flows of capital. Accurately representing the creative milieu of a bluegrass ensemble can prove altogether messy.

Bill Monroe filed the copyright for 'Uncle Pen' in 1951. By this time, institutions were already established for legally declaring authorship-cum-ownership of a song and charting the flow of royalties. Most significantly, private publishing companies provided the resources to promote a song, monitor its use, collect royalties, and distribute money to the author (after subtracting an agreed upon percentage for these services). By the early 1950s, two decades into his professional career, Monroe was familiar with the benefits of such institutions. What's more, influenced by mid-century recording industry culture and people like Eli Oberstein, Monroe was well-versed in business tactics such as publishing songs under pseudonyms and purchasing song rights directly from other composers. All that's to say, there were several institutional and strategic options available when Monroe asserted ownership of 'Uncle Pen'.

Despite using pseudonyms like James B. Smith and Albert Price just a year prior, Monroe filed the copyright for 'Uncle Pen' under his own name with the publishing company Hill and Range Songs, Inc.[46] While it is only possible to speculate on Monroe's rationale, his decision in this instance reflects shifts in his career and in the broader country music industry during the 1950s. At the end of 1949, Monroe left Columbia Records. Shortly after, in February 1950, he performed on his first recording session for Decca Records. Around this time Monroe began to record in Nashville, and indeed his transition to a new label was accompanied by the increasing professionalisation of a country music industry concentrated in that city. When he signed with Decca, he also formed relationships with Nashville-oriented institutions, such as the publishing conglomerate BMI and its affiliate, Hill and Range. During these transitional years Monroe likely used pseudonyms as a strategy to skirt contractual obligations to Columbia and the ASCAP affiliated publishing company Peer-Southern.[47] By the time he published 'Uncle Pen', however, it appears Monroe's relationship with Decca had been solidified. He was publishing under his own name and sometimes through his own publishing house, Bill Monroe Music. Indeed, by the early 1950s, Monroe was ensconced in the song-publishing culture of the burgeoning Nashville country music industry. The romantic assumptions about composition circulated within this industry would ultimately inform how we understand Bill Monroe as a songwriter.

By examining the collaborative composition and publication of 'Uncle Pen', the goal of this chapter has not been to diminish Monroe's status as a creative and original songwriter. Rather, this case study creates opportunities to question common assumptions about authorship, musical works, and the songwriting process. As an artist, Monroe was engaged with the music and styles that surrounded him. He experimented with these influences in his work as an instrumentalist, composer, and bandleader. In this way, his role as a 'synthesising creator' is best reflected in developing the bluegrass sound.[48]

Monroe, however, was also protective of his musical vision, and recording industry institutions provided the tools and legal principles to safeguard the work of the Blue Grass Boys. The publication of 'Uncle Pen' illuminates how romantic notions of authorship influence legalistic representations of songwriting and the business strategies that form around them. We see, for instance, the significance of (individual) names within the mechanisms of publishing. Interestingly, despite contemporary concerns with the oeuvre of 'great' songwriters, the prevalence of pseudonyms in the early recording industry suggests that the names tied to particular works had less to do with composer identity than with securing compensation through legal ownership. What's more, Monroe's navigation of and reliance on private publishing houses to affix his (or some other) name to a song demonstrates how the recording industry infrastructure privileges, if not demands, adherence to the rigid 'author→work' model. As Toynbee observes, 'most writers and composers are forced to sell on their copyright. No-one can make it without a publishing deal'.[49] Concerned primarily with the copyright that '*subsists* in songs'[50] – hence, approaching songs as property, which can be purchased, endowed, or revoked – corporate publishing conglomerates promote the notion of fixed 'works' and individual authors, both of which can be managed as concrete units of exchange. Such rigid categories overlook performative and collaborative modes of composition that are often more applicable to the creative exchanges within a bluegrass ensemble. Stepping outside of the 'author/genius model',[51] however, provides opportunities to explore alternative, flexible approaches to songwriting that, in many cases, more accurately reflect the social realities of songwriting in a popular music context.

Notes

1 Neil V. Rosenberg, 'From Sound to Genre: 1946–49', in *Bluegrass: A History* (Urbana and Chicago: University of Illinois Press, 2005), pp. 68–94.

2 Neil V. Rosenberg and Charles K. Wolfe, *The Music of Bill Monroe* (Urbana and Chicago: University of Illinois Press, 2007), p. xxiv.

3 Ibid.

4 Rosenberg, *Bluegrass: A History*, p. 28; Richard D. Smith, *Can't You Hear Me Callin': The Life of Bill Monroe, Father of Bluegrass*

(Boston: Little, Brown and Company, 2000), p. 15

5 Smith, *Can't You Hear*, p. 19.

6 Ibid., p. 20.

7 Ibid., p. 27.

8 Robert Cantwell, *Bluegrass Breakdown: The Making of the Old Southern Sound* (Urbana and Chicago: University of Illinois Press, 2003), p. 32.

9 Rosenberg, *Bluegrass: A History*, p. 28.

10 Cantwell, *Bluegrass Breakdown*, pp. 126–9.

11 Rosenberg, *Bluegrass: A History*, p. 29.

12 Rosenberg and Wolfe, *The Music of Bill Monroe*, p. 17.

13 Ibid., p. 2.

14 Ibid., p. 14. Publishing royalties are tied to a copyright and have the potential to generate continuous profit for artists and/or publishing companies as future artists and commercial interests continue to use a piece of music. Alternatively, sales royalties only materialise at the point of purchase and thus offer limited, often short-term opportunities to reap profit.

15 Rosenberg, *Bluegrass: A History*, p. 34.

16 Smith, *Can't You Hear*, p. 36.

17 Rosenberg and Wolfe, *The Music of Bill Monroe*, pp. 6, 15.

18 Ibid., pp. 8, 12.

19 Monroe continued playing with some manifestation of the Blue Grass Boys up until his death in 1996.

20 Rosenberg, *Bluegrass: A History*, p. 42.

21 Ibid., pp. 43–4.

22 Ibid., pp. 68–94.

23 Alan Lomax, 'Bluegrass Background: Folk Music with Overdrive', in Thomas Goldsmith (ed.), *The Bluegrass Reader* (Urbana and Chicago: University of Illinois Press, 2004), p. 132.

24 Many, including non-bluegrass artists, have performed and/or recorded Monroe's compositions. Most notable is Elvis Presley's up-tempo rendition of 'Blue Moon of Kentucky'.

25 Rosenberg and Wolfe, *The Music of Bill Monroe*, pp. 85–6.

26 David Gates, 'Annals of Bluegrass: Constant Sorrow – The Long Road of Ralph Stanley', in Goldsmith, *The Bluegrass Reader*, p. 330.

27 For accounts of 'Uncle Pen's' composition see Rosenberg and Wolfe, *The Music of Bill Monroe* and Smith, *Can't You Hear*.

28 Rosenberg and Wolfe, *The Music of Bill Monroe*, p. 85.

29 See Smith, *Can't You Hear*, pp. 104–5, 110, 112, 191.

30 Segments from the documentary film *Powerful: Bill Monroe Remembered* (2013) feature former Blue Grass Boys such as Bobby Hicks, Leslie Sandy, and Jimmy Martin sharing their memories of composing songs with Monroe while driving between performances.

31 Rosenberg and Wolfe, *The Music of Bill Monroe*, p. 85.

32 Ibid., p. 86. Harmonies in bluegrass music would become far more common through the 1950s and beyond.

33 Smith, *Can't You Hear*, p. 113. Monroe recorded the song on 8 April 1950, six months before the first recording of 'Uncle Pen'. See Rosenberg and Wolfe, *The Music of Bill Monroe*, p. 84.

34 Smith, *Can't You Hear*, p. 113.

35 For discussions of the author as 'genius' and musical 'works' see Peter Manuel, 'Composition, Authorship, and Ownership in Flamenco, Past and Present', *Ethnomusicology* 54/1(2010), pp. 106–35; Justin Morey and Phillip McIntyre, 'Working Out the Split': Creative Collaboration and the Assignation of Copyright Across Differing Musical Worlds', *Journal on the Art of Record Production* 5 (2011). At http://arpjournal.com/ (accessed 24 June 2014); and, Jason Toynbee, 'Musicians', in Simon Frith and Lee Marshall (ed.), *Music and Copyright* (Edinburgh: Edinburgh University Press, 2004), pp. 123–38.

36 Morey and McIntyre, 'Working Out the Split'.

37 Toynbee, 'Musicians', p. 127.

38 Rosenberg and Wolfe, *The Music of Bill Monroe*, p. 86.

39 For a discussion of Bill Monroe's creative leadership see Blake Williams, Curtis McPeake, and Mark Hembree's comments in the film *Powerful: Bill Monroe Remembered*. 2013. International Bluegrass Music Museum.

40 Rosenberg and Wolfe, *The Music of Bill Monroe*, p. 86.

41 Toynbee, 'Musicians', p. 127.

42 See Tom Ewing's comments in the film *Powerful: Bill Monroe Remembered*. 2013. International Bluegrass Music Museum.

43 See Mark Hembree's comments in the film *Powerful: Bill Monroe Remembered*. 2013. International Bluegrass Music Museum.

44 Lionel Bently, 'Copyright and the Death of the Author in Literature and Law', *Modern Law Review* 57/6 (1994), pp. 978–9.

45 Toynbee, 'Musicians', p. 124.

46 Rosenberg and Wolfe, *The Music of Bill Monroe*, p. 83.

47 Ibid., p. 78.

48 Smith, *Can't You Hear*, p. 113.

49 Toynbee, 'Musicians', p. 124.

50 Simon Frith and Lee Marshall, 'Making Sense of Copyright', in Frith and Marshall, *Music and Copyright*, p. 6.

51 Morey and McIntyre, 'Working Out the Split'.

4 Singer-songwriters and the English folk tradition

ALLAN F. MOORE

The subjects of this chapter are a heterogeneous collection of individuals, distinguished by far more than they share, but ultimately owing their greatest debt, and generally their identity, to the Second (British) Folk Revival and its inheritors.[1] The folk tradition, of course, is just that: marked by the encounter with traditional songs and dances, many of these musicians share(d) the desire both to maintain that tradition and keep it relevant to contemporary listeners. It is the primacy of that encounter, and of the continued commitment to the folk genre,[2] which marks out all the singer-songwriters I identify below. The English folk tradition,[3] from the early days of the Second Revival of the 1950s through to the present, has frequently blurred that apparent purity (in the way that folk traditions are assumed to modify their material), both implicitly and explicitly, and one outcome of this blurring is a particular line of singer-songwriters that it is the purpose of this chapter to survey. Historically, it is possible to divide these musicians into three generations. The first generation, those involved with the revival and its immediate aftermath,[4] tended to place more emphasis on the writing of a good song than on details of its performance. Politics is, perhaps, the dominant topic, although this comes in a number of guises. From the mid-1970s, and with the rise of the punk aesthetic, folk retreated to the margins of musical expression, and many writers appear to have become far less outspoken. From the late 1990s, partly with the rise of 'nu-folk', a new set of concerns and approaches can be discerned among the most recent, 'third', generation of singer-songwriters. Rather than stick to a historical narrative, I shall be most concerned, here, with the topics musicians have taken up (politics, geography, humour, emotional tone, the supernatural, and reference to the tradition), and with some stylistic generalisations concerning how these songs sound, broadly the move from songs conceived for live performance towards songs conceived for recorded arrangements. Since there is no comprehensive study of this music, my sources are generally the songs themselves, their recordings, articles in magazines like *fRoots* and *Musical Traditions* (see bibliography), a host of fan and artist websites, and the material I am developing for my own monograph on the English folk song tradition.

Origins

The starting-point for the renewal of this tradition is the work of Ewan MacColl and Bert Lloyd, effectively the instigators of the revival. MacColl worked initially with Joan Littlewood, forming Theatre Workshop as both actor and playwright, a role which incorporated some songwriting. He worked freelance for the BBC, a process which culminated in the famous *Radio Ballads*, broadcast between 1958 and 1964. An earlier programme spawned the Ballads and Blues club, forerunner of Britain's folk-club movement. An apologist for industrial folk song,[5] many of MacColl's own songs focused on aspects of the lives of the working class, but usually written from a position of immense familiarity with traditional song, ballads, work songs, lyric songs and others. Bert Lloyd learnt some of his repertoire from an early sojourn in Australia; working as a left-wing journalist in England he became considered the foremost expert on traditional song (and he had a similar interest in industrial song). As singers, both recorded widely, mainly in the 1950s and 60s, both separately and together, largely singing traditional material. MacColl's own songs could easily be listed. 'Shoals of Herring', written for the third of the *Radio Ballads*, has become a well-known 'Irish traditional' song under the title 'Shores of Erin' (exemplifying the glory of the non-notated folk process). It is written from the perspective of the herring fisherman. 'Dirty Old Town' envisages industrial blight as containing the seed of socialist revival, a far cry from the stereotypical naïve view of the subject of folk songs. Likewise, perhaps, 'The Ballad of the Big Cigars', written in praise of the Cuban Revolution. MacColl's socialist principles underpin all his work, although 'The First Time Ever I Saw Your Face', written for his beloved Peggy Seeger, is both more personal and apparently more universal, judging by the very different people who have recorded it. In opposition to MacColl's case, Bert Lloyd's songs cannot be listed. For years it was assumed he simply sang songs he had collected himself, or had found in obscure earlier collections.[6] In more recent years, it has become clear that he extensively rewrote many of the songs he sang, moving verses from song to song, filling in narrative gaps, often passing on the results to younger compatriots in the Revival. It is, however, impossible to trace all the cases, and details, of this rewriting. The creative approaches adopted by these two founding fathers come to represent two major forms of songwriting adopted by those in this line of tradition: writing from scratch (whether that means inventing lyrics to pre-existing melodies, or lyrics and melodies, alone, both of which were MacColl's approach, or whether that also means supplying chords and arrangement too); and surreptitious rewriting. This latter approach must not be sidelined, since in the tradition itself, it is and was engaged in by most experienced singers, consciously, and conscientiously, or not.

Politics

The politics of folk song in the 1950s and 60s was determinedly left wing, partly because of particularly MacColl's influence, and partly because so many traditional songs and broadside ballads are written from the perspective of the disenfranchised and the wage labourer. Leon Rosselson came to prominence as a songwriter on the first BBC satirical TV show, *That Was the Week That Was*.[7] As part of the early folk group The Galliards,[8] he had already recorded international folk songs and would work with such later luminaries as Martin Carthy, Roy Bailey and Frankie Armstrong. His songs spring directly out of his socialism, whether protesting particular disasters such as the Aberfan school tragedy of 1966 ('Palaces of Gold'), social relations ('Don't Get Married, Girls'), capitalism *tout court* ('Who Reaps the Profits? Who Pays the Price?') or celebrating movements such as the Diggers[9] ('The World Turned Upside Down') or individuals like the late Victorian socialist polymath William Morris ('Bringing the News from Nowhere'). Rosselson's songs are strong on lyrics (of which there are frequently very many) but do not fit conventional stereotypes. Some ('Who Reaps the Profits', for instance) show the definite influence of Georges Brassens and French topical song. Such political topics remain relevant, as shown by Devonian Steve Knightley's 'Arrogance, Ignorance and Greed' (2009),[10] which has already travelled widely. In the 1960s, Jeremy Taylor had been working as a young teacher in South Africa, falling foul of the authorities with songs like the comedic 'Ag Pleez Deddy' which questioned acquisitive culture. Back in the UK, many of his songs raise general problems through focusing on stereotypical individuals, such as 'Mrs Harris' (with its complex plot lampooning publicity-seeking do-gooders) or 'Jobsworth'. Both Rosselson and Taylor must communicate directly – lyrics are clear, melodies syllabic and unornamented, and guitar parts straightforwardly strummed, for the most part. The greater degree of arrangement apparent in Knightley's recording of his song (with his folk duo, Show of Hands) demonstrates a shift in perspective I shall return to. While some writers pursue their politics with anger and others with (very pointed) humour, Ralph McTell's approach is more one of regret. 'England 1914' captures a beautifully delineated scene which, only at the last, points up that war has already started, while the gay ignorance of the male protagonists off to war in 'Maginot waltz' is, in retrospect, still shocking.[11]

Indeed, the 1914–18 war often surfaces as a source for songs of social justice. Active since the mid-1960s, Harvey Andrews' 'Margarita' again contrasts a (distant) war with the last dance of a soldier off to the front. Mick Ryan's stunning 'Lark Above the Downs' contrasts the freedom of the lark with the first-person view of the execution of a young victim of shellshock, but it also illustrates another key feature of some singer-songwriters – Ryan, as singer, most usually works with accompanying instrumentalists – Paul Downes, as on the 2008 recording of this song, or Pete Harris. Ryan is better known in folk circles as a writer of 'folk operas', perhaps the inheritor of the 'ballad opera' genre relaunched by Peter Bellamy's influential *The Transports* of 1977. Scotland-born Australian writer Eric Bogle's 'Willie McBride' (1976) is equally powerful.[12] It takes the form of a one-sided dialogue between a contemporary sitting on the grave of young war victim McBride and the dead young soldier, a discourse which angrily questions both this, and all, conflict. Again, it illustrates another general factor, for the song was for years better known in others' versions (that of June Tabor most notably), and perhaps Bogle is not the best interpreter of his own material. Other wars are also mined for material. Martin Carthy, doyen of the Second Revival, took a set of anonymous lyrics from the Commonwealth period to create 'Dominion of the Sword' (1988) but, rather in the fashion of Bert Lloyd, cuts material and adds two new verses, on the politics of South Africa and Greenpeace. This may seem a strange mixture but, allied to a powerful Breton tune full of awkward cadences, they all strengthen the song's 'might is right' message. Among the younger generation of singer-songwriters, Gavin Davenport's 'False Knight' (2012) leans heavily on traditional balladry, while commemorating the death of his own grandfather in the 1939–45 war. Ewan McLennan's already celebrated 'Joe Glenton' (2012) narrates the tale of a soldier turned conscientious objector within the recent Afghanistan conflict, and notably his guitar accompaniment is simpler in this song, whose details are so important, than in others he sings.

We should not be surprised at the dominant presence of what I am calling political songs – the roots of the revival in socialism and CND marches to Aldermaston left a long legacy,[13] and songs which protest a situation remain common. Sometimes, the topic is profound, as in Dave Goulder's simple 'Easter Tree' (no later than 1977) which does little more than note ways people are killed by 'civilised' society. Well known as a dry-stone waller, Goulder's website catches the tone of so many of these musicians,[14] enumerating a rich, complex identity strong on community, and within which the description 'professional musician' is notably absent. In this song there is no moral, no conclusion, as in the best traditional songs: that is left up to you. But politics as the protestation of inequalities, of all kinds, can become too simple a topic. Ralph McTell's gentle 'Streets of London' became so well-known and widely performed in the 1970s that it has become almost unplayable now. Ralph May took his stage name from the American blues singer Blind Willie McTell, in homage to the ragtime/blues guitar style which was the bedrock of so many of the leading figures of the 1960s–80s. Roy Harper preferred a simple, strummed style as backdrop to a rich lyrical palette; his less specific 'I Hate the White Man' is still too potent to be easily taken up by any other singer. To listen to Bert Jansch, however, is to be beguiled by the intricate finger style and altered tunings which contributed so much to the distillation of an English folk-guitar style by the end of the 1960s:[15] his 'Needle of Death' is merely, perhaps, the best of those songs which take the side of the no-hoper. These latter songs typify what seem to be the two dominant attitudes in this repertory – the sheer commitment to a just cause which can turn to anger (in Harper's song) and compassion (in Jansch's). And, perhaps that explains why there are so very few songs within this tradition which explore the egotism of the singer/writer.

A further, much-mined political topic concerns the pace of change and/or ecological concerns. The gnomic, almost riddle-like structure of Yorkshireman Pete Coe's[16] 'Seven Warnings' (2004) conveys its power through an almost necessary distancing of the narrative from reality, otherwise too grim to bear. Richard Thompson's 'Walking Through a Wasted Land' (1985) is more matter-of-fact, while his direct delivery avoids any pleasantries. The resilience, part-feminist, part-mythic, hinted at in Karine Polwart's 'Follow the Heron' (2006) offers a more poetic take (more often found in what I identified above as the third generation), while many of her songs are concerned with a range of contemporary social concerns. West Country singer Nigel Mazlyn Jones' songs are frequently activated by an infatuation with the very earth, songs such as 'Behind the Stones' (1999). This concern for the ground, and by extension a certain groundedness, leads me to a second type of subject matter.

Locality

Traditional song is often strong on a sense of place. Sometimes specific locations are given, sometimes types of location (forest, ship, field, coalmine), but we are rarely left completely to guess. A similar emphasis can be found in much of the newly written material where the location can, occasionally, mythologise the entire land, Although no writer majors on this theme, individual examples are notable, such as Maggie Holland's 'A Place Called England' (1999, and well-known through June Tabor's recording), Ashley Hutchings' 'This Blessed Plot' (2003, with its use of those resonant phrases from John of Gaunt's speech in Shakespeare's *Richard II*) or Steve Knightley's 'Roots' (2006), which ties national identity to music. Despite the material reality of the songs' subject, the earth of England, there is also an insinuated mythic identity which few writers try entirely to deny.

More common than writing of 'England' is the presence of regional distinction. Particular writers are associated with, and often write about, regions and, in some cases, specific counties: to speak of established

writers, Northumbria for Jez Lowe and Peter Bond, Gloucestershire for
Johnny Coppin, Teesside for Vin Garbutt, Derbyshire for John Tams,
Wiltshire for Mick Ryan, Somerset for Fred Wedlock, etc. There is no
competitive element here, more normally an attempt to display com-
monalities of the singer's locale, thus Jez Lowe's humorous invention of
time spent in 'Durham Gaol', his sentimental recounting of pit ponies
in 'Galloways' (both 1985), or his study of the Newcastle writer Jack
Common in 'Jack Common's Anthem' (2007). Coppin offers an alternative approach, frequently setting the words of established Cotswold poets
(John Drinkwater, Ivor Gurney, W. H. Davies) in addition to writing his
own lyrics. Pete Morton's Leicester background creeps into the lament
that is 'Rachel' (1987), but the specificity of a local landmark gives the
song particular poignancy, as does Bob Pegg's curious transplanting of
'Jesus Christ Sitting on Top of a Hill in the Lake District' (1973). Perhaps
this suggests that the local resists the global in constructions of folk song,
in England at least. It is also important to note that some regional writers
remain regional. As a teenager going to folk clubs in Dorset I remember
how widely Mike Silver's 'Country Style'[17] was taken up, and yet now common knowledge of the song seems to be restricted to Germany, where
Silver has frequently worked.

Humour

A certain pointed humour is often apparent in traditional songs, usually
directed at pomposity, wealth and advantage. Fred Wedlock's 'The Vicar
and the Frog' (1973) is a contemporary take on this approach.[18] Sometimes,
humorous songs take the form of parodies, as in Scotsman Hamish
Imlach's 'Black Velvet Gland' (c. 1967),[19] while the ironic self-parody of
Adge Culter's 'I am a Zider Drinker' (1976) loses nothing through its lack
of subtlety. The comedy in Dave Goulder's 'The Sexton and the Carpenter'
(1971) is black indeed, but with plenty of forerunners within the tradition.
Many singers – McTell, Coe and Rosselson for example – have a large output of children's songs where, again, humour is often to the fore. Shows for
children, whether broadcast or live, remain an important avenue for the
folk writer. Other satirists, like Jake Thackray, worked at arm's length from
the tradition although his starting-place mirrored Rosselson's. Writers like
Mike Harding combine traditional material with humorous songs, such as
'The Number 81 Bus' (1972) which, again, relies on geographical specificity for some of its humour (Harding is now better known as a BBC radio
presenter). Even mainstream comedians like Jasper Carrott are part of
this story – the risqué parody 'Magic Roundabout' (1975) originated, like
many of his other songs, in his own Birmingham folk club.

Compassion

I suggested above that the dominant aesthetic positions to be found in this repertoire are probably those of anger and compassion. Anger, of course, is most appropriately found in a range of political song and usually needs striking imagery, beautifully countoured melody and very careful word choice (the culminatory 'again, and again, and again, and again' in 'Willie McBride', for instance) to avoid becoming an unsophisticated rant. An unconsidered compassionate tone, of course, can in turn become almost inconsequential: songs like Donovan Leitch's Dylanesque 'Catch the Wind' (1965) and Ralph McTell's idyllic 'Kew Gardens' (1970) demonstrate how careful a writer must be here. John Tams has had a long career as a theatre musician. In some of his songs ('Harry Stone' (2000), or the anthemic 'Raise Your Banner' (1986)), the tone of compassion for his subjects moves, by way of Tams' commitment, close to anger. Bill Caddick spent much of his career with musicians, including Tams, originating in National Theatre productions of the 1970s. His 'The Old Man's Song' (co-written with Tams in the 1980s) typifies the compassionate depth that some writers can go to in order to try to understand another's experience – there is little doubt that it takes as its subject 'growing old disgracefully'. As with any other first- or second-generation singer, the content, however, lies securely in the words, and to a lesser extent the melody, as we would expect from a song. A comparison with the much younger Lisa Knapp's 'Two Ravens' (2013) is instructive. Knapp's song is 'about' Alzheimer's disease, according to a number of sources, and yet this reading is far from obvious. She sings with a markedly compassionate tone, and the instrumentation of her recording is gentle, if the combination of sounds is slightly unconventional. But the sounds of the recording are at least as important as the 'song' in enabling the listener to make sense of the experience.

Personal experience

The degree of personal experience apparent in traditional song is moot. Where songs take a personal perspective, it is normally an anonymous, or anonymised, one. New songs often take this line, but are enabled to appear convincing because of the apparent life experience of the author. The career of Cyril Tawney is a case in point. Joining the Royal Navy immediately after the war, he became the first English 'professional folk singer' by the late 1950s. While his songs are written from personal experience, because so many of them speak of the life of many a sailor ('Oggie Man', 'Sally Free and Easy', or 'The Grey Funnel Line'), they retain a usability absent from the songs of some revivalist singers. This raises another issue particular to this repertory – the quality of a song is sometimes judged by the degree to which other singers take it up and modify it. Too personal and it fails this test. Many of Sydney Carter's[20] songs count here: 'The Crow on the Cradle', for instance, which at first hearing appears almost a lullaby (a tone most performers emphasise), turns out to be a vicious anti-war song. 'Lord of the Dance' is widely known, and widely used in some schools. The tune is taken from an old Shaker hymn,[21] and yet in its rewriting, mythologising aspects of the life of Christ, it clearly belongs in the folk tradition. Martin Simpson's 'Never any Good' (2007), essentially a personal biography of his father, but sung with great compassion, is sufficiently vague about its narrative that, combined with the wealth of rich imagery it offers, it becomes possible for amateur singers to pick it up. Other writers manage to catch this self-effacing tone, even in a folk rock context, particularly Richard Thompson ('Down Where the Drunkards Roll' (1974), 'I Misunderstood' (1991)) and Sandy Denny ('Who Knows Where the Time Goes?' (1968), 'One More Chance' (1975), 'Solo' (1973)). Both Thompson and Denny rose to notice with the band Fairport Convention: while Denny perhaps convinces a listener that her personal experiences have a core commonality, and while the same can be said of the experiences recounted in Thompson's songs, the consistent life failures of his protagonists suggests it is less likely the experiences are Thompson's own.

Mention of Thompson and Denny introduces yet another distinctive feature of these musicians. While some operate as soloists, or with a small number of backing musicians, as would be expected from 'singer-songwriters' in any other genre, the birth of folk rock in the late 1960s – an approach which remains current to the present – means that some singer-songwriters work in a band context. This was true of Thompson and Denny, of Ashley Hutchings, and later of Dave Swarbrick and Chris Leslie, all particularly with Fairport Convention. It became the case for Maddy Prior, particularly when working outside the band Steeleye Span (such as the songs on *Lionhearts* (2003) concerning Henry II and his sons). With a new (post-punk) folk-rock generation, it became the case for the Oysterband, with usual lyricist Ian Telfer, and for Joseph Porter's pointed history lessons for Blyth Power. Subsequently, it's become the case for Little Johnny England, for writers Gareth Turner and P.J. Wright.

The new tradition

Most writers who have come out of the tradition seem, at one time or another, to have felt a need to make that lineage explicit. Not only does this seem to be the best explanation for the plethora of faux traditional songs produced, but it explains why a very large majority of singer-writers still include traditional songs in their repertoire. Sometimes, the inauthenticity of faux trad songs is blatant for humorous effect (such as Paddy Roberts' 'The Ballad of Bethnal Green' from 1959), but equally historically located. Only rarely, I suspect, is there any attempt by a writer to pass off a newly minted song as a true traditional. The motive almost always appears to be one of homage to a canon consisting, in free-reed virtuoso John Kirkpatrick's words, of 'captivating stories told in beautiful language and extraordinary melodies'. A singer like Steve Tilston has made something of a speciality of this mode of working: 'The Naked Highwayman' (1995) pictures a narrative which could so easily have had an eighteenth-century origin, but probably didn't. 'Nottamun Town Return' (2011) takes off from the old evergreen 'Nottamun Town', adding a powerful contemporary slant. Richard Thompson's 'The Old Changing Way' (1972) invents a plausible travelling life with a final moral of what happens when you fail to 'share with your nearest'. Thompson's songs, while frequently alluding to the tradition in tone or musical arrangement, sit a little apart in being drawn so often from the mis-turnings of contemporary life. Chris Wood sometimes sets the lyrics of Hugh Lupton: their joint song 'One in a Million' (2005) completely rewrites a traditional tale, bringing it into the present – the narrative of a lost ring eventually recovered does not give the easy optimism of popular song, but the outcome is positive nonetheless.

Kate Rusby first rose to prominence in the mid-1990s, at the start of the latest generation. Known originally for her approach to traditional songs, some of her own songs could almost pass as traditional, with their slightly archaic language and narrative ('I Courted a Sailor', 'Matt Highland' (both 2001)), although the effortless virtuosity of her working band perhaps belies this. The same goes for the younger Bella Hardy's celebrated 'Three Black Feathers' (2007), her own take on the night-visiting song (less a genre in its own right than a group of genres). Mastery of both language and melodic contour is necessary to bring off such songs: it is tempting to identify them as pastiche, since they work against existing models, but this seems unfair in that the best of them certainly have an identity in their own right. This mastery is, perhaps, even more important for singers who adapt, in Lloyd fashion, pre-existing songs. I have already referred to Martin Carthy in this context, and shall do so again. Nic Jones, whose musical tastes went far and wide, and who insisted he became a folk singer 'by accident', was well known for rewriting lyrics and tunes ('Musgrave', 'Annan Water' (both 1970), 'Canadee-i-o' (1980)), to make them usable, or even simply to assuage his boredom at singing the same song the same way for gig after gig. Sometimes, the relationship between new and traditional material is more tangential – Bella Hardy's 'Mary Mean' (2009) takes just one verse from the song 'The Water is Wide', but it brings a striking sense to its new context.

The supernatural

Many traditional songs incorporate aspects of the supernatural, often in the guise of resurrected or reincarnated corpses, or of other-worldly beings. While there seems to be some resistance to incorporating such elements overtly in new songs, they do nonetheless appear in other guises. Dave Goulder's 'January Man' (1970) personifies the months of the year in the same way that a traditional song like 'John Barleycorn' personifies the process of beer-making. Martin Carthy's 'Jack Rowland' (1982) draws from a number of sources, including the traditional tale 'Child Rowland and Burd Ellen', but does not stint in its shape-changing climax. Interestingly, although details make clear that Jack's journey is into Elfland, this is not actually stated in the song. Some of Chris Wood's songs disport a wary wonder as he reworks this tradition in the context of a stark socialism: 'England in Ribbons' (2007), which takes its cue from mummers' plays before bringing the narrative up to date – the 'ribbons' are something England is both bedecked in, and torn into; or 'Walk this World' (2005), the beginnings of a modern-day wassail; or 'Come Down Jehovah' (2007) with its affirmation of the sacredness of everyday life, aligned to a love of the land to which I have already drawn attention. Among younger writers, Emily Portman's 'Hatchlings' (2012) takes as its topic the myth of Leda, but in a manner far from straightforward, and with a concern for musical arrangement more typical of contemporary writers than of previous generations.

Contemporary approaches

The most recent generation of folk singers seems to have developed a new relationship to tradition, in that their own intervention in the narratives they sing is far more marked than among earlier singers. Seth Lakeman has become emblematic of this approach, in his rewriting of widely known songs, an approach which seems to sit mid-way between MacColl's and Lloyd's. His 'The Setting of the Sun' (2006) revises the song sometimes known as 'Polly Vaughan'. He turns it from a third-person to a first-person perspective, in the process shearing the narrative of its branches and turning it into a streamlined account of disaster. Alasdair Roberts goes further, dismembering songs in order to create new situations. His 'I Fell in Love' (2003) seems to draw images and narrative elements from traditional songs 'The Elf Knight', 'Pretty Polly', and 'The Bows of London' without settling on any of them. In his narrative, the protagonist sings of dismembering his lover's body to create music, a metaphor for Roberts' own process, perhaps. Gavin Davenport's recent 'From the Bone Orchard' (2013) explicitly refers to the body of traditional song in a moment of lucid self-awareness, as had Richard Thompson's 'Roll over Vaughn [sic] Williams' four decades earlier (1972).

Perhaps the most notable recent development in this tradition concerns the distinction between singers and writers. In the 1950s, the early writers would also sing many traditional songs, indeed ones they themselves may well have collected or unearthed from nineteenth-century (or earlier) collections. From the early 1960s through at least to the 1980s, either one tended to be a singer-songwriter majoring on singing one's own songs, or one did not openly write. The current generation of singers, however, have frequently turned to writing (usually having made an impact as a singer). There are two different stories to tell here, too. Some major performers – Eliza Carthy and Jon Boden, for instance – seem to become serious songwriters at the point at which they produce albums which seem a long way from the tradition (respectively *Angels and Cigarettes* (2000) and *Painted Lady* (2006), for instance), bringing that writing experience back to folk performance. Earlier singers who became writers and moved away from folk (such as Al Stewart, Roy Harper, Richard Digance) did not generally return.[22] More recent singers who became writers – I have already mentioned Knapp, Polwart, Portman, MacLennan, Davenport, but many others too – work from within accepted approaches and standard 'folk' venues (folk clubs, arts centres, folk festivals).

In this chapter I have tried to identify the major features of songwriting within the tradition set by the Second Revival: the writing of complete songs and the intervention in pre-existing songs; the presence of singer-songwriters not only as soloists, and as not necessarily the best singers of their own material; the dominance of anger and compassion as modes of emotional expression; some degree of continuity of subject matter with traditional songs and the avoidance of the confessional, personal tone; both continuity and generational distinction across six decades of writing. Of these, it is perhaps the distinctive tone of the current generation of writers which might be regarded as most marked: in their emphasis on arrangement, on the ways these songs sound in rendition, found within this current generation, we may suspect that the practice of writing new folk songs will not remain unchanged for much longer.

Notes

1 The First Revival, also known as the late Victorian/Edwardian revival, is dated to (approx.) 1890–1920. While it was, perhaps more extensively, concerned with a revival of folk-dance practices, the Second Revival was far more concerned with re-utilising and re-imagining folk song.

2 By this I mean performing at venues and events for folk music, a continuity with traditional topics, manners of articulation and instrumentation, an unusually high level of accessibility to fans, participation in the virtual community of performers, etc.

3 More space would have enabled me to cover the Scots and Irish revivals specifically too – I have tended to be a little cavalier in not entirely excluding them from this chapter.

4 I.e. those working in the 1950s, 1960s, and early 1970s.

5 I.e. the songs emanating from cultures with new, post-rural, working practices, from the late eighteenth century onwards.

6 The earliest English collections of folk songs date to the sixteenth century, while individual songs could be found in print a century earlier, even though this is considered an essentially oral tradition.

7 Broadcast in 1962–3.

8 Active *c.* 1959–62.

9 A group of English agrarian socialists, active in 1649–50, far more influential through their historical memory than their actual activities.

10 Where I cite dates, they are dates of the first (available) recording rather than of writing, since the latter are not normally made known (and, in this genre, with its emphasis on live performance, the ontological distinction between writing a song and recording a track can broadly be maintained).

11 McTell's location of the Maginot Line in World War I well exemplifies the fictionality which operates between song and experience.

12 Sometimes known as 'The Green Fields of France' and 'No Man's Land'.

13 The Campaign for Nuclear Disarmament dates to 1958, and marches to the site of British nuclear weapons production in Berkshire. Fears of nuclear annihilation were rife throughout Europe during the 1950s and 60s and membership of CND came from all sections of society.

14 Available at: www.davegoulder.co.uk (accessed December 2014).

15 Other major contributors to the style included Davy Graham, John Renbourn, Dick Gaughan, and Martin Carthy. Jansch was, and Gaughan is, a Scot.

16 Coe is a veteran of the 1980s folk movement which tried, with little success, to argue against Margaret Thatcher's brand of politics.

17 I can find no precise date for this, a song which was long unrecorded, but memory situates it in the early 1970s.

18 I have in mind traditional songs like 'The Friar in the Well'.

19 This takes off the Anglo-Irish standard 'Black Velvet Band'.

20 A major writer of important songs coming out of the 1950s/60s movement, Carter himself rarely performed.

21 Many first-, and some second-generation writers would take established melodies as the basis for a new song. This practice is far rarer in the new millennium.

22 Digance plays annually at Fairport Convention's Cropredy Festival.

5 The Brill Building and the creative labour of the professional songwriter

SIMON BARBER

Introduction

The Brill Building is an eleven-story Art Deco-style office building located in New York City that has played an important role in popular music since the pre-World War II era, particularly as a home to music publishers and songwriters. By the early 1960s, the Brill Building housed more than 160 businesses operating in the music industries, and it is this period in its history, and the history of a neighbouring music publishing company called Aldon Music, that is the focus of this chapter.[1] As suggested by the title of this piece, sustaining a career as a professional songwriter is a precarious form of work.[2] However, from the Tin Pan Alley era to the present day, the friendly competition of the office environment has served as a productive context for songwriters in all manner of genres. For non-performing songwriters particularly, the organised approach to songwriting practised at companies like Aldon Music was key to nurturing ongoing success during the early 1960s, and it is no coincidence that similar modes of work can also be observed at successful labels and production houses like Motown, Fame Studios in Muscle Shoals, and latter-day enterprises like Xenomania and The Writing Camp.

This research explores how routinised approaches to creative work improve productivity, increase the likelihood of commercial success and reduce career instability. This is accomplished by examining the ways in which the work of professional songwriters is organised (usually by music publishers), and by situating this case study of the Brill Building era within a broader continuum of underlying stylistic and organisational continuities. My approach involves a synthesis of a cultural study of the professional practice of songwriters combined with a political economy of the music industries in which they work. I am informed by those that have defined the study of creative labour, such as Bourdieu, Negus, Hesmondhalgh, and Banks, as well as political economists like Golding, Murdoch, and Mosco, who have argued in favour of drawing together political economy and cultural studies to form this sort of 'dialogic inter-disciplinarity'.[3] Throughout this chapter, I draw on interviews that I have conducted for *Sodajerker On Songwriting*, a podcast devoted to the art and craft of songwriting.[4] The podcast features conversations with professional songwriters including Brill Building alumni such as Neil Sedaka, Barry Mann and Cynthia Weil, Jeff Barry, and Mike Stoller. These interviews present an array of life stories, reflections on professional development and practice, and perspectives on the industrial contexts of song production, all of which serve to evince the experiences of those carrying out this sort of creative labour. By studying the political, social and economic factors that shape the work of professional songwriters, we can better understand their importance, and in turn, more readily acknowledge them within popular music studies, media studies and other fields in the humanities and social sciences.

Historical context

Situated north of Times Square at 1619 Broadway on the northwest corner of Broadway and West 49th Street, the Brill Building was established in 1931 as the Alan E. Lefcourt building. It later came to be named after the Brill brothers, who owned a clothing store at the site and from whom the space had originally been leased. During the depression, the Brill brothers rented office space to music publishers, songwriters, composers and other agents, some of whom had ties to Tin Pan Alley, a historic centre of music publishing activity situated further downtown. Through the years, tenants at the Brill Building have included music publishers like the T. B. Harms Company, Mills Music Inc., Famous Music, and Hill & Range, as well as performers like Cab Calloway, Tommy Dorsey, Duke Ellington, and Nat King Cole.

The structure of the Brill Building is an example of 'vertical integration'; that is to say that publishers, songwriters, arrangers, producers and performers were located in such proximity, that the entire process of writing a song, arranging it, transcribing it, recording a demo, pitching the song to a label or artist, and contracting a 'plugger' to take the song to radio, could all be done in-house. Indeed, there are stories of songwriters who would start at the top of the Brill Building and visit every publisher on the way down until a song found a home, sometimes with more than one company.[5] Although the Brill Building is widely recognised as the epicentre of this kind of activity, a great deal of work took place at another office building across the street from the Brill Building, a block away at 1650 Broadway on 51st Street.[6] It was for a music publishing company at 1650 Broadway called Aldon Music, founded in 1958 by Al Nevins and Don Kirshner, that songwriting teams like Goffin and King; Sedaka and Greenfield; and Mann and Weil wrote many of their most celebrated songs.[7]

Nevins and Kirshner were music industry entrepreneurs who recognised the cultural impact of rock 'n' roll and hired a coterie of young songwriters to create music for the growing market of teenage music consumers.[8] With eighteen writers on staff by 1962, Kirshner and Nevins essentially recreated the Tin Pan Alley mode of production by hiring talented songwriters and providing them with cubicles to work in and pianos to write songs on. At Aldon Music, the songwriters were encouraged to make demos of their songs, and take an active role in the production of records.[9] In addition to simplifying the production process and reducing costs for music publishers and record labels, this gave songwriters the opportunity to develop their skill sets and their careers. Indeed, many of these employees became arrangers, producers and performers too (often recognised as 'singer-songwriters'). With the popular 45 rpm single as their target format, the songwriters of 1650 Broadway 'wrote records' that would speak directly to young people.[10] As such, 1650 Broadway is typically understood as a more dynamic environment than the Brill Building at 1619 Broadway, and one that was not as readily mired in the traditional cultures of Tin Pan Alley.[11]

As a predominantly white, Jewish workforce, these young songwriters imbued their work with progressive political and racial sensibilities. Their songs, which were typically recorded and performed by African American women organised into 'girl groups', were variously inspired by the sounds of 'classical music, jazz, doo-wop, African American music and Afro-Cuban music'.[12] Typically organised into two-person teams, writers like Carole King and Gerry Goffin; Jerry Leiber and Mike Stoller; Neil Sedaka and Howard Greenfield; Barry Mann and Cynthia Weil; Burt Bacharach and Hal David; Doc Pomus and Mort Shuman; Jeff Barry and Ellie Greenwich, and others, helped to define what is often described as the 'Brill Building sound'.[13] This was a sound that, until The Beatles arrived in America in 1964, dominated the charts, incorporating Latin rhythms, and progressive approaches to arranging, particularly through the use of string sections.[14] Emerson argues that these young tunesmiths were the 'last gasp in the grand tradition of the Great American Songbook' and should be understood as the 'heirs of Irving Berlin. Jerome Kern, George and Ira Gershwin and Harold Arlen'.[15] Collectively, these songwriters are responsible for a pop canon that has lasted more than fifty years and includes such titles as 'Will You Love Me Tomorrow', 'Some Kind of Wonderful', 'The Loco-Motion', 'Stand by Me', 'Be My Baby', 'Chapel of Love', 'Leader of the Pack', 'Save the Last Dance for Me', 'Viva Las Vegas', 'Twist and Shout', 'Magic Moments', 'Calendar Girl', 'Happy Birthday Sweet Sixteen', 'Breaking Up is Hard to Do', 'Saturday Night at the Movies', 'On Broadway', 'You've Lost that Lovin' Feelin'', and many others.[16]

Studying the Brill Building

In popular culture, there has been ongoing interest in the music of 1619 and 1650 Broadway and the lives and careers of those that worked in and around those spaces. In film, this has been depicted in documentaries such as *AKA Doc Pomus*, and in works of fiction such as *Grace of My Heart*, the tale of a Brill Building-era songwriter called Denise Waverly, whose career and personal life echo that of Carole King.[17] In the theatre, stage productions such as *Beautiful: The Carole King Musical, Smokey Joe's Café* (featuring the songs of Leiber and Stoller) and *They Wrote That* (the stories behind the songs of Mann and Weil) have attracted large audiences both on and off Broadway.[18] There have been memoirs published by songwriters such as Burt Bacharach, Carole King, and Leiber and Stoller, whilst biographers have awarded attention to the likes of Neil Sedaka, Doc Pomus, and Bert Berns.[19] Histories of the Brill Building and its neighbouring hubs of activity include Ken Emerson's work on the 'bomp and brilliance' of the era and Rich Podolsky's book on the career of music publisher Don Kirshner and his company, Aldon Music.[20]

Academic literature pertaining to the Brill Building has frequently highlighted its impact on popular culture. Inglis' work, for instance, is concerned with acknowledging the Brill Building's status as an influential force in pop music beyond its heyday. He asserts that the structures and cultures of the Brill Building helped to transform the emphases of music as a business and that it should be understood as central to the core of popular music. This is illustrated through a detailed analysis of the impact of the Brill Building on four examples from popular culture: the 'British invasion', Motown, the productions of Phil Spector, and soul music in general.[21] Scholars such as Fitzgerald and Scheurer have taken a highly focused approach to exploring the ways in which Tin Pan Alley and Brill Building composers influenced British rock acts.[22] Fitzgerald carries out a musicological analysis of songs by The Beatles, arguing that 'the transition to the British invasion era actually involved much greater continuity with the musical past than is often acknowledged'.[23] Scheurer regards The Brill Building and its eleven floors of music publishing offices as the 'last bastion of Tin Pan Alley' (*c.* 1890–1950) and makes a comparative analysis of Brill Building songs with those of The Beatles in order to demonstrate their common features in terms of structure and melody.[24] From a political economic perspective, Rohlfing's study of the importance of women to songwriting, arranging and recording during this period is a welcome addition to the field in that it calls for studies of songwriting and production to consider issues of race and gender in addition to economic relationships and class.[25]

Despite the range of literature about the creative output of the Brill Building, little attention has been paid to the nature of songwriting as a form of work, and the ways in which that work is organised in order to maximise the potential for success. In 1964, Leiber and Stoller's Red Bird label put out nine records that reached the top 100, four of which ascended to the top 10. As Emerson points out, seven of these were written by Jeff Barry and Ellie Greenwich, a record only surpassed by Lennon and McCartney of The Beatles, and Motown's Holland-Dozier-Holland.[26] Fitzgerald notes that when analysing top 40 hits from 1963–4, Barry and Greenwich, Mann and Weil, Goffin and King, and Bacharach and David account for forty-eight pop hits with thirty-two different performers.[27] To begin to understand how this sort of success was achieved, it is necessary to consider the methods adopted by these songwriting teams, and the ways their work was organised by music publishers.

The creative labour of the professional songwriter

With the general decline of rock 'n' roll towards the end of the 1950s, mainstream popular music in the United States during the early 1960s was dominated by songwriters at both 1619 and 1650 Broadway, who wrote pop songs for groups like The Ronettes, The Crystals, and The Drifters. At Aldon Music, Nevins and Kirshner 'made rock and roll a profession'.[28] By signing gifted young songwriters at a starting salary of $50 per week, Kirshner invested in the idea that teenagers could write songs that would resonate with other teenagers. Barry Mann, who along with his writing partner and wife, Cynthia Weil, wrote songs like 'You've Lost That Lovin' Feelin'', says: 'we thought of ourselves as the bridge between old pop and rock 'n' roll. We came along at just the right time.'[29] Cynthia Weil concurs: 'we were the right age at the right time, writing the right kind of material, and with the right kind of energy and thought processes'.[30]

There can be little argument with Emerson's suggestion that the great skill of these songwriters was their ability to 'articulate the anxieties of adolescence in ways that were neither condescending nor anachronistic'.[31] From the teen romance of songs by Barry and Greenwich, to the socially conscious messages of Mann and Weil's 'Uptown', 'Only in America' and 'On Broadway', the Brill Building songwriters, themselves young people, tackled a broad range of experiences. Weil remarks: 'It seemed back then that music was about ideas. When Barry educated me in rock 'n' roll, those were the subjects that I naturally wanted to write about. The atmosphere in our office was more about writing love songs, but we just went our own way and did what we did.'[32]

A popular way to characterise the work of these songwriting teams is to suggest that employees of Aldon Music 'cranked out hit after hit with assembly-line efficiency'.[33] Whilst the typical configuration of two-person teams encouraged collaboration and the rapid advancement of ideas, as Inglis has pointed out, the concept of the production line or 'songwriting factory' reduces the creative act of writing a hit song to a workaday task.[34] Barry Mann shares in the view that the 'factory' metaphor does not fully represent their work in this period. He argues: '"songwriting factory" is such a negative phrase. It gives you the idea that we wrote a song in twenty minutes and there it was, you had a hit record. We really thought of it as a songwriting school.'[35]

Though songwriters like Goffin and King and Mann and Weil learned a great deal from each other and imbued their efforts with creativity and passion, the organised approach inculcated by Don Kirshner was extremely effective in maintaining productivity and connecting songs with artists that could deliver the required performances.[36] Kirshner, who was only a few years older than most of his writers, would call his staff at home every week to tell them which artists were about to record, and who would need songs. For the writers, the aim then was to produce songs that could be hits for those artists. At the end of the week, all of the writers would gather in Kirshner's office to play their creations and solicit feedback. Barry Mann relates: 'what gave us a framework was knowing which artists were about to record. That's why we ended up learning how to write for different artists.'[37]

Echoing Mann's concept of the songwriting school and the importance of having an artist in mind for a song, Cynthia Weil agrees: 'it was homework, and sometimes someone else would record it and it would become a hit with someone else, but that was the impetus that got you to the piano, that so-and-so was going to be recording and Don Kirshner wanted a song for them in two days or three days.'[38]

Though these songwriting teams were highly motivated, there was no mandate that they had to write, nor that they should write in certain genres. Indeed, as Mann states, songs were often written for girl groups, and later reworked for male vocal ensembles:

> There were different writing teams and we would go home or just write there and we'd be in competition with each other, but we didn't have to. If we didn't want to write, we didn't write. And sometimes we just wrote for the hell of it, to see what would happen. When we wrote 'On Broadway', it wasn't written for a specific person. We wrote it for a girl group, until we rewrote it with Leiber and Stoller.[39]

Whilst the sparse writing cubicle inhabited by the professional songwriter has been a pervasive image throughout popular music history, Mann indicates here that Aldon songwriters worked at home just as often. At the office, or from the comfort of their homes, they experimented with different styles in order to respond to the opportunities that had been presented to them. Cynthia Weil acknowledges that this kind of stylistic fluidity was an important part of their ongoing success: 'today people think of themselves as a certain kind of writer, a country writer or a pop writer. We never were told: "you can't write country", so we wrote country.'[40]

There was also a great deal of competition among the writing teams, particularly in pursuit of writing suitable 'follow-ups' for artists that had recently had hit records. Mann and Weil and Goffin and King were regularly engaged in competition to write hit songs that would please their employers. Cynthia Weil describes the friendly competition that drove this rivalry: 'our best friends were Carole King and Gerry Goffin, who were the other married-couple songwriting team at the time. They were our fiercest competitors, but they were also our friends and we shared everything with them.'[41] Emerson suggests that Goffin and King and Mann and Weil built their entire lives around the process of writing songs and making demos, to the extent that they had time for few other friends.[42] Though Kirshner encouraged these friendly rivalries in order to generate new material for artists, he perhaps did not expect these two couples to vacation together in order to keep the competition fair.[43]

The first songwriters hired by Nevins and Kirshner were Neil Sedaka and Howard Greenfield, teenage collaborators from Brighton Beach, who had already achieved some success publishing songs. Sedaka, a Juilliard-trained pianist, and Greenfield, a poet and lyricist, insisted that Aldon place one of their songs on the charts before they would sign with the company. Once under contract with Aldon, they flourished, having hits like 'Stupid Cupid', 'Calendar Girl', 'Happy Birthday Sweet Sixteen', and 'Breaking Up is Hard to Do'. 'I wrote records', Sedaka says, 'you had to tell the whole story in two and a half minutes. Howie and I mastered that art form.'[44] Though Sedaka is confident about his accomplishments, he has always found the process onerous: 'you have to force yourself. As much as I have done it for sixty years, I'm still afraid of it.'[45] The routines that enabled the Sedaka/Greenfield partnership to accumulate new songs were similarly hard-won:

> In those days, we worked five days a week from ten in the morning until five at night. It was a great way to learn your craft. Some days you didn't come up with anything but you had a small piece of something that could develop the next day. I always had a tape recorder there, or otherwise I would forget it. It is a discipline thing.[46]

Writing on a regular basis, even when little usable material results, is a strategy also adopted by Mann and Weil. Cynthia Weil reports: 'We would have what we called 'slump songs', when we were in a writing slump and we just couldn't get anything, so we'd say "let's just write something so that we don't forget that we are writers."'[47] In a similar fashion, Bacharach and David maintained a routine of meeting daily at 11am in order to write songs for their publisher, Famous Music, based at 1619 Broadway. Contrary to Bacharach's legacy as a melodic innovator, the pair experienced a relatively unpromising start to their career.[48] They did, however, produce top-20 hits for Perry Como, Marty Robbins, and Patti Page using the methodology of a daily routine. Other techniques routinely adopted by songwriters during this period included rewriting an existing hit song 'sideways'; that is to say, changing enough of the melody and chords of a successful song until it becomes an original property. It was using this method on the song 'Little Darlin'' (made famous by The Diamonds in 1957) that produced the Sedaka/Greenfield hit 'Oh! Carol'.

Another practice among Brill Building-era songwriters was to swap partners for writing sessions. Jack Keller, who was not part of a songwriting team, maintained a routine that involved collaborating with different Aldon writers on different days of the week. He wrote twice a week with Howard Greenfield, who was often available due to Sedaka's busy touring schedule. Together they penned 'Everybody's Somebody's Fool' and 'My Heart Has a Mind of its Own', both of which were number-1 hits for Connie Francis. Keller wrote with Gerry Goffin on Tuesdays and Thursdays and with Larry Kolber on Fridays.[49] Together, Keller and Goffin penned 'Run to Him', a hit for Bobby Vee. With the exception of Mann and Weil, who wrote together exclusively, these sorts of collaborations were commonplace and can be understood as techniques employed to sustain the success rates of (mostly) non-performing songwriters.[50] As Podolsky notes, Carole King and Gerry Goffin failed to achieve success forty-five times before topping the charts with 'Will You Love Me Tomorrow'.[51] However, as a result of the methods used, the talent gathered by Nevins and Kirshner, and the environment they cultivated, extraordinary results were achieved. When Goffin and King's 'The Loco-Motion' reached number 1 on the charts in 1962, it knocked Sedaka's 'Breaking Up is Hard to Do' off the top spot. With two number 1s, eight top-10 hits and eighteen top-20 songs, two of which were on their own label, this organised approach to songwriting enabled Aldon Music to effectively dominate the charts.[52]

In 1962, to take advantage of their commercial success, Kirshner and Nevins established their own record label. Leiber and Stoller followed two years later. The consolidation of all of the aspects of recording, publishing and releasing records provided greater financial returns and led to the sale of Aldon Music to Columbia Pictures Screen Gems in April of 1963 for somewhere in the region of $2–3 million.[53] With Kirshner now fulfilling a new role at Screen Gems, there was less time to manage the careers of his writers. Many of the Aldon writing teams migrated to the west coast, but were generally now too old to target their material at an audience of teenagers.[54] With the arrival of The Beatles and an upsurge in rock 'n' roll acts writing their own material, it became increasingly difficult for non-performing songwriters to obtain cuts on records. Whilst singer-songwriters like Neil Sedaka and Carole King were able to achieve fame performing their own material as solo artists, life beyond the Brill Building era was less assured for those who relied on others to perform their songs.[55] By 1969, the community that Jack Keller once described as the 'Garden of Eden' for professional songwriters had essentially dissolved.[56]

Conclusions

As an economic model, the vertically integrated structure of the music businesses at 1619 and 1650 Broadway enabled close professional and personal relationships between songwriters, producers, publishers and promoters, ensuring the best opportunities for the records they produced. The strategies inculcated by Aldon Music to encourage the creation of new material increased opportunities for commercial success and developed the professional skill sets of its songwriters. As members of this 'songwriting school', the songwriting teams were motivated to compete with each other in a collegiate environment, striving to write the hit single that would afford them cuts on future albums. The philosophies and work routines adopted, including the necessary grind of writing 'slump songs' and regular collaborations outside of their established partnerships, were just some of the methods that provided them with continued success during the early 1960s.

Though the arrival of The Beatles in America (and the 'British Invasion' in general) is often used to symbolise the relegation of Brill Building songwriters, it should be understood that when The Beatles arrived in New York in 1964, Lennon and McCartney were 'continuing and reinforcing the traditions of the professional songwriter' and that they were inspired by the sounds they displaced from the charts.[57] In addition to being fans of Goffin and King, and occasionally covering their songs, Lennon and McCartney's approach to rhythm, structure, chords and melody was not dissimilar to that of the Aldon crew, particularly between 1963 and 1966.[58] Even in the throes of Beatlemania, America was not immune to the charms of pop singles sung by girl groups; Motown's Supremes achieved five consecutive number-1 hits between the summers of 1964 and 1965. Indeed, Fitzgerald argues that Motown 'updated and replaced' the Brill Building model for success in this genre, and the statistics bear out this claim, showing that Motown's Holland-Dozier-Holland equalled the success of Lennon-McCartney in 1965 and bettered them in 1966, by scoring twice as many top-10 hits and top-40 entries.[59]

Likewise, it should not be understood that organised approaches to songwriting were outmoded during this period, but that the underlying similitude of songwriting and production across different genres continued despite the ebb and flow of individual careers. Motown was, as Fitzgerald puts it, 'kind of a black Brill Building'.[60] Moreover, founder Berry Gordy was directly inspired by the Aldon Music model and told Don Kirshner of his intention to build a company like Aldon Music in Detroit.[61] Through its attention to a star-focused system, its round-the-clock studio practices, quality control meetings and emphasis on melodic songs married with social and political commentary, Motown blossomed, and sold millions of records to teenagers engaged by soul music. Just as Motown was an exclusive team of people brought together to produce songs through a series of structured processes, so too Xenomania, the British pop music production team behind number-1 hits for acts like Girls Aloud and Sugababes, benefits from this approach.[62] In the five decades since the sounds of the Brill Building dominated the charts, the routines and methods adopted by the music publishers and songwriters of that era have become part of an ongoing legacy furthered by those who continue to engage with organised approaches to the art of songwriting.

Notes

1 Today, the Brill Building is home to fewer music-related businesses, most notably Broadway Video, a production company operated by the television and film producer Lorne Michaels, and the offices of singer-songwriter Paul Simon. A 2013 article by David Dunlap noted the decline of music industry tenants, but described a renovation plan designed to attract technology and music-related companies to the building. David Dunlap, 'Half Empty but Full of History, Brill Building Seeks Tenants', *The New York Times* (24 July 2013). Available at: www.nytimes.com/2013/07/25/nyregion/half-empty-but-full-of-history-brill-building-seeks-tenants.html (accessed 23 February 2015).

2 Kim de Laat's 2015 article on managing conflict and reward in professional songwriting teams provides a detailed study of the 'doubly uncertain' nature of this career path. See also work in production studies: Vicki Mayer, Miranda J. Banks, John T. Caldwell (eds.), *Production Studies* (London: Routledge, 2009).

3 Natalie Fenton, 'Bridging the Mythical: Political Economy and Cultural Studies Approaches to the Analysis of the Media', in Eoin Devereux (ed.), *Media Studies: Key Issues and Debates* (London: Sage, 2007), p. 8.

4 The *Sodajerker On Songwriting* podcast, available in full at www.sodajerker.com/podcast/ is licensed via Creative Commons.

5 Alan Betrock, *Girl Groups: The Story of a Sound* (New York: Delilah, 1982). p. 39. See also: Mary Rohlfing, "'Don't Say Nothin' Bad About My Baby": A Re-evaluation of Women's Roles in the Brill Building Era of Early Rock 'n' Roll', *Critical Studies in Media Communication* 13/2 (1996), p. 104.

6 1697 Broadway at 54th Street, next door to the Ed Sullivan Theatre, is another site of activity that extends this misnomer even further geographically.

7 Aldon Music existed from the first week of April 1958 until 1963, the period between the emergence of Elvis Presley and the arrival

of The Beatles in the United States. See Rich Podolsky, *Don Kirshner: The Man with the Golden Ear: How He Changed the Face of Rock and Roll* (Milwaukee: Hal Leonard Corporation, 2012), p. xi.

8 Kirshner, whose first foray in the music business was discovering and managing the singer Bobby Darin, learned the music publishing business from Leiber and Stoller at the Carnegie Deli on 7th Avenue (Podolsky, *Don Kirshner*, p. 21).

9 Podolsky, *Don Kirshner*, p. 4.

10 Brill Building-era writers such as Mike Stoller, Jeff Barry and Neil Sedaka have elucidated a conceptual approach to writing specifically for this format (www.sodajerker.com/podcast/).

11 Ken Emerson, *Always Magic in the Air: The Bomp and Brilliance of the Brill Building Era* (London: Fourth Estate, 2006), p. 22.

12 Ibid., p. xi.

13 Although he is rarely contextualised as a Brill Building songwriter, Barry and Greenwich often wrote with producer Phil Spector, whose 'wall of sound' production style is symbolic of this period. Other key figures of the time include Jack Keller and Bert Berns.

14 Doc Pomus described the sound as 'Jewish Latin' (Emerson, *Always Magic in the Air*, p. 125–6).

15 Emerson, *Always Magic in the Air*, p. xii.

16 As an indication of the perennial nature of some of these songs, in the four decades following its creation, Mann and Weil's 'You've Lost that Lovin' Feelin'' was broadcast in the United States more than ten million times.

17 *AKA Doc Pomus*. 2014. Clear Lake Historical Productions. Dirs. Peter Miller and Will Hechter. *Grace of My Heart*. 1996. Cappa Productions. Dir. Allison Anders. See also: *Hitmakers: The Teens Who Stole Pop Music*. 2001. Peter Jones Productions. Dir. Morgan Neville.

18 *Smokey Joe's Café*, which opened in 1995, ran for 2036 performances, making it the

longest-running musical revue in Broadway history. Jessie Mueller, who portrays Carole King in the Broadway production of *Beautiful* received 'Best Performance by an Actress in a Leading Role in a Musical' at the 2014 Tony Awards.

19 Burt Bacharach (with Robert Greenfield), *Anyone Who Had a Heart* (London: Atlantic Books, 2013); Carole King, *A Natural Woman: A Memoir* (London: Virago Press, 2012); Jerry Leiber and Mike Stoller (with David Ritz), *Hound Dog: The Leiber and Stoller Autobiography* (London: Omnibus Press, 2009); Rich Podolsky, *Neil Sedaka: Rock 'n' Roll Survivor: The Inside Story of his Incredible Comeback* (London: Jawbone Press, 2013); Alex Halberstadt, *Lonely Avenue: The Unlikely Life and Times of Doc Pomus* (London: Jonathan Cape, 2007); Joel Selvin, *Here Comes the Night: The Dark Soul of Bert Berns and the Dirty Business of Rhythm and Blues* (Berkeley: Counterpoint Press, 2014).

20 Emerson, *Always Magic in the Air*; Podolsky, *Don Kirshner*. See also Betrock, *Girl Groups*.

21 Ian Inglis, '"Some Kind of Wonderful": The Creative Legacy of the Brill Building', *American Music* 21/2 (2003), p. 215.

22 Jon Fitzgerald, 'When the Brill Building Met Lennon-McCartney: Continuity and Change in the Early Evolution of the Mainstream Pop Song', *Popular Music & Society* 19/1 (1995), pp. 59–77; Timothy E. Scheurer, 'The Beatles, the Brill Building, and the Persistence of Tin Pan Alley in the Age of Rock', *Popular Music & Society* 20/4 (1996), pp. 89–102.

23 Fitzgerald, 'When the Brill Building met Lennon-McCartney', p.73.

24 Scheurer, 'The Beatles, the Brill Building', p. 90.

25 Rohlfing, '"Don't say Nothin' Bad About My Baby"', p. 94.

26 Emerson, *Always Magic in the Air*, p. 214.

27 Fitzgerald, 'When the Brill Building met Lennon-McCartney', p. 61.

28 Emerson, *Always Magic in the Air*, p. xiv.

29 Available at: www.sodajerker.com/episode-6-barry-mann-and-cynthia-weil (accessed 23 February 2015).

30 Ibid.

31 Emerson, *Always Magic in the Air*, p. xv.

32 Available at: www.sodajerker.com/episode-6-barry-mann-and-cynthia-weil (accessed 23 February 2015).

33 Emerson, *Always Magic in the Air*, p. xv.

34 Inglis, '"Some Kind of Wonderful"', pp. 217–218.

35 Available at: www.sodajerker.com/

episode-6-barry-mann-and-cynthia-weil (accessed 23 February 2015).

36 Podolsky calculates that between 1960 and 1963, twenty-seven of the thirty-one songs recorded by Barry Mann became hits. See Podolsky, *Don Kirshner*, p. 129.

37 Available at: www.sodajerker.com/episode-6-barry-mann-and-cynthia-weil (accessed 23 February 2015).

38 Ibid.

39 Ibid.

40 Ibid.

41 Ibid.

42 Emerson, *Always Magic in the Air*, p. 114.

43 Podolsky, *Don Kirshner*, p. 152.

44 Available at: www.sodajerker.com/episode-25-neil-sedaka (accessed 23 February 2015).

45 Ibid.

46 Ibid.

47 Available at: www.sodajerker.com/episode-6-barry-mann-and-cynthia-weil (accessed 23 February 2015).

48 Perhaps due to Bacharach's complex musical sensibilities, they didn't achieve a number-1 record until 1968 (Emerson, *Always Magic in the Air*, pp. 28 and 247).

49 Emerson, *Always Magic in the Air*, p. 110–11.

50 Interestingly, some of these co-writing sessions were enormously successful and yet were never repeated. For instance, the one-off combination of Carole King and Howard Greenfield produced 'Crying in the Rain', a 1962 hit for The Everly Brothers.

51 Podolsky, *Don Kirshner*, p. 82.

52 Emerson, *Always Magic in the Air*, p. 120.

53 Although the Aldon writers renewed their contracts, few of them made use of their new offices on Fifth Avenue because they did not have the atmosphere of the old cubicles on Broadway.

54 Emerson, *Always Magic in the Air*, p. 254–255.

55 Even Sedaka's career has been tumultuous enough to merit a book on the subject: Rich Podolsky, *Neil Sedaka: Rock 'n' Roll Survivor: The Inside Story of His Incredible Comeback* (London: Jawbone Press, 2013).

56 Podolsky, *Don Kirshner*, p. 149.

57 Inglis, '"Some Kind of Wonderful"', p. 222.

58 Fitzgerald, 'When the Brill Building met Lennon-McCartney', p. 69.

59 Ibid., p. 75.

60 Ibid.

61 Podolsky, *Don Kirshner*, p. 165.

62 Available at: www.sodajerker.com/episode-68-miranda-cooper (accessed 23 February 2015).

6 Forging the singer-songwriter at the Los Angeles Troubadour

CHRISTA ANNE BENTLEY

In 2007, on the fifty-year anniversary of one of Los Angeles' most storied music venues, singer-songwriters Carole King and James Taylor reunited in West Hollywood to commemorate Doug Weston's Troubadour club. For both King and Taylor, the club held extra significance as the place where they first collaborated on King's song, 'You've Got a Friend' (1971). Explaining his first encounter with the song, Taylor said, 'This is a Carole King tune – a pure Carole King tune. I heard it for the first time standing right there', pointing to the sound booth lofted above the stage. 'I worked it up on the guitar and got a version of it, and in an amazing act of generosity, she let me cut this tune first. I was amazed because she was cutting *Tapestry* at the time, and that she would let go what I thought was maybe one of the best pop tunes ever written.' Then Taylor joked, 'I didn't realise at that time that I would be singing that song every night for the rest of my life. But it's a great song to be known for, and I thank Carole for it.'[1] To close the concert, the two performed a duet version of the tune. King added a counter-melodic tag to the end of the song, singing:

> Here we are at the Troubadour
> We never thought we would do this anymore,
> but this was the place that opened the door.

What was it about the Troubadour that drew artists to its stage? How did this club 'open the door' and influence the careers of artists who played there? And how did this space shape the way that a generation of music fans understood that elusive quality of personal, authentic music?

This chapter explores the network of musicians, space, atmosphere, and histories tied to Doug Weston's Troubadour between 1968 and 1975, investigating the role the Troubadour played in constructing the meaning of the singer-songwriter identity. The venue fostered a dynamic culture of singer-songwriters, including Joni Mitchell, Jackson Browne, and Randy Newman alongside King and Taylor, and during this era the Troubadour became the Mecca for artists aspiring for a place in the singer-songwriter tradition. Not only did the group of performers influence the reputation of the Troubadour to make it the premiere club for singer-songwriter performance, but the practices and logistics of the venue itself helped frame the way audiences viewed, and continue to view, singer-songwriters.

For many audiences, a singer-songwriter does not simply refer to an artist who writes and performs original music. The term is imbued with meanings based in audience perceptions of intimate performance, storytelling, an artist's vulnerability, and a sense of immediacy between the listener and the artist's persona. Consider this example from Mark Bego's 2005 biography of singer-songwriter and lifelong Angeleno Jackson Browne, which opens with a description of one of Browne's contemporary performances:

> There is only one chair set up centre stage tonight … With the exception of a large area rug on which his chair is resting, the stage is unadorned … This is no 'pretender', this is pure unadulterated Jackson Browne, bare bones, singing his songs of love, or loss, or disappointments … Tonight there is no band. There is no opening act. There are no guest stars. It is just Jackson, casually dressed, yet emotionally naked. He sits alone: a troubadour and his songs.[2]

Bego paints a picture of the singer-songwriter as a solo, acoustic performer who needs no extravagant set design, and whose most important quality in performance is the ability to emotionally bare it all on stage. This image contains the signifiers and values wrapped up in the modern definition of the singer-songwriter that has persisted for more than three decades. And the solidity of those meanings came specifically from the singer-songwriter scene cultivated at the Troubadour.

Several practices at the Troubadour contributed to the audience perception of the club as the premiere location for singer-songwriter performance and ascribing authenticity to the music performed within the space. Most importantly, the Troubadour served as a social space where elite members of the music industry fraternised. The resulting community drew more and more aspiring artists hoping to rub elbows with industry insiders, or even get their music heard. A crucial aspect to the venue came from the astute way the club's management curated an atmosphere that allowed the social scene to thrive while maintaining an environment conducive to intimate performance. Additionally, the Troubadour's practices for recruiting talent created a platform for undiscovered artists. The layout of the venue fostered new rituals for the audience to signal their approval of an artist, and successful performances in this space were said to launch the careers of new singer-songwriters. Finally, the artists themselves perpetuate the venue's significance in their own authentication narratives, continuing to connect the values of the singer-songwriter identity with the Troubadour.

My premise is based on the idea of a musical scene, a term first used by Will Straw from the field of communication studies to show how networks of people can direct the development of new musical styles. Straw distinguished a musical scene from a musical community, explaining that the latter has 'a relatively stable composition and the music(s) performed should be rooted in some sort of geographic heritage'.[3] Alternatively, Straw sees a music scene as a 'cultural space in which a large range of musical practices coexist, interacting with each other within a variety of processes of differentiation and according to widely varying trajectories of change and cross-fertilization'.[4] By exploring a singer-songwriter scene, rather than an artist's individual history, this chapter shows how a coherent identity for the singer-songwriter crystallised at the Troubadour through the club's network and interactions between the artist and audience.

Getting to the Golden State

'The Troubadour was the first place I went when I got to LA', claimed the Eagles' Don Henley, who moved to California from small-town Texas in 1970.[5] Like Henley, many artists migrated to southern California throughout the 1960s, magnetised by the burgeoning music industry in Los Angeles as several recording companies relocated to West Coast offices. In addition to abundant recording studios, the city boasted a rich history of live performance, and touring acts passed through Los Angeles in between San Diego and San Francisco en route up the California coast on a circuit that continued through Oregon and Washington. Los Angeles cradled the beginnings of several home-grown genres developed during the 1960s, including the surf music of Jan and Dean and the Beach Boys, Phil Spector's Wall of Sound created at Gold Star Studios, and the folk rock of The Byrds and The Mamas and the Papas. At the beginning of the 1970s, two new sounds dominated the Los Angeles live music scene, the singer-songwriter movement and California country rock, which both formed at the Troubadour. But the history of the club has older roots with the folk revivalists who followed the music industry's migration to the Golden State at the end of the Beat Era.

Doug Weston, the idiosyncratic owner of the Troubadour, opened the venue in 1953 at a small space next to the Coronet Theater on Hollywood's La Cienega Boulevard.[6] The name of the club evokes a romantic image of Renaissance-era wandering poets, a moniker applied to travelling folk musicians and Beatniks. The simple room featured only a small stage in the back left corner and could seat no more than sixty audience members.[7] After four years, Weston relocated the venue to a larger space that could hold up to three hundred people on Santa Monica Boulevard on the border between Hollywood and Beverly Hills. But even at the larger space, Weston maintained the intimate atmosphere created in the tiny room.[8]

The Troubadour's new location touted two main rooms: the bar area and the performance space. Inside the performance space, tables filled the room, while wooden beams ran across the ceiling, adding warmth to the relatively unadorned space. The stage stood on the right-hand side as patrons entered the room. Approximately 5m by 8m, the stage was large enough to hold a small ensemble even though many artists opted to perform solo acoustic sets. In front of the stage, the audience sat at tables topped with red-checked gingham tablecloths and flickering candles, creating a 'shabby-chic' ambience. Behind the tables stood a second bar and kitchen, from which servers delivered patrons' orders off a menu featuring wines and cheese plates.[9] Lofted above the kitchen, Weston created more seating where audience members could squeeze-in on church pews. Even from this vantage, the stage was not far away, giving listeners a sense that they were still up close to the music. The sound and lighting booth sat at the back section of the loft next to the dressing room and Doug Weston's office, where performers would access the stage by descending a wooden staircase that led from the office. Each of these elements brought out the idea of warmth and intimacy crucial to the singer-songwriter identity.

However, the Troubadour's allure – attracting Henley and others to the club – came from the way Weston set up the new venue as a bar and social scene more than any specific musical catalyst. The location was geographically central to Hollywood recording studios and Laurel Canyon, the eclectic neighbourhood many Troubadour patrons called home. In addition to the prime location, the Troubadour bar offered the perfect mix of socialising and music that differentiated it from other Sunset Strip venues, whose bars were integrated into the performance space. An elite crowd of music industry executives and insiders began frequenting the Troubadour bar, where people could hang out for the price of a beer and not have to pay admission to the venue.

The Troubadour had a fluid clientele comprised of a core group of artists, producers, and critics based in Los Angeles and a rotating cast of musicians who came through town on tour or while recording, and the bar provided a space for these people to meet, exchange ideas, and forge collaborative partnerships.[10] Los Angeles-based singer-songwriters – King, Taylor, Browne, and Mitchell – encountered touring acts, including Chicago-native John Prine and New Yorker Laura Nyro, both of whom had great success at the Troubadour.[11] As Kate Taylor – recording artist and sister to James Taylor – explained to me, she could find her friends there on any given night.[12] Remembering the feeling of familiarity walking through the club's doors, Taylor recalled:

> It was this very intimate and comfortable place where you could see a lot of the same folks there every night, a lot of friends … It always seemed like it was crowded, and everyone always seemed excited … We were all very sociable and excitable, and we would talk about gigs, songs, records, and the news of the day.[13]

Taylor's memories of the environment demonstrate how the quotidian interaction fostered the scene's sense of community. Beyond the friendships fostered by the social scene, Troubadour regulars used the venue to form industry partnerships. Well-known producers like Lou Adler and David Geffen brokered recording deals for many of the major names from the club's growing singer-songwriter constituency. The Troubadour became such a legendary location because it functioned as a space where artists, even beyond the borders of Los Angeles, converged, and producers could funnel the talent into the music industry.

The Troubadour's business practices

'Bring your axe or whatever you swing with!' read an advertisement in 1962, publicising the Troubadour's open mic, or hoot night, during the folk revival of the early 1960s.[14] The hoot was a promising platform for artists longing for a chance to be heard by the venue's esteemed crowd. Along with Weston's practices for booking talent, this recurring event fed the club's impression as a launch pad for singer-songwriters.

Weston began the hoots in the early 1960s to fill a dead night on the calendar. Unlike contemporary concert culture, in which artists perform one night in each city on a tour, the Troubadour used to book an act for a six-night engagement, playing two shows a night Tuesday through Sunday. This left Monday night available for the open mic, which required minimal advance planning. Although the title of the event hearkens back to the hootenannies held for string bands in the Appalachian Mountains, the Troubadour hoot was less an open jam session and more a formal event. Starting Monday afternoon, hopeful songwriters and other entertainers would queue up outside the venue in a line that wrapped around Doheny Drive. Booking agents auditioned the acts while still in line and picked the top candidates to perform during the 9 pm show. Producing artists such as Jackson Browne and Tom Waits, the hoot created an eager audience at the Troubadour each Monday night.

Along with the hoot, Weston sought undiscovered acts for his weekly bookings, scouring through unreleased albums to find upcoming artists. Weston's willingness to take a chance on an unknown name compounded with the presence of powerful industry voices magnified the venue's influence, as Robert Hilburn – popular music critic for the *Los Angeles Times* throughout the 1970s – explained: 'The Troubadour could ignite careers because performers were, in many ways, auditioning for the entire record industry when they stepped on that small wooden stage. Every Tuesday night, some 300 to 400 industry insiders, including radio station programmers, critics, and concert bookers, showed up to pass judgement.'[15]

Performing for a discerning audience with the ability to influence opinions in the music industry elevated the idea of a Troubadour debut, and successful sets in this particular space were said to be instrumental in propelling a relatively unknown artist into the national spotlight.

Weston's own comments about the Troubadour reveal how he viewed the club's role in discerning an artist's authenticity. When Hilburn interviewed Weston for the *Los Angeles Times* in 1970, Weston affirmed the importance of performing in an intimate setting to establish 'validity'. During the interview, Weston pointed Hilburn to a list of performers printed on the Troubadour's menu:

> We like to think of that list as a sort of hall of fame … It represents some of the finest talent of our times. And we didn't bring them to the Troubadour with just money. We can't compete with the Santa Monica Civic Auditorium or Las Vegas or a college concert date in bidding for talent. What we do offer an entertainer is a place where he can check up on his own validity. All performers remember the days when they played to small houses. They remember the waves of emotion they felt in small clubs. The Troubadour gives them a chance to get back to that atmosphere and make sure their music is still valid. It is so much more satisfying than the big concert halls where the closest person in the audience is 50 to 100 feet away. The people who play our club are sensitive artists who have something to say about our times. They are modern-day troubadours. It is important for them to get away from the crowds and check their own validity once in a while.[16]

Weston saw the size of the club as the key to the Troubadour's status, allowing both the audience to experience the immediacy of the performance and the artist to receive audience feedback.

Infamous in Hollywood for driving a hard bargain, Weston also imposed strict control over his talent, forcing artists to sign his 'options', a contract that restricted performers from playing larger venues the next time they played in the Los Angeles area. Therefore, if an artist earned national attention after playing at the club, the artist remained contractually obligated to play the Troubadour a second time regardless of the artist's ability to sell out venues three times the size. From an outsider's perspective, this made the Troubadour appear as the preferred venue for singer-songwriters regardless of their popularity or ability to play to larger houses. In actuality, this repeat business came from Weston's grip on his new acts.

'People got quiet for her'

When 'the crowd goes wild', the volume of shouts and applause indicate the audience's enthusiasm, and in many genres performers have used this reaction to gauge audience approval. But at the Troubadour, the crowd developed a new set of rituals to deem a performance legitimate. Of course, a little applause never hurt anyone's ego, but the true mark of a successful set at the Troubadour became a silently enraptured audience during a singer-songwriter's performance. The audience reaction became one of the most influential markers of authenticity for the singer-songwriter identity, and critics would convey this aspect of the performance in their reviews, implying that the power to initiate an artist as a singer-songwriter came from the audience.

Many of these practices came from the layout of the venue and the logistics of navigating the social scene at the club. Weston's layout for the seating in the performance space, combined with the atmosphere and ambience of the club, primed the audience to expect the immediacy of a singer-songwriter performance. Comparing the venue to another folk club in Los Angeles called the Ash Grove, the multi-instrumentalist Chris Darrow, a regular on the Troubadour stage, remarked, '[The Troubadour] was a little bit more intimate than the Ash Grove, in a different kind of way because the room was set up differently, but it was about the same size.'[17] In his opinion, the difference came from the 'state of the room', describing how the rectangular shape of the Troubadour made for fewer rows that were longer, which allowed listeners to feel close to the stage even from the last row.

Even in the small space, patrons had to travel between the two sections of the Troubadour, which inspired unique ways for the audience to demonstrate their engagement with the music. For example, as servers navigated the small space to deliver drinks throughout the night, it caused a great amount of noise within the audience. Many patrons even carried on conversations during performances, escalating the noise level in the room. However, if an artist captivated the audience amid the noise and commotion, a quietude came over the audience that served as a tacit approval of the performer.

Such an ability to command silence from the audience became an important factor in Joni Mitchell's authentication when she first arrived in Los Angeles as a young folk singer. When Mitchell made her debut in August of 1968, Darrow commented, 'She had a presence, and people got quiet for her. She didn't have to ask for it. It came as a result of the presence that she had. She was obviously going to do something.'[18] *Billboard* reported on the performance the following week and placed a similar emphasis on the tacit approval of the audience, demonstrated through their silence, writing, 'Miss Mitchell achieved rapport with her audience. They sat attentively as she spun stories based on human experiences and personalities which have inspired her writing.'[19] When Mitchell played the club again six months later, reviews revealed that she had gained a national following. Stephen Braitman of the *Van Nuys News* reported, 'The crowd was larger, more expectant this time, as they waited for Joni Mitchell to mount the Troubadour stage Tuesday night and begin her return engagement. Since her last opening here … a virtual cult of Joni Mitchell followers has grown and moved the Canadian-born songstress into national prominence.'[20] For Mitchell and others, silence signalled the audience's respect and connection to the songs and stories of the artist and promoted an optimal environment for listeners to experience the immediacy of the performance.

Another indication of audience engagement unique to the Troubadour's layout arose from the club's limited restrooms, with only one set of bathrooms in the entire venue located in the performance space. As country-rock singer and Troubadour regular Linda Ronstadt described in her autobiography, *Simple Dreams*:

> The limited space of the Troubadour put the bathrooms in a back hall area off the performance space. That meant everyone from the bar had to travel through the room where the stage was in order to visit the plumbing. Even if you were an up-and-coming hopeful hanging out in the bar but too broke to pay the admission fee, you could get a rich sampling of what was happening on the stage every time nature insisted.[21]

Beyond the chance happening of needing to use the restroom, patrons would flood into the listening room on the auspices of 'visiting the bathroom' when the music inside sounded promising – a request that the bouncers could not deny even to bar patrons who had not paid the admission fee. As Jackson Browne recalled, 'If there was somebody everybody was waiting to see, the bar would empty out into the room for that person's set … If you could empty the bar into the house for part of your set, that was doing pretty well.'[22] Audience members and critics perpetuate the importance of this method of granting credibility as they retell the story of Elton John's debut performance, one of the most often mythologised stories of a Troubadour debut.

John's first performance at the Troubadour in August of 1970 was also his premiere in the United States. According to legend, on opening night of his week-long gig in Los Angeles, the young British artist accompanied himself on the piano to a small audience sitting in the performance space. The rest of the patrons were packed into the bar area. However, when John played his song 'Take Me To the Pilot', the bar crowd poured into the venue, captivated by his earnest performance and entertaining musicianship. The next morning, Hilburn published an unrestrained review in the *Los Angeles Times*. 'Rejoice. Rock music, which has been going through a rather uneventful period lately, has a new star. He's Elton John, a 23-year old Englishman whose United States debut Tuesday night at the Troubadour was, in almost every way, magnificent.' Hilburn declared John's music 'staggeringly original', comparing the artist's uniqueness to other Troubadour favorites Randy Newman and Laura Nyro and acknowledging John's place in the canon of singer-songwriters to emerge from the club. Hilburn concluded, 'By the end of the evening, there was no question about John's talent and potential. Tuesday night at the Troubadour was just the beginning. He's going to be one of rock's biggest and most important stars.'[23] The way that the story of John's premiere has lived on in the oral history of the venue reinscribes the importance of the event and the method that the audience used to ensure John's place in the tradition.

The Troubadour today

Today, artist memoirs and biographies contribute to the Troubadour's legendary status by pointing to their debuts as turning points in their careers. Carole King has continued to emphasise the Troubadour as a defining piece of her legacy. When King first made the transition from Brill Building songwriter to solo performer in 1970, her album, *Writer*, received little critical attention and low album sales. But after King took the Troubadour stage in 1971, Hilburn lauded her talent, writing, 'The marvelous reception being paid this week to Carole King at the Troubadour – where all tickets for her six-night engagement were sold out two weeks in advance – underscores the fact that singer-songwriters in all probability, have never had it so good in pop music.'[24] Following this performance, King's *Tapestry* (1971) broke industry sales records, lasting seventeen weeks on *Billboard*'s Hot 100 chart, and earned King four Grammy awards.

King's 2012 memoir, *A Natural Woman*, dedicates an entire chapter to her Troubadour premiere. King claims that during the time onstage, she learned how to overcome crippling stage fright, writing, 'The more I communicated my joy to the audience, the more joy they communicated back to me. All I needed to do was sing with conviction, speak my truth from the heart, honestly and straightforwardly, and offer my words, ideas, and music to the audience as if it were one collective friend that I'd known for a very long time.'[25] King accentuates the importance of the connection between artist and audience, facilitated by the size and atmosphere of the venue. 'I had found the key to success in performing. It was to be authentically myself.'[26] Claiming that the Troubadour allowed her to access this part of her artistry, King's language illustrates the perception of a singer-songwriter's authenticity based on an artist's display of honesty, vulnerability, and sincerity during a performance.

In recent years, the Troubadour has featured mainly local Indie groups, but the venue maintains its importance in authentication narratives for singer-songwriters. Performers continue to animate their sets at the club as a way to prove their place as an established singer-songwriter. For example, James Blake, an electronic artist from England, chose the Troubadour as the site for his US debut in 2011. The stories that emerged after Blake's performance echo the themes of Troubadour premieres forty years earlier, emphasising the importance of the venue's atmosphere and audience's spellbound silence. A review in *LA Weekly* by journalist Lainna Fader proclaimed, 'He used space and silence to great advantage in his short but mesmerising set, playing nearly an hour without more than a couple words. The soul in his music wrapped around every member of the silent crowd, who kept quiet all night', in language that even evokes the tone of Hilburn's effusive reviews.[27] At the performance, Blake paid homage to the Troubadour's legacy by ending his set with a cover of Joni Mitchell's 'A Case of You' (1971). The choice demonstrated his knowledge and proficiency within the canon of works by singer-songwriters that turned the venue into the institution it is today.

The version of the story published by *Los Angeles Times* critic August Brown further divulged that Mitchell herself was present for Blake's set, writing:

> Just before his encore at the sold-out Troubadour on Monday night, UK singer-producer James Blake had someone to thank. Introducing his last song, a lonely and lilting solo piano cover, he first lauded its songwriter. 'She's been such an influence on my writing for the last year or so, and that she might be here to hear this is such a massive honor.' Then he played Joni Mitchell's 'A Case of You', and at that the audience gasped a bit and searched around the room. Sure enough, in the upper VIP balcony, there was the Lady of the Canyon, watching over the proceedings.[28]

Blake's biography reiterates the importance of this event, reading 'It all started, says Blake, with Joni Mitchell. His favorite singer and songwriter came to see him at the Troubadour in Los Angeles two years ago and hung around afterwards to talk. "She's an oracle … I learned a lot just from meeting her."'[29] Mitchell's presence at his performance acted as validation of Blake, inducting him into the Troubadour hall of fame.

This exploration reveals how the Troubadour became the premiere establishment for singer-songwriters, and in turn, how that institution has framed the perception of the singer-songwriter. Initially, the mixture of powerful industry voices at the Troubadour and its reputation as a proving ground drew artists to the venue. Meanwhile, the club's atmosphere, curated by the management, reinforced the values connected with the singer-songwriter identity for the audience. The identity forged within the Troubadour's walls solidified the values of personal music, authenticity, vulnerability, and intimate performance as the defining marks of artists deemed singer-songwriters, and continues to inform the listener's perception of this category.

Notes

1 Carole King and James Taylor, *Live at the Troubadour*, Hear Music, HRM-32053, 2010.

2 Mark Bego, *Jackson Browne: Timeless Troubadour, His Life and Music* (New York: Citadel Press, 2005), pp. 1–2.

3 Will Straw, 'Systems of Articulation, Logics of Change: Communities and Scenes in Popular Music', in *Cultural Studies* 5 (1991): p. 373.

4 Ibid.

5 Joe Smith, ed. Michael Fink, *Off the Record: An Oral History of Popular Music* (New York: Warner Books, 1988) p. 351.

6 Since 2009, the Coronet Theater serves as the new location for Largo at the Coronet, a music and comedy club owned by Mark Flanagan, who keeps the original Troubadour open as 'The Little Room'.

7 Myrna Oliver, 'Doug Weston, Troubadour Founder, Dies', *Los Angeles Times*, 15 February 1999. Available at: articles.latimes.com/1999/feb/15/local/me-8369 (accessed 5 June 2014).

8 Today, this neighborhood is known as West Hollywood, incorporated as its own city in Los Angeles County in 1984.

9 Menu accessed through the personal collection of Henry Diltz housed at the Grammy Museum's Laurel Canyon Exhibit, May 2014.

10 This is consistent with Straw's definition of a scene in 'Systems of Articulation'.

11 Robert Hilburn, 'Prine Stealing the Show at the Troubadour', *Los Angeles Times*, 18 December 1971, p. B6. Pete Johnson, 'Laura Nyro at Troubadour', *Los Angeles Times*, 31 May 1969, p. A6.

12 Interview with author, Santa Monica, CA, 6 April 2014.

13 Ibid.

14 Advertisement from the personal collection of Tracy Newman.

15 Robert Hilburn, 'A Legend Rocks On', *Los Angeles Times*, 25 December 2007. Available at: articles.latimes.com/2007/dec/25/entertainment/et-troubadour25 (accessed 10 May 2014).

16 Robert Hilburn, 'Atmosphere, Talent Key To Club's Success', *Los Angeles Times*, 2 August 1970, p. M1.

17 Interview with author in Claremont, CA, 6 May 2014.

18 Ibid.

19 Eliot Tiegel, 'Joni Mitchell Clicks in "Turned On" Act', *Billboard*, 15 June 1968, p. 18.

20 Stephen Braitman, 'Joni Mitchell Starring at Troubadour', *Van Nuys News*, 24 January 1969. Available at: jonimitchell.com/library/view.cfm?id=1480 (accessed 20 June 2014).

21 Linda Ronstadt, *Simple Dreams* (New York: Simon & Schuster, 2013), pp. 117–18.

22 Richard Cromelin, 'Living Up to Their Legends', *Los Angeles Times*, 20 February 2009. Available at: articles.latimes.com/2003/feb/20/news/wk-cover20 (accessed 15 May 2014).

23 Robert Hilburn, 'Elton John New Rock Talent', *Los Angeles Times*, 27 August 1970, p. D22

24 Robert Hilburn, 'Carole King's New Role as a Singer', *Los Angeles Times*, 22 May 1971, p. A6.

25 Carole King, *A Natural Woman* (New York: Grand Central Publishing, 2012), p. 225.

26 Ibid.

27 Lainna Fader 'Live Review: James Blake at the Troubadour' on *LAWeekly*, 24 May 2011, www.laweekly.com/westcoastsound/2011/05/24/live-review-james-blake-at-the-troubadour, accessed 2 June 2014.

28 August Brown, 'Live Review: James Blake at the Troubadour', *Pop & Hiss,* The L.A. Times Music Blog, 24 May 2011. Available at: latimesblogs.latimes.com/music_blog/2011/05/live-review-james-blake-at-the-troubadour.html (accessed 1 June 2014).

29 James Blake 'Biography', Cat's Cradle Events, 13 May 2013. Available at: www.catscradle.com/event/261575-james-blake-carrboro/ (accessed 1 June 2014).

7 The 'professional' singer-songwriter in the 1970s

MICHAEL BORSHUK

When introducing his 2001 oral history of the Brill Building for *Vanity Fair* magazine, David Kamp suggests that the early 1960s marked a paradigm shift in American popular music, from the workmanlike output of New York's contracted composers to the more baldly personal material from the singer-songwriters that followed:

> The Brill Building sound was the *sound* of bigness and tidiness, of exuberance underpinned by professionalism – the fulcrum between the shiny craftsmanship of Tin Pan Alley and the primal energy of 60s soul and rock. It represented the last great era of assembly-line-manufactured pop – before the success of The Beatles and Bob Dylan lent a stigma to not writing your own material.[1]

Kamp's historical trajectory here corresponds tidily with a common narrative about popular music's changes in the 1960s.

In many listeners' views, that decade saw the ascendance of the introspective voice in songwriting, a tradition derived perhaps from Harry Smith's *Anthology of American Folk Music*, and best defined through the iconic examples of Bob Dylan, Paul Simon, and Joni Mitchell. For half a century, popular music had depended on a symbiosis between the offstage composer (a lineage that ran from Irving Berlin through George Gershwin to Jerry Leiber and Mike Stoller or Gerry Goffin and Carole King) and the celebrity performers of stage, film, and record. The late 1960s, on the other hand, merged these roles dramatically. From Dylan onwards, the story apparently goes, the singer was more likely to have written his own material, offering an emotional proximity and raw sincerity that eschewed overtly commercial gloss. Moreover, in this narrative, this ostensible earnestness continued into the following decade, with artists like James Taylor, Janis Ian, and Bruce Springsteen.

But the 1970s also saw the rise of a different kind of singer-songwriter: namely, the 'professional' composer. These artists were steeped less in the naked performance of the folk tradition than in the more businesslike conventions of Tin Pan Alley and the Brill Building, both of which Kamp perhaps too quickly presumed dead by the early seventies. In short, to remember that not all singer-songwriters after the mid-sixties aspired to unchecked autobiography or raw introspection is to complicate the monolithic narrative that Kamp and others propose.

This chapter will focus on three examples of representative artists in the more 'professional' vein of singer-songwriter during the 1970s – Randy Newman, Billy Joel, and the composing team of Walter Becker and Donald Fagen from Steely Dan. Newman and the Steely Dan team actually began their careers as contract songwriters in the late 1960s; Joel toiled as a working musician in the same period before earning notice as a solo performer. More importantly, each of these artists derived his style in the comprehensive manner that characterised Tin Pan Alley composition, drawing from diverse musical genres, exploring the wide range of formulaic song patterns that defines American popular music, and focusing on sophisticated arrangements and glossy studio recording.

I should be clear here that the brand of Tin Pan Alley composer I have in mind throughout this chapter is to be found among those songwriters who first composed mass-mediated popular music in the early twentieth century: namely, Irving Berlin, George Gershwin, Cole Porter, Richard Rodgers, Jerome Kern, and Harold Arlen. These composers, unlike their predecessors, were not merely writing for the American sheet-music market, but instead, provided the songs made famous in film and on record and radio between 1920 and 1960. And it was in this tradition, I suggest, that the 'professional' singer-songwriters of the 1970s developed their styles, even though none of them actually worked in the Brill Building proper, as the assumption is such professional songwriters often did.[2] Ultimately, this chapter will explain how, while our idea of the American singer-songwriter is shaped so much by so-called 'personal' artists, this other, more workmanlike approach was just as tangible an influence on 1970s popular music. Moreover, while I use this argument to offer an extended discussion of these artists' eclectic, incorporative use of musical style and existing song forms, I also suggest how this approach had unexpected social resonances, specifically with regard to American popular music's difficult engagement with racial expectations and aesthetic cross-fertilisation across ethnic lines.

Unlike many of their contemporaries, Newman, Joel, and the Steely Dan duo all cultivated their musical approaches in overtly commercial contexts. All three could give the illusion of intimacy, offering character-driven narratives that imitated the autobiographical style of folk-derived singer-songwriters.[3] But while the latter group seemed ostensibly 'authentic', unfettered by the artifice of popular music's purely 'manufactured' forms, the 'professional' singer-songwriters were less determined to mark their distance from the music's market history. That does not mean they sacrificed artistry for mercenary reasons, but rather, that each recognised the indivisibility of pop music from its economic context. For these artists, creativity and attention to detail were the vehicles for a comfortable working life, and all three developed their styles aware of the artistic benefits to be gained by working with commercial interests rather than posturing defiantly against them.

A brief survey of their early careers shows these artists' tangible connections to commerce. Newman, for example, inherited composing-for-hire as a family business. His uncles were Alfred, Lionel, and Emil Newman, brothers who wrote film music and boasted dozens of screen credits between them.[4] At seventeen, Randy Newman was signed to write for Los Angeles-based Metric Music, a division of Liberty Records. This early period featured some precocious success placing songs – as with Judy Collins' 1966 rendition of 'I Think It's Going to Rain Today' – but also some notable failures, like Frank Sinatra's rejection of 'Lonely at the Top', two years before Newman recorded the song himself on his 1972 album *Sail Away*. Even as Newman was making the transition from paid composer, he followed his famous uncles into writing for the movies, when Norman Lear contracted him to score the comedy *Cold Turkey*, released in 1971.

Similarly, Steely Dan began as professional songwriters: first in the final days of the Brill Building and then for ABC-Dunhill Records in Los Angeles.[5] Becker and Fagen met in the late 1960s, as undergraduates at Bard College. The two performed in bands in college, but after leaving Bard for New York City, they initially focused on writing rather than gigging. Seeking financial gain, Becker and Fagen cold-called music publishers in Manhattan but suffered numerous rejections. Just like Newman's experience with Sinatra, Becker and Fagen learned their quirky songbook was incongruous with many existing artists' styles. Finally, the pair caught a break when Kenny Vance of Jay and the Americans (and its Brill Building publishing subsidiary, JATA) took a liking to their material and offered to manage them. Under Vance's tutelage, Becker and Fagen recorded demos, toured briefly with Jay and the Americans, scored a low-budget film entitled *You Gotta Walk It Like You Talk It or You'll Lose That Beat*, but, alas sold only one song – a ballad called 'I Mean to Shine' – interestingly, to Barbra Streisand. By 1971, producer Gary Katz invited them to Los Angeles to write songs for ABC-Dunhill Records, as part of the label's attempt to exploit the 'underground' youth market. Again, though, the duo found their offbeat material unsuitable for other acts. Trying to recover on its investment, the label commissioned Becker and Fagen to assemble their own band and record the songs themselves. Steely Dan was born.

Unlike Newman, Becker, and Fagen, Joel's early apprenticeship did not include a stint as a staff composer, but his beginnings are no less coloured by the 'business' of music. As a teenager, Joel was already performing around his home town, Hicksville on Long Island, New York, when he entered the orbit of George 'Shadow' Morton, a producer who worked with artists ranging from Janis Ian to Iron Butterfly. In 1964, Morton secured a job writing for Leiber and Stoller's Red Bird Records by bringing them the demo for the soon-to-be Shangri-Las' hit 'Remember (Walking in the Sand)'. Uncredited, Joel, at age fourteen, performed the song's opening piano figure, from a part Morton hummed to him.[6] Over the next decade, Joel gigged in New York-area bands, eventually signing an ill-advised contract with Artie Ripp and his slapdash label, Family Records. When Ripp made a mess of Joel's first record, *Cold Spring Harbor*, by recording it at the wrong speed, Joel tried to elude his legal commitment by disappearing to Los Angeles. There he performed solo piano under the pseudonym Bill Martin, a tenure made famous in 'Piano Man'. His exile lasted several months, until finally he signed with Columbia Records – who negotiated a settlement with Family – and recorded the series of LPs that saw him ascend to pop stardom by the mid-1970s.[7]

I offer these snapshot biographies to show how these artists all came of age creatively within a commercial context that validated musical professionalism and the labour of art. The musical *zeitgeist* of the later 1960s and early 1970s honoured work that (at least on the surface) defied so-called crass commercialism and privileged ingenuous expression. Even an earlier Brill Building mainstay like King had been rebranded within this context. Note how, as King made the move from staff writer to performer, she appeared on the cover of her most famous album, *Tapestry*, barefoot and gazing solemnly at the camera. On the other hand, the 'professional' singer-songwriters – Newman, Joel, and Becker and Fagen – kept exaggerated earnestness at arm's length by meaningfully extending the more 'artificial' and 'manufactured' aesthetics of their Tin Pan Alley and Brill Building antecedents.[8]

All three artists used song forms and musical conventions drawn from early twentieth-century Tin Pan Alley. The most obvious was Newman, whose compositions sometimes sounded strikingly anachronistic. Take 'Yellow Man', recorded in the studio for 1970's *12 Songs*, and then again, with an audience, for the following year's *Randy Newman Live*. While the tune's lilting swing suggests the 1920s and 30s, the song's compositional shape also announces that historical connection, structured as it is around the 32-bar, AABA lyric form that dominated Tin Pan Alley. Newman's studio version solidifies the homage with a theatrically dated scat vocal section. Moreover, the tune's place in the sequencing on *12 Songs* completes a kind of American songbook suite – beginning with Newman's cover of Mack Gordon and Harry Revel's 'Underneath the Harlem Moon' from 1932, and continuing with 'Yellow Man' and a mordant parody of Stephen Foster's mid-nineteenth-century minstrel staple, 'My Old Kentucky Home'.

'Yellow Man' was not anomalous among Newman's compositions for its use of historical song form. One of Newman's best-known songs,

'Political Science' also uses the 32-bar, AABA Tin Pan Alley model, in a raucous number that comically imagines the United States obliterating most of the globe. The ironic effect – juxtaposing the primary form of American popular music's earnest past with an unabashedly malicious sentiment – is a signature element of Newman's style. As Jon Pareles notes astutely: 'Singing in a homely croak, he uses the nostalgic bounce of ragtime and the hymnlike chords of parlor songs to hold sentiments that would appall Stephen Foster. He also takes a craftsman's pride as he honors or smoothly disrupts verse-chorus-bridge song forms'.[9] Compositionally, 'Political Science' honours traditional form straightforwardly – using the 32-bar template, and appending an introductory 'verse'. Historically, most standards in the American songbook featured this element: a modified recitative that established the song's narrative before moving into the 32-bar 'chorus' that constituted the tune's more familiar shape. Since the latter half of the twentieth century, many singers have excised these verses in performance, with some notable exceptions. (Frank Sinatra, for example, seemed fond of the introductory verse to the Gershwins' 'I've Got a Crush On You'; Judy Garland, true to her musical theatre sensibility, restores these narrative song parts on her famous *Carnegie Hall* live LP of 1961.) Throughout his early writing, Newman used the Tin Pan Alley 'verse' as a framing element. Other examples include the funereal opening to the otherwise comic 'Davy the Fat Boy' (from his debut, *Randy Newman*), or the southern speaker's frustrated complaint, which opens 'Rednecks' (from the 1974 album, *Good Old Boys*.)

Even when Newman was not looking to the past compositionally, he still voiced that debt through performance, as with the ragtime piano flourishes on 'So Long Dad' (from *Randy Newman*) or 'Simon Smith and His Dancing Bear' (on *Sail Away*). But that's not to say the songwriter presented himself as a museum piece. On all of his records between 1968 and 1979, he also played more straightforward 'rock' material. (Notable examples include 'Mama Told Me Not to Come' on *12 Songs* or the slyly lascivious 'You Can Leave Your Hat On' on *Sail Away*.) The effect of these stylistic juxtapositions, I would suggest, was to argue against the idea of constant change in popular music. Instead, Newman consciously reminded audiences of professional composing's long tradition, and the commercial artistry contemporary songwriters had inherited. An obvious reminder occurs in the closing line of 'Sigmund Freud's Impersonation of Albert Einstein in America', from the 1977 album *Little Criminals*, when Newman directly echoes his forefather Berlin: 'May all your Christmases be white'.

Though perhaps less 'formally' obvious, Joel and Steely Dan could be similarly reverential. These artists generally eschewed a strict fidelity to earlier song forms, but did occasionally recreate sounds from previous eras. Two notable examples would be Joel's playfully antique 'Root Beer

Rag', from his album *Streetlife Serenade*, or Steely Dan's unironic cover of Duke Ellington's 1926 'East St. Louis Toodle-Oo' on *Pretzel Logic* from 1974.[10] Beyond these rarities, though, both artists' sounds were clearly rooted in the 1970s. In a 2012 interview, Fagen even self-consciously distanced his collaborations with Becker from the Tin Pan Alley tradition:

> I don't think Walter and I were songwriters in the traditional sense, neither the Tin Pan Alley Broadway variety nor the "staffer" type of the fifties and sixties. An attentive listening to our early attempts at normal genre-writing will certainly bear me out. It soon became more interesting to exploit and subvert traditional elements of popular songwriting and to combine this material with the jazz-based music we had grown up with.[11]

And yet, the distancing gesture here, I would argue, confirms Steely Dan's relationship to the history of American professional songwriting. Their subversion of 'traditional elements', that is, required a fairly academic awareness of those same qualities. Joel's awareness was no less studied. Even in the late stages of his career, when he has avoided producing new popular music, Joel still speaks admiringly about the tradition out of which he styled himself: 'I wanted to write something other than the three-minute pop tune even though that's an art form unto itself. Gershwin was incredible, Cole Porter was incredible, Richard Rodgers, great stuff … the three-minute symphony'.[12]

While Steely Dan and Joel avoided Tin Pan Alley's musical forms, they were certainly faithful to its incorporative ethos. Remember that the composers who defined the American songbook (Berlin, Gershwin, Rodgers, Arlen, and Porter) were all adept at commercially absorbing a broad range of source materials. As Ann Douglas summarises specifically of Irving Berlin: 'Berlin derived his style from dozens of sources – English music-hall songs, Irish ballads, Stephen Foster melodies, American marches, and the [African Americans] who created and played ragtime'.[13] Indeed, the composer's early success modelled the value of an attentive ear and an inclusive style – and many followed. Consider Gershwin's prescient use of jazz elements in 1921's *Rhapsody in Blue*, Porter's approximation of folk-country music for 1934's 'Don't Fence Me In' and the French café *chanson* in 1953's 'Allez-Vous En', or Rodgers' ability to generate a believable but ersatz Austrian folk song with 1959's 'Edelweiss' from *The Sound of Music*. As these songwriters realised, eclecticism could appeal to many audiences. And it is that comprehensive spirit that recognisably defines Joel and Steely Dan as songwriters in this long tradition.

In the catalogues of both, we hear a capacity for genre-blending, and the integration of incongruous elements into one stylistic whole. Consider, for example, Joel's range, from the cascading barroom sing-along of 'Piano Man', through the torch song of 'New York State of Mind', to the straightforward rock of 'Big Shot'. The opening track, appropriately enough, on Joel's *Streetlife Serenade*, the album that marked his return to New York, is 'Say Goodbye to Hollywood', which, from its introductory thumping drums to its wall-of-sound orchestration, impersonates Phil Spector's production from the 1960s. Indeed, Joel was always adept at incorporating existing elements, perhaps most obviously later, with 1983's *An Innocent Man*, a pastiche album that pays tribute to the doo-wop and early rock of his youth. Maybe his greatest talent, though, was not recreating the past, but, rather, making comprehensive use of musical styles in vogue. His most famous ballad, 1977's 'Just the Way You Are', with its Fender Rhodes piano and pop-jazz harmonic structure is genealogically related to Stevie Wonder's number 1 single 'You Are the Sunshine of My Life', from four years earlier; the neighbourhood narratives of *The Stranger* seem indebted to the working-class stories on which Bruce Springsteen rode to superstardom in the mid-1970s; and when New Wave erupted at the end of the decade, Joel turned to Farfisa organ and synthesisers to approximate The Cars and Elvis Costello on 1980's *Glass Houses*.

Steely Dan was no less eclectic or incorporative. While the group is largely heralded for its use of a harmonic complexity and instrumental vocabulary drawn from post-war jazz, Becker and Fagen brought a wider range of genres into their sonic mix. 'Pearl of the Quarter' and 'With a Gun', from 1973's *Countdown to Ecstasy* and 1974's *Pretzel Logic*, respectively, are essentially country tunes. 'The Fez' from 1976's *The Royal Scam*, and 'Glamour Profession' from 1980's *Gaucho* sound very much like disco. *Gaucho*'s lead track, 'Babylon Sisters' borrows from reggae music. Structurally, the genre that Becker and Fagen most frequently turned to was the blues, the basic I–IV–V, 12-bar form of which provided the architecture for many of their most famous songs: 'Pretzel Logic', 'Black Friday', 'Chained Lightning', 'Peg'. In all, Steely Dan's opportunistic eclecticism is hardly surprising, given many of their offstage remarks about musical influences. In his 2013 book *Eminent Hipsters*, Fagen, for example, remembers admiringly how adeptly Henry Mancini – one of the great professional composers in American entertainment – had appropriated various elements in vogue in post-war jazz to score television's *Peter Gunn*. 'The idiom he used', Fagen writes, 'was largely out of Gil Evans and other progressive arrangers plus the odd shot of rhythm and blues. . . For small groups, Mancini hijacked the elegant "locked hands" voicing style associated with pianists Milt Bucker and George Shearing'.[14] Fans of Steely Dan will recognise Fagen's use of the verb 'hijack' in this instance as complimentary, not pejorative. Case in point: called out in an 1980 interview about similarities between Steely Dan's recent song 'Gaucho' and a 1974 Keith Jarrett jazz tune entitled, 'Long as You Know You're Living Yours', Fagen gleefully remarked, 'Hell, we steal. We're the robber barons of rock and roll'.[15]

In addition, it is worth acknowledging the profound influence that these 'professional' songwriters drew from African American vernacular music. While that borrowing is hardly surprising for any white artist after rhythm and blues had been appropriated commercially into rock and roll, I would argue Newman, Joel, and Steely Dan used black music in a more complicated way. The 'professional' songwriters, that is, resemble their Tin Pan Alley ancestors more than they do Elvis Presley or The Rolling Stones. Within rock's swaggering ethos, the white performer seems perennially intent on legitimising his use of black musical style by staging a racialised rebellion, arguing against the accusation of theft by dramatising how 'black' he can be. Elvis' gyrations, Mick Jagger's strut: these are notable instances of the white performer's dramatisation of 'blackness', by imitating the exaggerated physicality white audiences have historically assumed of African Americans. (The historian Eric Lott suggests that this recurring spectacle is blackface minstrelsy's 'unconscious return'.[16]) Newman, Joel, and Steely Dan, however, all thoroughly incorporated black musical influence, but without the anxious theatrical baggage of racial masquerade. Swagger, dance, strut: none of these were key to these artists' onstage personae. Newman's stage demeanour, for instance, was almost self-consciously non-theatrical. Appearing always in glasses and semi-casual clothing, he appeared more professorial than glamourous. Joel, while slightly livelier, embodied the low-key spirit of lounge pianists everywhere throughout the seventies. Despite some touring early in the 1970s, Becker and Fagen avoided live performance altogether by the decade's second half. And yet, all of these artists are heavily indebted to black music. Newman's vocal style turns on blues singing's elision and rhythmic play; Joel often musically invokes Ray Charles; Steely Dan, beyond their obvious debt to blues and jazz, modelled the arrangements for tracks like 'Peg' and 'Josie' on the tightly coordinated charts they loved in early R&B music.[17]

In short, the 'professional' singer-songwriters turned to African American musical aesthetics for their sonic qualities, but not as a vehicle for racial rebellion. In this, they followed both their distant Tin Pan Alley antecedents and their more recent Brill Building forebears, all of whom understood the compositional possibility that the African American musical vernacular posed. Think, for instance, of the vogue for blues-based material in the 1920s and 30s, perhaps best exemplified by Arlen's 'Stormy Weather' of 1933. Recall, later, how Leiber and Stoller turned a commissioned assignment into an approximation of blues musical veracity when they wrote 'Hound Dog' for Big Mama Thornton in 1952. In these instances, the composers isolated the musical qualities – not the theatrical aspects – at the heart of African American music and turned these back to the world into something palatable to a broad, interracial audience. Similarly, Newman, Joel, and Steely Dan all understood that African

American music was less a medium for shocking middle-class parents – as Presley or Jagger might have implied – than the bedrock of American popular music.

Finally, beyond their studied use of songwriting conventions, the 'professional' songwriters were all masterful throughout the seventies in bringing a similarly academic sensibility to studio production values. Steely Dan, of course, is legendary for having run through dozens of takes at every stage of the recording process. But Newman's and Joel's meticulous arrangements suggest they were just as attentive to detail. Unsurprisingly, the credits for these artists' albums feature many of the same top-flight studio musicians. And yet, while this approach extended a legacy of craftsmanship that had run from Berlin through Goffin and King, changing currents in popular music conspired to limit its historical window. With music marketing's shift to the visual in the culture of 1980s MTV, for instance, note that Joel was alone among these artists in maintaining a widespread popularity, aided no doubt by the appearance of his supermodel wife, Christie Brinkley, in his videos.[18] If, as David Kamp suggested in *Vanity Fair*, changes in popular music sped the death of a Tin Pan Alley-derived approach to songwriting, maybe the growing intimacy between visual culture and the recording industry after the 1970s was, ultimately, the more momentous paradigm shift.

Notes

1 David Kamp, 'The Hit Factory: An Oral History of the Brill Building', *Vanity Fair*, November 2001, p. 248. Available at: davidkamp.com/2006/09/the_hit_factory.php (accessed 1 May 2015). While Kamp's narrative focuses much on popular music's shift towards privileging the 'authenticity' associated with performers singing their own compositions, others argue that changes in musical taste came just as much from audiences' attraction to the 'primal energy' of rock and soul performance to which Kamp also alludes here. As such, these critics suggest that the 1950s, not the 1960s, was the more significant decade. For example, in his book *Tin Pan Alley* (New York: Donald Fine, 1988), David Jasen credits the shift to rock and roll's emergence in the mid-1950s, since the new genre privileged the vivacity of performance over songwriting craft. Similarly, William G. Hyland writes of the 1950s: 'The gap between the music of Rodgers and Berlin and rock and roll grew ever wider until it was a chasm. And into this gap came television with its own insatiable appetite for visual effects, for charismatic personalities, and for new music and new performers'. William G. Hyland, *The Song is Ended: Songwriters and American Music, 1900–1950* (New York: Oxford University Press, 1995), p. 294.

2 Just as I have tried to be clear about what I mean by 'Tin Pan Alley' – that is, to refer more to a generation of composers and the style of songwriting they inaugurated than to the actual geographical section of Lower Manhattan that housed commercial music publishers – I also wish to point out here that the idea of 'the Brill Building' has come to be used in a similarly metonymical fashion. The Brill Building is an actual architectural structure in midtown Manhattan, but the term's use has come to refer to the mid-century songwriters who worked in that location and those (like Neil Sedaka, or Goffin and King) who toiled at 1650 Broadway just a few blocks away (See Chapter 5 in this volume).

3 Think, for instance, of Newman and Joel's most naked-sounding piano ballads like 'I'll Be Home', and 'She's Always a Woman', respectively, or Steely Dan's angst-ridden first-person narratives like 'Dr. Wu' or 'Deacon Blues'.

4 Alfred contributed soundtracks to many canonical Hollywood films, including *All About Eve* (1950), *The Seven Year Itch* (1955), and *The*

Greatest Story Ever Told (1965). Emil and Lionel composed for less well-known films, but all three were firmly entrenched in the business, including a broad range of conducting and musical direction work.

5   While it is difficult to eulogise the Brill Building with chronological exactness, Kamp dates its demise to the early 70s, when many staff songwriters moved to Los Angeles, often to pursue their own recording and performing careers (Kamp, 'The Hit Factory', p. 248). Notice that Becker and Fagen's careers unintentionally paralleled this broader narrative, as I discuss below.

6   'Bumpy, Bikers and the Story Behind "Leader of the Pack"'. (*Fresh Air*. NPR Radio. 26 September 2013.) Available at www.npr .org/2013/09/26/200445875/bumpy-bikers-and-the-story-behind-leader-of-the-pack (accessed 30 August 2014). In Jay Warner, *American Singing Groups: A History from 1940s to Today* (New York: Hal Leonard, 1992), Warner confirms that Joel was the piano player on Morton's demos, but also casts doubt on the apocryphal story that Joel played on the actual session for The Shangri-Las' 'Leader of the Pack', p. 447. (Joel himself has made this claim at times, only to waver and suggest his contributions might not have made it to the actual record.)

7   Billy Joel, interview with Tom Hoving. (*20/20*. ABC-TV.1 May 1980.) Available at www.youtube.com/watch?v=i-gUgyf1-3w (accessed 30 August 2014).

8   In some cases, though, record covers still created the illusion of autobiographical intimacy. Early album covers for Newman's eponymous debut and *Sail Away*, or Joel's *Cold Spring Harbor* and *Piano Man* feature the same kind of unadorned photographic closeness to the artist I see in King's *Tapestry*. From the mid-70s onwards, though, their album art was much more self-consciously theatrical. Steely Dan, on the other hand, never appeared on the front of an LP sleeve.

9   Jon Pareles, 'Songs for All Occasions, But Sparing Ground Zero'. *The New York Times* 14 June 2002. Available at www.nytimes .com/2002/06/14/movies/pop-review-songs-for-all-occasions-but-sparing-ground-zero. html (accessed 30 August 2014).

10   Steely Dan often paid tribute to their jazz influences through musical allusion. The piano figure that opens the early hit, 'Rikki Don't Lose That Number', for instance, directly echoes Horace Silver's 'Song for my Father'. The instrumental section that closes 'Parker's Band', a memorial to bebop saxophonist Charlie Parker, is a quotation from Parker's own 'Bongo Bop'.

11   Bruce Pollack, 'Donald Fagen Interview'. *The Steely Dan Reader: Four Decades of News and Interviews* 7 November 2012. Available at steelydanreader.com/2012/11/07/ donald-fagen-interview/ (accessed 30 August 2014).

12   Andrew Goldman, 'Billy Joel on Not Working and Not Giving Up Drinking'. *The New York Times* 24 May 2013. Available at www .nytimes.com/2013/05/26/magazine/billy-joel-on-not-working-and-not-giving-up-drinking. html (accessed 30 August 2014).

13   Ann Douglas, *Terrible Honesty: Mongrel Manhattan in the 1920s* (New York: FSG, 1995), p. 357.

14   Donald Fagen, *Eminent Hipsters* (New York: Viking, 2013), pp. 16–17.

15   This interview was conducted by David Breskin for the March 1981 issue of *Musician* magazine. It is reprinted online at *The Steely Dan Reader: Four Decades of News and Interviews*. Available at steelydanreader. com/1981/03/01/steely-dan-interview (accessed 30 August 2014).

16   Eric Lott, *Love and Theft: Blackface Minstrelsy and the American Working Class*. (New York: Oxford University Press, 1993), p. 5.

17   Greil Marcus makes this comparison between Newman's vocal style and blues singing in *Mystery Train: Images of America in Rock 'n' Roll Music* (New York: E. P. Dutton, 1975), pp. 112–36. Joel commented on his debt to African American music at his 1999 induction to the Rock and Roll Hall of Fame. After acknowledging a long list of African American musical influences, Joel quipped as follows about the occasional accusation that he is a derivative artist: 'Let me just suggest this: if anyone who was derivative like I'm derivative should be automatically excluded from this institution would mean that there wouldn't be any white people here'. Finally, the black guitarist Vernon Reid comments on Steely Dan's relationship to black music in an interview with journalist Greg Tate. Calling Steely Dan 'the redemption of the white Negro', Reid distinguishes them from other white artists by suggesting that Steely Dan accept an 'outsider-elite' position in their use of African American musical influence, trying to approximate the marginalised genius of, say, the trained jazz musician, rather than using black music merely as a rebellious pose. See 'Steely Dan: Understood as the Redemption of the White Negro', in *Nothing But the Burden*, ed.

Greg Tate (New York: Broadway Books, 2003), pp. 110–15.

18 That's not to say that Newman's and Steely Dan's careers were commercially over by the 1980s. Newman's primary turn to film composing from the late eighties onwards – especially for blockbuster animated films like *Toy Story* and *Monsters, Inc.* – earned him a different popular audience within an even more unabashedly commercial context. Steely Dan returned to recording after a twenty-year hiatus with 2000's *Two Against Nature*, an album that won a surprising Grammy for Album of the Year. As Fagen suggests in *Eminent Hipsters*, though, their audience now is a niche population rather than the broad following they attracted in the 1970s.

PART II

Individuals

8 Thomas D'Urfey

TŌRU MITSUI

Thomas D'Urfey (1653–1723) was a very popular poet/songwriter and a productive dramatist in the period between the closing years of the reign of Charles II (r. 1660–1685) and the years of the reign of Anne (r. 1702–1714). Nevertheless, he lost his fame in the late eighteenth century, with the disparity between popularity and oblivion being exceptionally striking.

In the mid-nineteenth century, more than a hundred years after D'Urfey's death, William Chappell introduced him to the readers of his two-volume book, *Popular Music of the Olden Time* (1859).[1] Then, in 1923, two established literary periodicals published bicentennial memorial essays,[2] and a decade later, in 1933, a book of D'Urfey's songs was published. Twenty-six songs, selected out of some five hundred, were edited by Cyrus Lawrence Day, with music reproduced in facsimile.[3] On the whole, the historians of English literature have paid only cursory attention to his poetry and songs, and, if he has been known at all, it has been as the editor of *Wit and Mirth: or Pills to Purge Melancholy* (1719–20), a six-volume collection of popular songs of the time.[4]

The works of D'Urfey

In addition to songs, the works of Thomas D'Urfey include dramatic works and poems of political satire.[5] These total thirty-two in all and make him the most prolific dramatist of the time, and his plays did indeed enjoy great success around the decade 1691–1701,[6] but his friends apparently preferred his songs. In the late seventeenth century he also wrote a variety of narratives both in prose and verse, whose literary quality is negligible.

It was in the genre of songwriting that D'Urfey showed himself at his best. In particular, he was blessed with the ability to grasp and express in his songs what the general public desired. His success was also due to his appropriate selection of tunes. According to the traditional method, he adopted the tunes of songs – popular songs and folk songs – with which the general public were already familiar, often also using tunes written by renowned contemporary composers, such as Henry Purcell. Moreover, he had an unparalleled gift not only in the writing of songs but also in singing them in a resonant bass voice, and hence the term singer-songwriter can be applied to him, though not specifically in the way in which the term began to be used in the late 1960s. Day remarks that 'Those of his songs that appear in more than one of his collections often show changes which represent the way he was in the habit of singing them,'[7] and also 'the titles of many … songs in D'Urfey's early collections record the names of the places where he entertained the court'.[8]

The popularity of D'Urfey

When his third play, and his first comedy, *Madam Fickle*, was staged in November 1676, both Charles II and Duke of Ormonde praised it highly.[9] The praise led to him being presented to Charles by the Duke and to win a name for himself, after which, as 'Tom Durfey', he was increasingly favoured by the king and his courtiers. Bestowed with a ribald and unreserved wit, D'Urfey was happy to play antics and make himself a laughingstock, and Charles joyously kept him company. The songs D'Urfey wrote and sang were the kind of witty songs that appealed to the libertine king, who even sang with the singer-songwriter D'Urfey, as he himself delightedly boasts in the preamble to his song 'Advice to the City': 'a famous song … so remarkable, that I had the Honour to Sing it with King CHARLES at Windsor, He holding one part of the Paper with Me'.[10]

Charles' successor James II (r. 1685–1688) was 'of a temper too saturnine for the frivolous pleasures',[11] and D'Urfey had difficulty in behaving in such a way as to enjoy his support, but patronage endured in the age of William and Mary who were jointly on the throne at the time of the Glorious Revolution (William III (r. 1689–1702); Mary II (r. 1689–1694)). Queen Anne (1702–14) also appreciated his competence in composing lyrical songs, and Caroline, the wife of George I (r. 1714–1727), showed quite an interest in them while her husband, who succeeded Anne, did not.[12] His popularity, particularly among the courtiers, gave him supreme confidence. As can be seen in the occasional attacks in his work on fellow poet Thomas Shadwell, he assumed that he, not Shadwell, would succeed John Dryden to the position of Poet Laureate.[13]

For nearly forty years, D'Urfey made himself agreeable to aristocrats at banquets and parties, while the general public also talked about him in an excited way. His popularity was not limited to London, as was evidenced by Addison: 'Many an honest Gentleman has got a Reputation in his country, by pretending to have been in Company with *Tom d'Urfey*'.[14] For their part, intellectuals of the time did not openly welcome his songs, and apparently any mention made of him was contemptuous – although in its way that contempt is a reflection of his immense popularity. The Duke of

Buckingham derided him: 'And sing-song Durfey, placed beneath abuses/ Lives by his impudence, and not the Muses'.[15] Thomas Brown, his contemporary as a writer of abusive satires and his strongest competitor, refers to what D'Urfey said, without giving his name: 'The Town may dada – da – damn me for a Poet, says Chærilus, but they si – si – sing my songs for all that.'[16] (D'Urfey had a stammer.[17]) Nevertheless, such denigration must have come, in large measure, from a moral standpoint, for D'Urfey wrote and sang scores of songs which are unreservedly licentious, easily incurring the displeasure of men of strict morals.

When D'Urfey became actively involved in writing, the England of Charles II, who had returned from exile in France to ascend the throne, was in reaction to the puritanical administration of Oliver Cromwell. Under the reign of this extravagant and womanising king, nicknamed 'Old Rowley' (after the then-famed stallion), the new age was characterised by a hedonistic lifestyle in which people laughed away chastity and virginity. This trend held up until the early eighteenth century, and, unusually, writers of witty and bawdy songs thrived as well as vintners.

Types of D'Urfey song

A considerable number of D'Urfey's songs were included in various collections of poems and songs published from 1683[18] to the early eighteenth century, and his most popular songs were published repeatedly in many songbooks up to the end of the eighteenth century. Alongside these there were five books devoted solely to his songs, and D'Urfey himself put those songs together with other unpublished songs, making a total of three hundred and fifty in all, to form the two-volume *Songs Compleat, Pleasant and Divertive* (1719). Soon afterwards this became the first two volumes of *Wit and Mirth: or Pills to Purge Melancholy* (1719–1720). He tried his hand at any type of lyrical songs known to the age, and his songs can be classified, as Day suggests, in three groups – political songs, court songs, and country songs.[19]

The first group, political songs, is dominated by satirical songs as a matter of course, since the literary age in the late seventeenth and early eighteenth centuries, known as the age of Dryden, was distinguished by satires. Many of the tunes D'Urfey adopted were from long-lasting folk and popular songs as well as from other familiar songs sung in contemporary plays and operas, and his lyrics often retained some phrases from the verses which were originally combined with the tune. D'Urfey was apparently the foremost among the songwriters of political satires, aptly reflecting the spirit of the times in his songs and in his singing. In 'The King's Health' (written in 1681, when he was twenty-eight years old) he extolled Charles II, likening the king to Cæsar and siding with the Tories, in four strains:[20]

The First Strain.
JOY to Great Cæsar,
Long Life, Love and Pleasure;
'Tis a Health that Divine is,
Fill the Bowl high as mine is:
Let none fear a Feaver,
But take it off thus Boys;
Let the King Live for ever,
'Tis no matter for us Boys.

The Second Strain.
Try all the Loyal,
Defy all,
Give deny all;
Sure none thinks his Glass too big here,
Nor any *Prig* here,
Or Sneaking *Whig* here,
Of Cripple *Tony*'s Crew,
That now looks blue,
His heart akes too,
The *Tap* won't do,
His Zeal so true,
And Projects new,
Ill Fate does now pursue.

This song was as popular as 'Lilliburlero',[21] a renowned satirical song set to an Irish jig, which appeared a few years later.

In the Restoration period, such prodigal courtiers as the Earl of Rochester (John Wilmot), Sir Charles Sedley, the Earl of Dorset (Charles Sackville), and Sir George Etherege wrote poems and songs as 'wits', and their jovial and sensuous works, typified by the idea of 'love is sex', established the Restoration style of lyrics which persisted until the early eighteenth century. D'Urfey competed with those courtiers in the technical approach to lyrical poems and songs. His subject matter also concerned love and his amorous songs are similar to those by courtly poets, as is evident in a song beginning with 'When first Amyntas', and the first stanza of which runs as follows:

WHEN first *Amyntas* su'd for a Kiss,
My innocent Heart was tender;
That tho' I push'd him away from the bliss,
My Eyes declar'd my Heart was won:
I fain an artful Coyness wou'd use,
Before I the Fort did Surrender:

But Love wou'd suffer no more such abuse,
And soon alas! my cheat was known:
He'd sit all day, and laugh and play,
A thousand pretty things would say;
My hand he'd squeez, and press my knees,
Till farther on he got by degrees.

Example 8.1. D'Urfey, 'When first Amyntas', *Wit and Mirth* (1719–20), vol. 1, pp. 334–5.[22]

It is now widely known that this tune was composed by Henry Purcell. Many amorous songs were given a country-life setting. These belong to the long tradition of pastorals which had been the mainstream of English lyrical songs, and the court poets frequently wrote in this style also. D'Urfey's songs of this type are generally vulgar but cheerful and robust, dealing with dalliance between country lads and lasses. However, the most outstanding of his songs in the courtly fashion, may well be 'A Dirge', a non-love song, which was inserted in his extremely successful play, *The Comical History of Don Quixote* (performed in 1694).

In addition to 'A Dirge', D'Urfey deserves immortality through some songs which can be classified as country songs. A wholehearted passion permeates the song which begins with 'The Night her Blackest Sable Wore', the popularity of which ensured the fame of the tune's composer, Thomas Farmer. The song 'The Farmer's Daughter' (generally known as 'Cold and Raw'), which unaffectedly expresses natural feelings, became so popular that John Gay used it in *Beggar's Opera*, while the song that begins 'Sawney was tall and of Noble Race', inserted in the third act of D'Urfey's comedy, *The Virtuous Wife* (1679), was printed as a broadside and grew in popularity in no time, not only in England but also in Scotland (as did many of his songs). Various songs, including political ones, were written to the tune of this song, which Farmer 'undoubtedly composed',[23] and ballad operas continually used it. The final line in the first stanza, expressing melancholy without indulging in sentimentality, became the name by which the tune is known:[24]

Example 8.2. D'Urfey, 'Sawney was tall and of Noble Race'.

Sawney was tall and of Noble Race,
And lov'd me better than any eane;
But now he ligs by another Lass,
And *Sawney* will ne'er be my love agen:
I gave him fine *Scotch* Sarke and Band,
I put 'em on with mine own hand;
I gave him House, and I gave him Land,
Yet *Sawney* will ne'er be my Love agen.

As a whole, D'Urfey's songs are coarse and unreserved but they are never devoid of lyricism, in contrast to the pseudo-classicism of the day, in which the display of refinement and formality was at the cost of emotional depth. If his modern-day readers find his songs dull and slovenly as verse, it must be, for one thing, because they do not sing them. An anonymous, sympathetic writer stressed in 1923: 'Read with the tunes, these songs explain their own popularity by their spirit, their vigour and their movement.'[25] At the same time, 'irregularities of rhyme and metre', often left in his texts, 'that interfere with the reader's enjoyment' disappear when the songs are sung.[26]

Putting D'Urfey in historical perspective

D'Urfey's work belongs to a time in English cultural history when poems and songs were not yet clearly differentiated, though the division had begun to be made. For instance, Robert Herrick, noted for a song beginning with

'Gather ye rosebuds while ye may,/ Old Time is still a-flying' and described by Swinburne in about 1890 as 'the first in rank and station of English songwriter',[27] died in 1674, when D'Urfey was in his early twenties. This division was in parallel with 'a dissociation of sensibility', as famously noted by T. S. Eliot: 'In the seventeenth century a dissociation of sensibility set in, from which we have never recovered; and this dissociation, as is natural, was aggravated by the influence of the two most powerful poets of the century, Milton and Dryden'.[28] However, even Dryden himself, who died in 1700, can be regarded in a way as a child of his age. He wrote ninety-two songs, as admirably represented by *The Songs of John Dryden*, which Cyrus Day edited a year before editing D'Urfey's songs, affirming that 'practically all of Dryden's songs were set to music and sung in plays or at concerts before they were printed and offered to the reading public'.[29]

As a leading songwriter, D'Urfey was shortly followed by the prolific Henry Carey (1687–1743), whose 'Sally in Our Alley' became an all-time favourite. Then Charles Dibdin (c. 1745–1814) wrote numerous songs among which patriotic sea-songs were particularly influential. Both Carey and Dibdin were also dramatists while being active to some extent in singing their songs. The tradition continued in Scotland with Robert Burns (1759–1796) and in Ireland with Thomas Moore (1779–1852). Subsequently, in the new English-speaking world, Stephen Foster (1826–1864) stood out as the greatest songwriter, shadowing another productive songwriter, Henry Clay Work (1832–1884) known for 'Grandfather's Clock'. In the twentieth-century United States, eminent singer-songwriters (e.g. Woody Guthrie (1912–1967)) came out of a folk-music tradition, foreshadowing the recognised singer-songwriter tradition from the late 1960s and 70s.

Notes

1 William Chappell, *Popular Music of the Olden Time*, vol. 1 (London: Cramer, Beale, & Chappell, 1859), pp. 305–9; vol. 2, pp. 490, 495–6, 611–12, and 618–23.

2 Anonymous, 'Thomas D'Urfey: died February 26, 1723', in *The Times Literary Supplement*, 22 February 1923, p. 121, and Montague Summers, 'Thomas D'Urfey (1653–1723)', in *The Bookman*, March 1923, pp. 272–4.

3 Cyrus Lawrence Day (ed.), *The Songs of Thomas D'Urfey* (Cambridge, MA: Harvard University Press, 1933). Day wrote a PhD thesis at Harvard University in 1930 on D'Urfey entitled 'The Life and Non-dramatic Works of Thomas D'Urfey'. It should be pointed out that, in the introduction to *The Songs of Thomas D'Urfey*, Day oddly never refers to the two bicentennial memorial essays, with

ample information, to which he must have been indebted.

4 *Wit and Mirth: or Pills to Purge Melancholy* was first edited and published by Henry Playford in 1698. It was in such good repute with the public that it was repeatedly enlarged as well as being reprinted, and finally a definitive edition in six volumes, containing 1144 songs and poems, was compiled by Thomas D'Urfey in 1719–20 and published by J. Tonson in London. In 1876 this 1719–20 edition was 're-typed', page by page, by an unidentified printer in London. The reprint transferred the staff-notational conventions of the seventeenth-century to the modern notation, but it 'is in some cases obscure, ungrammatical or a mistake', according to Anonymous, 'Tunes and Traditions', in *Times*

Literary Supplement, 20 May 1960, p. 316 – a review of the facsimile reproduction of the 1876 reprint of *Wit and Mirth* in three volumes, published in 1959 by Folklore Library Publishers in New York.

5 With the exception of his songs, his other published output (e.g. satire and dramatic works) were of low quality. Montague Summers, a scholar of the seventeenth-century drama, laments at the beginning of the second paragraph of a bicentennial essay: 'Tom D'Urfey! There are perhaps in the whole history of English literature few of any writers of equal output and such high contemporary fame, who have fallen into completer oblivion than "that ancient Lyric", friend Tom' – Summers, 'Thomas D'Urfey (1653–1723)', p. 272.

6 Day (ed.), *The Songs of Thomas D'Urfey*, pp. 19–22.

7 Ibid., p. 123.

8 Ibid., p. 8.

9 Ibid., p. 6.

10 D'Urfey, *Wit and Mirth* (1719–1720), vol. 1, p. 246.

11 Day (ed.), *The Songs of Thomas D'Urfey*, p. 9.

12 D'Urfey says that 'I have perform'd some of my own Things before their Majesties King *CHARLES* the IId, King *JAMES*, King *WILLIAM*, Queen *MARY*, Queen *ANNE*, and Prince *GEORGE*, I never went off without happy and commendable Approbation', in the third page of the unpaged 'Dedication' in the first volume of *Wit and Mirth* (1719–1720).

13 Day (ed.), *The Songs of Thomas D'Urfey*, pp. 15–16.

14 From *The Guardian*, no. 67 (28 May 1713) in *The Works of the Right Honourable Joseph Addison, Esq.* (London: Jacob Tonson, 1721), vol. 4, p. 131.

15 Quoted in Anonymous, 'Thomas D'Urfey: died February 23, 1723'.

16 *The Fourth and Last Volume of the Works of Mr Thomas Brown* (London: Printed for Sam. Briscoe, 1715), p. 117.

17 'Contemporary allusions to his stuttering are very numerous' in Day (ed.), *The Songs of Thomas D'Urfey*, p. 6.

18 This was the year when D'Urfey added an apostrophe to his name and capitalized the second letter to make known his presumably self-styled aristocratic French origin: Day (ed.), *The Songs of Thomas D'Urfey*, p. 17.

19 Day (ed.), *The Songs of Thomas D'Urfey*, p. 34.

20 *Wit and Mirth* (1719–1720), vol. 2, pp. 152–6. The music which precedes the lyrics is too long to be quoted here. The old long 's' in the song text is here changed to the modern 's' as well as in the following song-text quotations.

21 Day (ed.), *The Songs of Thomas D'Urfey*, p. 128.

22 Two notations in the present chapter are reproduced using Finale. However, it should be noted that the fourth bar in the present tune by Purcell is obviously misrepresented. The first note should be G♯ and the second one E.

23 Chappell, *Popular Music of the Olden Time*, vol. 2, p. 618.

24 *Wit and Mirth* (1719–1720), vol. 1, pp. 316.

25 Anonymous, 'Thomas D'Urfey: died February 26, 1723'.

26 H. J. Byrom, review of *The Songs of Thomas D'Urfey*, in *Review of English Studies*, 10/40 (1934), p. 471.

27 Algernon Charles Swinburne, 'Robert Herrick', p. 260, in *The Complete Works of Algernon Charles Swinburne* (London: William Heinemann, 1925–7), vol. 15 (1926).

28 Anonymous [T. S. Eliot], 'Metaphysical Poets', review of *Metaphysical Lyrics and Poems of the Seventeenth Century: Donne to Butler* edited by Herbert J. C. Grierson, in the *Times Literary Supplement*, 20 October 1921, p. 669.

29 Cyrus Lawrence Day (ed.), *The Songs of John Dryden* (Cambridge, MA: Harvard University Press, 1932), p. xiii.

9 Leadbelly

JOSEP PEDRO

Huddie Ledbetter, better known as Leadbelly (1888–1949),[1] was one of the most unique, fascinating and influential singer-songwriters of the foundational American blues and folk traditions – a starting point of the contemporary singer-songwriter development. Born in 1888 on Jeter Plantation, near Mooringsport, Louisiana, he belonged to the first generation of blues artists – formed by itinerant African American musicians with outsider lifestyles, seeking social advancement in spite of the Jim Crow south. Stylistically, however, his extensive and varied repertoire has earned him a differentiated and sometimes peculiar status in blues studies and popular music history, as he is often considered a songster rather than a bluesman.[2]

A multi-instrumentalist who could play guitar, piano, mandolin, harmonica, violin and accordion, Leadbelly gained notoriety as the 'the King of Twelve-String Guitar', developing a distinctive, powerful drive that has had a profound impact on the evolution of popular music. Throughout the decades, his obscure and appealing persona has constantly inspired further reinterpretations of material he composed or first popularised by musicians from different scenes and styles, ranging from the mid-twentieth century folk revival, roots and surf rock of Pete Seeger, Creedence Clearwater Revival, and The Beach Boys respectively, to the more recent grunge and garage rock sounds of Nirvana and the White Stripes.[3]

Leadbelly's case poses significant challenges for any researcher, writer or reader discussing his music, life, and legend. Many episodes of his life remain unclear, others have been interpreted in contradictory ways, and the artist himself continuously reconstructed his persona through malleable stories. The aim of this chapter is to offer a reliable and nuanced framework for approaching such a complex character, based on the most relevant stages of Leadbelly's artistic and life trajectory. In this process, I will refer to significant events and circumstances, relating them to particular songs and styles, and incorporating previous discussions about the musical, socio-political, and racial meanings and implications of his remarkable journey.

Figure 9.1. Leadbelly (Huddie Ledbetter), New York, 1944–5.

Rambling singer-songwriters in the deep south

Leadbelly grew up around Caddo Parish, Louisiana, a frontier, rural area that hosted one of the highest concentrations of African Americans west of the Mississippi River.[4] As a strong, rambunctious young man, he proved to be an effective agricultural worker, picking cotton and learning about farming and cowboy culture, and, by the time he was fourteen, he had won a local reputation for his guitar playing and singing. His relentless progression, however, would soon be inextricably bound to problems with the law.

In 1903, after having seen him returning home with cuts and bruises from fights, his father gave him a Colt pistol; 'a typical coming-of-age present in the frontier South' that came with some rather ambiguous advice in favour of self-defence.[5] A few weeks later, Leadbelly got into a dispute over his girlfriend Eula Lee, which ended with him pistol-whipping a young boy on the side of the head. Fortunately, the sheriff let him go with a $25 fine for carrying a concealed weapon.

Anxious to see the outside world, Leadbelly continuously defied his parents by travelling nineteen miles from Mooringsport to Shreveport, where he explored the exciting and often troubled nightlife of the red-light district. It was centred on Fannin Street, a row of saloons, brothels, dance halls, and gambling houses that operated legally between 1903 and 1917. Leadbelly's experience in the more competitive, crowded, and celebratory environment of Fannin Street made him grow personally and artistically. The popular barrelhouse piano players and their rolling-bass technique made an impact on his already dynamic guitar picking and songwriting. Moreover, blues became a bigger part of his repertoire, as it was more popular in this 'sinful' environment than the country-folk songs he had generally been singing. A groundbreaking formative experience, his time in Shreveport inspired the composition 'Fannin Street', which dealt with the acts of defying his mother and sister, and proving his growing independence. It also served Leadbelly to affirm himself as a singer-songwriter, and express his already self-conscious rambling character. Overall, the song manifested the intense contrast between the correctness of family life in respectable, small communities, and the thrilling, instinct-liberating ambiance of Fannin Street and, more generally, of the musician's life.

For a brief time Leadbelly returned home, but at eighteen he started wandering again, mainly through West Texas. After a period of promiscuity which culminated in his contracting gonorrhoea, he decided to settle down and married Lethe Henderson in 1908. The couple moved to Dallas in 1910, where Leadbelly met his greatest partner and mentor: Blind Lemon Jefferson, a blind singer-guitarist who would later become the first country blues recording star. Both musicians met each other around Deep Ellum, a thriving area similar to Shreveport's Fannin Street where 'hobos invariably landed and where African American, Hispanic, and white cotton pickers were picked up'.[6] Like Leadbelly, Lemon had an eclectic repertoire ranging from old ballads to gospel songs, though he was first and foremost a blues singer. Together they played topical songs about historic events and localised situations of the day such as 'The Titanic', 'Boll Weevil Song', and 'Fort Worth and Dallas Blues'; as well as celebrated blues standards such as 'C.C. Rider' and 'Matchbox Blues', which would later be extensively covered by blues, rhythm and blues, and rock 'n' roll performers.

Leadbelly also learnt new techniques from Lemon, most notably the slide guitar, and recorded several songs in tribute to his beloved friend. The most special one was his composition 'Silver City Bound', a travelling song which remembered their trips around Texas. In the spoken introduction to the recording, Leadbelly expressed the desire for freedom entrenched in blues lives: 'We get out two guitars; we just ride ... anything. We didn't have to pay no money in them times. We get on the train; the driver takes us anywhere we want to go.'

Finally, he also explained some of their business 'planning', typically related to women and money: 'There's a lot of pretty girls out there [Silver City], and that's what we were looking for. We like for women to be around, 'cause when women's around, that brings men and that brings money.'[7]

Accommodation and resistance in the Jim Crow era

Due to his living circumstances and volatile temper, Leadbelly was incarcerated several times in Texas and Louisiana, a background that became fodder for the construction of his myth,[8] and his presentation in the college concert and folk circuits of northern cities.[9] Surprisingly, unlike the vast majority of inmates, Leadbelly was able to contradict the restrictive statues of Jim Crow, and gain his freedom repeatedly through several formulae, most notably through the creativity and persuasive powers of his pardon songs.

In 1915 he was arrested, allegedly for attacking a woman who had rebuffed his advances. He was convicted of carrying a pistol, and sentenced to thirty days in the Harrison County (Texas) chain gang. Three days into his sentence, however, Leadbelly managed to escape. His adventure may be pictured and understood through the heartfelt and ironic lyrics of 'Take this Hammer', a prison song which he popularised in the early 1940s:

> Take this hammer, carry it to the captain (x3), tell him I'm gone (x2)
> If he asks you was I runnin' (x3), tell him I was flyin' (x2)
> If he asks you was I laughin' (x3), tell him I was cryin' (x2)
> They wanna feed me cornbread and molasses (x3), but I got my pride (x2)

After a brief stay in New Orleans, Leadbelly returned to north-eastern Texas and changed his name to Walter Boyd. He survived picking cotton and playing music occasionally, but in 1917 found himself in trouble again, and was charged for murder and assault to murder. Though the circumstances remain unclear, he was sentenced to 'a minimum of seven years and a maximum of thirty years in the notorious Texas penal system'.[10] After two failed attempts to escape, he was transferred to Sugarland Prison, a state prison outside Houston which became associated with the traditional folk song 'Midnight Special'. Told in the first person, the lyrics referred to the everyday conditions of prisoners, warned about the dangers of travelling to Houston, and talked about receiving news of deceased wives. Despite this, the prisoner ultimately finds a powerful glimpse of hope in the shining, 'ever-loving light' of the Southern Pacific passenger train, the Midnight Special. Its light represented salvation, and the train itself symbolised mobility and travel which provided the most tangible evidence of freedom for African Americans, a community emerging from a harsh history of enslavement and oppression.[11]

In 1924, the Governor of Texas Pat Neff initiated a tour around different prison camps, which often included entertainment shows by talented inmates like Leadbelly. Armed with his twelve-string Stella guitar and dressed up in a special white suit for important occasions, Leadbelly performed traditional African American songs, pleased the governor with hillbilly tunes, and even danced 'The Sugarland Shuffle', a parody of a frantic (black) man chopping cotton.

Once he established a strategic self-deprecating rapport with the authority audience, Leadbelly started singing a pardon song (later recorded as 'Governor Pat Neff') in which he pleaded for his liberation:

> Please, honourable governor, be good and kind,
> If I don't get a pardon, will you cut my time?
> If I had you, Governor Neff, like you got me,
> Wake up in the morning, I'd set you free.

Delighted with this apparently improvised tune, Neff – who had actually campaigned against pardons – agreed to set him free before leaving his office. Throughout the following year, the Governor returned several times to celebrate crowded parties with guests and inmate entertainers. Finally on 16 January 1925, he signed a full pardon for Leadbelly, who had served a bit more than six and a half years of his seven-to-thirty-year sentence.

Gordon Parks' film *Leadbelly* (1976) provides an unmatched cinematographic rendition of Leadbelly's southern experiences, including a dramatic, caricaturised yet complex scene of the pardon plea to the Texas governor. Broadly situated in the context of the 1970s Blaxploitation cinema, the film inscribed Leadbelly's figure in the problematic and paradoxical post-civil rights movement era, and presented him as an inspirational model, 'as an example of a black man who survives, who uses his art to aid in that survival and to overcome the dominance of violence in his life'.[12]

The feeling of self-affirmation, masculinity and agency is particularly intense in the film's final scene, where the fictionalised Leadbelly, longing for his freedom, exclaims: 'And after seven years you ain't broke my body, you ain't broke my mind, you ain't broke my spirit.'

Liberation, mobility, and New York's folk revival

In 1930, five years after his release, Leadbelly got into a knife-fight over an argument with Dick Ellet, a respectable white citizen of Mooringsport, and was convicted of assault with intent to murder. He was sentenced to six to ten years of hard labour at the Louisiana State Penitentiary at Angola, 'a facility that made Sugarland look like easy time'.[13]

Immersed in their committed search for the uncontaminated 'purity' of African American folk songs, father and son folklorists John and Alan Lomax visited Angola in 1933 and 1934, making pioneering recordings of Leadbelly, as well as of other inmates and farmers throughout the south. Among Leadbelly's recordings was 'Governor O.K. Allen', a new pardon song addressed to the Governor of Louisiana that was personally delivered to him by the Lomaxes. Leadbelly was effectively liberated in 1934 and the popular legend – backed by both the Lomaxes and the artist himself – made the white 'ballad hunters' responsible for the black man's liberation. However, this version, which was widely accepted and reproduced at the time, was not accurate and has been contested with evidence showing that Leadbelly was actually released under Louisiana's 'good time' laws.[14]

Upon his release, Leadbelly and John Lomax formed a groundbreaking, mutually beneficial, and highly controversial partnership, which would ultimately expose the complexities of intercultural dialogues and relationships between different social and 'racial' groups. Leadbelly became Lomax's chauffeur and field-expert recording assistant in his prison investigations, and through him Lomax was also able to bring life to his recently published *American Ballads and Folk Songs* (1936) and upcoming *Negro Folk Songs as Sung by Leadbelly* (1936).

Their northern conquest began with their presentation at the annual meeting of the Modern Language Association in Philadelphia – a leading professional association for scholars of literature and language. Almost immediately, they were invited to a New Year's Eve party at the Greenwich Village apartment of two committed enthusiasts of folk culture, where Leadbelly performed for a bohemian audience 'of New York tastemakers, Village intellectuals and artists, reporters, and faculty from Columbia and New York University'.[15] Although his new white audience had difficulties understanding his southern dialect, Leadbelly was, according to Alan Lomax's description, 'the performer everyone thought of when they wanted honesty, authenticity and power'.[16]

Press coverage emphasised the artist's origins and extraordinary life story, and was generally marked by a blatant sensationalist tone, which reflected the intrigued fascination, exotic appeal and marketing potential of Leadbelly's figure in this new public sphere. The New York *Herald Tribune*, for instance, published a significant article with the lead line 'Sweet Singer of the Swamplands Here to do a Few Tunes Between Homicides'.[17] Moreover, *Time* magazine produced a newsreel of *The March of Time* with Leadbelly and John Lomax themselves, where the former appeared willingly submissive to his 'boss'.

Leadbelly was certainly attracted by the urban landscape of the 'Big Apple', as reflected in his own composition 'New York City' (1940). He naturally explored the black nightlife of Harlem, where he ran into Cab Calloway's band and made friends with writer Richard Wright. Wright portrayed him in the *Daily Worker* newspaper as a talented and fearsome folk singer, and accused John Lomax of cultural colonisation.[18] But it was in the developing, leftist folk scene where Leadbelly achieved a venerated and inspirational status, as he embodied a powerful political symbol in the emergent African American Civil Rights Movement, a modern John Henry, an authentic heroic figure otherwise unattainable in the inherited white, middle-class experiences. 'Bourgeois Blues' (1938), a race and class-based critique of Washington DC; 'Scottsboro Boys' (1938), a civil rights song in which he advises black people not to go to Alabama; 'Mr Hitler' (1942), a cry against Hitler which reinforced his American citizenship; and 'Jim Crow Blues' (1944), a protest song about the shameful widespread of Jim Crow discrimination, provide useful examples to explore his overtly political songs.

In 1939 Leadbelly was arrested in Manhattan for allegedly stabbing an intruder who had been harassing his wife Martha Promise. By then, his relationship with John Lomax was over due to distrust, fatigue, and problems over money, but Alan, then twenty-four, left his ethnomusicology studies at Columbia University for a semester and raised money for the singer. He also arranged commercial recordings with Musicraft and RCA, and invited him to his radio show *Back Where I Come From*, which he produced with film director Nicholas Ray.

Focused in New York's burgeoning integrated musical scene, the groundbreaking radio programme featured musically and socially related artists like Woody Guthrie, Sonny Terry & Brownie McGhee, Pete Seeger, and Josh White, with whom Leadbelly actually formed a duo that enjoyed a very successful six-month engagement at the historic Village Vanguard. The influence of these folk revival founding fathers was long-lasting and would reach the peak of its visibility during the 1960s with the rise of upcoming stars like Bob Dylan.

Transatlantic crossover

In May 1949 Leadbelly travelled to France and performed several shows, most notably at the Paris Jazz Fair. He became the first country blues singer to visit Europe, initiating an influential trend that was followed by Josh White and Big Bill Broonzy in the early 1950s, but became ill before completing the tour and ultimately died in New York on 6 December 1949, at age sixty-one. The commercial impact and influence of his work and artistic persona continued to grow, inspiring endless renditions that reflect Leadbelly's far-reaching and versatile position in popular culture, as well as the intricate problems of discussions about music, 'race' and performance.

About a year after his death, The Weavers, a folk quartet formed by Pete Seeger, recorded a version of 'Goodnight Irene' which peaked at number 1 in the Billboard Best Seller chart. Other performers like Frank Sinatra or country musicians Ernest Tubb and Red Foley also obtained hit records with their versions. In Britain, Lonnie Donegan, the 'King of Skiffle' who earned his success appropriating material from folk-blues artists, recorded several versions of Leadbelly songs, including 'Rock Island Line' (1955), which sold three million copies, 'John Henry' (1955), and 'Pick A Bale of Cotton' (1962). Though it would have certainly been interesting to see his reactions and evolution throughout the decades, Leadbelly was not able to see the widespread success of his songs – many of which he picked up from family members, partners, inmates and recording musicians – in the hands of other artists.

Hopefully, this chapter serves to enrich the debate addressing Leadbelly's accomplishments, trials, and contradictions, and brings greater attention, acknowledgement, and present discussion about his contributions. Embodying the outlaw bluesman archetype, his case illustrates the intimate relationship between popular music and biography, as his life story and artistic trajectory arguably represent the full potential of musical performance in contrasting social settings, providing insights on the history and hybridity of popular music, the complexities of 'race' relations and geopolitical dialectics between north and south, and the unstoppable search for authenticity.

Ultimately, Leadbelly's legacy will continue to resonate in popular culture, extending an ongoing and stylistically varied historical and spatiotemporal dialogue with the era that he helped to define and represent, as he emerged as a legendary storyteller who consolidated a decisive link between the southern working-class tradition and the progressive urban Bohemia.

Notes

1 Over the years, Huddie Ledbetter's nickname has been spelled both as 'Leadbelly' and as 'Lead Belly'. During the 1930s and 1940s it was generally written as two words, but current conventions have standardised the single-word use 'Leadbelly', which I follow here. See Charles Wolfe and Kip Lornell, *The Life and Legend of Leadbelly* (New York: Da Capo Press, 1992), p. xv. Throughout this article I rely on the biographical data offered in this exhaustive work.
2 The use of the term 'songster' over 'bluesman' emphasises the stylistic variety of a given

performer, often including diverse folk, work and spiritual songs. Nevertheless, it should be remembered that the work of early country blues artists generally transcended the most currently standardised forms of blues music (i.e. I-IV-V chord progression). A searching and creative musician, Leadbelly drew on different branches of the southern oral traditions, transforming and popularising many songs, and also creating his own compositions.
3 'Leadbelly songs', those composed or 'originally' associated with Leadbelly, have been

covered extensively and periodically in popular music, as shown by the following examples: the folk group The Weavers covered 'Goodnight Irene' in 1950 achieving a great success; Brook Benton made 'The Boll Weevil Song' a pop hit in 1961; Creedence Clearwater Revival recorded 'Midnight Special' and 'Cottonfields' in their album *Willy and the Poor Boys* (Fantasy, 1969); that same year 'Cottonfields' also afforded The Beach Boys' their most widespread international success; and a year later Led Zeppelin recorded 'Gallow's Pole' ('The Gallis Pole') in their album *III* (Atlantic, 1970); In 1993, Nirvana's MTV unplugged interpretation of 'Where Did You Sleep Last Night' (also titled 'In the Pines') exposed Leadbelly's material to new generations and audiences, a trend that would continue through other singular bands and artists like The White Stripes, who covered 'De Ballit of de Boll Weevil Song' and 'Take a Whiff on Me' in their live DVD *Under Blackpool Lights* (Third Man, 2004), and Tom Waits, whose compilation *Orphans: Brawlers, Bawlers & Bastards* (ANTI-, 2006) includes a cover of 'Goodnight, Irene'.

4 Wolfe and Lornell, *Life and Legend*, p. 6.

5 Ibid., p. 27. 'Now son, don't you bother nobody, don't make no trouble, but if somebody try to meddle with you, I want you to protect yourself.'

6 Alan Govenar, *Texas Blues. The Rise of a Contemporary Sound* (College Station: Texas A&M University Press, 2008), p. 92.

7 Leadbelly, 'Silver City Bound', in *Lead Belly's Last Sessions*. Smithsonian Folkways, 1994.

8 For more details on accommodation and resistance during the Jim Crow Era, see R. A. Lawson, *Jim Crow's Counterculture. The Blues and Black Southerners 1890–1945* (Baton Rouge: Louisiana State University Press, 2013).

9 As shown throughout the article, Leadbelly's northern conquest was mainly defined by his performances in Philadelphia, New York and Washington, which took place at a variety of settings ranging from scholarly reunions to bohemian nightclubs.

10 Wolfe and Lornell, *Life and Legend*, p. 75.

11 Angela Y. Davis, *Blues Legacies and Black Feminism* (New York: Vintage Books, 1998), p. 67. The pleasures alluded to in the sexual double-meaning in the lyrics are also arguably another symbol of freedom.

12 Maurice L. Bryan Jr, 'Good Morning Blues: Gordon Parks Imagines Leadbelly', in Tony Bolden (ed.), *The Funk Era and Beyond. New Perspectives on Black Popular Culture* (New York: Palgrave McMillan, 2008), p. 135.

13 Wolfe and Lornell, *Life and Legend*, p. 99.

14 Ibid., p. 120. His discharge was a routine matter under the 'good time law' which applied to all first and second offenders.

15 John Szwed, *Alan Lomax. The Man Who Recorded the World* (New York: Viking, 2010), p. 65.

16 Ronald D. Cohen (ed.), *Alan Lomax. Selected Writings 1934–1997* (New York: Routledge, 2003), p. 198.

17 Wolfe and Lornell, *Life and Legend*, p. 139.

18 Ibid., pp. 200–2.

10 Region and identity in Dolly Parton's songwriting

JADA WATSON

As she entered the studio in September 1972 to begin recording her eleventh solo album, Dolly Parton's career was at a crossroads. Parton and duet partner Porter Wagoner had achieved considerable success with both the syndicated television programme *The Porter Wagoner Show* and their duet recordings. They were also named the Country Music Association's Vocal Duo of the Year in 1970 and 1971. Despite these successes, tension was mounting between the duo behind the scenes over Wagoner's attempts to control her career, and Parton's lack of commercial success with her solo albums. When Parton joined *The Porter Wagoner Show* in 1967, Wagoner convinced the young singer-songwriter to leave Fred Foster at Monument Records and join him at RCA Victor. Wagoner personally shaped this next stage in her career: he produced their duets and all of her early RCA Victor solo albums, controlling album content and musical arrangements.[1] Wagoner also owned 49% of her publishing company (Owepar), and they co-owned Fireside Recording Studio in Nashville.[2] Under his guidance, however, Parton had only achieved one number 1 hit with 'Joshua' in 1971. Having left her family in Sevierville, Tennessee, to pursue a career as a singer-songwriter in Nashville eight years earlier, Parton was becoming increasingly anxious to make her mark on the country industry. Frustrated and homesick, she assembled a collection of songs about her rural upbringing in the Smoky Mountains for her 1972 recording sessions, and for the first time included only her own songs. The result was an autobiographical concept album and homage to her homeplace, childhood, and familial bonds on *My Tennessee Mountain Home* (1973).

As Nancy Cardwell stated in the opening chapter of her 2011 monograph on Dolly Parton, 'It's been said that where you're from has a lot to do with who you are'.[3] With this statement, Cardwell captures perfectly the important role that the Smoky Mountain region has played in Parton's life, music, and identity. The fourth of twelve children born to a sharecropper and his wife in Sevierville in January 1946, Parton was steeped in the traditions and culture of her southern rural-mountain origins. Life was challenging for the Partons in the late 1940s and early 1950s; they did not have electricity, running water, indoor plumbing, or a telephone.[4] They grew their own food, made their own clothes and toys, and always managed to make enough money to stay off welfare. Music played an integral role in daily life in rural Appalachia, where families like the Partons struggled to make a living. Surrounded by a family of talented singers, musicians, and songwriters, Parton received her musical education at home, at family gatherings, and in church. Her mother introduced her to the repertoire of religious hymns, old-time songs, and tragic Appalachian ballads. The challenges of growing up in this poor southern rural-mountain region, and the Appalachian ballads, had a tremendous impact on Parton and her songwriting. She demonstrated from a young age that she could write in a style similar to these 'old mountain melodies' and make a 'song that's brand new sound like it's old'.[5] Rural Appalachia became the setting of many candid recollections about the hardships of growing up in the region.

Within the country music genre, there exists a songwriting tradition of artists using place-based narratives to reveal aspects of their artistic identity. As I demonstrated in a recent article on country music and place, these narratives do not just describe geographic regions; rather, they also define the relationship between individuals and their surrounding environment and community, unveiling elements of an artist's character, values, and beliefs. Perhaps the most complicated relationship within place songs is that between an artist and the 'homeplace'. While place, and home in particular, can signify safety, belonging, and familial togetherness, it can also represent a space of limitations from which an artist struggles to escape.[6] For Parton, homeplace symbolises the duality of these tensions, representing security and limitations, belonging and isolation, simplicity and hardships/suffering. She articulates these tensions throughout *My Tennessee Mountain Home*'s overarching narrative, exploring the hardships of southern rural living, while also reflecting nostalgically on a simpler way of life. Despite the fact that Parton dreamed of escaping the poverty of her southern rural upbringing from a very young age, her songwriting has continually revealed the influence of the culture and traditions of the region. They also capture her childhood memories and familial relations, suggesting that it is not just the region and its musical traditions, but also the people embedded in this region that have contributed to shaping Parton's character and identity.

For many place-themed songs, especially those by Parton, the concept of autobiography is a particularly relevant point of discussion. These songs communicate an artist's life experiences, revealing the values and lessons learned from the challenges of growing up in a specific geographic region. Loretta Lynn had done the same in 1969 with her reflection on growing up a poor 'Coal Miner's Daughter' in Butcher Holler, Kentucky. According to Pamela Fox, autobiography is linked in country music's historiography with the notion of 'authentic sincerity'.[7] She argues that the published celebrity autobiography affords artists the opportunity to abandon performative guises in order to honour their southern poor and 'working-class roots in (some variant of) the mythic rural past'.[8] While autobiographical narratives often reflect nostalgically on a simpler way of life, they also reveal the hardships of rural living at a specific time and place, and reflect on issues concerning class marginality of the southern poor. These texts demonstrate not just that artists identify with southern working-class culture, but, perhaps more importantly, that they have fulfilled the patterns of rural southern people seeking a better existence in towns throughout the south.[9] Like the literary autobiography, the autobiographical song maps out the transition from an artist's humble origins to life as a country star, insisting upon the notion that these origins remain an integral component of his/her identity.

Autobiographical songs seek to accomplish the same goal as chapters in a book, relying on the musical setting to evoke the imagery lost in a photograph. Scholarship on music and place demonstrates how musical codes and style conventions can represent or characterise geographic space. In *Music and Urban Geography*, Adam Krims emphasises that musical setting plays an important role in highlighting, embracing, and/or critiquing the environment described in the lyrical narrative.[10] Travis Stimeling has also considered the ways in which musical styles associated with a particular geographic region can allow an artist to establish a sense of regional identity and articulate relationship to place.[11] In *My Tennessee Mountain Home*, Parton provides a lens into aspects of her identity, and draws on musical conventions associated with both her Appalachian roots and the 'countrypolitan' production values of the Nashville Sound to map out the journey from her southern rural homeplace to her urban life in Nashville. Through this fusion of old and new musical styles, Parton created a musical language that appealed to the working-class population of the folks back home and displaced southerners living in urban centres.

My Tennessee Mountain Home

An autobiographical concept album, *My Tennessee Mountain Home* offers a bittersweet look back at the poor life and rural Smoky Mountain traditions from which Parton was determined to escape at a young age. Interestingly, very few Nashville artists used the concept album in the early 1970s, as country music's major labels saw the long-playing record (LP) as a means to collect and distribute songs by a single artist, and not as a large-scale compositional format.[12] For Parton, however, the concept album provided a fitting format for her over-arching autobiographical narrative, as she could incorporate elements of her story into every detail of the album: individual songs became chapters in her story, and the album jacket was transformed into a family photo album complete with inscriptions from her parents. The album's cover featured a photo of the original Parton home: a weathered, one-story cabin and a front porch stretched across the front with wash tubs and other artefacts that suggest simple rural, mountain living. The inside of the LP sleeve presents a page of the Parton family scrapbook, with a photo of a four-year old Parton playing in the yard of her 'Tennessee Mountain Home', the school picture in which she wore her 'Coat of Many Colors', and paintings of the family home and her daddy's work boots. The sleeve also introduces her family and the doctor that delivered her, honouring the people and life in the mountains. Parton's parents, Avie Lee and Robert Lee Parton, authored the album's liner notes. Their thoughtful inscriptions comment on Parton's 'kind, gentle, loving, and understanding' character, and highlight the challenges that their family faced. Perhaps most importantly, Parton's father emphasises the importance of family and homeplace:

> With all her success she has never changed at all. She is just as warm and kind as ever. She loves her TENNESSEE MOUNTAIN HOME where she grew up, and her family and friends are very dear to her heart. And I want to say I know she will never change.[13]

Their inscriptions describe the singer-songwriter as an ordinary person, who continues to uphold the values and traditions of her humble origins.

Music Row's studio practices also made it challenging for artists to consider the concept album format because they demanded that sessions produce four songs in strict three-hour blocks. In her sessions for *My Tennessee Mountain Home*, however, Parton observed their practices; using her studio time efficiently, she recorded three to four songs per session, grouping them based on instrumentation (and possibly availability of session musicians) instead of album ordering (Table 10.1). This allowed her to then be involved in post-production sequencing of the album's autobiographical narrative (Figure 10.1).[14] The album opens with a recitation of the first letter she wrote to her parents back home just a few days after arriving in Nashville. Accompanied by the lonesome melody of the harmonica playing the nineteenth-century traditional English ballad 'Home, Sweet Home', Parton tells her parents that she didn't realise how much she would miss her family and how hard it would be to leave home, until she embarked upon her journey to Nashville. In an effort to calm her parents' nerves about their daughter living alone in the city, Parton informs them that she has already found employment singing on the *Eddie Hill Show* and reveals that some singers have already expressed interest in her songs. This letter draws on a traditional country narrative in which an artist from a small town expresses disillusion with the big city: Nashville, she says, was not exactly what she thought it was going to be, and relates her initial pangs of homesickness upon arrival. Through this performance, Parton

Table 10.1 My Tennessee Mountain Home *Recording Sessions*

Session date	Song	Album location
1 September 1972	My Tennessee Mountain Home	Side B, Track 1
	The Wrong Direction Home	Side B, Track 2
	Daddy's Working Boots	Side A, Track 4
	[Sacred Memories]	[NA]
5 September 1972	Old Black Kettle	Side A, Track 3
	Down on Music Row	Side B, Track 5
	The Letter	Side A, Track 1
2 October 1972	Dr. Robert F. Thomas	Side A, Track 5
	In the Good Old Days (When Times Were Bad)	Side A, Track 6
	Back Home	Side B, Track 3
3 October 1972	I Remember	Side A, Track 2
	The Better Part of Life	Side B, Track 4
12 December 1972	Overdub Session for 1 and 5 September recordings	

Location: RCA Studio B, Nashville, TN; Bob Ferguson (Producer)

1. The Letter
2. I Remember
3. Old Black Kettle
4. Daddy's Working Boots
5. Dr Robert F. Thomas
6. In the Good Old Days (When Times Were Bad)
7. My Tennessee Mountain Home
8. The Wrong Direction Home
9. Back Home
10. The Better Part of Life
11. Down on Music Row

Figure 10.1. Final Track Listing of *My Tennessee Mountain Home*

invites her audience to witness her revisit an emotional moment from her past, allowing them to hear the tender way in which she speaks to her family, her reservations about leaving, and the loneliness she felt in her first days in Nashville. An act of 'performed' sentimentality, 'The Letter' provides a backdrop for the album, and reinforces the important role that family and southern rural values play in the songwriter's life.

Side A recounts stories about the hardships of growing up in the Smoky Mountains, focusing predominantly on her memories of her parents and how hard they worked, and emphasising the values that they instilled in her as a child. Imagery is an important songwriting device in this half of the album narrative, as objects like her mother's 'Old Black Kettle' (Track 3) and her 'Daddy's Working Boots' (Track 4) become symbols of the loss of the simple things in life and the sacrifices made to provide for a large family (respectively). She also pays tribute to the town's physician that delivered her, 'Dr. Robert F. Thomas' (Track 5). Parton closes the first half of the album narrative with a slowed down re-recording of her 1968 single 'In the Good Old Days (When Times Were Bad)', which reflects on the challenges that her family faced in order to survive in the isolated region of east Tennessee.[15] The song outlines the long hours of work in the fields, the impact of unpredictable and harsh weather on crops, and the physical ailments her parents endured to provide for their children. These ailments demonstrate not just the challenges that they faced living in an isolated region, but also the gender roles at play in rural southern communities: her father's bleeding hands and stiff body were a result of his manual labour in the fields, while her mother's suffering was due to the lack of adequate medical care during pregnancy, labour, and delivery. In the chorus, Parton reveals that while no amount of money could buy these memories from her, no amount of money could pay her to live through it again. Parton drew on a combination of Appalachian and 'countrypolitan' conventions to support this song's narrative. She evokes her heritage through both her acoustic guitar strumming and style of vocal delivery, which maintain the feel of storytelling so important to the Appalachian tradition. Parton uses a guitar strumming technique similar to that of Maybelle Carter, a thumb-brush pattern in which she strums the strings with the back of her nails. The thumb-brushing remains at the core of the song setting, and is reinforced through the rhythmic layering of the drum kit, bass guitar, and electric banjo. While the presence of the drum kit is certainly a departure from Appalachian country-folk style, it's the addition of the Nashville Edition background vocals in the chorus with their 'oohs' and 'aah' – a signature of the 'countrypolitan' style – that points strongly to Nashville recording studios.[16] It is not just the cultural and stylistic differences between rural and urban Tennessee's musical tradition that are illuminated by the musical setting, Parton also highlights the temporal distance between her childhood memories and life as a country star. By merging these old and new styles, Parton finds a unique way to modernise the traditions of her youth, making them accessible to a wider audience, while also bringing visibility to the vanishing traditions of her region.

Side B opens with the album's title track and only single, 'My Tennessee Mountain Home' in which Parton expresses her love for the simple lifestyle of the Smoky Mountains. She opens the narrative by describing a typical summer afternoon of children chasing insects, the fragrance of a honeysuckle vine, and songbirds in the distance. Parton describes a peaceful mountain life, one that is in direct contrast to the hardships and struggles of the previous song. While 'My Tennessee Mountain Home' also draws on a combination of Appalachian and 'countrypolitan' styles, the background vocals are used for a different effect in the song's chorus. In 'My Tennessee Mountain Home' Parton draws on Appalachian vocal traditions of southern gospel singing to praise her homeplace and close-harmony singing to describe the region's tranquillity. By highlighting two of the region's vocal practices in the chorus setting, Parton honours the group, religious, and close-harmony singing traditions of her childhood. After painting this idyllic scene about her homeplace, the next three songs on the album explore the depths of her homesickness. Parton contemplates the fragility of time and the enduring memories of their simple past ('Wrong Direction Home', Track 8), expresses a desire to return home ('Back Home', Track 9), and reflects nostalgically on the memories of her childhood ('Better Part of Life', Track 10). Parton's desire to return home, however, is metaphorical: her songs do not reveal a desire to physically return to east Tennessee, but rather, they demonstrate her longing for an earlier, simpler time – to the homemade toys and clothes, the musical gatherings, and to the strong familial bonds of her childhood.

From the southern rural-mountain region of her childhood to the urban setting of Music City USA, the album's concluding track is the only song to consider her *new* homeplace. 'Down on Music Row' relates Parton's first days in Nashville, when she was eager and determined to share her songs on Music Row. While the preceding songs on this side describe serene landscapes and wildlife, this song points to landmarks on Music Row including the steps of RCA Victor, the fountain in front of the original Country Music Hall of Fame and Museum, and the walkway of stars, important cultural landmarks in country music's history – all of which Parton wanted to (and eventually would) join.[17] As in 'The Letter', she hints at her disillusionment with the reality of the music business when she first arrived in Nashville, but remains determined to achieve her goals. She concludes the song with a nod to her RCA Victor producers Chet Atkins and Bob Ferguson for listening to her songs.[18] The musical setting offers additional commentary to the narrative, reinforcing rural and urban spaces throughout 'Down on Music Row'. The song opens with only the acoustic guitar as Parton sings the chorus, creating a prologue to this story, as though told from her home in east Tennessee. The drum kit enters the accompaniment in the first verse with a 'train' beat that references her journey, while the harmonica and the pedal steel signify nostalgia and rural spaces as she leaves home.[19] The harmonica and pedal steel drop from the setting as Parton walks down music row, but return when she reveals her frustrations over finding an audience for her music (again, revealing nostalgia for home). As she mentions 'Chet and Bob' at RCA, the background singers sing vowel sounds ('ahhh') to point to the creators of the 'countrypolitan' style. The accompaniment seems to offer not just a musical narrative of her journey, but also a critique of place: the use of harmonica and pedal steel are used to symbolise Parton's longing for her rural home, while the 'countrypolitan' conventions characterise the urban setting and country music industry, suggesting that this is the sound of being a country star 'Down on Music Row'.

Parton's Appalachian roots remain at the core of every song on the album through her easy folk style vocal delivery and the thumb-brush strumming. These stylistic elements (drawn from the 'old mountain music' of her origins) function as musical codes that mark out region and solidify relationship to the homeplace. Although the 'countrypolitan' style was traditionally used as a way to 'sophisticate' country by removing strong markers of rusticity like the fiddle, pedal steel, and banjo so that it would appeal to a crossover pop audience, Parton retained these instruments and incorporated elements of the urban Nashville Sound on this album in a way that enhances her Appalachian influences. Although these regional styles represent the clash of rural values with the urban commercialisation of country music, their combination emphasises rurality. Combining the Appalachian with the 'countrypolitan' style conventions of RCA Victor allowed Parton to keep one foot firmly rooted in her past, revealing that the culture and traditions of east Tennessee have left an indelible mark on Parton's music and identity. More importantly, the album brought awareness to issues impacting the southern working class, and mapped out not just Parton's move from Sevierville to Nashville, but also the pattern of migration of rural southerners to urban centres across the American south. Parton's album captured the lonesomeness of this journey, and provided cultural grounding for an audience composed of displaced working-class southerners nostalgic for their rural homes and the communities of their upbringing.[20]

Conclusions

To say that her poor, rural-mountain origins have left a mark on Parton's identity would be an understatement. Home has maintained an important role in Parton's life, as the location of her memories, familial relations, and identity. She has even built a business empire on her family's story, notably in the construction of *Dollywood*, a theme park that features traditional crafts and music of the Smoky Mountain region. The park also includes a replica cabin of her Tennessee Mountain Home, at which Parton revealed the important role that this home and geographic location played in shaping her career in the following inscription: 'These mountains and my childhood home have a special place in my heart. They inspire my music and my life.'[21]

Although she would pen her literary autobiography, *Dolly Parton: My Life and Other Unfinished Business* in 1994, Parton first turned to song-writing to document her story. She shared the first piece of her story in 1968 with 'In the Good Old Days (When Times Were Bad)', followed by 'Coat of Many Colors' in 1971, which relayed the story about how her mother stitched together a coat for young Parton out of rags given to the family. On *My Tennessee Mountain Home*, Parton explored more deeply her complex relationship with the region; she recounted the challenges her family faced and her desire to leave east Tennessee, while also proclaiming her love and appreciation of the region and her family and a desire to return back home. These conflicting tensions result in an intense sense of longing and nostalgia not for the limitations of the life she was born into, but for the loss of the simpler way of life, traditions of her Appalachian roots, and her family. As country music historian Bill Malone observes, songs about the homeplace have 'provided emotional release and security for people who have moved into a complex world rife with uncertain loyalties and shifting moral values'.[22] The evocation of her poor, rural upbringing at this pivotal moment in her career suggests that, amidst the success and tension with Wagoner, Parton's lack of control over her professional life may have contributed to a need not just to mark out her place within the industry, but also to unveil elements of her identity, and build (or rebuild) ties to her poor, southern rural origins. The confessional nature of the autobiographical narrative allowed Parton to tell *her* version of her story, to share her life experiences, and document her journey from Sevierville to Nashville. Parton continued to turn to her childhood memories and Appalachian roots in her songwriting throughout her career; her discography reveals an array of character sketches, memories, and emotions about her childhood in east Tennessee.[23] A singer-songwriter first and foremost, Parton's songs reveal to her audience that underneath the sparkly wardrobe, big wigs, makeup, acrylic nails, and urban-centred production values, the poor little mountain girl and her rural Appalachian roots remain.

With *My Tennessee Mountain Home*, Parton entered into a long tradition of country singer-songwriters exploring their origins and relationship to place through song. Like Loretta Lynn, Merle Haggard, and (the perhaps lesser-known) Butch Hancock, Parton's album invoked confessional autobiographical narratives to explore issues of regional identity through song. For Parton, bound to the production values associated with her label and producer, the countrypolitan style of *My Tennessee Mountain Home* often masks the confessional nature of the song narratives in which she explores her roots, heritage, and the hardships of growing up in rural Appalachia. Yet her album marked an important shift in country songwriting, wherein the genre's singer-songwriters began turning to place-based narratives to explore local and regional issues.[24] Parton helped transform the autobiographical narrative into an important platform for considering deeper connections to family, community, and place. In sharing her personal experiences about growing up in rural Appalachia, Parton demonstrated the ways in which songwriting could be used to interrogate issues related to the traditions and culture of place, helping to establish a sense of regional identity.

Notes

1 Stephen Miller, *Smart Blonde: Dolly Parton* (New York: Omnibus Press, 2008), pp. 164–76.

2 Parton and her uncle Bill Owens created Owepar in 1964. After he left the business, Parton transferred Owens' 49% to Wagoner as a Christmas present in 1969 (see Jerry Bailey, 'Dolly Parton Wants to Glitter as a Musician', *Country Music* (February 1973), p. 30). It was common practice in Nashville for producers to have a controlling part of publishing and co-authorship in exchange for helping a younger artist. Following her departure from their partnership in 1975, Wagoner sued Parton for breach of contract. They settled out of court, and in addition to Parton agreeing to pay Wagoner a $1 million settlement and record one final album together, Wagoner returned his half of Owepar to Parton and she returned her half of Fireside. See Dolly Parton, *My Life and Other Unfinished Business* (New York: Harper Collins, 1994), pp. 184–5.

3 Nancy Cardwell, *The Words and Music of Dolly Parton: Getting to Know Country Music's 'Iron Butterfly'* (New York: Praeger, 2011), p. 7.

4 Bill DeMain, *In Their Own Words: Songwriters Talk about the Creative Process* (Connecticut: Praeger, 2004), p. 29.

5 Quoted in Miller, *Smart Blonde*, p. 29.

6 Jada Watson, 'Dixie Chicks' "Lubbock or Leave it": Negotiating Identity and Place in Country Song', *Journal of the Society for American Music* 8/1 (2014), pp. 50–2.

7 Pamela Fox, *Natural Acts: Gender, Race, and Rusticity in Country Music* (Ann Arbor: University of Michigan Press, 2009), p. 114.

8 Ibid., p. 115.

9 Warren R. Hofstra and Mike Foreman, 'Legacy and Legend: The Cultural World of Patsy Cline's Winchester', in Warren R. Hofstra (ed.), *Sweet Dreams: The World of Patsy Cline* (Urbana: University of Illinois Press, 2013), p. 22.

10 Adam Krims, *Music and Urban Geography* (New York: Routledge, 2007).

11 Travis Stimeling, "Music, Place, and Identity in the Central Appalachian Mountaintop Removal Mining Debate', *American Music* 30/1 (2012): pp. 1–29.

12 Parton was not the only artist to pursue a concept album in the early 1970s; Willie Nelson had explored the format a year earlier with his final RCA Victor project, *Yesterday's Wine* (1971). See Travis Stimeling, '"Phases and Stages, Circles and Cycles": Willie Nelson and the Concept Album', *Popular Music* 30/3(2011): pp. 389–408.

13 Dolly Parton, *My Tennessee Mountain Home*. RCA Nashville, Legacy 82876815292. 2007.

14 A group of core musicians were present on each of the four session dates for *My Tennessee Mountain Home*, including Jimmy Colvard and Jerry Stembridge (guitar), Bobby Dyson (bass), Jerry Carrigan (drums), Pete Drake (Steel), Mack Magaha (fiddle), Buck Trent (banjo), and the Nashville Edition (background vocals). Hargus 'Pig' Robbins (piano) attended the first 3 sessions, with Ron Oate taking his place at the fourth session. See recording session personnel listing in Dolly Parton, *My Tennessee Mountain Home*. RCA Nashville, Legacy 82876815292. 2007.

15 Merle Haggard recorded 'In the Good Old Days (When Times Were Bad)' on *Mama Tried*. His album was released in October 1968, just one month before Parton released the song as a single.

16 Joli Jensen, *Nashville Sound: Authenticity, Commercialization, and Country Music* (Nashville: Country Music Foundation Press & Vanderbilt University Press, 1998), p. 83.

17 The original Country Music Hall of Fame and Museum opened on Music Row on 1 April 1967, and moved to their current location in downtown Nashville on 17 May 2001. For more on the institution and its programs, see Diane Pecknold, *The Selling Sound: The Rise of the Country Music Industry* (Durham: Duke University Press, 2007), pp. 195–6; pp. 238–9.

18 Neither producer played a role in Parton's early recording career in Nashville. Atkins was even hesitant to sign her when approached by Wagoner in 1967. They were, however, highly influential producers behind the creation of the Nashville Sound, and producers of her RCA Victor work.

19 Another 'countrypolitan' song that used its musical setting to enhance the lyrical narrative is Mac Davis' 'Texas in My Rear View Mirror' (1981). See Watson, 'Dixie Chicks' "Lubbock or Leave it"', pp. 64–5.

20 Bill C. Malone, 'Patsy Cline and the Transformation of the Working-Class South', in. Hofstra. *Sweet Dreams*, pp. 31–5.

21 Inscription on the replica cabin of Parton's Tennessee Mountain Home at *Dollywood*. Dollywood, 'Rides & Attractions'. Available at: www.dollywood.com/themepark/rides/Smoky-Mountain-Home.aspx (accessed 1 May 2014).

22 Bill C. Malone, *Don't Get Above Your Raisin': Country Music and the Southern Working Class* (Urbana: University of Illinois Press, 2002), p. 54.

23 Parton addresses her homesickness in 'Sacred Memories' (1972/2007), 'Tennessee Homesick Blues' (1984); childhood memories in 'Coat of Many Colors' (1971); and character sketches/cultural traditions on 'Down from Dover' (1969), 'Applejack' (1977), and 'Smoky Mountain Memories' (1994).

24 Notable examples of concept albums dealing with issues of regional identity include, Butch Hancock's 1978 *West Texas Waltzes and Dust-blown Tractor Tunes*, Terry Allen's 1979 *Lubbock (On Everything)*, and Andy Eppler's 2009 *Disease in the Heartland*. These albums are discussed in Watson, 'Dixie Chicks "Lubbock or Leave it"', pp. 62–6. One might also consider the discography of Canadian country artist Corb Lund, who explores issues of southern Albertan identity as well as his family heritage in the region.

11 Authorship and performance in the music of Elton John

PHIL ALLCOCK

Elton John has become a brand, a term under which a range of activities and values are grouped together. This chapter will focus specifically on how Elton John's role as an author is influenced by notions of performance and performer, creating a nexus of characteristics that encompass the figure of the singer-songwriter. Having changed his name by deed poll, the man formerly known as Reginald Dwight is now indistinguishable from 'Elton John', the global music icon. The person and the onstage artist are no longer separate. More than a popular music artist, he is a philanthropist, a gay rights campaigner, gay icon, art collector, and composer for films and musicals. Through the mixing of the person and the stage persona, the longevity and success of his career, and interests outside of popular music, Elton John is exemplary of how authorship in popular music draws upon elements of both the intramusical and extramusical.

Songwriting partnership

Elton John and Bernie Taupin have an unusual songwriting partnership. Taupin writes lyrics (without any verse/chorus structure) and posts them to John. Throughout their career they often write their respective parts of a song in separate rooms, a fact that was the inspiration for the title of the 1991 tribute album *Two Rooms*. The 1975 album *Captain Fantastic and the Brown Dirt Cowboy* also referred to the John/Taupin songwriting partnership, with John as 'Captain Fantastic' and Taupin as the 'Brown Dirt Cowboy'. In contrast to other songwriting partnerships such as Lennon and McCartney, they never switch roles and only one is consistently the performer.

In comparison with the most commercially successful popular music artists, Elton John is noteworthy as a singer-songwriter. At one end of the composer–performer spectrum are artists and groups such as Madonna and Michael Jackson, The Beatles, Led Zeppelin, and Pink Floyd, that have significant authorial voices. At the other end are those like Elvis Presley for whom, although he wrote some of his own songs, most of his material was written by others (such as Leiber and Stoller, and Otis Redding). Or to put it another way, the interaction of intramusical and extramusical features of Elvis Presley's songs would take into account that in most cases he was the performer but not the composer. As a singer-songwriter Elton John is between the two groups, as John is a portion of the songwriting partnership, albeit a crucial one. Furthermore, for some, John's persona as virtuosic performer and entertainer (particularly in his early career) may also create a sense of separation between performer and composer. As performing persona, while audience members are likely to be aware of his songwriting partnership with Bernie Taupin (as well as other lyricists on occasion), during a performance the spotlight is focused solely on Elton John.

Performance

Live performances are a test for any artist, even one as experienced as Elton John. The live setting strips back much of the collaborative preparation that got the artist there in the first place. The hairstylists, make-up artists, and roadies cannot help the performer if they play a wrong chord or say the wrong thing. There is no safety net. This humanising experience helps emphasise the personal connection an artist will have with the audience in live performance. Unlike a film star who can film a scene again and again, the music star, once on stage, has to cope with the pressure and play things correctly on the initial attempt. One could read this pressure and risk of error as symbolic of everyday individual struggle. The audience can relate to the artist through this struggle, arguably making the connection more intimate while adding to the 'anything can happen' excitement of live performance. Liveness, and the virtuosity and heroism thereby inscribed, reaffirms the artist's humanity.

While Elton John usually records and performs with a band, he also performs solo and has undertaken entire concerts without any other musicians supporting him. Whilst other singer-songwriters of Elton John's stature may perform an individual song as a solo number, it is highly unusual for this to be done for an entire concert. This 'unplugged' effect gives him the ability to connect with the audience on a much more personal and intimate level than most popular music artists can achieve. Furthermore, the use of the piano distinguishes his performances from rock groups or guitar-based singer-songwriters.

In addition to lyrical authorship, the subject of the lyrics could also distance John from perceived authorship. But when Elton John performs a song, even narrated in the third person, John is still the performer. The performing subject, therefore, becomes strongly part of the narrative despite authorship or topic. At times, Elton John makes this clear through extravagant costumes, set designs bearing his name, or musical virtuosity (piano and/or voice). The focus is clearly on him. Elton John is a curator, or an auteur. As Till writes: 'Pop stars' performances are assumed to be real, the emotions they portray, the lyrics they sing, the answers they give in interviews are supposed to portray the real lives of these liquid stars, no matter how plastic their public facades, how well constructed their media-friendly masks are.'[1] In other words, Elton John's performances are attributed to him, despite Bernie Taupin (or occasionally others') lyrical authorship. Perhaps it is the way in which the songwriting partnership between Elton John and Bernie Taupin operates that allows this sense of realism to exist. With the music being composed and performed solely by Elton John (with supporting musicians as necessary) his role as a curator or auteur – bringing together a range of ideas (music, lyrics, staging, etc.) – negates the creative conflict between songwriting partnership and sole performing artist.

Stardom and celebrity

Stars are brands, representing a set of values and expectations. In a film, even a major star has to share the limelight with other actors, the director, and the plot. In popular music the artist is telling the story, and as far as the audience are concerned the artist is directing the performance, with the other musicians supporting the artist – they are not equals. When an actor plays a role in a film they are, more often than not, perceived as separate from the role. In contrast, this distinction does not exist for popular music artists. The popular music artist is the person, performer, and director (who controls the performance) all rolled into one. Till writes of how a level of fame reaches the most popular of stars:

> For a star to progress to a point where they are described as a popular icon requires their achievement of a level of fame at which they are treated with the sort of respect traditionally reserved for religious figures … Such popular icons have generally had critical success, have gained financial independence, have achieved a high level of fame, receive unconditional audience adulation, and crucially they are usually known by only one name … The importance of image in this process has meant that an artist's image has become as important to success within popular music as the quality of their music. Indeed it has meant that for some artists the careful handling of branding, marketing and image has been the dominant factor in, and feature of, their success. However, most musical artists who have sustained iconic status also have gained recognition at some point for the quality of their music. To identify a popular music star as having achieved iconic status, one would look for identification by a single name, critical success, financial success, international audience recognition and fame, as well as a musical career that is successful in the long term.[2]

Till's categorisations of the status markers of the popular music icon align with Elton John's career. He is instantly recognisable by his first name, and often builds this fame into his set design. 'Elton' has been critically successful over a period of six decades, becoming one of the bestselling artists of all time with record sales reaching an estimated 300 million. As a result, he has bought a number of houses across the world, has built one of the largest private photography collections in the world, and he contributes millions of pounds to charity each year. Through his charity work as well as his music career, Elton is recognised internationally (including through his own Elton John AIDS Foundation); not to mention his high profile 1997 performance at the funeral of Princess Diana, performing new lyrics to 'Candle in the Wind', which became the best-selling single of all time.

Elton's status as a popular music icon impacts greatly upon his work, in particular his longevity of success. His avoidance of retirement, despite being financially secure to do so, has implications for how the audience interpret Elton as a music artist. His authenticity is boosted through his seeming desire to perform concerts and record albums for their own sake and for the audience's benefit. For twenty years Elton has donated all royalties from singles to charity. For the audience, these facts reduce critiques of commercialism in Elton's music, and his status can lend weight to any related projects.

The Internet has been a key element in the rise of celebrities over the last twenty years or so, and has allowed supplementary information about an artist to be readily available to the public. Through the use of his own website and Twitter account, members of the public are able to access instantly up-to-date information about Elton John. Information from such sources has a strong focus on Elton John as a music star, even though they may discuss other aspects of his life (such as the birth of his children or marriage to David Furnish). In contrast, an artist beginning their career now is likely to incorporate social media into their star image in a far more symbiotic way. The flooding of the music market has led to artists needing to be more active in differentiating themselves from others. As a result, the public is demonstrably allowed more access into their private lives, far more openly and freely than for an artist of Elton John's generation.

Gender and live performance

As the 1960s transitioned into the 1970s, many male artists dressed in an explicitly gendered way, even when that meant questioning gender norms (such as men with long hair). Like those in the emerging 'glam rock' scene, Elton John wore comic and/or extravagant costumes. For those performers who chose a less masculine or more androgynous appearance (such as

David Bowie), there were ways in which they could counterbalance this elsewhere in their performance. The use of conventional rock instruments such as drums and guitar, with their connotations of masculinity, was one way to achieve this. Movement and physical gestures are another way to perform gender. Vocalists can control the microphone to claim power – the vocalist is often described as 'taking the lead', being the 'leader of the band', or being the 'frontman'. Instrumentalists could boost the volume of their instrument in the mix to gain similar power and dominance. Most members of a band stand up to perform, and so they can move about the stage and use physical gestures which have sexual overtones. In contrast, Elton John is more limited than performers with smaller instruments – the piano is a static object (though this is similar to singer-songwriters who sit with their acoustic guitar). Furthermore, Elton John does not control the microphone in the same manner as some artists. Because both hands are occupied with playing the piano, he cannot hold the microphone. In this way, it is more difficult for him to reposition himself towards the audience for greater intimacy. Also, he cannot move the microphone to alter his performance. If he wishes to produce a more intimate sound (such as that found on 'Your Song', analysed by Katherine Williams in Chapter 20), Elton John has to move closer to the microphone – the microphone does not move closer to him.

The piano is a large, opaque object, and makes it difficult for the performer to move on as large a scale as someone like Mick Jagger or Freddie Mercury, for example. Indeed, the piano could be seen as an extension of, or as, John's body. Whether he is wearing a costume (which makes his gender performance more ambiguous) or a suit, the obscuring of his bottom half gives a different impression than artists who primarily stand up on stage (though this is not to say that Elton never stood up to play, especially in his more flamboyant 1970s performances). The point is that, unlike a guitarist or a vocalist, his body can be less visible and has more restricted mobility than other artists who do not play the piano. A guitarist, with their body visible, can potentially adopt similar positioning to those standing in the audience. They can move to the very front of the stage to get closer to the audience, and can use their bodies to react to the music and interact with the audience. This may have a significant impact on how the audience relates to Elton John, and how Elton John is perceived as a star and celebrity.

Costumes, instruments, and positioning are important to consider when exploring the link between songwriting and performing, and the ways that singer-songwriters retain performative authorship of their songs. In the case of Elton John, the notion of authorship is heightened by the way in which he has drawn together different aspects of his existence as a popular music artist, singer-songwriter, and person, to create a global music icon. He has been able to create a distinctive artistic identity for himself. The audience do not interact with a singer-songwriter within a cultural vacuum. They are aware of the many facets that combine to form the artist, and this is the environment in which the singer-songwriter composes and performs their songs.

Elton John has created a distinctive artistic identity and authorship in spite of the fact that he writes music to lyrics others have authored. He has achieved this identity through his unique combination of roles as a virtuosic performer, 'professional' singer-songwriter (given his ability to work quickly at setting music to lyrics), and popular music star and celebrity. Elton John's position as a popular music icon has brought these roles together into a single author identity.

Notes

1 Rupert Till, *Pop Cult: Religion and Popular Music* (London: Continuum, 2010), p. 46.

2 Ibid., p. 47–9.

12 Depicting the working class in the music of Billy Joel

JOSHUA S. DUCHAN

Singer-songwriter Billy Joel (b. 1949), an American musician whose career spanned the 1970s through to the present, is perhaps most famous for ballads and love songs such as 'Piano Man' (from *Piano Man*, 1973) and 'Just the Way You Are' (from *The Stranger*, 1977). A closer look at Joel's musical output, however, reveals not only an autobiographical impulse familiar to many twentieth-century popular musicians, but also a keen ability, common among singer-songwriters, to render larger cultural trends as compelling musical narratives. This chapter examines one of the themes on which Joel has mused throughout his career, the working class, and its musical manifestations in three songs that span his catalogue, 'Ain't No Crime' (from *Piano Man*), 'Allentown' (from *The Nylon Curtain*, 1982), and 'The Downeaster "Alexa"' (from *Storm Front*, 1989). Although they vary stylistically, each song offers the composer's observations of, and commentary on, working-class and broader American culture in the late twentieth century.[1]

Joel was raised on New York's Long Island in the town of Hicksville, one of the earliest examples of a 'Levittown', in which thousands of identical, inexpensive houses were constructed and sold to veterans returning from World War II. While taking piano lessons as a child there, he would master classical pieces by ear and even offer his own improvisations on them.[2] The influence of classical music can be seen in several of his pieces, including 'The Ballad of Billy the Kid' from *Piano Man* and 'This Night' from *An Innocent Man* (1983).[3] The Beatles' 1964 appearance on the *Ed Sullivan Show* inspired him to pursue a future in popular music and to compose songs that exhibited varying degrees of 'Beatlish compositional, vocal, instrumental, and studio-technical production'.[4] He achieved commercial success with his second album, *Piano Man*, whose title track peaked at number 25 on the *Billboard* Hot 100 chart. But it was *The Stranger* that established the suburban New Yorker as a household name, yielding four hits in the top twenty-five and two Grammy awards.[5]

'I came from a blue-collar area', Joel said in a 2007 interview. 'You know, some people think that because I came from the suburbs I lived in a privileged area, very hoity-toity. Well, it wasn't. It was a working-class town'.[6] Thus, throughout Joel's catalogue one finds pieces that engage with working-class life from a variety of angles and with varying degrees of directness. He tends to approach these songs by singing either as a distanced narrator describing working-class life (e.g. 'Ain't No Crime' and parts of 'Allentown'), or as a working-class protagonist (e.g. parts of 'Allentown' and 'The Downeaster "Alexa"'). Occasionally, he also conflates songs about the working class with attempts to write folk music.[7] Across Joel's working-class songs is a consistent attempt to capture the challenges and perspective of everyday people in a world they cannot fully control.

Blues, gospel, and collectivity in 'Ain't No Crime'

'Ain't No Crime' begins by cautioning: 'nine o'clock coming without any warning and you gotta get ready to go'. Later lyrics reveal that there is little in the protagonist's life aside from work and the occasional diversion of drunken revelry. The unwelcomed return to a 'nine-to-five' job is paired with a sense of youthfulness vis-à-vis parental disapproval. It is unclear whether Joel's use of the second-person address ('you') is directed at the subject of the song or the listener. In either case, the previous night's overindulgence was an enjoyable distraction but, as the song concludes, ultimately only that: the wind will continue to blow, the grass will still grow, so 'you gotta keep goin' and the Lord have mercy on your soul'.

Lyrical and musical choices reinforce the interpretation of 'Ain't No Crime' as implicitly espousing a working-class perspective by hinting at both blues and gospel styles.[8] The narrative, about a person with little sway over his circumstances yet still including a glimmer of hope, recalls the spirit of many blues songs, while the religious sensibility of the final lyric suggests a gospel approach. Like much blues music, the harmony emphasises a tonic–subdominant relationship. The melody highlights the flattened third scale degree, one of the common 'blue' notes, which also functions as a flattened seventh or ninth in relation to the supporting harmony. Formally, however, the song differs from the archetypical blues, as its two verses contain three 6-bar phrases that move from tonic to subdominant, while the chorus comprises three 4-bar phrases, each beginning on the subdominant and resolving to tonic. Thus, Joel does not entirely commit to the blues genre but adopts enough generic markers to make the allusion clear.

Joel's signature piano lays the foundation for 'Ain't No Crime', and the end of each phrase during the verses features a quick, three-beat melodic fragment outlining the tonic chord with fast grace and passing notes, played solo. Along with the rest of the rock band's rhythm section, the song also features an organ, whose presence suggests a church setting. During much of the melody a mixed choir sings with or behind Joel's lead, exhibiting several markers of gospel, including a wide vibrato and high levels of intensity and volume. These elements connote a sense of group solidarity, as disparate vocal timbres sing cooperatively to support and assist in the delivery of the song's message. This sense of community links Joel's expression of a working-class perspective with Aaron Fox's observations that in working-class music, 'vocalization performs … an intertwining of self and other, and an aesthetic and ethical projection of the self into the experience of the other that is the basis for sociality'.[9] The use of blues and gospel styles in 'Ain't No Crime' thus presents a combination of voices evoking a sense of community but drawing no conclusion other than that, despite any entertaining distractions, one must always return to the quotidian routine of work.

Industrial decline and unfulfilled promises in 'Allentown'

As the opening track on *The Nylon Curtain*, 'Allentown' announces itself with a screaming steam whistle signalling the beginning or end of a factory shift – appropriate, since the Pennsylvania city for which the song is named was an important part of the American industrial boom following World War II. This song angrily laments the subsequent industrial decline, however, declaring straight away that 'they're closing all the factories down'.[10] 'Allentown' focuses less on the company's plight than on rank-and-file, blue-collar workers, expressing their frustration at a loss of work and identity, and a sense that their home town is dying. Moreover, Joel's lyrics convey a bitter sense of betrayal. After all, many steelworkers of the 1970s were Baby Boomers, taught to believe in the promise that, 'if [they] worked hard, if [they] behaved', they could expect a better life, a steady job, and decent working conditions. Yet this promise amounted to little when compared with 'what was real: iron and coke, chromium steel', the economics of what was now an international industry in which American companies were flailing. As the situation disintegrated, 'the union people crawled away', as Joel sings, spitting the *p*'s with disgust and holding on to the last word to draw out the union leaders' retreat.

With 'Allentown' the scope of Joel's perspective on working-class life expands beyond just a story of a hung-over youth from 'Ain't No Crime'. For Joel, even the name 'Allentown' signified something quintessentially American; he called it a 'heartland name'.[11] Indeed, the song, which reached number 17 on the *Billboard* Hot 100 chart, is a blue-collar anthem, a rallying cry for those abandoned by big companies whose work gave them an identity and offered them purpose. The bridge describes how each child 'had a pretty good shot' to at least match his or her parents' socioeconomic status. When that goal proves elusive, Joel notes how 'they threw an American flag in our face', perhaps a corporate attempt to soften the blow by appealing to a (fading) sense of national pride. Although the first and second verses are sung using the pronoun 'we', implying a sense of community for which the protagonist sings, after the fury of the bridge the final verse adopts the first-person 'I', suggesting resignation and isolation.[12] He is, in the end, a narrator at some distance from the action.

Musically, 'Allentown' features regular, pounding piano chords that create a sense of steady forward motion, the rhythm of an assembly line. Unlike in 'Ain't No Crime', Joel sings alone, his voice sounding against the clanging of factory machinery and a fuller band, comprising electric guitar, electric bass, and drums emphasising the backbeat. The short delay applied to the vocal track creates a slightly unnatural, cold, and mechanistic quality, enhancing the anger in the lyrics.

Harmonically, the song remains tonally uncertain, suggesting at times both C and G major while also including passages in D and F. This ambiguity extends to the lyrics as well, as the title appears at the beginning of some phrases and the end of others. Thus, as Robert Schultz writes, 'the intricate search for identity with regards to tonal and lyrical structure in "Allentown" very effectively embodies the struggle for personal identity in small-town, blue-collar America portrayed in the lyrics'.[13]

The struggle evoked in 'Allentown' is echoed in the iconography of the album's cover art, which pictures a row of identical houses like those found in suburban American communities of tract housing, including the one in which Joel was raised. The indistinguishable nature of the homes matches Joel's views on the monotony of suburban life, which made it all the more difficult to distinguish oneself. 'You're a nothing, you're a zero in the suburbs', Joel told Dave Marsh. 'You're mundane, you're common'.[14] Thus, in 'Allentown' compositional choices align to support a narrative – of anger, frustration, loss, and loneliness in an increasingly mechanised, globalised, and post-industrial world – that would seem at home in the tradition of American folk music stretching back through Bob Dylan to Pete Seeger and Woody Guthrie. Indeed, in the music video for 'Allentown', Joel is seen observing the action, strumming an acoustic guitar while wearing a faded plaid shirt and a beat-up fedora. Yet, as A. Morgan Jones points out, these folk signifiers are at odds with the video's choreographed dance and the music's rock-and-roll instrumentation and style.[15]

Struggle and resignation aboard 'The Downeaster "Alexa"'

While 'Allentown' dealt with the American rust belt, 'The Downeaster "Alexa"', released seven years later and reaching number 57 on the *Billboard* Hot 100, sets its sights on the fishing industry off the coast of Long Island

and New England, closer to Joel's home. The lyrics are peppered with references to locations to which one could sail (the Block Island Sound, Gardiners Bay, Martha's Vineyard, Montauk, Nantucket) and maritime tasks (charting a course, taking on diesel fuel, working 'with the rod and the reel'). Joel sings from the perspective of a lonely, beleaguered fisherman, who must sail ever greater distances from shore in search of swordfish. The work is gruelling but he continues out of a strong sense of obligation to his family. He comes from a long line of fishermen, but the nature of the work has changed; the future looks grim 'for a man who works the sea'. (His boat's name gives the song its title and also references Joel's daughter.)

Whereas 'Allentown' could serve as a metaphor for American industry in general, 'The Downeaster "Alexa"' is more specific. The song points to two sources of the fisherman's woes: government regulation of once-endangered Atlantic striped bass ('since they told me I can't sell no stripers') and demographic shifts wherein wealthy urbanites displace long-time residents of Long Island's blue-collar fishing communities ('there ain't no island left for Islanders like me'). Moreover, unlike 'Allentown', 'The Downeaster "Alexa"' offers no nostalgic reflection on 'glory days'.[16] Here, there is nothing but stark reality.

Musically, 'The Downeaster "Alexa"' is a strophic ballad. After a harmonically stable introduction in A minor, which later reappears as transitional material, the song modulates to C major for the verses. The C-major sonority prevails for the first half of the verse, which describes the forward-looking present, while a shift towards the subdominant accompanies the second half, which looks backwards to the past. Later instrumental passages shift back to A minor, with a brief foray in E minor.

Addressing a much older vocation, this song about fishing includes more folk elements than the blues and gospel of 'Ain't No Crime' or the driving rock of 'Allentown', yielding the closest alignment of narrative and musical style. Three such folk signifiers are especially pertinent: metre, instrumentation, and vocal texture. Metrically, the song emphasises the first and third beats within its common-time signature, contrasting the backbeat of the pieces discussed earlier in this chapter and most of Joel's catalogue in general. Furthermore, 'The Downeaster "Alexa"' sees changes in the way Joel employs his accompanying instruments. For example, the piano is completely absent. While an electric guitar is present, it is more ornamental and atmospheric than melodic or harmonic, playing distorted descending glissandi suggestive of a lament. More prominent is the accordion, an instrument that carries strong folk connotations.[17] As Marion Jacobson points out, 'the traditions of the accordion are seen as cultural remedies for the shallowness of American popular music'. Its status as a 'low-tech, antipostmodern antidote to synthesizer saturation' was especially strong during its revival in the 1970s and 80s – when Joel was writing 'The Downeaster "Alexa"' – as it was often used, in Jacobson's words, to 'humanise' rock music and harmonise 'working-class sensibilities' with the rock aesthetic.[18]

In the second half of the third verse, Joel sings vocables ('ya-oh') accompanied by an improvisatory fiddle (played by an uncredited Itzhak Perlman).[19] Both reappear after the song's final verse, but the vocables are expanded and reminiscent of a sea shanty ('ya-ya-ya-oh' over a repeating I–V–vi harmony in C major). Jones argues that these features, plus sound effects evoking seagulls, reinforce the song's folk qualities and its sense of authenticity.[20] Like many work songs, sea shanties were often sung in call-and-response fashion; vocables were frequently used in the responses. In 'The Downeaster "Alexa"', we hear only one part of this antiphonal vocal texture. The absence of the other voice(s) helps convey the sense of loneliness the captain feels, with the crying gulls his only companions. The image pictured on the cover of the song's single release sends the same message iconographically: bundled in a dark coat against a dark sky, Joel stares, stolid and unsmiling, past the viewer and off into the distance. Aside from a single seagull soaring over his shoulder, he stands alone against a cold world.

These three songs illustrate how, despite varied musical styles, Billy Joel sings from the point of view of, and about, hard-working people whose circumstances are worsening and who have little control over the forces that affect their lives. This sense of singing for (and representing) others fits nicely with Allan Moore's concept of 'authenticity of execution', or 'third-person authenticity', in which 'a performer succeeds in conveying the impression of accurately representing the ideas of another, embedded within a tradition of performance'.[21] Over the course of his career, Joel's working-class songs grow darker and more resigned even as they achieve, in their performance, greater consistency in their lyrical and musical techniques: 'Ain't No Crime' is premised on a night of fun and includes stylistic markers of blues and gospel without wholly adopting either; 'Allentown' mentions weekend getaways on the New Jersey shore amidst its expression of frustration, portraying Joel as witness to and bearer of the folk tradition while retaining mainstream rock instrumentation; and 'The Downeaster "Alexa"' offers little optimism but employs most thoughtfully folk signifiers in its metre, instrumentation, and texture. Ultimately, then, Joel's songs about the working class examine, comment on, and allow him to vocally embody parts of society and the historical and economic forces at work in people's lives.

Notes

1 For more on Joel in the context of a 'professional' composer, see Borshuk's Chapter 7 in this volume.

2 Billy Joel, quoted in Tony Schwartz, 'Billy the Kid', *Newsweek* 11 December 1978.

3 Walter Everett, 'The Learned vs. The Vernacular in the Songs of Billy Joel', *Contemporary Music Review* 18/4 (2000), pp. 110–11.

4 David and Victoria Sheff, 'Playboy Interview: Billy Joel', *Playboy* May 1982,

pp. 71–2; Everett, 'The Learned vs. The Vernacular', p. 107.

5 The hits were 'Just the Way You Are', 'Movin' Out (Anthony's Song)', 'Only the Good Die Young', and 'She's Always a Woman'. Joel won Grammy awards for Record of the Year and Song of the Year (for 'Just the Way You Are').

6 Len Righi, 'Billy Joel Revisits "Allentown"', *The Morning Call* (Allentown, PA), 28 November 2007, accessed via PopMatters (www.popmatters.com/article/billy-joel-revisits-allentown) on 15 May 2014.

7 A. Morgan Jones, 'The Other Sides of Billy Joel: Six Case Studies Revealing the Sociologist, The Balladeer, and the Historian' (PhD diss., University of Western Ontario, 2011), pp. 211–12. Jones describes how the visual signifiers in the music video for 'Allentown' conjured a sense of folk that was at odds with the song's rock instrumentation. However, he argues that Joel's video for 'The Downeaster "Alexa"' effectively matches visual signifiers of folk with musical ones.

8 The association between the blues, gospel, and the working class is deep. David Evans lists 'work' among the subjects often addressed in blues songs ('Blues: Chronological Overview', in Melonee V. Burnim and Portia K. Maultsby (eds.), *African American Music: An Introduction* (New York: Routledge, 2006), p. 85), while Tea Hunter describes the many forms of the blues in the twentieth century as sites for 'African American working-class self-understandings in the modern world' in *To 'Joy My Freedom: Southern Black Women's Lives and Labors After the Civil War* (Cambridge, MA: Harvard University Press, 1997), p. 169. The association also extends to musicians, as David Grazian's ethnographic study finds that 'most successful Chicago blues musicians are expected to comport themselves as working-class black men who have lived a life of hard labor' ('The Production of Popular Music as a Confidence Game: The Case of the Chicago Blues', *Qualitative Sociology* 27/2 [2004], p. 145). Jerma Jackson describes how both blues and gospel musicians 'were rooted in rural communities and working-class urban enclaves' in *Singing in my Soul: Black Gospel Music in a Secular Age* (Chapel Hill: University of North Carolina Press, 2004), p. 23.

9 Aaron A. Fox, *Real Country: Music and Language in Working-Class Culture* (Durham: Duke University Press, 2004), p. 321.

10 Bethlehem Steel, one of the country's largest steel producers (located in nearby Bethlehem, Pennsylvania), faced increasing foreign competition and rising retiree pension and healthcare costs that made it emblematic of the broader decay in American manufacturing in the 1970s. By the time of *The Nylon Curtain*'s release, the company reported an annual loss of $1.5 billion and accelerated its factory closures.

11 Righi, 'Billy Joel Revisits "Allentown"'. Joel also notes that the song's melody and harmony were composed 'probably in the '70s', but he 'didn't write the song' – presumably referring to the lyrics – 'until '82'.

12 Jones, 'The Other Sides of Billy Joel', p. 157.

13 Robert D. Schultz, 'Beethoven's Pop Legacy: Classical Structure in the Music of Billy Joel', in 'Three Analytical Essays in Twentieth-Century Music' (MA Thesis, University of Washington, 2005), pp. 46–51.

14 Billy Joel, quoted in Dave Marsh, 'Billy Joel: The Miracle of 52nd Street', *Rolling Stone* 14 December 1978, p. 72.

15 Jones, 'The Other Sides of Billy Joel', pp. 166, 211–12.

16 Ibid., p. 182.

17 The accordion features prominently in a variety of European and North American folk traditions. In the Americas, the accordion's association 'with immigrant, ethnic, and working-class expression' has remained strong since the 1880s (Helena Simonett, *The Accordion in the Americas: Klezmer, Polka, Zydeco, and More!* (Urbana, IL: University of Illinois Press, 2012), pp. 8–9). See also Charles and Angeliki V. Keil, *Polka Happiness* (Philadelphia: Temple University Press, 1992).

18 Marion Jacobson, *Squeeze This!: A Cultural History of the Accordion in America* (Urbana, IL: University of Illinois Press, 2012), p. 211.

19 Richard Scott, *Billy Joel: All About Soul* (New York: Vantage, 2000), p. 71.

20 Jones, 'The Other Sides of Billy Joel', pp. 186, 188–9.

21 Allan F. Moore, 'Authenticity as Authentication', *Popular Music* 21/2 (2002), p. 218.

13 Musical gesture in the songs of Nick Drake

TIMOTHY KOOZIN

British songwriter, singer, and guitarist Nick Drake is known for his intro-spective songs and innovative acoustic guitar style based on alternative tun-ings and elegant finger-picking techniques. His three studio albums created between 1969 and 1972 continued to rise in popularity after his tragic death in 1974. More recently, larger audiences have been introduced to Nick Drake's music through the many film soundtracks, television episodes, and particularly, television commercials that have featured his music.[1]

We might imagine the act of songwriting starting with a melody, lyric, some chords, or an instrumental riff. But in abstracting aspects of a song, we may not account for the role of the body in the creative process. We can enrich our understanding of musical, expressive, and cultural processes operating in a song, and perhaps uncover aspects of the songwriter's craft, by locating the creative impulse in an embodied action: a musical gesture. This chapter explores the relationship between Drake's varied choices in guitar tuning and the gestural movements of guitar performance he employs to create unusual textures, dissonances, and modal harmonic patterns, showing how Drake created an optimal idiomatic approach that minimises necessary physical motion on the fretboard while effectively engaging the resonance of open strings.[2] Drake's characteristic timing in delaying the vocal melody results in an expressive temporal dislocation between the guitar and voice. This often takes the form of an afterbeat gesture, in which the voice seems to rebound off the guitar rhythm, like a musical agent commenting on events already past. This enhances Drake's recurring narrative strategy of projecting the vocal persona of a conflicted and detached observer of the world.

Drake's producer and mentor, Joe Boyd, writes of an encounter prior to their collaboration on Drake's first album, *Five Leaves Left* (1969):

> One evening, Nick played me all his songs. Up close, the power of his fingers was astonishing, with each note ringing out loud – almost painfully so – and clear in the small room. I had listened closely to Robin Williamson, John Martyn, Bert Jansch and John Redbourn. Half-struck strings and blurred hammerings-on were an accepted part of their sound; none could match Nick's mastery of the instrument. After finishing one song, he would retune the guitar and proceed to play something equally complex in a totally different chord shape.[3]

Robert Kirby, arranger for instrumental ensembles heard on the album, has also commented on Drake's guitar tunings and chord voicings:

> I used to then sit with him and go through exactly how he played his chords, because he always de-tuned his guitar. He used strange tunings, not proper guitar tunings, and not the ones like people use in D tunings. He had very complicated tunings. Very complicated. Sometimes a low string would be higher than the string above. And so it would be very important for me to write down exactly how he played each chord, and every bar. And I would do that with him, that sometimes annoyed him I think, because it took a long time.[4]

Strategic decisions in guitar tuning were clearly integral to Drake's creative process. Choices in tuning and actions in performance resulted in unique chord voicings with attributes specially suited to each song. Kirby understood that close study of the actual voicings of chords would be necessary in creating instrumental arrangements that could effectively blend with Drake's own vocal–guitar performance. Both Boyd and Kirby describe closely observing Nick Drake to better understand what he was *doing* in performing his songs. In following his musical actions while listening, they were attuned to his musical gestures. The six songs selected for this study each employ a different guitar tuning, illustrating how Drake employed a consistent gestural approach in creatively exploring the expressive possibilities offered though different guitar tunings. The chapter further explores how Drake's gestural strategies are coded with meaning, projecting topical signifiers rooted in pastoral, blues, British folk, Baroque, and Classical musical traditions that are integral to Drake's style.

'Pink Moon'

In Nick Drake's 'Pink Moon' (Example 13.1), sustained open strings project a continuous sonic environment, so that each change engaging a stopped string is foregrounded for attention.[5] Drake strategically employs a variant of open-chord tuning in the song, so that the unfretted third string provides a ringing fourth or 'sus4'. Movement with one finger can resolve the dissonance upward, bringing the wayward string into consonance with the major triad. Fretting a higher string can suggest a ninth or eleventh chord, while fretting lower strings can imply the supertonic or other harmonies. The grasping and shaping of the chord, with one or two fingers depressed to bring voices within the chord into focus, constitutes a crucial part of the physical gesture that enlivens guitar melody and rhythm, creates harmonic motion, and adds dissonant colour. This basic gesture is a crucial component of the riff heard throughout the song.

Example 13.1.   Nick Drake, 'Pink Moon', *Pink Moon* (1971).

Tuning: CGCFCE (capo 2nd fret)

"One-finger" chord changes (shifting from 4th, to 3rd, to 2nd string)

000200   00200x   0200xx

I   ii   IV

Intro   Verse
                              "I saw it written..."   "It's a pink moon"

I   (ii IV)   V   IV   I   (ii IV)   I

I saw it writ-ten and I saw it say,   Pink moon ___ is on its way. ___

And none of you __ stand so ____ tall.   Pink moon __ gon-na get you all. ___   It's a pink moon.

Chorus
      "Pink pink pink pink, pink moon."
Em9   G/D   D

ii   IV   I   (ii IV)   I

Piano interlude
D   em9   G   D

I   ii   IV   I

As the song unfolds, the basic gesture expands to form a large-scale gesture that is thematic, form-producing, and connected to imagery expressed through the lyrics and singing.

Chord changes in the introduction are effected with one finger crossing strings on a single fret, providing unbroken continuity of sound with highly economical physical movement. Cross-string motions with one finger are also heard melodically. The pentatonic underpinnings of the introduction riff are expanded later in the piano–guitar interlude.

The lyrics personify the moon with human-like attributes while aligning the singer's persona with the mythical power of the moon, bringing about an expressive convergence between the individual and the moon:[6]

> I saw it written and I saw it say, [dominant]
> Pink moon is on its way. [subdominant]
> And none of you stand so tall. [dominant]
> Pink moon gonna get you all. [subdominant]
> It's a pink moon. [tonic]

The open-chord tuning with added melodic inflection on a single string allows for patterns that can be shifted whole to another fretboard location by means of a barre chord. While all strings are stopped with the index finger to form a main chord, other fingers are free to add local inflection. In 'Pink Moon', the larger motor movement of the arm choreographs motion through the whole phrase of the verse, from the dominant, to subdominant, to tonic. In the lyrics, actions, and references involving people ('I', 'you') are accompanied with the dominant. The second and fourth lines express anticipation that the pink moon is 'on its way' and 'gonna get you all'. This can be interpreted to represent human mortality, since death is always approaching and no one will outlast the moon.

Ironically, the reference to the moon as a possible harbinger of death is not overtly sinister, but playful, as if we are engaged in a game with the moon. This ambivalence towards fate, the passage of time, and the inevitability of death is a prevalent theme in Drake's songs. The final line in the verse, which simply observes the pastoral image of the pink moon, is associated with open guitar strings and the tonic chord. In this way, harmony and embodied action in guitar playing are directly related to the narrative and imagery presented through the song's words: the 'willed' harmonies on dominant and subdominant requiring moves higher on the fretboard are associated with human interactions while the natural resonance of the open chord, requiring less human intervention, is aligned with the imagery of the moon. In Drake's quiet and subdued vocal, he consistently employs a rhythmic delay, so that his vocalisation seems always to follow after the downbeat. Not a single word is punctuated on a downbeat until the verse ends on the words, 'pink moon'. In this way, Drake deflects attention from himself rhythmically and prioritises the image of the pink moon.

The chorus metaphorically represents a ritualistic engagement with imagery of the moon low in the sky. The presence of the moon is doubly marked, not just as different from the light of day, but as an unusually rare 'pink moon'. For this privileged moment, Drake sings with perhaps his most unusual vocal sound, so low in his range that the voice barely speaks, 'Pink, pink, pink, pink, pink moon'. In an expressive convergence of cross-domain mapping, the low guitar strings tuned down and stopped on the second fret are heard resolving to resonant open strings. The unusual timbre of the low guitar sounds paired with Drake's low vocalisation provide an embodied representation of the mythically charged evocation of the pink moon.

The ritualistic alignment of human life with elemental natural entities including the moon, sun, sea, and wind is a recurrent theme in Drake's music. Here, as in other Nick Drake songs, the transvaluation of myth interrogates cultural hierarchies while connecting the individual with a transcendent pastoral experience.[7] The pressures and fears of modern human life are diminished as the individual claims a small, but not wholly insignificant, place within the natural world. Drake's delayed metrical timing, low vocalisation, and self-effacing, quiet manner deflect attention away from his engagement a singer, as if he is a detached observer. From the first line, 'I saw it written and I saw it say', he quietly presents himself as a kind of oracle of nature, observing significances others don't notice. In contrast to the subdued vocalisation, the guitar is rhythmically energised and clearly directed in harmony and melodic line. It could be said that Drake projects the guitar as the dominant 'voice' so that he is at liberty to comment vocally as if from a distance.

The alignment of the individual with the moon is celebrated in the instrumental interlude. Drake overdubbed a single-note piano melody, pairing this with a guitar melody that moves down the fretboard on one string while other guitar strings openly resonate. This can be interpreted as a musical embodiment of the observer and the moon unified as a pair. Lateral moves down the guitar fretboard expand the pentatonic riff that was confined to one hand position in the introduction. In this way, the melody is a motivic and gestural expansion that breaks out feely from the confines of the intro and verse while projecting the pastoral-moon metaphor into a passage of purely instrumental sound.

Pastoral expression in the song is clearly leveraged in the 1999 Volkswagen Cabrio commercial that features 'Pink Moon', during which two young couples drive by moonlight. Images of the full moon and the travellers' faces aglow in moonlight depict the bucolic pleasure of driving in the convertible with the top down. They arrive at a party – their apparent destination – but choose not to go in, opting instead to continue their moonlit journey. Through formal oppositions signified in the pastoralism of the ongoing nocturnal ride and the return to urban social life represented in the arrival at the party, the commercial enlists Nick Drake's music to project a pastoral discourse.[8]

'One of These Things First'

'One of These Things First', from Drake's second album, *Bryter Layter*, uses open-E guitar tuning, tapping into guitar traditions of blues and folk music Drake is known to have admired.[9] In the introduction, the elaboration of tonic harmony with the subdominant would be typical in blues

Example 13.2. Nick Drake, 'One of These Things First', *Bryter Layter* (1970).

styles, but the unusual dissonant passing motion marked with slurs in Example 13.2 resists harmonic categorisation. The resulting linear chords can be readily understood, however, as deriving from a basic guitar move, shifting with two fingers one fret at a time to form a linear embellishing melody in parallel sixths, as shown in the harmonic reduction and guitar tab. The resulting descending chromatic line may communicate a hint of the irony Drake projects in this deceptively upbeat song.

The song plays on vagaries of self-identification, time, and memory, observing the seemingly random twists of fate that might shape who we are, have been, and may yet be. Perhaps more to the point is the way the song presents an almost stream-of-consciousness succession of images depicting how one might mentally construct and label an identity. This is presented with playful irony, almost as a child's game of make-believe, drawing attention to the game-like play of roles we assume in life:

> I could have been a sailor,
> Could have been a cook.
> A real live lover,
> Could have been a book.

As in 'Pink Moon', variants on a basic guitar riff shift to other fretboard locations, so that the larger arm movement choreographs a pathway
marking changes in musical structure and the trajectory of lyrics. Parallel
shifts in guitar patterning are marked with arrows in Example 13.2. Shifts
to the subdominant, mediant, and supertonic accompany increasingly
abstract conjecture on possible identities, now represented as inanimate
objects. Very long, sustained vocal notes delay linear melodic motion to
form a suspension with a dissonant tritone interval on the word, 'signpost'.
The effect seems to dislocate the singer from the immediacy of the repetitive temporal patterning in the guitar:

> I could have been a signpost,
> Could have been a clock.
> As simple as a kettle,
> Steady as a rock.

The instrumental-like quality of the vocal line, particularly in the use of
rhythmic delay in attacking and releasing vocal notes, is comparable to
techniques employed by jazz vocalists and instrumentalists. It is known
that Drake admired the music of Miles Davis and may have been influenced by Davis' approach to modality and rhythm as well as his character-
istically muted tone.[10]

More directed harmony leading towards the dominant accompanies a
rhetorical shift as the protagonist considers the responsibilities of a relationship and riddles of consciousness itself:

> I could be,
> Here and now.
> I would be, I should be,
> But how?

Resolution of dominant harmony with closure on the tonic completes
the trajectory of large-motor movement down the fretboard to the open
strings, possibly implying resignation and an acceptance of the mysteries
of time, fate, and self-identity:

> I could have been
> One of these things first.
> I could have been
> One of these things first.

The song can be interpreted as an ironic subversion of social pressures
typically experienced in adult life. The presentation of past, present, and
future identities, real or imagined, as a kind of playful game is expressed
through the interplay of the guitar and vocal, with very long sustained
vocal notes heard against the quick and repetitive triple rhythm patterning in the guitar. Like a nursery rhyme, the song provides for a ritualistic

sharing of communal experience, with serious adult concerns of self-identity and responsibility submerged in a game-like contemplation of the cyclic temporal mysteries of life. The second verse, in particular, seems to be tinged with regret ('I could have stayed beside you, Could have stayed for more') as Drake contemplates love and time itself from a detached observer's position. By the end of the song, an ironic contradiction is apparent in the instrumental setting for the vocal. The guitar, piano, bass, and drums are interactive, exuberant, and rhythmically charged while the vocal melody is subdued and inwardly directed. Superimposed duple and triple cross-rhythms typical of jazz highlight the immediacy of expression in the instrumental combo, while the singer's persona is clearly absorbed in contemplating the past. Drake's song is ironically upbeat, as if the lively instrumental setting provides a means for the singer to avoid his own failures and self-doubt. In questioning how he could be more grounded in the present moment ('I could be, Here and now'), perhaps the singer-songwriter is consciously questioning his own engagement in the moment of performance, wondering what his own creative utterance 'could have been'.

'Rider on the Wheel'

Another song that is both fatalistic and playful is Nick Drake's 'Rider on the Wheel'.[11] A game of riding on a wheel represents cycles in time and in human relationships. Example 13.3 illustrates how the guitar texture in 'Rider on the Wheel' divides the upper and lower strings of the guitar into two registrally separated fields of action in the introduction. Melodic

Example 13.3. Nick Drake, 'Rider on the Wheel' (c. 1968).

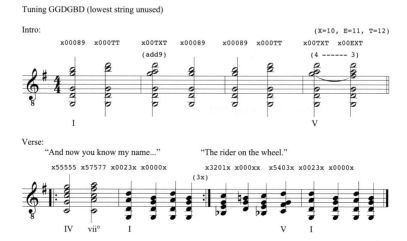

motions on upper strings are heard in opposition to sustained resonant pedal tones on lower strings, facilitated through the open-G guitar tuning.[12]

Like the merry-go-round metaphor in J. D. Salinger's *Catcher in the Rye*, the wheel is a nostalgic device implying childlike innocence and resistance to the adult passions and responsibilities that pull at the protagonist. By the third verse, life, love, and perhaps Drake himself as the singer-poet are conflated in a self-referential, nursery rhyme-like song about a song:

> And round and round we go.
> We take it fast and slow.
> I must keep up a show
> For the rider on the wheel,
> For the rider on the wheel.

Drake again employs a gestural strategy of shaping local harmonic and melodic shifts with movements of one or two fingers on the fretboard and broader phrase-delineating moves through arm motions along the fretboard to grasp barre chords. In the verse, the arm choreographs a kind of cyclic motion between the fifth fret, for the subdominant, and the open strings, for the tonic, forming a literal enactment of the singer-songwriter moving 'round and round' to 'keep up the show'.

'One of These Things First' and 'Rider on the Wheel' are both playfully ironic songs that conflate the songwriter's creation and performance with the individual's creation of self-identity. In claiming the distanced objectivity to be aware of illusions others might perceive as reality, the songwriter-performer ironically resists the illusion of his art, fatalistically accepting life's consequences while at the same time satirising the superficiality of the singer-poet's perceived identity. Drake was very likely influenced by the self-referential, carnival-like social critiques found in Bob Dylan's music: each in their own way, Dylan and Drake ironically project the persona of an artist engaged in subversion of an illusion he is clearly invested in creating.

'Clothes of Sand'

While Nick Drake's highly personal songs may defy categorisation as folk music, he nonetheless had important contacts with British musicians that negotiated boundaries between traditional, progressive, and folk rock music. Members of the British folk rock bands Fairport Convention and Pentangle played on Drake's *Five Leaves Left*. 'Clothes of Sand' is an out-take from the *Five Leaves Left* sessions. The song evokes the expression of a traditional Anglo-Scottish ballad. The elegiac pastoral mood, modal melodic inflections, and alternations of question and answer in the verse and chorus structure are signifiers through which Drake constructs

Example 13.4. Nick Drake, 'Clothes of Sand' (c. 1968).

connections to English folkloric traditions. The song also projects a Baroque topical reference in the chorus, through use of a descending chromatic bass line reminiscent of the lament bass in a Baroque aria. This recurring device used by Drake will be examined below in three songs: 'Clothes of Sand', 'Day is Done', and 'Fruit Tree'.

The EADGAE guitar tuning, a variant of tunings in fourths and seconds found in Celtic guitar music, facilitates chords of open fifths that shift by whole steps to the modal subtonic in the introduction, as shown in Example 13.4. The archaic-sounding open chords, with colouristic alternations of one note sounded on different strings, highlight mournful and elegiac pastoral elements in the text:

> Who has dressed you in strange clothes of sand?
> Who has taken you far from my land?
> Who has said that my sayings were wrong?
> And who will say that I stayed much too long?
>
> Clothes of sand have covered your face,
> Given you meaning but taken my place.
> So make your way on down to the sea,
> Something has taken you so far from me.

The song is most tragic and poignant in the chorus at the major subdominant chord, as the bass line descends at the words 'down to the sea'. Slurs in Example 13.4 mark the chromatic descent in the bass from the tonic to the dominant, a formation that evokes the lament bass in a Baroque aria. Raymond Monelle discusses the chromatic descending fourth in the lament bass as a gesture of grief perhaps derived from the *pianto*, the effect of iconically representing the moan of a person weeping with the descending semitone.[13] In this song, the descending bass line is an elaboration of the mournful semitone bass motion on G♭ to F heard earlier. Nick Drake lingers a moment on the brighter G♮, before continuing the tragic descent through G♭, as if to represent the singer's persona, lingering on the memory of a loved one now unattainable, before relinquishing the image to the engulfing sea.

The song uses an elegiac mode of expression to explore loss on multiple levels, whether it be in mourning the actual death of a loved one, or the feeling of lost connection in an estranged relationship, or an introspective loss of self-identity. There is also a veiled connection to the psychedelic culture of the late 1960s, as if 'silver spoons and coloured light' might refer to truths obscured through use of drugs. Closely voiced dissonances clash against sustained open strings in the guitar, enhancing the treatment of lyrics depicting the trappings of illusion that might 'clothe' our deeper true identities. The arm literally travels outward, away from the body, during the stepwise descent on the lowest guitar string, forming an embodied metaphor for one departing. ('So make your way down to the sea. Something has taken you so far from me'.) The understated singing and historicised style of the song ironically represent the persona of one out of touch with ordinary reality. Through his embodied expression in guitar playing and vocalisation of the lyrics, Drake connects imagery from an archaic folkloric past to a tragic depiction of modern alienation and dysfunctionality.

'Day is Done'

Like 'Clothes of Sand', 'Day is Done' is another song from the *Five Leaves Left* sessions that that shares characteristics with a ground bass aria. A repeated bass-line pattern suggestive of the lament bass topic is heard in each verse, with variants to allow for added lines in some verses and cadences that alternate in closing on either the dominant or tonic. The song combines Drake's vocal and guitar with a string quartet. Conceiving his arrangement for strings as an homage to George Martin's setting on 'Eleanor Rigby', Robert Kirby stated, 'Mozart was my favourite composer but The Beatles ran him a close second'.[14] The song sadly depicts an

Example 13.5. Nick Drake, 'Day is Done', *Five Leaves Left* (1969).

Tuning: standard (capo 5th fret)

Bass line

awareness of time running out on a life that has been spent in superficial pursuits represented as a race, a game, or a party. In this way, the song can be heard as a cautionary parable urging the listener to seek meaningful fulfillment in life while there is still time. Through the continuous repetition of the bass line and the varying texture in the strings and guitar, the expression in the lyrics is formalised and presented in the stylised context of its own dramatic world, as one also finds in late Beatles songs including 'Day in the Life' and 'She's Leaving Home'.

The guitar work is active, even virtuosic, projecting an agency and engagement that is at odds with the downcast expression of the singer. As the guitar work provides ironic resistance to the vocal expression, Drake is depicted as an observer of his own life predicament. Artistic distance seems to relieve the pressures of his own personal investment in life's outcome.

'Fruit Tree'

'Fruit Tree' is perhaps Drake's most formally developed song to enlist a chromatic descending bass line in the poetic contemplation of death. Example 13.6 shows the guitar patterning modelled as an expanding gesture with a descending trajectory. The tuning, BBDGBE, provides for a minor tonic chord with the top guitar three strings ringing open, a pre-dominant chord played as a barre on the second fret, and a dominant built on the lowest two open strings. As in all of Drake's music, the guitar tuning is strategic, here providing for high ringing open strings on the minor tonic and low open strings on the dominant. The succession of chords forms a sliding gesture that moves incrementally down the fretboard from the tonic to the dominant with economy of motion and the sustained resonance of open strings. The bass line in the verse presents a descending chromatic line not unlike that found the Baroque lament bass aria. The song is prophetically self-referential in declaring that the artist is under-appreciated while alive and more revered after death, as was Nick Drake himself. Creative in its natural state, the fruit tree is an idealised representation of the artist, bearing its fruit without regard for whether it is appreciated.

In setting the lyrics, the life of the tree is associated with the minor tonic chord. The trajectory of the guitar then passes through intermediary chords in moving down the fretboard towards the dominant, the goal at phrase endings associated with death and remembrance in the lyrics. In approaching the final section of the song, sustained chords on the dominant accompany the vocal line expressing death as a 'womb' where you will be 'safe in your place deep in the earth'. This remarkable passage builds to the climax of the song, with words that welcome death while bitterly rejecting those who fail to appreciate creativity in life. The descending gesture is expanded most fully and dramatically in the final phrases of the song. As the singer-poet consoles the fruit tree – an idealised representation of himself – the harmonic rhythm broadens, with chords built on the descending chromatic tetrachord heard in a rhythmic augmentation.

Example 13.6. Nick Drake. 'Fruit Tree', *Five Leaves Left* (1969).

Conclusion

It has been documented that Drake may have used at least a dozen different guitar tunings on his recordings.[15] This study has shown Nick Drake's songwriting process to be one of experimentation and invention, in which he mapped idiomatic gestures of guitar playing on to differently tuned fretboard configurations to form new expressive possibilities in each song. A focus on Drake's approach to musical gesture in singing and playing the guitar has also shed light on dramatic and psychological dimensions in his songs, his use of myth and topic, and his blending of folkloric, jazz, blues, and classical musical traditions. Tablature renderings have provided a tool to examine and communicate aspects of physical motion in guitar performance, in an effort to model practices evidenced in Drake's recordings. As in any analysis, this is an act of interpretation: an attempt to more richly imagine what Nick Drake may have been doing in conceptualising and playing his music. The search for a deeper understanding of how Drake used the guitar in creating and performing songs has provided a means to track elements of his embodied musical expression and explore his unique approach to musical gesture.

Notes

1 This includes the 1999 Volkswagen commercial that featured 'Pink Moon' and the 2010 commercial for AT&T with Nick Drake's 'From the Morning'.

2 For more on musical gesture and the guitar, see Timothy Koozin, 'Guitar Voicing in Pop-Rock Music: A Performance-Based Analytical Approach', *Music Theory Online* 17/3 (2011). Available at: www.mtosmt.org/issues/mto.11.17.3/mto.11.17.3.koozin.html (accessed 24 February 2015).

3 Joe Boyd, *White Bicycles: Making Music in the 1960s* (London: Serpent's Tail, 2006), p. 6.

4 From an interview with Robert Kirby posted at The Nick Drake Files website, www.algonet.se/~iguana/DRAKE/NDinterviews.html#KIRBY (accessed 24 February 2015).

5 All musical examples are renderings by the author based on listening and exploration in singing and playing the songs.

6 Lyrics by Nick Drake appear in this chapter with the kind permission of Bryter Music, The Estate of Nick Drake.

7 Transvaluation as a component in the structure of myth is formulated in James Jakób Liszka, *The Semiotic of Myth: A Critical Study of the Symbol* (Bloomington: Indiana University Press, 1989) and explored in the analysis of musical narrative in Byron Almén, *A Theory*

of Musical Narrative (Bloomington: Indiana University Press, 2008).

8 See the video at www.youtube.com/watch?v=BIOW9fLT9eY (accessed 24 February 2015). For more on pastoral discourse, see Michael Klein, *Intertextuality in Western Art Music* (Bloomington: Indiana University Press, 2005), pp. 68–71.

9 Nick Drake's mastery of formative blues and folk influences is evident in listening to his home recordings compiled on the 2007 *Family Tree* album, which includes his performances of songs by Bob Dylan and Bert Jansch as well as several traditional blues songs.

10 Nick Drake played saxophone, clarinet, and piano before taking up guitar and was known to appreciate the music of Miles Davis and John Coltrane. Biographer Trevor Dann specifically cites the modal structure in Miles Davis' *Kind of Blue* as an influence on Nick Drake. See *Darker Than the Deepest Sea: The Search for Nick Drake* (Cambridge, MA: Da Capo Press, 2006), p. 108.

11 'Rider on the Wheel' and 'Clothes of Sand' are out-takes from the *Five Leaves Left* sessions recorded July 1968 to July 1969. They are included on the compilation albums, *Time of No Reply* (1986) and *Made to Love Magic* (2004).

12 GGDGBD guitar tuning is known to have been used by Joni Mitchell in 'This Flight

Tonight', 'Electricity', 'For the Roses', and 'Hunter'.

13 Raymond Monelle, *The Sense of Music: Semiotic Essays* (Princeton, NJ: Princeton University Press, 2000), pp. 67–9. See also Ellen Rosand, 'The Descending Tetrachord: An Emblem of Lament', *The Musical Quarterly* 65/3 (1979), pp. 346–359 and Janet Schmalfeldt, 'In Search of Dido', *The Journal of Musicology* 18/4 (2001), pp. 584–615, for studies of the lament bass in the Baroque aria. The special moment marked for attention with the major sixth scale degree in the bass (on G♮, at 'down to the sea') in Drake's 'Clothes of Sand' parallels a similarly poignant moment in the most famous of all lament bass arias, Dido's Lament from Henry Purcell's *Dido and Aeneas*, at the climax of the song on the words, 'remember me'.

14 Robert Kirby, as quoted in Peter Paphides, 'The Inner Life of Nick Drake', *The Observer* (24 April 2004).

15 See, for example, the list by Chris Healey at The Nick Drake Files website, www.algonet .se/~iguana/DRAKE/tunings.html (accessed 24 February 2015).

14 Sampling and storytelling: Kanye West's vocal and sonic narratives

LORI BURNS, ALYSSA WOODS, AND MARC LAFRANCE

Numerous scholars have identified hip-hop as rooted in the practice of storytelling.[1] Nelson George describes rap 'as a showcase for the art of verbal dexterity and storytelling', while Tricia Rose has discussed its 'ability to use the powerful tradition of black oration and storytelling to render stylistically compelling music'.[2] We hope to contribute to an understanding of the hip-hop singer-songwriter by revealing Kanye West's lyrical and musical strategies as aligned with the characteristics of the singer-songwriter genre: hence, we consider how he communicates about life experiences and delivers social commentaries; we trace numerous social themes and concerns at the core of his lyrical expression throughout his work; we examine how he creates an intimate space through his musical expression and recording practices; and we discuss how he uses technology as his instrument in order to develop innovative vocal and sonic expressive strategies.

Throughout his career, West has consistently engaged with the themes of fame and celebrity, the music industry, consumerism, class and race. Some tracks develop these themes in a 'braggadocio' style (e.g., 'Good Life'), while others reveal his struggle with the negative consequences of fame (e.g., 'Everything I Am'). Our aim is to examine how West communicates his social messages with a sense of immediacy by means of innovative musical strategies and technologies. We also aim to illustrate how West extends and deepens his cultural critique of fame, consumer culture, race and class through these same strategies and technologies. More specifically, our analysis focuses on his much-acclaimed work in the domain of sampling and production where we see him connecting closely and intimately with the process. West's work has been widely received as innovative in terms of how it expands the conventions of hip-hop production. In what follows, we concentrate on his selection of samples as well as their manipulation in the context of his song structure, design, and expression.[3]

After gaining success as a producer (notably on Jay-Z's 2001 album *The Blueprint*), West became a rapper in 2002. Damon Dash, the CEO of Roc-A-Fella, found it hard to imagine marketing West as a rapper.[4] In addition to his style of dress, his middle-class upbringing set him apart from many MCs.[5] As Jay-Z states, 'We all grew up street guys who had to do whatever we had to do to get by. Then there's Kanye, who to my knowledge has never hustled a day in his life. I didn't see how it could work.'[6] Insofar as mainstream rap has tended to construct itself in opposition to bourgeois norms and values, it has in the past eschewed 'preppy' suburban images like West's while celebrating more 'street-based' images such as those of Jay-Z. While West could not position himself as a 'gangsta', his injury from a serious car accident became a tale of struggle on the track 'Through The Wire' (the first single from *The College Dropout*, 2004).[7] At an early point in his career, this track revealed his own lived experience of aspiring for fame and acceptance.

For our analysis of a track from this early period, we have chosen the first single from *Late Registration*. 'Diamonds From Sierra Leone' – which samples Shirley Bassey's performance of John Barry and Don Black's 'Diamonds are Forever' (1971) – is a self-critical examination of celebrity and consumerism, while the video linked to the 2006 film *Blood Diamond* uses the material to confront the damaging effects of the diamond trade.

A turning point in his career, the album *808s & Heartbreak* (2008) stands out as a break with hip-hop conventions. West relies heavily on the Auto-Tune device and a singing style instead of a typical MC rap delivery. At the same time, the songs are arranged for the iconic 808 drum machine, creating a sparse texture and sense of longing and nostalgia for 1980s hip-hop.[8] From this album, we analyse 'Welcome to Heartbreak', a track that shows the subject to be struggling with the damaging effects of fame on his personal life.

West's *808s* provoked a strong critical response in the entertainment media.[9] When questioned about his decision to sing instead of rap, he defended his creation of a melodic album:

> I always knew that the melody drives the record so much; if you think about my biggest records, 'Stronger', 'Gold Digger', 'Diamonds are Forever', 'Good Life', they always had that [sings melodic line]. And this was the big thing that connected internationally, the reason why I'm one of the big artists, because they're always gonna get that melody. And I was like … I'm just gonna make it be all melody.[10]

Not only does the album feature singing rather than rapping, it also relies much less on sampling than his previous work – a stylistic feature that did not go unnoticed by reviewers.[11] West explains this feature:

> this album doesn't have a lot of like labels on it or samples, things to stand next to it, to say, hey I'm cool 'cause I down [sic] with that funk … But to be able to … write outright songs and melodies, it's just a greater challenge, because you're not standing on all of these things that make you cool and stuff, it's really like a naked approach … And I think the song-writing, to have melody in it, makes it more powerful at the end of the day.[12]

Invoking the notion that the album is 'made from scratch'[13] West distances himself from sampling, despite its foundational role in hip-hop musical expression.[14] He thus positions himself as the sole creator of the music, invoking singer-songwriter authenticity. He goes so far as to declare *808s* as the forerunner of an original genre: '*iTunes* didn't choose to use it, but the genre for this sound is called pop art. That's what I want it to say on *iTunes*: pop art.'[15] Continuing this line of thinking in a New Zealand press conference, he claims that 'I'm delivering art in its purest form … I think that everything that I deliver is fully art, it is sonic art, and this is my project and I believe there are songs on it that will affect culture, which is the end goal of a true pop artist'.[16] With comments such as these, West communicates an intense desire to connect with his audience on his terms and extend his cultural reach.

Emerging out of the *808s* period of genre experimentation, West's fifth and sixth albums, *My Beautiful Dark Twisted Fantasy* (2010; hereafter *MBDTF*) and *Yeezus* (2013), feature a range of expressive styles, from aggressive rapping to melodic Auto-Tuned singing. While West maintained creative control, forty-two people were involved in the songwriting, recording, and production of *MBDTF*.[17] Critics observed the influence of West's previous styles on *MBDTF*: 'In some ways, it's the culmination of Kanye West's first four albums, but it does not merely draw characteristics from each one of them. The 13 tracks … sometimes fuse them together simultaneously.'[18] His sampling references on the album are diverse, from soul (Smokey Robinson in 'Devil in a New Dress') to progressive rock (King Crimson in 'Power') to indie folk (Bon Iver in 'Lost In the World'). While the album moves beyond hip-hop conventions to experiment with diverse genres and electronic textures, it still holds mainstream appeal. West himself indicated that it contained 'songs that are blatant radio hits, it's like I'm speaking with today's texture'.[19]

By contrast, West has stated that his intention with *Yeezus* was to create an album that stood out within the genre: 'I feel I was able to start making exactly what was in my mind, again. And not having to speak with the textures of the time.'[20] In comparing the two albums, West stated: '*Dark Fantasy* can be considered to be perfect. I know how to make perfect, but that's not what I'm here to do. I'm here to crack the pavement and make new grounds sonically and in society, culturally.'[21] *MBDTF*'s extensive genre reach is also evident on *Yeezus*, as West expands his sonic palette into minimalist textures and industrial sounds. Intense electronic sounds are underpinned by samples from artists as diverse as Nina Simone (jazz), Capleton (reggae), and Omega (progressive rock).[22] From *Yeezus*, we have chosen 'Black Skinhead' for its dark and oppositional statement on racism in the music industry.

For each of the three chosen tracks, we analyse lyrics, music and video images. In order to respect the narrative flow of our chosen tracks, our analyses are presented sequentially, in order to capture the listener's experience of the song's narrative flow, sonic events and vocal expressive strategies.

'Diamonds From Sierra Leone', *Late Registration* (2005)

West's sampling of 'Diamonds Are Forever' is a straightforward example of his early song production.[23] Bassey's chorus, which extols the enduring quality of diamonds in comparison to the fragility of romantic love, is integrated as the chorus of West's song. Her chorus is juxtaposed with his rapped lyrics, which draw the listener into a reflection on his financial success and burgeoning career status. Not only does he describe the effects of his commercial success (i.e., a reference to his Porsche), he also refers to several negative public events, culminating in an account of his disappointing loss at the 47th Annual Grammy Awards, where the track 'Through the Wire' did not receive the award for Best Rap Solo Performance. Interestingly, 'Diamonds from Sierra Leone' would go on to receive the Grammy for Best Rap Song the following year.

The title of the sampled song conveys multiple meanings in relation to the themes that West explores: 1) 'Diamonds' are the material subject of his critique of the 'blood diamond' trade in the music video; 2) 'Diamonds' also stand as a symbol for success, a central theme in West's song; 3) The diamond is the iconic symbol for Roc-A-Fella Records;[24] 4) In the lyrics, diamonds stand for the songs that he produces; and 5) The chorus hook, 'Diamonds Are Forever', invokes longevity, a status that West implicitly claims in this song. Developing these themes, West offers a multi-layered exploration of their iconic and symbolic meanings.

West's track begins with a sampled passage from the original song's introduction [00:09–00:34]. Maintaining its majestic texture, the vocal is prominent and lush, while the brass jabs are softened through the effects of reverb. At the first statement of West's chorus [00:15–00:34], his voice is more forward, and the Bassey sample is further back in the mix. In the passage from Bassey's final outro [02:14–02:34], she repeats 'forever' in a motivic leap from B^3 to $F\sharp^4$, and then rises to a climactic high C^5 that resolves to B^4. The C major–B minor progression that supports Bassey's resolution stands out as an expressively marked Phrygian II, occurring in the song whenever the lyrics refer to the darker side of romance ('desertion', 'hurt', 'lies', 'death'). As Bassey resolves to B, a majestic trombone line rises to a $C\sharp$ as an added ninth over the closing B minor tonic.

West maintains the powerful brass line beneath Bassey's final resolution, as well as the active groove of the hi-hat, however he adds a deep synthetic bass kick and a high harpsichord sound as downbeat accents.

In addition to these textural enhancements, he manipulates the original phrase to intensify his own chorus. In response to Bassey's repetition of the word 'forever', he repeats 'ever' in a series of rising statements [00:26–00:33], culminating in his own strained B^3.[25] The rise in vocal pitch (unusual for an MC in 2005), the harmonic progression, and the instrumental gestures allow West to reach a peak of intensity at the end of his chorus. In his treatment of the final cadence we hear Bassey's C–B resolution, but the sample fades before we can hear the trombone's dissonant C♯. Instead, West introduces a high harpsichord gesture that lands on the C♯ as a downbeat accent to the beginning of the ensuing verse.

As he develops his song structure, West intensifies the standard verse–chorus alternation by disrupting the chorus that follows verse 2: although Bassey's chorus begins as expected, West presses onwards with his rap, leading directly into verse 3 in a seamless lyric delivery. The extended verse section (i.e., verse 2 – disrupted chorus – verse 3) allows the uninterrupted rap flow to build in intensity [01:34 – 03:13], the emerging story beginning with an account of his father taking him to church, then shifting to a concern for the quality of songs ('diamonds') that are being mass-produced. West's juxtaposition of Bassey's chorus hook with his emotionally charged rap creates a formal tension that disrupts the rhetorical effect of the chorus; that is, while Bassey's chorus is directed towards a climactic resolution, West's rap intensifies and denies resolution in its own rhetorical sphere. The final verse leads to a close with West asserting his power as a songwriter and producer. The song ends with a chorus and outro that features West repeating his insistent harpsichord gesture.

The music video for 'Diamonds from Sierra Leone' (directed by Hype Williams) juxtaposes images from the diamond mines with an up-scale diamond store. An elegantly dressed West is seen on the streets of Prague and inside an ornate church. The Porsche that is mentioned in the lyrics appears as a visual emblem of wealth, not only his own as a successful artist, but also implicitly the kind of wealth that emerges from the diamond trade. The video climaxes when West drives the Porsche, with a child labourer as his passenger, into the window of the diamond store. They jump from the vehicle before crashing and run away with a group of other children. The video closes with the running group (including West), heading into the church, creating a narrative of resistance and liberation for the child labourers. A second image of West as performer concludes the song at the harpsichord, suggesting that he remains caught up in the performance world.

With this track, West invites his listeners to engage with a complex intersection of words, music and images. Lyrically, the song introduces and interrogates events in West's professional life that have shaped his media reception. Musically, he creates a dialogue between his voice and

Bassey's sampled voice. For West as a hip-hop producer, the lush production values of the original track become the instrument over which he develops his own dynamic expression. His unconventional modes of vocalisation and intensification of the musical form are heard in relation to the repetitive sampling of the original song. The images of the video situate his struggles with fame in a larger social context as he confronts the economic inequalities bound up with the 'blood diamond' trade. The lyrics, music, and video images intersect to convey West's social critique of consumer culture: although the lyrics point to a self-reflexive or 'internal' modality, the video reveals his understanding of the external forces that drive the cultural phenomena of interest to him.

'Welcome to Heartbreak', *808s & Heartbreak* (2008)

This song offers a meditation on life's dreams and values in the face of the challenges of fame and commercial success. In the form of an intimate communication, West's lyrical narrative expresses the isolation that the subject experiences as a result of his celebrity lifestyle. Symbols of wealth ('sports cars' and 'cribs') are juxtaposed with symbols of family life ('report cards').[26] The introspective dialogue is continued in the chorus by guest vocalist Kid Cudi who sings about a vision of 'real' life that the famous individual can dimly perceive as though through a fog.[27]

West sculpts a sonic texture and vocal melody that reinforces the lyrical self-reflection. A dark and slow-moving 8-bar phrase in the cello is metrically ambiguous until the entry of the kick and Taiko drums in the last bar. The full instrumental arrangement is established in the second phrase, featuring a pitch-modulated synth bass on the cello melody, the kick on beats 1 and 3, a distorted backbeat snare crash, running rim shots creating a 'ticky' groove, and an active keyboard that develops motives from the cello melody. As the first verse explores his longing for fatherhood, the subject's emotional emptiness is reinforced by a mechanical and distant but reverberant vocal. The keyboard drops out, leaving a hollow space between the low bass, the high synth wash, and the aggressive backbeat snare. West's voice occupies this space in an Auto-Tuned delivery that masks his natural sung expression. The delay effects at the tail of each phrase create a stark contrast to the strident backbeat snare. West's overt critique of the celebrity lifestyle is delivered in a vocal style that maintains a connection to the conventions of rap by centring his vocal delivery on the tonic, but departs from rap by sustaining his pitches in a singing tone. He infuses the limited melodic range with expressive tension and a sense of directionality by moving to the second and third degrees of the G-Aeolian scale (A and Bb) and treating these as tendency tones that descend to the G tonic.

The dark soundscape of West's verse contrasts with Kid Cudi's gently sung chorus vocals, which are overdubbed at a higher pitch level, phased, and split to the left and right channels. In the centre of the mix, West's strained, high-pitched 'ooo' emerges, a full octave higher than his verse. The lyrics, when combined with West's intensified vocal expression, communicate a sense of urgency around the subject's need to change his life.

After a second verse and chorus, the bridge offers a dramatic vocal intensification as West leaps to a higher register and is accompanied by a string arrangement. His vocal line symbolises his frustration and resignation by opening the phrase with the high-pitched plaintive call (a leap to F^4), but closing with the familiar gesture to the low G^3 tonic. In contrast to the intensity of the bridge, verse 3 offers a sparse texture as the percussion drops out and a low synth wash reinforces the loneliness expressed by the lyrics. As he describes being late for his sister's wedding, the contrast between the subject's affective landscape and that of his sister drives home the alienation that characterises his existence. The outro and final chorus communicate a desperate and sorrowful sentiment of being trapped in this lifestyle, as West repeats the lyrics, 'No, I can't stop'.

The video portrays an image of West, trapped by the symbols of celebrity status, struggling to unmask himself. The video, directed by Nabil Elderkin,[28] is characterised by a post-production technique referred to as 'data moshing', which maintains the outline and shape of a subject within an image, but transforms the figure with a mixture of colour and design elements from the background using pixel bleeding.[29] In this process, the lines between the body (what is ostensibly real) and the background become blurred and, at times, erased, as in the effect of camouflage; bodies and faces are masked and merged.[30] In the context of this particular music video, data moshing becomes a visual complement to the audio interference created by the Auto-Tune device, which, in turn, depicts the subject's struggle with his own fame and materialism. The result is a simultaneous manipulation of image and sound that compels the audience to question what is seen and heard. Thematically, the video treats and represents data moshing and sound interference as technological 'problems' that connote disconnection and resonate with the theme of alienation. The video is also characterised by its use of numerous effects associated with television, for instance, distortion, light flickering, pixilation and the colour test pattern. At the bridge section, which is also the climax of the video, West breaks through the glass of a television screen and the screen dimensions change from wide-screen video format to traditional television proportions. These television mediation strategies emphasise the artifice of a materialist society, and point to the complexities of authenticity as they relate to media exposure.

With this track, West tells a story about the damaging effects of celebrity status. Musically, he breaks from rap's norms by featuring a sung vocal presentation, underscoring the emotional lyrics, and mediating his voice through the Auto-Tune device, further depersonalising the artist and distancing the individual from the deeply personal and contemplative lyrics. This becomes readily apparent in the video where West and Kid Cudi fade in and out of existence through the art of data moshing. The vulnerability expressed by West on this track, and on *808s* as a whole, represents a marked departure from hip-hop's musical and cultural norms.

'Black Skinhead', *Yeezus* (2013)

This track references a number of significant rock songs: Marilyn Manson's industrial rock track, 'The Beautiful People' (1996); Gary Glitter's glam rock track, 'Rock and Roll' (1972); and Depeche Mode's alternative rock track, 'Personal Jesus' (1990).[31] Building upon these references, West offers a harsh and frank commentary on American racial and religious politics in relation to the hip-hop industry. He criticises the hypocrisy of the mainstream audience, as his race is held up as both an attraction and a threat. Popular culture is criticised for its portrayal of the black man as an enforcer ('goon'). In the face of condemnation for his behaviours and artistic work, he insists upon his work's integrity ('I've been a menace … but I'm devoted'). He resists a religion-based censorship with the assertion of his status, turning religious symbolism on itself ('I'm aware I'm a King, back out of the tomb'). Taking on the accusation that he is 'possessed', he reinforces this notion by identifying with the figure of the wolf, and with the power of the Roman army, which West conflates with the Spartans, as portrayed in the film *300*.[32]

The track opens in a manner reminiscent of the Marilyn Manson track with the highly distorted 2-bar guitar riff (left and right) that is answered by the galloping 4-bar kit phrase. A reverberant floor tom, tuned low, is heard in stark contrast to the white noise effect of the crash cymbal and the heavy thud of the bass drum. The second phrase ushers in a dryer ambiance, and incorporates rhythmic breathing, the heavy kick, resonant toms, and backbeat handclaps in a gesture that invokes Glitter's rhythmic shuffle and call, as well as Depeche Mode's rhythmic breathing. These sounds appear to travel unpredictably across the stereophonic spectrum, creating a 'chaotic' effect. For instance, during the passage [00:17 – 00:25], we hear the abrupt cutting off of the sound to create the feeling of stopped breath, distant ululations to the left and right, crisp toms panned hard to the left, as well as a mechanical wipe that is heard to the right. To close this introductory section, the distorted guitar riff returns for the last two bars, once again split left and right. With this introduction, West appears to contrast natural sounds with mechanical effects: the breathing, handclapping and ululations communicate at the level of embodied human expression, while the crisp drums, distorted guitar, and mechanical effects suggest a harsh industrial context. The breathing draws the listener in, creating a sense of intimacy, while the distorted and mechanical instrumental sounds create a sense of urgency leading into the first verse.

During his rapped verse, West uses a variety of strategies to create lyrical emphasis. His opening line, 'For my theme song', is doubled and panned, creating a sense of depth and breadth. As the verse continues, his line is centred, highly articulate, and quite dry (minimal reverb). Around his voice we hear the active kick drum and snare in a shuffle pattern (centred), the panned ululations and wipe, and accented interjections of a centred mechanical voice saying 'black'. The latter vocal effect creates a 'dehumanised' voice in relation to West's main vocal. As he describes the danger of a black man being seen with a white woman, expressed through a reference to King Kong, the distorted guitar riff returns and creates a strident counterpoint against his rapped vocal line.

The chorus features a sudden bass drop, with a low F♯ that is repeated on the downbeat for four bars against West's intense vocal delivery. Given the sparse texture, the sharp intake of breath is an audible effect at the end of each bar-long vocal phrase. The lyrical content here conveys urgency ('They say I'm possessed') and hyper-sexuality ('Three hundred bitches, where's the Trojans?'). For the second set of four bars, the galloping drum and cymbal pattern returns, as well as the ululations, while West's vocal rises in spoken pitch and intensity, his final line accentuated by a vocal call ('ah'), which arrives on the downbeat of the next phrase. This vocal call ushers in an after-chorus phrase of eight bars, in which a reverberant call – treated with a delay effect – is heard in relation to West's desperate responses ('I'm outta control').

The after-chorus leads to a return of the distorted guitar riff and a repeat of the chorus, followed by verse 2, chorus, after-chorus, and final outro. The outro is based on the guitar riff over which we hear West's repeated statement, 'God'. The riff-based formal structure of this song is worth noting for West's mobilisation of a form derived from rock; with this structure, and with the references to industrial rock, alternative rock, and glam rock, West once again extends hip-hop practices.

West's 'Black Skinhead' video, filmed by photographer Nick Knight, focuses primarily on West, with his body treated to a variety of production and post-production effects. The black and white video opens with the image of three black Ku Klux Klan-inspired hoods. As the image zooms in on these hoods, their white background becomes a frame for the ensuing video scenes, creating the effect of 'teeth' around the images. Immediately following the three KKK figures, we see the eyes and mouths of three vicious dogs, whose mouths are sometimes shown throughout the video in extreme close-up.

The film focuses on the torso of Kanye West through a variety of camera angles, perspectives, and fragmentations that encourage the fetishisation of his body. We see a talc-covered (thus whitened) torso, a computer-modified image of West wearing a heavy gold chain, a metallic monster, a possessed figure with glowing eyes, a tribal figure with sub-dermal implants, and a hulk figure, with exaggerated musculature. As we examine the bodies from all angles, we discover that the figure with the sub-dermal implants also bears scars from a whip on his back. With these images, West exposes and positions himself in a variety of representations, suggesting that if we want to consume his image, he can become whatever we wish him to be: the hip-hop artist in black leather jeans and heavy gold chain, the muscular body who remains faceless, or the tribal body, bearing the scars of slavery. During the final section of the song (at the repetition of the word 'God'), the camera remains fixed upon a faceless head and torso with gold chain. To close, the black hoods return and the eyes from several hoods meet the spectator's gaze. In this final shot, there is no white background, so the only light on the screen is that which emanates from the eyes.

In the lyrical domain, 'Black Skinhead' communicates a message of resistance to fame, scrutiny, and censorship, while in the visual domain, the images of West's fetishised body appear to pose a fundamental contradiction: instead of creating images that resist the all-consuming gaze of the spectator, West invokes the stereotypes and mythologies around African American masculinity. And yet, the aggression of the images and the resistance of the lyrics combine with the urgent industrial aesthetic of the music to establish that this video is not meant to pander to, but rather to challenge, the mainstream. By positioning himself at the centre of his cultural commentary, West forces his viewers to witness that the social norms, values, and logics constituting the mainstream consumption of hip-hop are underpinned by racist representations of the black man as monstrous spectacle, rooted in and haunted by a particularly American iconography of slavery.

Conclusions

Many hip-hop artists are storytellers. Their narratives can be personal and convey a sense of intimacy to the listener, while their music is often driven by social and political concerns in narratives referred to as 'conscious rap'.[33] This analysis of Kanye West's work is offered as a case study of the hip-hop artist as singer-songwriter. Our analysis suggests that West portrays intimate personal experiences in the context of broader commentaries on largescale social issues. Throughout his career, he has consistently focused on themes of race, gender, class, fame, and consumer culture, writing himself into the stories in order to contextualise his own lived experiences within larger political contexts.

This chronological approach, has enabled us to track a shift in both tone and content across West's work. The first three albums explore his initial desire for and gradual accumulation of fame. His fourth album offers an anxious reflection on the damaging effects of fame, characterised by increasing isolation and despair. With his fifth and sixth albums, West embarks on a harsh critique of race and class in relation to American consumerism and the music industry.

We have also interpreted West's musical contributions in relation to the singer-songwriter tradition of forging distinctive vocal and instrumental strategies. As a singer and producer, West manipulates his strategically chosen samples to yield new meanings in the domains of lyrics and music, creating complex and multi-dimensional social commentaries. In his role as singer-songwriter, he challenges dominant hip-hop conventions, extending traditions by sampling materials from a range of styles and genres, and by expanding the modes of hip-hop vocality to include melodic vocals and Auto-Tune technology. Ultimately, these strategies serve to create a dynamic musical expression that encourages immediacy between artist and listener.

Notes

1 See, for example, Nelson George, *Hip Hop America* (New York: Penguin Publishing, 1998); Imani Perry, *Prophets of the Hood: Politics and Poetics in Hip Hop* (Durham: Duke University Press, 2004); Tricia Rose, *The Hip Hop Wars* (New York: Basic Books, 2008); Adam Bradley, *Book of Rhymes: The Poetics of Hip Hop* (New York: Basic Civitas, 2009).
2 George, *Hip Hop America*, p. xiii; Rose, *The Hip Hop Wars*, p. ix–x.
3 We attribute authorial intention to West, although we recognise that he typically works with multiple writers/producers. We ascribe ultimate author status to West, since these albums are presented as solo albums, his name is generally listed first in the song-writing credits, and he holds executive producer status.
4 Josh Tyrangiel, 'Why You Can't Ignore Kanye: More GQ than Gangsta, Kanye West is Challenging the Way Rap Thinks About Race and Class – and Striking a Chord with Fans of All Stripes', *TIME* 166/9 (29 August 2005), p. 54.
5 MC is synonymous with rapper (some say for 'mic controller' but some also for 'master of ceremonies'), dating from the days when the DJ was in charge and the MC had more of an announcing role.
6 Tyrangiel, 'Why You Can't Ignore Kanye', p. 54.

7 West centres this track around a sample of Chaka Khan's 'Through the Fire'. Sped-up 1970s soul vocal sample became West's trademark early in his career. The technique ('Chipmunk Soul') has been used by other producers but remains most closely associated with West due to its prevalence on *The College Dropout*.
8 *808s* does not feature a great deal of sampling, although 'Coldest Winter' is based on Tears for Fears' 'Memories Fade', 'Robocop' features a brief sample from Patrick Doyle's 'Kissing in the Rain', and the percussion in 'Bad News' bears close resemblance to Nina Simone's 'See Line Woman'. 'Kissing in the Rain' is an orchestral piece from the *Great Expectations* soundtrack (1998).
9 See, for example, Tom Breihan, 'Music: Post-Graduate Depression', *The Village Voice* 53/48 (2008), p. 64; Clover Hope, 'The 100 Problems of Kanye West', The Village Voice 54/4 (21–27 January 2009), p. 72; Jody Rosen, 'After a Hard Breakup, Kanye Writes His Own "Blood on the Tracks,"' *Rolling Stone* (11 December 2008), pp. 91–2; Sean Fennessey, 'Pride (In the Name of Love)'. *Vibe Magazine* 17/2 (February 2009), p. 80.
10 Kanye West, 'Singapore Press Conference, 3 November 2008'. Available at: www.youtube .com/watch?v=VTNe5xcv3Y0&feature=player_embedded (accessed 16 July 2012).

11 For example, see Emma Carmichael, 'Kanye's 808s: How A Machine Brought Heartbreak to Hip Hop', *The Awl* (21 September 2011). Available at: www.theawl .com/2011/09/kanye's-808s-how-a-machine-brought-heartbreak-to-hip-hop (accessed 16 July 2012).

12 Kanye West, "New Zealand Press Conference, 1 December 2008, part 2" Available at: www.youtube.com/watch?v=vtscn03scig (accessed 23 September 2015).

13 Fennessey, 'Pride (In the Name of Love)', p. 83.

14 For a discussion of the significance of the sample to hip-hop music and the concept of musical authenticity attached to the sample, see Andrew Bartlett, 'Airshafts, Loudspeakers, and the Hip-Hop Sample', in Murray Forman and Mark Anthony Neal (eds.), *The Hip-Hop Studies Reader* (London: Routledge, 2012), especially p. 573; and Joseph Schloss, *Making Beats: The Art of Sample-Based Hip-Hop* (Middletown, CT: Wesleyan University Press, 2004), especially Chapter 3.

15 West, 'Singapore Press Conference'.

16 Kanye West, 'New Zealand Press Conference, 1 December 2008, part 1' Available at: www.youtube.com/watch?v=fbzu8znDWoA (accessed 23 September 2015).

17 Andy Kellman, 'My Beautiful Dark Twisted Fantasy Album Review', AllMusic.com, 21 November 2010. Retrieved from: www .allmusic.com/album/my-beautiful-dark-twisted-fantasy-mw0002022752 (accessed 28 July 2014).

18 Kellman, 'My Beautiful'.

19 Zane Lowe, '*BBC Radio 1* Interview with Kanye West'. Retrieved from: www.xxlmag .com/news/2013/09/kanye-west-says-mbdtf-perfect-yeezus-advancing-culture/ (accessed 28 July 2014).

20 Vernon Coleman, 'Kanye West Says MBDTF was "Perfect", Yeezus is Advancing the Culture', *XXL.com* (3 September 2013). Retrieved from: www.xxlmag.com/ news/2013/09/kanye-west-says-mbdtf-perfect-yeezus-advancing-culture/ (accessed 28 July 2014).

21 Lowe, '*BBC Radio 1* Interview'.

22 'Blood on the Leaves' samples Nina Simone's performance of 'Strange Fruit' (1965) as well as 'R U Ready' (2012) by electronic/hip-hop producers TNGHT who co-produced the track with West. 'New Slaves' relies on a sample of Hungarian rock band Omega's 'Gyöbgyajú Lány' (1969), and the melodic contour of featured artist Frank Ocean's vocal line is closely connected to Omega's original melody.

23 The single version was included as a bonus track on the album *Late Registration*, and was the source for the music video, directed by Hype Williams. A remix of the song, with an additional verse by Jay-Z, was used as Track 13 on the album.

24 As he refers to his rhymes and 'the Roc', the video shows West to be making a diamond shape with his hands, the common gesture representing Roc-A-Fella Records.

25 It is also worth noting that his gesture here suggests a performance reference to Outkast's 'Ms. Jackson' from their 2000 album *Stankonia*.

26 During a 2009 interview with Sway on *The Morning Show*, West described an incident where 'Dave from MTV' was showing him pictures, 'and there was nothing that I could pull out or show him that could top what he was doing …. You know what just shuts everything down for anybody who's thirty years old? Somebody showing you their kids if you don't have kids.'

27 Kid Cudi gained the attention of the hip-hop community with his 2008 mixtape *A Kid Named Cudi*. West signed him to his label Good Music.

28 Nabil Elderkin (vimeo.com/nabilelderkin/ videos) collaborated with Kanye West for the videos 'Paranoid' and 'Coldest Winter' and has directed videos for a number of acclaimed artists (e.g., Frank Ocean's 'Novocaine', and Bon Iver's 'Holocene').

29 See Peter Kirn, 'Data Moshing the Online Videos: My God, It's Full of Glitch', *Create Digital Motion* (18 February 2009). Retrieved from: createdigitalmotion.com/2009/02/data-moshing-the-online-videos-my-god-its-full-of-glitch/ (accessed June 29, 2012).

30 Chairlift's 'Evident Utensil' (2009), directed by Nabil Elderkin, uses data-moshing to a more playful and pleasure-oriented effect. www .youtube.com/watch?v=mvqakws0CeU

31 These musical references are not actual samples, but rather intertextual references. Multiple musical elements are borrowed from the existing track in order to create a sonic link.

32 The theme of the monstrous has emerged throughout the latter part of West's career. Notable songs include 'Amazing' (*808s*), 'Monster' (*MBDTF*)

33 Common, Nas, Talib Kweli, Lupe Fiasco fall within this category. Adam Krims refers to this rap genre as Jazz/Bohemian Rap; see Adam Krims, *Rap Music and the Poetics of Identity* (New York: Cambridge University Press, 2001) pp. 65–70. We should note that Krims' use of the term bohemian is problematic as it implies an association with a white cultural movement rejecting certain conventions of dominant culture that would not necessarily be embraced by black artists.

15 James Blake, digital lion

MADISON MOORE

Genre-defying British electronic musician James Blake is a fairly emotional type of guy – at least that's what reviews of his 2013 Mercury Prize-winning sophomore album *Overgrown* tell us. Writing for *The Telegraph,* music critic Neil McCormick gave *Overgrown* an enthusiastic four out of five stars, describing the record as music full 'of emotion and imagination'.[1] Bob Boilen, of NPR Music, similarly called it 'breathtakingly emotional music'[2] and Erik Harvey at Pitchfork found it full of 'emotional resonance'.[3] The brushstrokes in his so-called 'post-dubstep' sonic palette, those of throbbing bass lines, silence, arresting soundscapes, and beautiful vocals set up the emotional power of his music.

But is there a singer-songwriter who does not use their songbook to dig into the pockets of human emotion? The content of Blake's music should come as no surprise to anyone, particularly as the singer-songwriter is typically a solo artist who plays her or his own instruments and who often writes songs about love and heartbreak. Where Blake differs in the genre, though, is in how his 'post-dubstep'[4] sound embraces and emerges out of digital technologies and club culture.

James Blake studied Popular Music at Goldsmiths, University of London, an art school of great renown that has produced other British stars like Katy B and Damien Hirst. Between 2009 and 2010, while still at university, Blake began releasing a string of dubstep EPs and singles straight out of his bedroom, including his much-loved 2009 debut 'Air and Lack Thereof' and EPs *CMYK* and *The Bells Sketch*. These recordings were all exercises in UK dubstep, a genre *Interview* magazine once described as so powerful that 'you can only get the full picture in person, when the bass is so enormous it actually makes your clothes flap'.[5]

Although Blake has always sung and played piano, his early EPs and remixes focus more on abstracted soundscapes, dubstep-beat pastures (loops layered over muffled-sounding beats), and technologies of sampling than on clear vocals, choruses or discernible lyrics. As musicologist and scholar of DJ culture Mark Katz has described, digital sampling allows musicians to use software or personal computers to recontextualise pre-existing content into brand-new musical ideas. For Katz, 'sampling works like a jigsaw puzzle: a sound is cut up into pieces and then put back together to form a digitised "picture" of that sound'.[6] This sometimes extra-musical content can come from anywhere – a voice, a part of a song, or a field recording. But once transformed into data these musical ideas can be infinitely manipulated, meaning they take on the character of whatever new space they find themselves in.[7] Sampling is not just about technology but about transforming – poaching – ideas and recirculating them in a wholly different creative context.

One characteristic of Blake's musical style is how he samples his own voice. On the chillingly minimal 'I Never Learnt to Share', from his self-titled debut LP, an unaccompanied Blake sings 'My brother and my sister don't speak to me. And I don't blame them.' Crucially, these are the only lyrics of the entire song and they are looped throughout. The second time he sings the phrase he sings it over himself and loops the recording over muffled beats. This technique is particularly striking when performed live as audiences immediately recognise the sultry opening words and end up having their own screams and shouts recorded into the sample and looped back to them, a subtle reminder of that moment being *live*. Blake's use of looping and sampling is a clear nod to his experience in DJ culture and his earlier dubstep productions.

Post-production and the art of sampling

As a DJ, producer and singer-songwriter James Blake represents what the art theorist Nicolas Bourriaud has called a 'postproduction artist', or an artist who uses technology and pre-existing material to create exciting new pathways through culture. He sees the DJ as a theoretical model to explore the type of intervention post-production artists make. For Bourriaud, 'the DJ activates the history of music by copying and pasting together loops of sound, placing recorded products in relation with each other'.[8] The slickness of Blake's 'CMYK', for instance – a title drawn from the four colours typically used in colour printing (cyan, magenta, yellow, and key/black) – lies in how he takes two popular tracks from the late 90s and transforms them so deeply they are recognisably unrecognisable. Blake's voice is cut up and thrown into the mix with samples from Aaliyah's 1998 Timbaland-assisted 'Are You That Somebody?' and 'Caught Out There' by American recording artist Kelis – the well-known single from 1999 where she screams 'I hate you so much right now!' As with any sampled track, the pleasure of 'CMYK' has to do with how listeners recognise the sampled parts, rediscovering songs they thought they knew as they listen to how drastically they have been distorted as a post-production text.

Where Blake shines as an artist, and where he also defies genre, is in the way he mixes the techniques of electronic music production with the qualities of the singer-songwriter. This style is even more pronounced on his sophomore LP *Overgrown*, where each track showcases either his skills as a singer-songwriter or his chops as a producer of electronic music. On 'Our Love Comes Back', for instance, Blake leads with his voice and soft piano work before a crescendo into beautifully melodic hums and coos that make the listener want to sing along, or hold a lighter up in the air, as much as it makes her want to move.

But the real masterpiece from *Overgrown*, and perhaps of Blake's entire catalogue, is the epic 'Retrograde', a haunting sing-along tune. Within the context of Blake's output 'Retrograde' is one of his most structured pop tracks and also one of the most beautiful, a beauty that lies in the way it plays with the minimal and the maximal. 'Retrograde' opens modestly with Blake's signature voice and piano work before slight handclaps are added, giving the track a sense of forward motion. Most remarkable though is how the chorus, already a rarity for a James Blake song, suddenly explodes into a giant wall of sound. A pulsating beat and a bombastic synthesiser line climbs down from its peak step-by-step, turning even a simple melodic line into a beat. The sound is so huge that the listener is compelled to turn the volume all the way up because we are not able to hear the fullness of the song at a lower output. Once Blake has gotten us so high, in an emotional bait-and-switch suddenly everything drops out from underneath us and we are returned back to the simple opening claps and vocal coos we were given at the beginning.

James Blake is neither the only artist nor even the first English artist to marry electronic music and singing-songwriting. A website called 'Post Dubstep Tumblr'[9] chronicles new and established artists from Mount Kimbie and Jai Paul to The xx and Banks, artists who also combine electronic music with soulful vocals. This is a busy musical intersection many artists have approached through the use of the vocoder. The vocoder was originally invented in Germany in 1939 as a way to transmit secure voice signals over copper telephone lines and was used to scramble conversations between Winston Churchill and FDR. Since its incorporation into the music industry the vocoder has been produced by leading electronic instrument manufacturers like Korg, Roland, E.M.S., and Moog.[10] As Kay Dickinson has observed, Stevie Wonder, Devo, Jean-Michel Jarre, and Laurie Anderson were among the earliest adopters of the vocoder as instrument.[11] By 1974 Kraftwerk featured the vocoder as a technology capable of musically transforming and distorting the human voice on their LP *Autobahn*, and disco purveyor Giorgio Moroder used the vocoder in many of his early productions, particularly 1977's *From Here to Eternity*. Imogen Heap has been a pioneer of electronic music, especially her signature 'Hide and Seek' from 2005, a track with multiple harmonies that sounds as if it is sung by an entire a cappella group even though it is in fact performed live by one performer with a keyboard synched to a vocoder.[12] Blake winks to Heap's 'Hide and Seek' with 'Lindesfarne I' and 'Lindesfarne II' from his self-titled debut – stripped back tracks where Blake's voice is distorted and harmonised with itself.

Silence as instrument

The clearest example of his work at the leading edge of the singer-songwriter and electronic music is his cover of Feist's 2007 'The Limit to Your Love', which Blake covered and released as a single in November 2010 and which appeared on his self-titled debut LP in 2011. As cultural critic Michael Awkward has argued, artists at the beginning of their career often cover songs by more established artists.[13] For Awkward, most song covers 'do not strive merely to pay tribute to and replicate beloved performances. Indeed, versions can serve as ways for skilful artists to develop and display distinctive styles and voices.'[14] Offering a skilful reinterpretation of an established song shows off an artist's technical ability as well as the depth of her or his creativity.

Whereas Feist's original version of 'Limit to Your Love' opens with soft drum work and a delicate tremolo, the James Blake version announces itself right away with strong piano chords. Blake's interpretation is stripped bare and slowed down for greater emotional impact – not unlike a number of early Prince records, 'Purple Rain' for instance – and the first few bars focus only on his vocal prowess and piano work. Where Blake leaves his signature stamp is not how he sings or what he does with the piano but with his commanding use of *silence* as an instrument. After teasing the listener with an intimate opening several bars later we are suddenly plunged into a deafening silence that lasts eight beats when, just as suddenly, deep, rib-shattering bass kicks in and Blake continues singing where he left off.

One of the most compelling aspects of Blake's oeuvre is his use of minimalism, sparseness, and silence as musical instruments. On Brian Eno-assisted 'Digital Lion', from Blake's critically acclaimed 2013 LP *Overgrown*, Blake returns to the power of the beat and silence. As in 'Limit to Your Love', Blake pulls the bass out again and uses the power of a 16-count relative silence before shoving a circular, gyrating beat back into the mix. This haunting track is not built around choruses or traditional song structures but in fact echoes his earlier play with sound texture, soundscapes and musical impressionism. It is an effect that allows his music to breathe instead of being filled up with walls of sound. 'He works mostly by subtraction', Brian Eno said during a 2013 lecture at the Red Bull Music Academy in New York. 'He takes lots of stuff out and ends up with very skeletal pieces.'[15] The emotional effect of this approach is powerful because it draws the listener in as much as it makes her eagerly anticipate and be surprised by the succession of sounds.

Blue-eyed soul

Although Blake's work defies simple genre and classification, many critics have located his music within a school of 'blue-eyed soul', soul or gospel-styled music sung by white artists. 'For me, when people say 'soulful', one music journalist said in a 2011 interview referring to how critics have framed Blake's music, 'it feels like they're saying, 'Oh, it's a white person who can sing like they're black.'[16] But the question of white artists appropriating black styles is a concern we should take seriously. 'Are Whites Stealing Rhythm & Blues?', a 1999 issue of *Ebony* magazine asked.[17] White artists have long appropriated black singing styles and sounds, and have achieved greater commercial success than black artists making similar styles of music.[18] Even Madonna, at the height of her fame, told *Rolling Stone* she wished she were black. 'When I was a little girl, I wished I was black … I was incredibly jealous of all my black girlfriends because they could have braids in their hair that stuck up everywhere. So I would go through this incredible ordeal of putting wire in my hair and braiding it so that I could make *my* hair stick up. I used to make cornrows and everything.'[19]

Recent commercial music history sees white UK artists like Amy Winehouse, Adele, Jessie J, Katy B, and Jessie Ware as singers who have adopted a black singing style. Cultural critic Daphne Brooks sees Amy Winehouse's performance as a blackface act, but one built on the stylised elegance of iconic black musical eras, iconised by that big 'bouffant, satin gowns, vintage cocktail dresses and little black gloves [which] clearly reference the styles of everyone from Lena Horne to The Shirelles'.[20] Gayle Wald termed the process of white artists selling black music back to white audiences 'the triumph of white supremacist sensibilities'.[21] Simply, this is about the way whiteness affords agency within the global music industry, meaning whiteness allows for greater artistic fame and economic prowess. For Wald there is 'cultural revivalism', the nostalgic appropriation of historical black singing styles, and the constant ability of white performers to make profit where black artists cannot.[22] To that end it is crucial to note that other contemporary black artists, like FKA Twigs, XXYYXX, Blood Orange, and The Weeknd, occupy a similar space in the field of 'indie R&B' or 'post-dubstep'.

It might be useful to remember Paul Gilroy's theory of blackness and of black performance culture as a deeply profane practice. Blackness has long been sold back to black *and* white audiences, as much to legitimise and naturalise racial difference as to profit on black performance innovations at their expense. Black performance culture has always been appropriated for commercial gain, and perhaps its most distinctive quality is in how widely it is spread or, as Gilroy put it, 'promiscuity is the key principle of its continuance'.[23] While James Blake does fit into the broader tradition of white musicians appropriating a black singing style, from gospel to soul, the most compelling feature of his work is not his soulful voice. It is the way he mixes and deconstructs genre through space, minimalism, anticipation, and beat strokes.[24]

Club vibrations

James Blake, the emotional singer-songwriter, emerges from the underground club scene, having partied everywhere from Berghain to London dubstep night FWD>> at Plastic People, and the club scene itself has had a noticeable impact on his sound and musical style. He told art critic Julie Baumgardner in *Interview* magazine that,

> I like my music to have a club feel, because I find the club atmosphere is really easy. I mean, they are weird places, because on a personal level, people are relating not unnaturally, but as if they're in a parallel universe. Weirdly, I feel very comfortable in places like that ... We do play a lot [of] tunes that have a definite groove, and I love to add the club feel to our set. We do play a lot [of] beats in a live set that are designed to make people move.[25]

This dance floor vibe is felt on a number of tracks in Blake's repertoire and amplified even further during his live sets, from the beat-driven 'At Birth' to the surprise crescendo at the tail-end of 'I Never Learnt to Share', to the more recent 'Voyeur (dub)' from *Overgrown*.

Since Blake arrived on the international music scene, crackdowns on nightlife in the UK have spread year by year due to gentrification, increased regulations, and council restrictions. London's Hackney Council recently announced it would restrict the number of bars and clubs that could open in Dalston, an über-trendy neighbourhood currently home to the FWD>> dubstep night at Dance Tunnel, because the number of clubbing options in the area has reached a 'saturation point'.[26] A recent article in *The Guardian* asked readers if they mourned the demise of nightclubs, and most readers equated nightlife with crime, drugs, noise, and other moralising qualities.[27]

But this negative approach to nightlife and dance music culture overlooks the fact that club culture is also a space of creative freedom and artistic experimentation, a place where artists like James Blake draw inspiration for their cultural productions.

Nightlife has long been a space for creative innovation and artistic expression, an aesthetically safe space where brand new ideas in fashion, art, and music are tested out. For Blake, these ideas are experimented on in his remixes as Harmonimix, a riff on 'Harmonix', the commercial name of the vocoder, as well as in his DJ sets and his own London club night-cum record label 1-800-Dinosaur. 'It just means that I've got somewhere to write tunes for', Blake once said during a live performance on Seattle's KCRW. 'We've all got something to play. Ben [Assiter] DJs, Rob [McAndrews] DJs, and my manager Dan [Foat] DJs with us, and a guy called Klaus. We play anything really – it's dance music. It's fun.'[28]

Conclusion

James Blake, a 'digital lion', is a singer-songwriter who occupies the leading edge of electronic music and powerful vocals. Through his use of space, minimalism, and colourful beat work, his entire oeuvre encourages us to think creatively about the category of singer-songwriter, particularly as his earlier productions featured little discernible vocal content and even his recent work is lyrically sparse. As Blake becomes more popular – Kanye West reportedly wants to work with him[29] – how will his artistic vision mesh with the pressures of commercial success? His early career has demonstrated his abilities as an independent artist committed to relatively non-commercial songs rich in emotional content, creative sampling, sound texture, and vocal prowess. Through this, what Blake offers is a new way of thinking about what it means to be a singer-songwriter in the twenty first century.

Notes

1 Neil McCormick, 'James Blake, Overgrown, Album Review', *The Telegraph*, 31 October 2013, available at: www.telegraph.co.uk/culture/music/cdreviews/9960024/James-Blake-Overgrown-album-review.html (accessed 17 November 2014).
2 Bob Boilen, 'James Blake, Live In Concert', *NPR Music*, 23 May 2013, available at: www.npr.org/event/music/185510193/james-blake-live-in-concert (accessed 17 November 2014).
3 Eric Harvey, 'James Blake', *Pitckfork*, 9 April 2013, available at: pitchfork.com/reviews/albums/17842-james-blake-overgrown/ (accessed 17 November 2014).
4 Dubstep is a style of dance music born in South London in the late 1990s that emerged out of UK garage music and combines heavy bass wobbles with syncopated rhythms. Prominent dubstep artists include Benga,

Loefah, Digital Mystikz, Skream, and DJ Hatcha. Post-dubstep is a term used to describe ambient indie R&B that borrows from dubstep. Post-dub artists include Mount Kimbie, James Blake, Fantastic Mr Fox and Kelela.
5 Alex Needham, 'The London Dubstep Scene', *Interview* Magazine, available at: www.interviewmagazine.com/music/the-london-dubstep-scene/#_ (accessed 23 December 2014).
6 Mark Katz, *Capturing Sound: How Technology Has Changed Music* (Berkeley: University of California Press, 2010), p. 147.
7 Katz, *Capturing Sound*, p. 148. For more on electronic music and sampling see Aram Sinnreich, *Mashed Up: Music, Technology, and the Rise of Configurable Culture* (Amherst: University of Massachusetts Press, 2010); Joseph Schloss, *Making Beats: The Art of*

Sample-Based Hip-Hop (New York: Columbia University Press, 2004); DJ Spooky, Rhythm Science (Cambridge: The MIT Press, 2004); and Lawrence Lessig, Remix: Making Art and Commerce Thrive in the Hybrid Economy (New York: Penguin, 2009).

8 Nicolas Bourriaud, Postproduction. Culture As Screen Play: How Art Reprograms The World (New York: Lukas & Sternberg, 2002), p. 19.

9 'Post Dubstep Tumblr', at www.postdubstep .tumblr.com, accessed 14 November 2014.

10 Kay Dickinson, Dickinson, '"Believe"? Vocoders Vocoders, Digitised Female Identity and Camp', Popular Music, 20/3 (2001), p. 333.

11 Dickinson, '"Believe"?', p. 334.

12 For more on the history of the vocoder, see Dave Tompkins, How to Wreck a Nice Beach: The Vocoder from World War II to Hip-Hop (Chicago: Stop Smiling Books, 2010).

13 Michael Awkward, Soul Covers: Rhythm and Blues Remakes and the Struggle for Artistic Identity (Durham: Duke University Press, 2007), p. 7.

14 Awkward, Soul Covers, p. 12.

15 Brian Eno, 'Lecture', Red Bull Music Academy, 2013, available at www .redbullmusicacademy.com/lectures/brian-eno (accessed 17 November 2014).

16 Mark Pytlik, 'James Blake', Pitchfork, 21 March 2011, at pitchfork.com/features/ interviews/7941-james-blake/ (accessed 17 November 2014).

17 Zondra Hughes, 'Are Whites Stealing Rhythm & Blues?', Ebony, November 1999, 72–80.

18 For more on black music and appropriation, see Eric Lott, Love and Theft: Blackface Minstrelsy and the American Working Class (New York: Oxford University Press, 1993).

19 Bill Zehme, 'Madonna: The Rolling Stone Interview', in Madonna: The Ultimate Compendium of Interviews, Articles, Facts and Opinions (New York: Hyperion, 1997), p. 106.

20 Daphne Brooks, '"This Voice Which is Not One": Amy Winehouse Sings the Ballad of Sonic Blue(s)face Culture', Women & Performance: A Journal of Feminist Theory, 20/1 (2010), pp. 39–40.

21 Gayle Wald, 'Soul's Revival. White Soul, Nostalgia, and the Culturally Constructed Past' in Monique Guillory and Richard C. Green, Soul: Black Power, Politics, and Pleasure (New York: New York University Press, 1998), p. 142.

22 Wald, 'Soul's Revival', p. 140.

23 Paul Gilroy, '… To Be Real': The Dissident Forms of Black Expressive Culture' in Catherine Ugwu (ed.), Let's Get It On: The Politics of Black Performance (Seattle: Bay Press, 1995), p. 16.

24 For more on the appropriation of black gospel music by white audiences, see E. Patrick Johnson, Appropriating Blackness: Performance and the Politics of Authenticity (Durham: Duke University Press, 2003).

25 Julie Baumgardner, 'Blake, Eerie', Interview Magazine, 12 May 2011, available at: www .interviewmagazine.com/music/james-blake#_ (accessed 17 November 2014).

26 'Council Reveals Clampdown on New Bars and Clubs in Dalston', Dalstonist, 24 July 2013, available at: dalstonist.co.uk/council-clampdown-on-new-bars-and-clubs-in-dalston/ (accessed 17 November 2014).

27 'Do You Mourn the Demise of Nightclubs?' The Guardian, 10 November 2014, available at: www.theguardian.com/commentisfree/2014/ nov/10/mourn-demise-nightclubs-bar-promoters (accessed 17 November 2014).

28 'James Blake Live on KCRW's Morning Becomes Eclectic', KCRW, 24 April 2014, available at: www.youtube.com/ watch?v=gMhTrVxs7Sc (accessed 17 November 2014).

29 'James Blake Collaborating With Kanye West And Bon Iver In New Album Sessions', SPIN, 15 June 2014, available at: www.factmag .com/2014/06/15/james-blake-kanye-west-new-album-bon-iver/ (accessed 17 November 2014).

16 Outside voices and the construction of Adele's singer-songwriter persona

SARAH SUHADOLNIK

The singer-songwriter label can suggest a distinctive artistic persona. Dark, brooding, or simply self-absorbed, these musicians are widely known as practitioners of confessional songwriting – artists who seem to bare the secrets of their soul in introspective prose and appropriately moody harmonies. How might such expectations weigh on the creative pursuits of the singer-songwriter? Are there situations in which the promise of emotional vulnerability can overwhelm individual artistic intentions? With whom do audiences truly connect – the singer, the song's protagonist, or the songwriter? The following ponders these questions as they relate to the example of Adele Adkins, a mainstream popular music sensation who has achieved considerable success in the early twenty-first century as the 'Queen of Heartbreak'.[1] In the public eye, it is largely the strength of Adele's voice – rather than her songwriting credits – that has made the artist's personal misfortunes into an integral component of her musical signature. Nevertheless, recurring themes in fan commentary (see Figure 16.1) consistently point to the sounds of sincere, heartfelt angst as a primary draw.

Both *19*, her 2008 debut, and *21*, her 2011 sophomore release, were conceived of as break-up albums, inspired by (different) failed romantic relationships. Adele's vocal style – alternately characterised as bluesy, soulful, and raw – has conspired with memories of anonymous ex-boyfriends in the creation and maintenance of an emotionally volatile artistic identity. Despite a stylistic departure from the more traditional singer-songwriter aesthetic of *19*, Adele continued to perform for audiences who yearned for the perpetually melancholy version of the heart-on-her-sleeve singer they first encountered in her music. In an effort to better understand the nature of the underlying conspiracy between emotive voice and anonymous ex, I approach more constrained views of Adele and her music as a manifestation of the impact traditional conceptions of singer-songwriters can have on an artist and their work. Through an examination of the narrative contributions of the anonymous friend characters who make appearances on both albums, I illustrate the extent to which outside voices have intervened in the ongoing construction of what I call Adele's singer-songwriter identity.

A word cloud based on iTunes reviews of *19* and *21* submitted by iTunes users.

Figure 16.1. A sampling of Adele fan commentary: a word cloud based on iTunes reviews of *19* and *21* submitted by iTunes users.

Interpreting Adele

Opting to address Adele's artistic persona as that of a singer-songwriter engages with the shared sense of intimacy, or knowing, that exists between artist and audience. Allan F. Moore parses this connection – an idea of the individual to whom we are listening – as distinct layers of musical experience and modes of self-presentation. I employ his ecological approach to artistic persona to identify different facets of Adele's singer-songwriter identity, showing that the roots of her 'Queen of Heartbreak' reputation exist outside the realm of her complete creative control. More specifically, in adopting this methodological framework, we can begin to see why *21*, an album that showcased the talents of an artist exploring other dimensions of her creative range, ultimately remained bound by the lovelorn figure that inspired it. Unpacking Adele's artistic persona in the way that Moore outlines – examining Adele as *performer*, *song character*, and *artistic persona* in particular – allows for a better understanding of how listeners relate to Adele through her music, and how fans might come to resent or reject musical choices that upset that relationship.

Adele as performer

Adele Laurie Blue Adkins (b. 5 May 1988) – the *performer*, or 'real person' – is who the artist is known to be outside the context of her records, 'an individual who has an observable historical position and identity', according to

Moore.[2] Outside more formal affiliations (e.g. BRIT School for Performing Arts and Technology), Adele situates herself as a performer through declared influences, identified through repertoire choices and in public interviews. On record, the singer-songwriter has paid tribute to recording artists as wide ranging as Bob Dylan and The Cure, couching her covers in childhood musical memories, artistic praise, or both. In an interview with *Jazziz Magazine*, she explained, 'I listened to Etta [James] to get a bit of soul, Ella [Fitzgerald] for my chromatic scales and Roberta Flack for control.'[3] One of many such comments, Adele consistently cites the influences of other esteemed artists when discussing the roots of her vocal prowess. More to the point, Adele has also drawn clear distinctions between her instrument and her self, constructing a performer identity that is generally obscured by her music. Ask her, as *Vogue* did in 2012, about what it is like to be a girl who 'sings her own blues', and she will likely respond that she is the total opposite of her records. In the extensive interview, Adele characterised herself as 'chatty, bubbly and kind of carefree really'.

Adele as song character

Inside her songs, fans know Adele as the (heartbroken) protagonist, or Adele the *song character*. As a recurring narrator and generally wronged woman, this Adele engages in a series of open-ended dialogues with her anonymous exes. Individual songs (on both albums), place the song character in emotionally turbulent settings, or scenarios, which act as a vehicle for the thoughts and feelings commonly associated with a romantic break-up. 'Turning Tables', for instance, employs colourful imagery as a larger metaphor for a turbulent relationship (rather than describe specific events or episodes that may have inspired it):

> Under haunted skies I see you,
> Where love is lost your ghost is found.
> I braved a hundred storms to leave you,
> As hard as you try, no, I will never be knocked down.
> I can't keep up with your turning tables,
> Under your thumb I can't breathe.

Adele's subjectivity gives meaning to otherwise nondescript 'you' and 'I' subject positions and otherwise ambiguous phrases, but specific tracks do not necessarily correspond to scenes from the performer's troubled past. Instead, they often represent an opportunity for Adele to step into a character that allows her to emote, reflecting on what has transpired.

The artistic persona

Persona is an amalgamation of performer and song character, the Adele for which boundaries between voice, song character, and artistic agenda become blurred. Musicologist Ian Biddle explains this idea as 'a way of grounding a certain kind of fantasy', a means of bringing together the inner and outer worlds of song and songwriter in an articulable relationship that extends to artist and audience.[4] Adele's freewheeling approach to media demonstrates this notion, inscribing her accessible break-up story in song in a way that has helped to sustain her distinctive public reputation – that of an unlucky in love, uncharacteristically earthy, pop diva. Consistently adopting a playful attitude towards the broad-based commercial appeal of this identity, Adele has postulated, 'It would be fucking awful if my third album was about being happily settled down, and maybe on my way to being a mom, and all the critics were, like, "Yeah it's fucking shit. Can you be miserable please?" And all the fans were going, "I just don't like you anymore. I don't bond with you anymore".[5]

'My Same', *19*

While reflecting on *19* in a 2008 interview with *The Observer*, Adele mused: 'I will sit in my room on my own for ages because otherwise I am rude to people. I can't be around anyone, I have to be on my own. And I'll write. That's how that atmosphere [in the songs] gets created.'[6] Along these lines, *19* paints a more traditional picture of a singer-songwriter. Some tracks explore feelings of heartbreak, while others augment the central break-up narrative with other introspective explorations that engage with the relationship theme more broadly. Throughout, Adele serves as a meandering narrator, blurring the boundaries between performer and song character in a way that invites listeners to accompany her on different journeys of self-discovery. The song 'My Same', for example, transforms nonsensical bickering between childhood friends into a moment of serious self-reflection. Sparse background vocals and an intermittent countermelody in the electric guitar create an airy, playground-like atmosphere, in which memories of banter between Adele and a childhood friend act as a veiled metaphor for self-criticism. The lyrics – delivered in a bluesy, singsong fashion – unfold in a type of point-counterpoint (as seen in Table 16.1).

These, alongside a series of other accusations aimed at Adele's character flaws, relay a strong confessional subtext. While it may seem as if the song recounts a conversation between Adele and an old childhood friend, the reality of the situation is that the childhood friend is actually her foil, building to the song's playful conclusion,' I don't know who I'd be if I didn't know you'.[7] The implied sense of intimacy between friends extends to Adele's audience, allowing the listener to feel as if they are Adele's confidante – acting as a witness to private, personal revelations.

Table 16.1 *'My Same', opening exchange*

Adele's Friend	Adele
You say I'm stubborn and I never give in,	
	I think you're stubborn 'cept you're always softening.
You say I'm selfish, I agree with you on that,	
	I think you're given out and way too much in fact.
	I say we've only known each other a year,
You say I've known you longer my dear.	
You like to be so close,	
	I like to be alone.
	I like to sit on chairs
And you prefer the floor.	
Walking with each other you'd think we'd never match at all, but we do …	

'Rumour Has It', *21*

Unlike *19*, *21* is framed as a more opened-ended emotional stand-off, and was more carefully engineered for mainstream audiences. The *21* track-by-track interview widely disseminated through YouTube, and made available on Adele's website, outlines a different sort of creative process. Without fully relinquishing the status of songwriter, clips of artist commentary and atmospheric shots of Adele in the recording studio reinforce a new emphasis on the artist's vocal talents. For instance, after claiming ownership of 'Rolling in the Deep', explaining, 'I guess it's sort of my musical equivalent of saying things in the heat of the moment', Adele goes on to describe the integral contributions of co-songwriter Paul Epworth:

> I went with Paul with it, Paul Epworth, and, um, it was exactly the kind of thing he had in mind to do with me I suppose. I wasn't really expecting anything out of the session just because he's known for being very indie, um, and I'm known for being very pop, so I wasn't sure if it would work too well, but it ended up being a match made in heaven really.[8]

In line with Joe Bennett's work on the power dynamics of collaborative songwriting, Adele positions herself as a creative lead, even while suggesting Epworth was largely responsible for the end result.[9] With the backing and managerial influence of a major label, the artist now appeared to be moving in a new direction. Observing this change, Jeff Smith, music director at Radio 2 in the UK publicly insisted, 'There is a lot more reality

Table 16.2 *'Rumour Has It', lyric substitution (*emphasis added)*

Chorus 1	Chorus 2	Tag
She made your heart melt, but you're cold to the core, now rumour has it she ain't got your love anymore.	You made my heart melt, yet I'm cold to the core, but rumour has it **I'M** the one **YOU'RE** leaving **HER** for.	… but rumour has it **HE's** the one **I'M** leaving **YOU** for.

to it than [Top-40 oriented] music, but it's still a lot more A&R-ed than people give it credit for'.[10] Combining a new approach with the equally new production values of 'a transatlantic Columbia dream team', *21* reimagined Adele as a mainstream pop sensation.[11]

As a reflection of this shift, 'Rumour Has It' relays a different sort of break-up song experience, creating considerable distance between Adele and her 'friends' in the process. The song depicts a battle for control of a rumour mill fuelled by lingering tensions between estranged partners. Although the narrative progression from Chorus 1 to Chorus 2 (as shown in Table 16.2) implies the couple in question may be getting back together, simple lyric substitution in the song's witty tag causes the storyline to shift, reversing the expected outcome. The ease with which the proverbial relationship tables are turned reveals gossip to be the song's true subject; not Adele's inner psyche. According to the artist, it is meant to be a tongue-in-cheek reaction to the ways in which her friends used to gossip about the men in her life.

For some audiences, an overwhelming attachment to Adele's artistic persona (a creative amalgamation of song character and performer) supports a different understanding of the track, demonstrating, as David Brackett has suggested, that fans can contribute an alternative authorial voice to a record. A number of reviewers, forum participants, and active YouTube users embraced 'Rumour Has It' as a bitter revenge anthem, a reaction that Brackett would characterise as part of a moment in which a song presented a range of affect that exceeded the composer/performer's intentions. While Adele claimed to be joking around at the expense of her friends, mixed public reception suggested a popular fixation on a cathartic fantasy in which the perpetually wronged Adele is allowed to win the upper hand (albeit briefly).[12] In other words, a visible attempt on the part of the artist to step outside her characteristic heartbreak persona was met with equally visible displays of resistance on the part of her listeners.

No stunts

Given the nature of these different facets of her artistic persona, it is my contention that the persistence with which audiences cling to Adele's singer-songwriter identity is best explained in relation to the landscape of mainstream contemporary pop. Sometimes, as Moore indicates, the artistic persona is best understood as a reflection of the broader environment in which it operates; an interplay of 'melody and accompaniment', or 'voice and setting', as Keith Negus would assert.[13] For many, the powerful young vocalist has served as the 'anti-Lady Gaga', a welcome alternative to hypersexualised, spectacle-driven pop.[14] Characterised as 'pretty and proudly Rubenesque' in 2008, 'determined to circumvent the starmaking machinery that befalls many pop singers', Adele, the newly minted star, still earned the same praise.[15] She has remained, in the eyes of her admirers, a 'triumph of restraint'.[16]

Directly engaging with her anti-Gaga status, Adele has consistently responded to the elaborate concert productions of her colleagues with a deliberately stripped down approach. On her 2012 concert DVD, for example, *Adele Live at the Royal Albert Fucking Hall*, she can be seen (and heard) ending a concert with the following bout of playful banter:

> This isn't really my last song. I just pop off stage and pretend I'm not coming back on. Just adding drama to my show. There's no dancing, no fires, no greased-up men … might get some of them for later in the tour … just in the dressing room, not on stage. Anyway, so, the last song of the night, wink, wink.

Dressed in her signature black dress, the message is clear: singer, songwriter, or singer-songwriter, Adele does not do stunts and her fans love her for it. As such, Adele's example teaches us that sometimes even the lonesome islands we call singer-songwriters can be a product of circumstance more than they are a reflection of fiercely individualistic creative pursuits. After sweeping the 2012 Grammy Awards, she more or less walked off the industry stage proclaiming, 'At least now I can have enough time to write a happy record … And be in love and be happy'. Now, presently awaiting her next album – *25*, rumoured to be released by the end of 2015 – one cannot help but wonder, how many fans, critics, and producers hope she wrote another moody (read 'real'), emotionally accessible, megahit instead?

Notes

1 Over the course of five short years, Adele Adkins (Adele) has boasted record-breaking sales figures and amassed four Brit Awards, nine Grammys, an Oscar, and a Golden Globe.
2 Allan F. Moore, *Song Means: Analysing and Interpreting Recorded Popular Song* (Burlington: Ashgate, 2012), p. 180.
3 Kara Manning, 'Lady Adele', *Jazziz* 25/6 (2008), p. 46.
4 Ian Biddle, 'The Singsong of Undead Labor: Gender Nostalgia and the Vocal Fantasy of Intimacy in the New Male Singer/Songwriter', in Freya Jarman-Ivens (ed.), *Oh Boy! Masculinities and Popular Music* (New York: Routledge, 2007), p. 130.
5 Aaron Hicklin, 'Lady Sings the Blues', *Out* 19/10 (2011), p. 118.
6 Sylvia Patterson, 'Mad About the Girl', *The Observer* (26 January 2008).
7 See Ingrid Monson's *Saying Something: Jazz Improvisation and Interaction* (Chicago: University of Chicago Press, 1996) for more on

the creative and cultural potential of this style of musical elaboration.

8 '21 Track by Track Interview', *Adele* website. www.adele.tv/trackbytrack/archive/ (accessed 24 February 2015).

9 See Joe Bennett, '"You Won't See Me" – In Search of an Epistemology of Collaborative Songwriting', *Journal on the Art of Record Production* 8 (2008), arpjournal.com/ "you-won't-see-me"-in-search-of-an-epistemology-of-collaborative-songwriting/-in-search-of-an-epistemology-of-collaborative-songwriting/ (accessed 24 June 2014).

10 Eamonn Forde, 'The Exception That Proves the Rule', *The Word* (2011), p. 73.

11 For the production of *21*, Columbia assembled a team that harnessed the collective talents of Rick Rubin, Paul Epworth, Ryan Tedder, and Francis 'Eg' White, among other well-known industry professionals.

12 YouTube videos of Adele giving the middle finger at the 2012 BRIT awards went viral as a similar breach of character. In interviews after the fact the artist explained that the gesture was directed at what she described as the 'suits' that cut her off before she was able to thank her fans for their support, but many were surprised by the uncharacteristic edginess of the gesture.

13 Keith Negus, 'Authorship and the Popular Song', *Music and Letters* 92/4 (2011), p. 619.

14 Dylan Jones, *The Biographical Dictionary of Popular Music: From Adele to Ziggy, the Real A to Z of Rock and Pop* (New York: Picador, 2012), p. 12.

15 Manning, 'Lady Adele', p. 48.

16 Jim Irvin, 'Someone Like You', *The Word* 108 (2012), p. 96.

17 Joanna Newsom's 'Only Skin': authenticity, 'becoming-other', and the relationship between 'New' and 'Old Weird America'

JO COLLINSON SCOTT

Be a hobo and go with me, from Hoboken to the sea,
Be a hobo and go with me ...[1]

These were the lyrics of the refrain that closed *Welcome to Dreamland* – a *Perspectives* show at the Carnegie Hall, New York, in February 2007, curated by David Byrne. The aim of the evening was to showcase the best of the world's 'new folk' movement. As a performer that night, I sang those words alongside Devendra Banhart, Vashti Bunyan, Adem, Coco Rosie, Vetiver, and David Byrne himself,[2] and together we closed the show climactically by entreating the thousands in the audience to 'be' something that they were not (Ben Ratliff of the New York Times described the audience that night as, 'models and rock stars and people with money').[3] Since then, I have often wondered: what was the meaning of that request? Can models and rock stars become hobos? What would it look like for a person to 'become' something other? What is this 'becoming' that the new folk movement recommends to us?

I hope to demonstrate that this notion of 'becoming' is especially relevant to critical questions surrounding the new folk movement. I will suggest that Deleuze and Guattari's notion of 'becoming-other'[4] might help us explore such questions regarding the nature of 'becoming' as stated above, and can be used as a particularly effective model through which we can try and understand the complex associations of authenticity related to this genre and its musical output. More specifically, I am going to examine the use of the genre term 'New Weird America' (which was a prevalent early description of new folk music) and focus on the work of one artist in particular – Joanna Newsom – who is the most widely known singer-songwriter of the genre.

'New' and 'Old Weird America'

The first significant use of the term 'New Weird America' (hereafter NWA) to describe a musical genre, was by David Keenan in his cover article for

Wire magazine titled, 'The Fire Down Below: Welcome to the New Weird America'.[5] In this article, Keenan described a, 'groundswell musical movement', based in improvisation, and 'mangling' a variety of American genres of different ages, including mountain music, country blues, hip- hop, psychedelia, free jazz, and archival blues. Keenan's construction of the description 'NWA' was an explicit reference to Greil Marcus' term, 'Old Weird America' (hereafter OWA). This was used prominently by Marcus in reference to Harry Smith's *Anthology of American Folk Music*: an album which Keenan says documents the specific, 'recurrent archetypal forms', that are being 'mustered' by musicians at the start of the NWA movement.[6]

Smith's *Anthology* was a collection of commercial recordings of American folk that were initially released in the 1920s and 30s, some of which were relatively successful. The *Anthology* itself was released in 1952, after which it is understood to have become the most important recorded source of inspiration for the urban folk revival from which the commercial singer-songwriter genre was born.[7] The *Anthology* was then re-released again in 1997, and went on to influence modern singer-songwriters within the new folk movement. Smith's compilation now has the status of a double, even triple canonisation: as a re-release of a compilation of re-releases; as a revival of the touchstone of the folk revival; and as a kind of short-circuiting of the historical lineage of the American singer-songwriter movement. There is therefore what Deleuze and Guattari might call an 'assemblage' of time that occurs with relation to the music of NWA, and it is this 'assemblage' and the understandings of the nature of the work of artists who traverse it that is the focus of the rest of this chapter.

Joanna Newsom is one of the most well-known and critically addressed singer-songwriters of the NWA genre and as such, her work is received as related both to OWA *and* to key figures of the modern singer-songwriter genre who arose out of the urban folk revival of the 60s and 70s (each with their own musical relationship to OWA). Newsom's initial reception as part of the NWA genre categorisation meant that her work would constantly be compared and associated with folk recordings of an earlier era. This served to focus critical reception of her work around two key themes, both related to authenticity: firstly, the charge that her work (along with other new folk artists) is based on shallow appropriations of cultural traditions and artefacts from the past, and secondly, that the nature of her vocal performance is imitative and affected. Let us take each of these critical assertions in turn.

A number of strong critics of new folk posit that the relationship between Newsom's early work and OWA is one of shallow imitation, where Newsom appropriates sounds of American traditional musics of the past purely in order to make her own sound more interesting. One of the most strident criticisms of the work of Joanna Newsom (and other new folk artists) along these lines has come from Simon Reynolds in his book *Retromania*.[8] Here Reynolds characterises Newsom's work as purely 'retro', thus translating her relationship with OWA into a charge of 'exoticism'.[9] Reynolds sees 'freak folk' as pure surface – the use of materials of the past simply for the extraction and assumption of an air of difference and 'hipness'.[10] He also places what he describes as 'freak folk'[11] in contrast to the work of more traditionalist British folk musicians.

Putting aside broader problems with Reynolds' project as a whole (including his self-confessed clear bias towards specifically modernist notions of linear progress),[12] with these descriptions he resurrects notions of folk authenticity based on 'primality'.[13] Indeed, the simple dichotomy that Reynolds builds between new folk and 'authentic folk' ignores strong critiques of such a narrative from those such as Mark Willhardt.[14] These critiques point out the questionable nature of the assumption that there is anything approaching a 'pure' folk music to be able to contrast with a more hybrid form particularly in an age of recording.

Newsom doesn't recognise the description of a gap between herself and the folk performers of a bygone era followed by a sudden desire on her part to listen to folk in order to glean something new from it. What she does recognise is merely a resurgence in interest in this kind of music, which chooses to focus on her:

> There is as much of a connection between my music and some of the people I'm being grouped with as there is between it and music that has been made for the last 30 years. I just think it's awkward. There isn't a new folk, there's just a new resurgence of media interest in a kind of music that has been this way for 30 years or more.[15]

Reynolds' notion of a clear linear narrative structure to time with artists reaching back or pointing forward along a line does not relate to Newsom's understanding of a more interconnected pattern of influence. This seems more clearly related to Deleuze and Guattari's descriptions in *A Thousand Plateaus* of music being the product of multiple rhizomatic connections across superimposed strata. Here they describe time not as 'chronos' – a great plot in sequence, something that divides up into epochs – but as 'the time of aion', where many layers are juxtaposed or superimposed.[16] Their notion of music as a product of 'becoming' means that the artist makes connections between or across these superimposed strata creating, 'a sort of diagonal between the harmonic vertical and the melodic horizon'.[17]

The distinction between a mere form of imitation reaching back across a linear sense of time, and a more complex 'becoming' is one that is very important in this discussion. Deleuze and Guattari describe the nature of the artist as a 'becomer': someone who somehow passes *between* territories across an assemblage to become a hybrid that is able to articulate a new kind of refrain (an original music). They describe 'becoming' in this sense as: 'Neither an imitation nor an experienced sympathy, nor even an imaginary identification. It is not resemblance ... [It is] not the transformation of one into the other ... but something passing from one to the other.'[18] This important distinction draws near to discussions continuing in the field of 'world music' focused on the politics of cultural borrowing–for example exchanges relating to 'hybridity' between George Lipsitz, Georgina Born and David Hesmondhalgh, and Timothy Taylor.[19]

In this context, Born and Hesmondhalgh have called for a more complex, problematised, or multiplied notion of identities involved in cultural musical exchanges (such as between NWA and OWA). Although criticised by Born and Hesmondhalgh for his suggestion of the possibility of a 'strategic anti-essentialism' at play in such work, George Lipsitz describes a potential process by which musicians can create 'immanent critique' of systems within commercial culture. This acts to 'defamiliarise' their own culture and then 'refamiliarise' it via new critical perspectives.[20] I suggest that the model of 'becoming-other' (indicated by Lipsitz's use the of Deleuzian language of 'deterritorialization' and 'reterritorialization') can open up the possibility of there being a form of 'strategic anti-essentialism' that retains the kind of crucial complexity that Born and Hesmondhalgh describe.[21] 'Becoming' cuts across the question of intention and appropriation, casting ideas of hybridity and cultural identification in a different, much more complex light. It is also peculiarly appropriate to Joanna Newsom's work, situated as it is, between notions of personal identity and layers of complex cultural borrowings from past and present 'others'.

To return now to the second key critique of Newsom's work – that the nature of her vocal performance style is an affectation – this criticism can also be shown to be related directly to a type of 'becoming'. Newsom's voice is frequently referred to in the critical literature in terms related to children ('childish'), or a sinister form of femininity ('witch-like'). It is important to note in this context that the specific form of 'becoming' that Deleuze and Guattari lay out in *A Thousand Plateaus* as associated with radical artistry is a becoming-*woman*, -*child*, or -*animal*.[22] Ronald Bogue explains why Deleuze chooses women, children and animals in particular:

> Social coding operates by way of asymmetrical binary oppositions in Western societies through an implicit privileging of male over female, adult over child, rational over animal, white over coloured etc. A becoming deterritorialises such codes and in its operations necessarily engages the underprivileged term in each of these binary oppositions ... A becoming-woman, becoming-child or a becoming-animal however, does not involve the imitation of women, children or animals – an action that would merely reinforce social codes – but an unspecifiable, unpredictable

disruption of codes that takes place alongside women, children, and animals, in a metamorphic zone between fixed identities.[23]

The remainder of this chapter will be dedicated to exploring how reception of Newsom's early work presented in her 2006 album *Ys* and, in particular, aspects of the track 'Only Skin', can be understood in the context of her work as a form of 'becoming-child' and 'becoming-woman'.[24]

'Becoming-child'

Newsom's voice is frequently described in the press as 'childlike'. Take for example this review from the *Independent* in 2004: 'Newsom sings like a four-year-old witch. With her scratchy squawk, not unlike the noise a cat makes when there are fireworks outside, delivering words that sound as though they were chosen for their cuteness from some old-fashioned rhyming dictionary, she risks appearing irredeemably pretentious.'[25] Newsom herself rails against this repeated description, but only insofar as it minimises the seriousness of what she is trying to achieve. In 2006 she countered the charge in a press interview: '[T]he songs are really dark. Not just dark, they're adult. They're actual heavy shit.'[26]

Contrast this with the themes of childhood scattered throughout *Ys* (as with all of her records) that attest to Newsom's preoccupation with childishness. Often, Newsom quotes nursery rhymes, children's tales, childhood memories (such as climbing a tree house, tramping through the poison oak, having pockets full of candy), and creates childish neologisms and characters such as, 'Sibyl sea-cow all done up in a bow'. In the closing section of 'Only Skin'– the duet with Bill Callahan – Newsom echoes the form, the rhythm and some of the sentiment of the children's song 'There's a Hole In my Bucket', with falsetto female voices answering the male questioning. During this section she also makes lyrical reference to 'Rock-A-Bye-Baby' and even hints at the nursery rhyme 'Old Mother Hubbard'.

Besides these references, we also have repeated statements and metaphorical suggestions of a deep desire to be taken back into the womb. In 'Emily' (another song from *Ys*) the narrator describes herself, 'In search of a midwife who can help me, who can help me, help me find my way back in'. This is reflected too in the most pervasive theme in the whole album: the multiple and repeated references to being submerged in water. The album is named after the myth of *Ys* – a city submerged in the ocean – and in this context submersion is typically representative of a womb-like state where the foetus floats suspended in amniotic water.

Despite the superficial impression of these simple lyrical references to childhood, it is clear that the child-theme in Newsom's work is not related to a romantic, pastoral idea of a past innocence. On the contrary – it can be seen as a subversive act of becoming, as Deleuze and Guattari would describe it. This becomes particularly clear with relation to Newsom's use of what is portrayed as 'childish' vocal tone/gesture and received accordingly as 'affectation'. As the following quote from Newsom suggests, her vocals are not an imitation of a child, but the political act of someone questioning the affectation of the institution of singing itself: 'I was like: I'm going to sing my heart out, as crazy as it sounds, and I'm not going to care because there's no hope of sounding anything like what people consider beautiful. I sure as hell wasn't affecting anything. I mean, the institution of singing is inherently an affectation.'[27] The assumption implicit in criticisms of the inauthenticity of Newsom's voice is the equation of 'natural' with a particular style of singing (controlled, smooth, non-nasal, 'in-tune', utilising vibrato), and 'affected' with anything else. But Newsom's argument here is that it is the trained Western singing voice in fact that is the construction. Her efforts therefore are not to imitate a childish or OWA Appalachian voice, but to reject the inauthentic constructions of the trained Western voice.

John Alberti's description of the work of the 'faux naif' is enlightening here. He explores the work of Jonathan Richman – an artist extremely influential in the punk movement – as a 'strategic invocation of childhood' that 'can be read as a gesture towards the concept of pre-ideological space as a point of radical disruption of the mainstream consumption of rock music'.[28] There is a strong and enduring political subversiveness to Richman's invocation of childishness, which Alberti maintains is a strategic action.[29] The same is patently the case in Newsom's work, where she consistently 'becomes-child', and sings with a voice that questions and radically disrupts territorial notions of identity and cultural institutions (for example, the constructedness of the institution of the trained singing voice).

This action also disrupts notions of the singer-songwriter's voice as the site of communication of personal confessional meaning. There is widespread understanding of the singer-songwriter as a performer of 'self' i.e. presenting inherently confessional work that represents the personal identity of the singer. In this context, the voice, as a site of personal identity, becomes a site of contention where that voice is conceived to be, 'not the singer's own'.[30] I would like to suggest then that Newsom's vocal sound is the product not of an intentional and therefore inauthentic act of imitation, but a *becoming* that occurs via the composer's affinity with practices of 'others' that reflect a different (subversive) perspective on aspects of her own practice.

'Becoming-woman'

Where Newsom's identity-obfuscating vocal strategies work against notions of the singer-songwriter as having an emotive confessional identity, her recordings also serve to work against damagingly stereo-typical understandings of the 'femaleness' of the singer-songwriter genre. Such stereotypes are exemplified by the following quote from Ronald Lankford, describing the history of the female singer-songwriter as one of apolitical, emotional self-exploration:

> Because the singer-songwriter style was ultimately harmless regarding its social impact it also provided a safe and acceptable place for women who wished to enter the music business. A woman who expressed her personal feelings about love and life while accompanying herself on piano or acoustic guitar had little room to flaunt her sexuality or protest an unequal gender system.[31]

Newsom's work in 'becoming-woman' in her recording of 'Only Skin' is contextualised via numerous clear lyrical references to femaleness. Twice we hear direct repeated exhortations to 'be a woman', echoed in its repetition by a warning of the perils of 'being a woman' ('knowing how the common folk condemn what it is I do to keep you warm, being a woman, being a woman'). The narrator also speaks of being the 'happiest woman among all women' i.e. the epitome of a woman.

In this context, i.e. the lyrically stated context of a becoming-woman, I am going to propose that 'Only Skin' is indicative of what Deleuze and Guattari would describe as 'transverse becomings', which are a flux between and across non-fixed identities. The structure of 'Only Skin' is such that we constantly flux back and forth between the binary opposi-tions Air/Earth, Water/Fire, East/West, and, less conspicuously, Woman/Man, Adult/Child. Table 17.1 displays these relations with regard to the structure of the song. I have described each section as: Air / Earth / Water / Fire / East / Woman / Child, and I have apportioned these sections largely with relation to melodic and rhythmic content, but also with regard to lyrical themes and vocal gesture.

This table differs somewhat from the mapping of the form of 'Only Skin' given by John Encarnacao.[32] As he suggests himself, his structural break-down refers only to melodic/harmonic content and therefore misses some of the nuances of arrangement etc., to which the breakdown in Table 17.1 pays attention. The summary represented here is based on a consideration of structure that takes into account a range of structuring features (i.e. not only melodic and harmonic repetitions, but lyrical themes and vocal ges-ture), and therefore, as is the case with any analysis of artistic content, the distinctions are not always clear-cut and there is some overlap between sections. One example of the kinds of distinctions being considered along with the melodic and harmonic content is vocal gesture. So where the lyri-cal imagery predominantly or prominently relates to flight, air, looking up, sky, climbing, height (i.e. mountaintops), or life, and where the vocal

Table 17.1 *Joanna Newsom's 'Only Skin'*

Time	Lyrical themes	Vocal tone, and melodic gesture	Section	Section descriptor
0.07	Above, airplanes flying	Soft, breathy.	A	AIR
0.38	Sand, bricks	More strident, throaty.	B	EARTH
1.03	Alive, airplanes	Soft, breathy.	A	AIR
1.33	Death, craziness, beneath the clover, cold clay	More strident, throaty.	B	EARTH
2.18	Fishing pole, swimming hole, riverside	Repeated descending melody, contrary motion with ascending harp part.	C	WATER
2.43		Rapidly becoming soft, breathy, hushed.	A	AIR
3.16	'Press on me, we are restless things'	Wavering breath control, obvious breaths, cracking to a whisper.	D	WOMAN
3.56	'Lazy cinder smoking'	'Smoky' vocal tone.	E	FIRE
4.27	'Fire moves away, fire moves away, sun/son'		F	FIRE
5.02	'Scrape your knee, it is only skin' 'Cut your hair', 'Happiest woman among all women'	Constantly wavering vocal, uncontrolled diaphragm, obvious shaking breaths, constricting throat (as in the start of tears).	D	WOMAN
5.37	Shallow water, knee deep, 'seagull weeps "so long!"'	Moment of traditional trained vocal control on, 'So long!'	(A)	Transition
6.07	'Out at the edge of town', 'being a woman', blossoms, 'blooming cherry trees'	Minor pentatonic scales, imitation of the sound of the Erhu on violin and in deliberate vocal vibrato on highest note of scale, constant flowing ascending then descending scales.	G	EAST
7.40	'Spray of the waves', 'tide rose'	Repeated oscillating interval of minor third.	H	WATER
7.57	'Sybil sea cow', 'toddle and roll', the shore, sassaphras, Sisyphus		I	WATER
8.14	'Are you mine, my heart?'		(A)	Transition
9.13	'Nowhere to go save up', 'where the light undiluted is weaving', 'bats bringing night in'	Softening vocal tone, breathy, some wavering associated with emotionality.	A	AIR
9.59	Description of dying bird	More strident, throaty.	B	EARTH
10.46	Climbing up to treetops with dying bird	Repeated descending melody in contrary motion with ascending harp part.	C	WATER
11.34	'Life is thundering blissful towards death in a stampede of his fumbling green gentleness'	Soft but occasionally strident vocal tone, breathy, wavering associated with emotionality, erratic breath control.	A	AIR

(Continued)

Table 17.1 (*Continued*)

Time	Lyrical themes	Vocal tone, and melodic gesture	Section	Section descriptor
12.07	'I was all alive'	Increasingly wavering and bodily vocal, obvious breaths, uncontrolled vibrato.	D	WOMAN
12.44	Stoke, flames, 'fire below, fire above and fire within'	Breathy, smoky main vocal with piercing throaty harmony vocal.	E	FIRE
13.14	'Fire moves away, fire moves away sun/son/some'	Softer tone, with soft, higher harmony on 'why would you say'.	F	FIRE
13.48	Woman: cherry stone, cherry pit, cherry tree, 'think of your woman who's gone to the West' Child: 'cold cold cupboard', 'when the bough breaks', 'a little willow cabin to rest on your knee'	Childlike call and response, harsh 'witchy' childish vocal tone most prominent in the 'response' harmonies (in contrast to deep smooth male vocal), prominent accelerando (associated with performance of strophic children's songs).	D	WOMAN / CHILD
15.38	'Fire moves away, fire moves away sun/son'	Soft, breathy, smoky vocal tone.	F	FIRE
16.15	Fire, fire, fire, woman, heights		A	AIR / FIRE / WOMAN

tone becomes largely breathy and mellow in combination with particular melodic and harmonic themes, the section is labelled as 'Air'. Such a relationship can be heard, for example, in the recording at 1.07, where Newsom sings, 'took to mean something run, sing; for alive you shall ever more be'. Compare this to the harsh, nasal, Appalachian vocal tone present at 14.36 when Newsom sings, 'when the bough breaks what will you make for me, a little willow cabin to rest on your knee' (contrasted markedly to the smooth, deep, controlled vocal tone of Bill Callahan) which I have characterised as 'Child'. This comes in the context of the call and response mimicking of the childhood song, 'There's a Hole in my Bucket' and with lyrics echoing other nursery rhymes such as 'Rock-a-Bye Baby'.

The section marked 'Woman' relates more to the vocal gesture than the lyrical content, and here we hear the vocal tone as markedly swayed by excitement or sadness via shallow, erratic breath control and wavering tone. This gives the vocal performance an impulsive and moving quality, where breathing is obvious and there is the wavering and constricting of voice that is associated with the beginning or end of tears. This eruption of the bodily in the voice would be associated with the feminine by theorists such as Julia Kristeva, who characterises the 'semiotic' in opposition to the 'symbolic'. The semiotic (suppressed by the symbolic) resurfaces in language as rhythms, pulses, intonation, the bodily qualities of the voice, the bodily qualities of the word, silences, disruptions, gestures, contradictions, and absences. In becoming-female then, one might expect that an artist would allow a focus on these aspects of language that have been repressed by the symbolic.[33]

Looking at the overall structure of the song as mapped out in the table, we can see the constant fluctuation between sections – particularly between air and earth. This motion or waving between oppositions, represents what Deleuze and Guattari equate with 'becoming-woman' – 'the molecular': a flux between non-fixed identities.

Within the sections labelled 'Water' the melodic structure also illustrates a constant waving motion with insistently ascending and descending passages, sometimes in long sweeping repeatedly descending vocal melodies which are placed in contrary motion to ascending scalar harp accompaniment (for example at 10.45 where Newsom sings, 'then in my hot hand she slumped her sick weight'), and sometimes in repeated single intervals (for example the oscillating movement across a minor third at 7.38 as Newsom sings, 'we felt the spray of the waves we decided to stay 'til the tide rose too far'). The frequent word-use relating to directionality that is persistent throughout the track merely serves to emphasise this sense of perpetual motion.

It is this flux – in the form of what we might call meta-sound-waves – that creates the music of 'becoming-woman'. The complex structure of the song, which constantly waves between identity-based themes, is complemented by Newsom's use of vocal tone and gesture, which flows from timbre to timbre in association with the type of transverse movement she is implying at any point. This constant rise-and-fall, back-and-forth movement between identities is complemented by the wave-like theme of water running throughout *Ys* (which I referred to earlier with relation to becoming-child) and is exemplified in the lyrical image of Sisyphus (who constantly rises and falls).

It is always a form of wave that creates music, and as such, Deleuze and Guattari maintain that music is the product of a flux of transverse 'becomings' across time and identities. In this way I have shown how Newsom's music can be perceived to be created out of this form of flux, and thus demonstrates a 'becoming'. The persistent waving back and forth between images of masculine and feminine identities in 'Only Skin' I would argue, is therefore central to the effect of the song as a whole. I have attempted to show how this is effected via vocal gesture, melodic and harmonic thematic structuring, specific melodic shaping, and in relation to explicit lyrical themes.

To answer the question that opened this chapter, it is clear from this analysis that the 'becoming' that NWA might recommend to us is not always a case of imitating other- or past- cultures (i.e. OWA), but can be a more complex process of traverse and flux between multiple identities.

Newsom's work does not succumb to Reynolds' critique of shallow borrowing from the past, but rather it displays a complex form of strategic anti-essentialism that involves the crossing between numerous multiple identities. This process can cross stable political boundaries and linear conceptions of both time and identity in a way that, far from reinforcing cultural hegemonies, serves to destabilise them. Negative critical reception of this work that casts it as purely 'retro' or 'inauthentic' can thus indicate (and also mask) more complex actions at work within the music and between the music and the modern listener.

Notes

1 Lyrics of a Moondog song titled 'Be a Hobo' (1971). 'Moondog', or Louis Thomas Hardin, was an outsider-artist and a street performer, who was based in New York in the 1940s to 1970s. Dressing as part-Viking, part-Native American, and drawing on cultural influences from European classical music, jazz, and American folk musics, Moondog's work (and persona) was a strong influence on much 'New Weird America' or 'new folk'.

2 David Byrne selected the performers Devendra Banhart, Adem, Coco Rosie, and Vetiver, in his role as curator of this show, which was part of a series of showcases of emerging genres. These artists are all considered by Byrne to be key figures in the new folk movement. It was in my capacity as multi-instrumentalist in Vashti Bunyan's band that I was invited to contribute to the concert.

3 Ben Ratliff, 'Free Spirits in a Groove That's Folky and Tribal', *The New York Times* (05 February 2007). Available at: www.nytimes.com/2007/02/05/arts/music/05drea.html (accessed 28 December 2014).

4 Gilles Deleuze and Felix Guattari, *A Thousand Plateaus: Capitalism and Schizophrenia* (London: Continuum, 2004).

5 David Keenan, 'The Fire Down Below: Welcome to the New Weird America', *The Wire* 234 (August 2003), pp. 33–40.

6 Keenan, 'The Fire Down Below', p. 34. Greil Marcus, 'The Old, Weird America', in Various Artists, *Anthology of American Folk Music* (ed. Harry Smith), Smithsonian Folkways Recordings reissue, 1997. Liner notes, p. 5.

7 The singer-songwriter genre can be seen to be born in earnest, from the *Anthology*-influenced Cambridge musicians who experimented with fusions of traditional forms and wrote their own songs to augment those passed down through generations. See Michael Brocken, *The British Folk Revival 1944–2002* (Farnham: Ashgate, 2003), pp. 84–5. For more on the *Anthology*, see Katherine Skinner, '"Must

Be Born Again": Resurrecting the Anthology of American Folk Music', *Popular Music* 25 (2006), p. 71.

8 Simon Reynolds, *Retromania: Pop Culture's Addiction to its Own Past* (London: Faber and Faber, 2011).

9 'Exoticism' as defined recently by Locke for example, can be understood in terms of borrowing from the past as well as appropriation from non-Western musics of the present. Ralph P. Locke, *Musical Exoticism: Images and Reflections* (Cambridge University Press, 2009).

10 Reynolds, *Retromania*, p. xxxi.

11 Reynolds here uses the terms 'free folk' and 'freak folk' interchangeably. These are both subcategories of new folk, and Reynolds later speaks specifically of Joanna Newsom as a freak folk artist.

12 Reynolds, *Retromania*, p. 404.

13 Allan F. Moore, 'Authenticity as Authentication', *Popular Music* 21 (2002), p. 213.

14 Mark Wilhardt, 'Available Rebels and Folk Authenticities: Michelle Shocked and Billy Bragg', in Iain Peddie (ed.), *The Resisting Muse: Popular Music and Social Protest* (Aldershot: Ashgate, 2006), pp. 30–48. Reynolds also demonstrates a lack of any depth of engagement with the work of Newsom and other new folk artists. For example, he states that there is *zero interest* from freak folk artists in the work of veterans from the urban folk revival era, particularly American ones, which is patently not the case (Reynolds, *Retromania*, p. xxxiv). See Lauren Dukoff, *Family* (San Francisco: Chronicle Books, 2009), a book of documentary photographs which demonstrates this cross-generational collaboration.

15 Cited in Marc Masters, 'Harp of Darkness', *The Wire*, 251 (January 2005), p. 25. Reynolds also frequently points to the rupturing action of the punk movement as being the last genuinely transformative force; Reynolds, *Retromania*, p. 240. Additionally, many new folk artists have

a background in underground punk scenes and John Encarnacao has convincingly identified numerous ways in which new folk continues on a cutting edge punk aesthetic, where this has become commercialised and stereotyped on acceptance in wider rock culture. John Encarnacao, *Punk Aesthetics and New Folk: Way Down the Old Plank Road* (Burlington: Ashgate, 2013).

16 Quoted in Ronald Bogue, *Deleuze on Music Painting and the Arts* (New York: Routledge, 2003), p. 16.

17 Deleuze and Guattari, *A Thousand Plateaus*, p. 327.

18 Gilles Deleuze and Felix Guattari, *What Is Philosophy?* (New York: Columbia University Press, 1994), p. 169.

19 George Lipsitz, *Dangerous Crossroads: Popular Music, Postmodernism and the Poetics of Place* (New York: Verso, 1994); Georgina Born and David Hesmondhalgh, *Western Music and its Others*; Timothy Taylor, *Beyond Exoticism: Western Music and the World* (London: Duke University Press, 2007).

20 Lipsitz, *Dangerous Crossroads*, p. 161; Meghan Winsby makes a similar point with regard to the potential of white women's authentic performance of the blues via shared experiences of oppression; Meghan Winsby, 'Lady Sings The Blues: A Woman's Perspective on Authenticity', in Jesse R. Steinberg and Abrol Fairweather (eds.), *Blues-Philosophy for Everyone: Thinking Deep About Feeling Low* (Hoboken: Wiley-Blackwell, 2012), pp. 155–66.

21 Born and Hesmondhalgh, *Western Music and its Others*, p. 30.

22 Deleuze and Guattari, *A Thousand Plateaus*.

23 Ronald Bogue, *Deleuze on Music Painting and the Arts* (New York: Routledge, 2003), pp. 34–5.

24 Joanna Newsom, *Ys*. Drag City DC303CD, 2006.

25 Gulliver Cragg, 'Ridiculous, Then Sublime', Review of Joanna Newsom, ICA, London. *The Independent* (9 November 2004). Available at: www.independent.co.uk/arts-entertainment/music/reviews/joanna-newsom-ica-london-19329.html (accessed 28 December 2014).

26 E. Williamson, 'Joanna Newsom', *VenusZine* 30(2006), cited in Encarnacao, *Punk Aesthetics*, p. 199.

27 As cited in Eric Davis, 'Nearer the Heart of Things', *Arthur Magazine*, 25 (Winter, 2006). Available at: arthurmag.com/2006/12/23/nearer-the-heart-of-things-erik-davis-on-joanna-newsom-from-arthur-no-25winter-02006/ (accessed 28 December 2014).

28 John Alberti, '"I Have Come Out to Play": Jonathan Richman and the Politics of the Faux Naif', in Kevin J. H. Dettmar and William Richey (eds.), *Reading Rock and Roll: Authenticity, Appropriation, Aesthetics* (New York: Columbia University Press, 1999), p. 175.

29 Alberti, 'I Have Come Out to Play', p. 181.

30 Nicola Dibben, 'Subjectivity and the Construction of Emotion in the Music of Björk', *Music Analysis* 25 (2007), pp. 171–97.

31 Ronald D. Lankford, *Women Singer-Songwriters in Rock: A Populist Rebellion in the 1990s* (Plymouth: Scarecrow Press, 2010), pp. xi–xii, xv.

32 Encarnacao, *Punk Aesthetics*, Table 9.5, p. 219.

33 Julia Kristeva, *La Révolution du Langage Poétique : L'avant-Garde à la Fin du XIXe Siècle, Lautréamont et Mallarmé* (Paris: Éditions du Seuil, 1974).

PART III

Men and women

18 Gender, race, and the ma(s)king of 'Joni Mitchell'

KEVIN FELLEZS

I thought I was black for about three years. I felt like there was a black poet trapped inside me, and ['The Jungle Line'] was about Harlem – the primitive juxtaposed against the Frankenstein of modern industrialization; the wheels turning and the gears grinding and the beboppers with the junky spit running down their trumpets. All of that together with that Burundi tribal thing was perfect. But people just thought it was weird.   (JONI MITCHELL)[1]

Art is short for artificial. So, the art of art is to be as real as you can within this artificial situation. That's what it's all about. That's what art is! In a way, it's a lie to get you to see the truth.   (JONI MITCHELL)[2]

Joni Mitchell has always been weird, even by her own account. Personifying as well as versifying the tensions, contradictions, and affinities between the footloose and the fenced-in that is a main theme running through her work, she has remained one of pop music's enduring enigmas despite over five decades in the music business.[3] By turns, she has described herself or been characterised by others as an idiosyncratic singer-songwriter, the 'consummate hippy chick', 'Annie Hall meets urban cowgirl', the 'babe in bopperland, the novice at the slot machines, the tourist, the hitcher', a poet, a painter, a reluctant yet ambitious superstar.[4] Who, in fact, are we confronting in a 'self-confessional singer-songwriter' who withholds her 'real' name?

Born Roberta Joan Anderson to parents preparing for a son named Robert John on November 7, 1943, the artist better known as Joni Mitchell concocted her name through a combination of youthful pretensions and her first, brief marriage. Eschewing Roberta, Joan became Joni at the age of thirteen because she 'admired the way [her art teacher, Henry Bonli's] last name looked in his painting signatures'.[5] Her marriage in June 1965 to older folk singer, Chuck Mitchell, when she was a twenty-one-year-old unwed mother, lasted less than two years yet she has continued to use Mitchell publicly for more than five decades (further, published accounts indicate she is called 'Joan' by intimates in her everyday life).[6] Her acts of performative alterity reflect a lifelong interest in exploring the possibilities as well as testing the limits of identity claims, performed years before she harboured any concrete thoughts regarding a professional music career.

Her identity play does not stop with name games. In 1976, on her way to a Halloween party thrown by Peter and Betsy Asher, Mitchell was inspired by 'this black guy with a beautiful spirit walking with a bop', who, while walking past her, declared, 'Lookin' good, sister, lookin' good!' Mitchell continues, 'I just felt so good after he said that. *It was as if this spirit went into me*. So I started walking like him'.[7] Stopping at a thrift store on the way to the party, she transformed herself into a figure her party companions assumed was a black pimp. Not simply a 'black man at the party', Claude-Art Nouveau was a 'pimp', a detail that Miles Grier considers in a thoughtful essay on Mitchell's use of black masculinity to earn 'her legitimacy and authority in a rock music ideology in which her previous incarnation, white female folk singer, had rendered her either a naïve traditionalist or an unscrupulous panderer'.[8] Importantly, Grier notes that Mitchell achieves this without having to pay full freight on the price of living in black skin or, I might add, the ease with which she can revert back to whiteness and its privileges, unlike avowed black-skinned models such as Miles Davis.

Entering the party unrecognised, Mitchell was delighted by her ruse and the masked anonymity it offered her, connecting her to the ways the burnt-cork mask of blackface minstrelsy, including its cross-gendered performance practices, allowed the predominantly working-class Irish male performers of the nineteenth century to perform in public in ways otherwise prohibited by bourgeois norms (see Figure 18.1).[9] Despite (mis)representing 'themselves', blackface was a way for black performers to appear on public stages in the nineteenth century. As with those black minstrels, Art Nouveau was a way to be in public without having to expose herself – a veil, to spin Du Bois' metaphor, which allowed Mitchell to hide in plain sight.

This blackface drag persona is said to be so important to Mitchell that her four-volume autobiography (as yet unpublished) purportedly begins with

Figure 18.1. Joni Mitchell as 'Claude' at the Ashers' Halloween party, 1976.

the words, 'I was the only black man at the party'.[10] As a female rock musician, Mitchell's responses to music industry inducements and demands
were meant to defend her status as an artist without attracting pre-emptive
gendered (dis)qualification. Her creative work, which not only fused musical genres but also synthesised music, painting, and verse, is complicated
further by being caught within the contradictions of her (trans)gendered
and (cross)racialist adoptions, co-optations, and appropriations.

Additionally, Mitchell invites interpreting her creative work as antago-
nistic to the notion of an art and popular culture opposition by challenging
the music industry's view of her creative output as pop commodity (while
unapologetically accepting its material rewards) and simultaneously
using jazz, visual art, and poetics as high cultural practices and discourses
through which she argues she is more properly understood. Mitchell admitted to Mary Dickie, 'I'm a fine artist working in the pop arena. I don't pander; I don't consider an audience when I work; I consider the music and the
words themselves, more like a painter'.[11] It is another question, of course,
of whether the literati view her work in the same way they understand the
work of, for example, Bob Dylan (an artist whose public name and persona
reveal little of the 'real' Robert Zimmerman yet has not faced the same criticisms that Mitchell has encountered regarding inauthenticity; indeed, he
is often praised for his chimerical persona), Jean-Michel Basquiat, Laurie
Anderson, or Kara Walker, artists who have straddled a similar popular/
art divide. Mitchell navigated the troubled waters between autonomous
art tendencies and more mundane commercial considerations, plying the
waves between high art aesthetics and a popular music career. Importantly,
Mitchell accomplished this partially on the backs of black bodies, including her own in blackface drag – a figure of shadows and light.

On one hand, Mitchell often speaks somewhat obliviously to the hierarchical nature typically implied between the museum and the nightclub –
as if 'good pop' such as hers easily transcends such demarcations. On the
other hand, Mitchell's categorisation of her music as a 'popular art music'
questions the masculinist orientation of aesthetic values, which valorises
certain values (intellectual rigor, discipline, technical virtuosity) while
concurrently 'feminising' and devaluing others (emotional capacious-
ness, delicate or sensitive sensibilities, intuitive spontaneity).

As noted in the second epigraph to this chapter, Mitchell has used 'art
as artifice' as a means to convey and express emotional and intellectual
truth(s). But she also recognises its double-edged utility. In a 1979 *Rolling
Stone* interview, Mitchell proclaimed,

> People get nervous about that word. Art. They think it's a pretentious word
> from the giddyap. To me, words are only symbols, and the word "art" has
> never lost its vitality. It still has meaning for me. Love lost its meaning to
> me. God lost its meaning to me. But art never lost its meaning. I always
> knew what I meant by art.[12]

Mitchell's self-conscious merging of Romantic ideals of the artist as autonomous creator coupled to Modernist conceptions of art's role in disrupting
social norms begs questions about the relationship between authenticity
and artifice in her work. Placing her internal black junkie poet musician
in a space of art as artifice, as 'the lie that gets us to see the truth', is part of
a larger programme that complicates easy accusations of minstrelsy, but it
does not designate her blackface performances 'innocent' either.

Lady of the Canyon

Mitchell's gender positioning is illustrated by the distance between her
public persona as produced through promotional campaigns and her
efforts to define herself as an artist. Mitchell had the good fortune to have
published songs under her own name for a publishing company in which
she was an owner prior to signing with Reprise, a record label originally
created as a vanity label for Frank Sinatra. Notably, in addition to retaining her publishing rights, she was granted total artistic control, including
choice of album artwork and repertoire, from her debut recording.

She evinced little control over her promotional campaigns, however.
Mitchell's image became deeply imbricated within the somewhat clumsy
yet effective overlapping of the discursive regimes of the counterculture and marketing departments at record labels; in no small part due
to music industry employees often identifying record labels as countercultural in some fashion. An advertisement in *Rolling Stone* for her third
release, *Ladies of the Canyon* (Reprise 1970), can serve as an example of
the intersecting ways in which the music industry and the counterculture
framed Mitchell as an *authentic* 'hippie chick folkie singer-songwriter'.
The ad describes Amy, a twenty-three year old 'quietly beautiful' woman,
as despondent because her recently departed boyfriend is moving quickly
to marry a fellow employee at Jeans West, a well-known denim clothing
store at the time. She begins to feel better when a grocery delivery boy,
Barry, compliments her collage of Van Morrison images. Offering him
a drink of 'Constant Comment [tea] with orange honey mixed in', Barry
offers Amy, in return, to smoke a joint (marijuana cigarette) with her and,
noticing her 'far out' stereo system, the opportunity to listen to a recent
purchase, which just happens to be Joni Mitchell's latest recording, *Ladies
of the Canyon*. As they both became 'quite mellow indeed', Amy begins to
feel better because she hears in Mitchell a sense that 'there was someone
else, even another canyon lady, who really knew' her situation, easing her
sense of painful isolation.[13]

This advertisement articulated the merging of consumerist culture
signifiers (Jeans West, Constant Comment, stereo components) with

countercultural ones (Van Morrison, marijuana, Joni Mitchell) indicating how, by obscuring the fact that this narrative is actually an advertisement for their new commercial release, Reprise's publicity department hoped to market *Ladies of the Canyon* as a recording for young listeners who were similarly inclined to create their own artwork, listen to other countercultural artists (besides Van Morrison, Neil Young plays an important role in the advertisement; not surprisingly, all were Warner Brothers artists at the time), and lead lives wherein 'alternative consumer culture' was not an oxymoron or contradiction.

Reprise ran another advertising campaign in the early 1970s, revealing the role gender and sexuality performed in marketing Mitchell at the time by declaring 'Joni Mitchell Takes Forever', 'Joni Mitchell is 90 Per Cent Virgin', and 'Joni Mitchell Finally Comes Across'. Recalling her career trajectory, Mitchell revealed that

> [b]y the time I learned guitar, the woman with the acoustic guitar was out of vogue; the folk boom was kind of at an end, and folk-rock had become fashionable, *and that was a different look*. We're talking about a business [in which the] *image is, generally speaking, more important than the sound, whether the business would admit it or not.*[14]

While Mitchell recognised the roles gender and image played in the popular music market, she rejected feminism: 'I was never a feminist. I was in argument with them. They were so down on the domestic female, the family, and it was breaking down. And even though my problems were somewhat female, they were of no help to mine'.[15] Reading feminism as anti-men more than pro-women, Mitchell explicitly positioned her musicking as androgynous: 'For a while it was assumed that I was writing women's songs. Then men began to notice that they saw themselves in the songs, too. *A good piece of art should be androgynous.* I'm not a feminist. That's too divisional for me'.[16] Women artists, she asserts, do not necessarily share aesthetic or musical affinities and therefore music should be evaluated without regard to the gender of its producer(s). Yet, her play for 'androgynous art' echoes the liminal space her music occupies – neither female nor male, Mitchell grounds her music in the space spanning genders. In a recent interview, Mitchell responded to a question about her image as 'hippie folk goddess' sardonically:

> Well, we need goddesses but I don't want to be one. Hippie? I liked the fashion show and I liked the rainbow coalition but most of the hippie values were silly to me. Free love? Come on. No, it's a ruse for guys. There's no such thing. Look at the rap I got that was a list of people whose path I crossed. In the Summer of Love, they made me into this 'love bandit'. In the *Summer of Love*! So much for 'free love'! Nobody knows more than me what a ruse that was. That was a thing for guys.[17]

A 'Hollywood's Hot 100' spread in the 3 February 1972 issue of *Rolling Stone* displayed her name surrounded by lips with arrows connecting her to various male musicians, represented with simple boxes framing their names – no lips, alas, for male musicians. The previous year, the magazine listed her as 'Old Lady of the Year for her friendships with David Crosby, Steve Stills, Graham Nash, Neil Young, James Taylor, et al.'. In the 'Hot 100' graphic (see Figure 18.2), David Crosby, James Taylor, and Graham Nash share images of a halved heart in separate connections to Mitchell's lips. Mitchell is one of four females listed on the page though the only one with a special graphic image and given an equivalent 'star billing' position to the male musicians.[18] Reflecting on it over twenty years later, Mitchell admitted, '[*Rolling Stone*'s chart] was a low blow [and] made me aware that the whore/Madonna thing had not been abolished by that experiment'.[19]

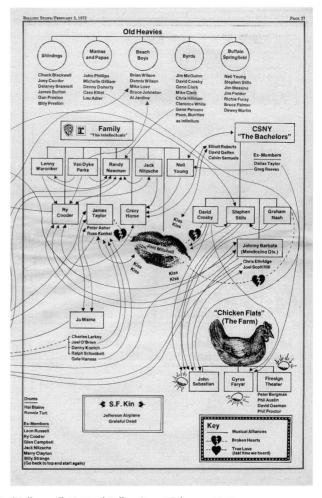

Figure 18.2. 'Hollywood's Hot 100' *Rolling Stone* 3 February, 1972.

Yet, as Mitchell related to Cameron Crowe:

> If I experience any frustration, it's the frustration of being misunderstood. But that's what stardom is – a glamorous misunderstanding ... I like the idea that annually there is a place where I can distribute the art that I have collected for the year. That's the only thing that I feel I want to protect, really. *And that means having a certain amount of commercial success.*[20]

Acknowledging the contradictory pressures and privileges of commercial success, codified within her conflicted triangulation of artistic experimentation, mass popularity, and financial success, Mitchell's artistic and commercial 'independence' is not based on a feminist agenda but on the claims to an art space 'beyond' the considerations of gender. Disavowing 'the lie' of the feminist movement, she argues that even well-meaning assessments that privilege women musicians' expressive qualities miss too much, replying with a question of her own:

> Do you think [the listening public] accepts [emotional expression] from a woman [as opposed to a man]? I don't know. The feedback that I get in my personal life is almost like, 'You wanted it, libertine!' I feel like I'm in the same bind. That's not going to stop me, I'm still going to do it but *I don't feel like I have the luxury [to openly express myself] because of my gender ...* I wouldn't go putting it into a gender bag, at all.[21]

Mitchell's claims for artistic authority rest on a 'gender-blind' – or, to use the term she prefers, androgynous – aesthetic. It is no compliment to be called a 'female songwriter' as it 'implies limitations [which have] always been true of women in the arts', who are seen as 'incapable of really tackling the important issues that men could tackle'.[22] Her programme is not to deny her position but 'in order to create ... a rich character full of human experience [for her songs] ... you have to work with the fodder that you have'.[23] Indeed, songwriting liberated her:

> I never really liked lines, class lines, you know, like social structure lines since childhood, and there were a lot of them that they tried to teach me as a child. 'Don't go there.' 'Why not?' 'Well, because they're not like us.' They try to teach you those lines ... And I ignored them always and proceeded without thinking that I was a male or a female or anything, just that *I knew these people that wrote songs and I was one of them.*[24]

In 1975's *The Hissing of Summer Lawns* (Elektra-Asylum, 1975), Mitchell's supine swimming body appears alongside the albums lyrics and liner notes (see Figure 18.3). By contrast, the liner notes were cryptic: 'This record is a total work conceived graphically, musically, lyrically and accidentally as a whole. The performances were guided by the given compositional structures and the audibly inspired beauty of every player. The whole unfolded like a mystery. It is not my intention to unravel that mystery

Figure 18.3. *The Hissing of Summer Lawns* (Elektra-Asylum, 1975).

for anyone, but rather to offer some additional clues'. Her ambiguity ultimately fails to displace the fundamental ideological role patriarchy plays in
ascertaining musical value because it leaves male privilege untouched and,
arguably, placing this text above her bikinied body plays into gendered differential power relations. Male privilege is simply obscured but not eliminated in 'gender-blind' aesthetic discourse or when masculinity is described
as merely another 'choice' among gender positionings. Simply judging
artistic works against a standard that is embedded within and implicated
by patriarchal Western standards immediately compromises those artists
who fall outside of those norms – as Mitchell does, despite her intention to
produce androgynous art.[25]

Art Nouveau

In (re)naming her 'inner black' character Art Nouveau, Mitchell referenced an early twentieth century art movement that strove to beautify

ordinary, everyday objects. The original Art Nouveau movement sought to aestheticise, in the sense of 'making beautiful', the everyday objects of ordinary life as a way to beautify an increasingly industrialised world.[26] Driven by a similar impulse, Mitchell meant to transform subalternity through an engagement with art. Thus, Mitchell can be seen 'making beautiful' the street hustler, the con, the pimp. Certainly, we can also view it as racist condescension – who is she, to 'make beautiful' those whose racialised bodies encounter material conditions she has never had to even consider, let alone face? As Mitchell claims in the first epigraph to this chapter, she thought she 'was black for about three years ... like there was a black poet trapped inside me'.[27] Similar to Norman Mailer's white Negroes,[28] and as Grier has also noted, Mitchell capitalises on her white privilege in accessing black masculinity in order to transcend, in her case, femaleness, generic limitations, and conventional popular music categorisations.

In this context, one of Mitchell's paintings blatantly signalled her use of black sexuality and, in particular, the black phallus, that play into tropes of black male hypersexuality, pointedly in its symbolic power over white masculinity, which is feminised in its presence, the fount of the white fear of, and desire for, blackness.[29] Mitchell met percussionist Don Alias when he was hired for the *Don Juan's Reckless Daughter* (Elektra-Asylum 1977) sessions, beginning a nearly four-year relationship. Mitchell had painted a number of her partners and she painted one of Alias in his bathrobe. Alias describes it: 'It was me, with my bathrobe open with – bang! like this – a hard-on sticking out'.[30] While she eventually succumbed to his pleas about the painting, countering that it was a 'testament to his sexuality', transforming the penis into a flaccid appendage, she displayed it 'smack-dab in the middle of the living room of the loft' they shared in New York. Perhaps Mitchell was so insistent about this painting because it served as a self-portrait of sorts, recording her self-transformation from blonde waif to black stud, from hippie chick to bebop poet.

Mitchell's black phallic fixation speaks to all the criticisms her recklessness with racialised, sexualised, and gendered performances might deserve but her eagerness to display the picture 'smack-dab in the middle of the living room' reveals a typically confrontational stance. Her imperviousness to any criticism of her appropriation of subordinate identities and cultures was brought into literal sharp relief by her artwork for the cover of *Don Juan's Reckless Daughter* (see Figure 18.4). Against a bare red and blue backdrop suggesting a desolate red landscape and an equally barren blue sky, Mitchell mounted a number of blue-toned black-and-white photographs, cut-and-pasted from a number of different photography sessions. Art Nouveau, leaning

---

Figure 18.4. *Don Juan's Reckless Daughter* (Elektra-Asylum, 1977).

back, sunglasses obscuring his eyes, is physically mimicking what one imagines was the bodily stance of Mitchell's Halloween admirer, slyly speaking the title, 'Don Juan's Reckless Daughter', to us, unambiguously naming her audacity and hinting at his possible role in her adventures. As Gayle Wald asks in an insightful discussion of another 'white Negro', jazz musician Milton 'Mezz' Mezzrow, 'To what degree do individuals exercise volition over racial identity, or how is volition over the terms of identity itself a function of, and a basis for, racial identity and identity-formation … and to what degree is such imagined racial or cultural mobility itself predicated upon a correspondingly rigid and immobile conception of "blackness"?'[31]

Grier answers Wald's question, noting critically, 'Mitchell has shown that her transcendence of racial boundaries, at least, depends upon *others*' upholding their essential functions … Wisdom is of the North and the white race; heart comes from the soulful blacks of the south. Clarity is the gift of the East's intelligent yellow race and introspection from the spiritual red men of the West',[32] locating Mitchell's racial crossing as another instance of white privilege. Yet while dependent on non-white essentialisms, Mitchell has often complicated this relationship. At an infamous 1970 Isle of Wight Festival performance, she was interrupted by an acquaintance of hers named Yogi Joe, who was subsequently taken off the stage by stage hands – an action which prompted boos and yells of disapproval from the audience. In her emotional response to the crowd, Mitchell explicitly disconnected ethnic or racial background from cultural authenticity in her appeal that the audience calm down and let her perform: 'Last Sunday I went to a Hopi ceremonial dance in the desert and there were a lot of people there and there were tourists ... and there were tourists who were getting into it like Indians and there were Indians getting into it like tourists, and I think that you're acting like tourists, man. Give us some respect'.[33] Her delineation between 'tourists' and 'Indians' as 'inauthentic' and 'authentic' experiences drain those categories of conventional, even normative, essentialisms and transposes them in a similar way that her blackface persona, Art Nouveau, highlights the constructedness of blackness and masculinity.

But it also reveals the fragility of artifice in the service of art. The self-awareness of the artifice involved in Mitchell's appeal to her audiences is never adequate to the task of 'saving' her. Mitchell, describing her aesthetic at the time of *Don Juan's Reckless Daughter*, positioned herself outside of musical norms:

> Even though popularly I'm accused more and more of having less and less melody, in fact the opposite is true – there's more melody and so they can't comprehend it anymore. So I'm an oddball, I'm not part of any group anymore but I'm attached in certain ways to all of them, all of the ones that I've come through. I'm not a jazz musician and I'm not a classical musician, but I touch them all![34]

Mitchell's sense of 'non-belonging' from conventional musical categories can be seen in Ariel Swartley's review of *Mingus* for *Rolling Stone* magazine: 'It's been a long time since her songs had much to do with whatever's current in popular music. (She would prefer we call them art-songs.) But then, she doesn't so much come on as an outsider, but as a habitual non-expert. She's the babe in bopperland, the novice at the slot machines, the tourist, the hitcher'.[35]

Mitchell, however, argues that rather than 'habitual non-expert', she is a 'consistent non-belonger', declaring:

> If you want to put me in a group – I tell you, nobody ever puts me in the right group ... I'm not a folk musician ... You know, melodically, folk musicians were playing three-chord changes. *[I had] the desire to write [lyrics] with more content with a desire for more complex melody – [that] was my creative objective. That is not folk music.*[36]

Conclusion

In an interview at the time of the release of the *Mingus* recording, Mitchell cited Mingus' 'If Charlie Parker Was a Gunslinger, There'd Be a Whole Lot of Dead Copycats' as an example of her position on this issue:

> Sometimes I find myself sharing this point of view. He figured you don't settle for anything else but uniqueness. The name of the game to him – and to me – is to become a full individual. I remember a time when I was very flattered if somebody told me that I was as good as Peter, Paul and Mary. Or that I sounded like Judy Collins. Then one day I discovered I didn't want to be a second-rate anything.[37]

As a quick perusal through interviews and reviews reveals, she has also been called self-indulgent, opinionated, over-reaching, and pretentious – often by individuals who find her music appealing (at least some of it, most of the time). As Janet Maslin tersely summed up in her review of *Don Juan's Reckless Daughter*, 'These days, Mitchell appears bent on repudiating her own flair for popular songwriting, and on staking her claim to

Figure 18.5. *Shadows and Light* (Elektra-Asylum, 1980).

the kind of artistry that, when it's real, doesn't need to announce itself so stridently'.[38]

The cover of the live concert recording, *Shadows and Light* (Elektra-Asylum 1980), provides us with a final arresting visual image (see Figure 18.5). Centred on a black background, a double-exposed photographic image places Mitchell and Alias together within the small frame. Mitchell's face is slightly obscured as it merges with Alias' cymbals, his face hidden behind hers. His body is somewhat visible and the result is a jarring image of Mitchell's profile sitting atop a black male body. Is this yet another case of Mitchell's racial and gender masking or passing, another fanciful self-portrait? Undermining Maslin's accusatory dismissal, the image is both revealing and cryptic, unfolding 'like a mystery [though Mitchell has no] intention to unravel that mystery for anyone', a figure of shadows and light.[39]

Notes

1 Vic Garbarini, 'Joni Mitchell Is A Nervy Broad', *Musician* (1983), p. 52.
2 Jian Ghomeshi, 'Joni Mitchell on Q'. *Q with Jian Ghomeshi* Canadian Broadcast Company (2013). Available at: www.cbc.ca/player/AudioMobile/Q/ID/2390721282/ (accessed 1 January 2014).
3 Mitchell is the subject of the chapter, 'Don Juan's Reckless Daughter', in Kevin Fellezs, *Birds of Fire: Jazz, Rock, Funk and the Creation of Fusion* (Durham: Duke University Press, 2011).
4 The first quote is from Laura Campbell, 'Joni Chic', *Sunday Telegraph* (08 February 1998). Available at: jonimitchell.com/library/view.cfm?id=367&from=search (accessed 20 September 2003); the second quote is from Ariel Swartley, 'The Babe in Bopperland and the Great Jazz Composer', *Rolling Stone* (6 September 1979), pp. 53–5.
5 Karen O'Brien, *Joni Mitchell, Shadows and Light: The Definitive Biography* (London: Virgin Books, Ltd., 2002), p. 30.
6 Mitchell gave the baby up for adoption while married. The father of her daughter, Kilauren Gibb, is Brad MacMath.
7 Quoted in Katherine Monk, *Joni: The Creative Odyssey of Joni Mitchell* (Vancouver, Toronto, and Berkeley: Greystone Books, 2012), p. 4, added emphasis.
8 Miles Park Grier, 'The Only Black Man at the Party: Joni Mitchell Enters the Rock Canon', *Genders* 56 (2012), p. 1.
9 For a brilliant analysis of blackface minstrelsy and the continuing resonance of its legacy, see Eric Lott, *Love and Theft: Blackface Minstrelsy and the American Working Class* (Oxford University Press, 1993).
10 Mitchell, as quoted in Monk, *Joni*, p. 1. Sheila Weller, however, has Mitchell saying, 'I was the only black man in the room', in Sheila Weller, *Girls Like Us: Carole King, Joni Mitchell, Carly Simon and the Journey of a Generation* (New York: Washington Square Press, 2008), p. 425.
11 Mary Dickie, 'No Borders Here', *Impact* (1994). Available at: jonimitchell.com/library/view.cfm?id=628, accessed on 22 September 2015 (originally sourced at www.jmdl.clm/articles/print.cfm?id=628, accessed on 22 December 2003).
12 Cameron Crowe, 'Joni Mitchell', in Peter Herbst (ed.), *The Rolling Stone Interviews, 1967–1980: Talking with the Legends of Rock & Roll.* (New York: St. Martin's, 1981), p. 381.
13 All quotes from advertisement in *Rolling Stone*, 14 May 1970, no. 58, p.17.
14 Dickie, 'No Borders Here', added emphasis.
15 Malka Marom, *Joni Mitchell: In Her Own Words, Conversations with Malka Marom* (Toronto: ECW Press, 2014), p. 62.
16 Gerri Hirshey, 'Women Who Rocked the World', *Rolling Stone*, 13 November 1997, p. 64, added emphasis.
17 Ghomeshi, 'Joni Mitchell on Q', n.p.
18 The only other females are Michelle Gilliam (Phillips), Cass Elliot, and Merry Clayton, one of the few non-whites on the page, which speaks to the assumed reader and editorial perspective of the rock-oriented *Rolling Stone* magazine.
19 Barney Hoskyns, 'Our Lady of the Sorrows', *Mojo*, December 1994. Available at: jonimitchell.com/library/view.cfm?id=193 (originally sourced at www.jmdl.com/articles/view.cfm?id=193, accessed 20 September 2003).

20 Crowe, 'Joni Mitchell', 386–7, added emphasis.

21 Bill Flanagan, 'Joni Mitchell Loses Her Cool', *Musician*, December 1985, pp. 70, 72, added emphasis.

22 Lindsay Moon (transcriber), 'Words and Music: Joni Mitchell and Morrissey', quotations from an interview conducted by (Steven) Morrissey of The Smiths, originally published in *Rolling Stone*, 6 March 1997; a fuller version of the interview was subsequently released on a promotional CD by Reprise Records to radio stations to promote her twin releases at the time, *Hits* and *Misses*. The quotations I take are from the promotional CD, transcribed by Lindsay Moon, whose transcription can be accessed at: jonimitchell.com/library/view.cfm?id=678 (originally sourced at www.jmdl.com/articles/view.cfm?id=678, accessed 18 September 2003).

23 Ibid.

24 Ibid.

25 This is the reason I attend to the gendered dynamics circulating within the discursive arena in which Mitchell operated, quite unlike Lloyd Whitesell's decision that 'while I would like to draw attention to the hierarchy of prestige within popular music, according to which women's intellectual production has been historically undervalued, I agree wholeheartedly with the view that Mitchell's accomplishment should stand or fall on its own merits, without respect to gender'; Lloyd Whitesell, *The Music of Joni Mitchell* (New York: Oxford University Press, 2008), p. 5. As noted in the text, this does little to challenge the differential gendered power dynamics that frame aesthetic evaluations which, I argue, Mitchell's work directly opposes and which deserves our critical attention.

26 For a comprehensive analysis of the Art Nouveau movement, see Maly Gerhardus, *Symbolism and Art Nouveau: Sense of Impending Crisis, Refinement of Sensibility, and Life Reborn in Beauty* (Oxford: Phaidon, 1979), English translation by Alan Bailey.

27 Garbarini, 'Joni Mitchell Is A Nervy Broad', p. 52.

28 See Norman Mailer, 'The White Negro: Superficial Reflections on the Hipster', originally published in the summer 1957 issue of the journal, *Dissent*.

29 See David Roediger, *How Race Survived US History: From Settlement and Slavery to the Obama Phenomenon* (New York: Verso, 2008) for a cogent historical analysis of race and racism in the US, particularly in the ways white supremacy maintains its hegemonic status.

30 All quotes this paragraph from Weller, *Girls Like Us*, p. 430, original emphasis.

31 Gayle Wald, 'Mezz Mezzrow and the Voluntary Negro Blues', in Harilaos Stecopoulos and Michael Uebel (eds.), *Race and the Subject of Masculinities* (Durham: Duke University Press, 1997): 116–37, at p. 117.

32 Grier, 'The Only Black Man at the Party', p. 10.

33 Quoted in the film, *Message To Love: The Isle of Wight Festival 1970* (directed and produced by Murray Lerner, Castle Music Pictures, 1997), as well as on the sound recording of the same name (Columbia/Legacy C2K 65058).

34 Anthony Fawcett, *California Rock, California Sound* (Los Angeles, CA: Reed, 1978), pp. 57–8.

35 Swartley, 'The Babe in Bopperland', p. 55.

36 Lindsay Moon (transcriber), 'Joni Mitchell Interview for Canadian Broadcast Company "Magazine"', added emphasis. Moon's transcription is available at: jonimitchell.com/library/view.cfm?id=904 (originally sourced at www.jmdl.com/articles/view.cfm?id=904, accessed 18 September 2003).

37 Crowe, 'Joni Mitchell', p. 388.

38 Janet Maslin, 'Joni Mitchell's Reckless and Shapeless "Daughter"', *Rolling Stone* 9 March 1978, p. 54.

39 Mitchell, liner notes to *The Hissing of Summer Lawns* (Elektra-Asylum 1975).

19 Gender, genre, and diversity at Lilith Fair

JENNIFER TAYLOR

It was the mid-1990s and Sarah McLachlan had been on the road promoting her *Fumbling Towards Ecstasy* (1993) album. At the time, a growing number of female singer-songwriters, such as Tracy Chapman, Jewel, Tori Amos, and Liz Phair, were experiencing significant commercial success. This gave McLachlan an idea. She suggested to her promoters that singer-songwriter Paula Cole be added to the bill as an opening act. Promoters balked and McLachlan quickly realised she had overlooked one crucial yet astoundingly superficial factor: Paula Cole is a woman. For decades, major record labels in the North American popular music industry have operated under the assumption that multiple women on a single concert bill would simply not be a profitable venture.[1] It is assumed audiences would not want to hear more than one female voice in an evening. Rather than accept this logic, McLachlan railed against convention and founded Lilith Fair.

Lilith Fair was an all-female music festival that toured North America during July and August of 1997, 1998, 1999, and 2010.[2] McLachlan was accompanied by a rotating line-up of approximately eleven to twelve female or female-led acts as the festival travelled to various cities, playing between thirty-five and fifty-five shows, depending on the year. The festival played one or two dates in each city it travelled to, the performances beginning in the afternoon and lasting through the evening. Lilith Fair quickly defied the music industry's logic by outselling all other North American touring music festivals of 1997. The commercial success of the inaugural Lilith Fair allowed the festival to expand its roster from just over fifty female performers in 1997 to well over one hundred in subsequent years.

As Lilith Fair began touring in 1997, it was apparent that the festival's 'celebration of women in music', as it was billed, was a celebration of a particular type of woman: white, female, singer-songwriters. In 1997, the lineup consisted of fifty-two acts. Thirty-nine of these acts were singer-songwriters, and thirty-six of these women were white. African American singer-songwriter Tracy Chapman would be the only non-white performer included on the Main Stage of Lilith Fair that year.[3] Various news outlets and music publications picked up on this point, Neva Chonin accusing Lilith Fair of having a 'whitebread, folkie focus'.[4] Academics were also swift to critique the festival's definition of women. Gayle Wald has argued Lilith Fair was a universalising recuperation of white women's music/performance as women's music/performance.[5] Lilith Fair positioned white female singer-songwriters as representative of all women in popular music, much like the women's liberation movement of the 1960s and 1970s situated the experiences of white middle-class women as normative. For other critics, the festival missed an opportunity to challenge traditional gender roles as they relate to music-making by privileging singer-songwriters over rock musicians, an issue that will be interrogated later in this chapter.[6]

These criticisms have merit. Lilith Fair's 'celebration of women in music' was based on a limited definition of female musicians. What is missing from these discussions of Lilith Fair is a detailed consideration of the festival that moves beyond teasing out its shortcomings. Although not the first all-female music festival,[7] Lilith Fair was the first all-female music festival to tour North America, and in 1997 it did outsell the rock-dominated tours that largely excluded female musicians. Robin D.G. Kelly suggests that if the success of radical movements is judged by whether or not they meet all of their goals; 'virtually every radical movement failed because the basic power relations they sought to change remain pretty much intact'.[8] It would be an overstatement to describe Lilith Fair as a radical movement, but Kelley's point resonates nonetheless. Lilith Fair did not set out to revolutionise the music industry and challenge how women are represented in popular music. Lilith Fair was a mainstream event with a commercial agenda and because it did not reject the corporate structure which contained it, the festival straightforwardly engaged the politics of representation in the popular music industry that intersect with gender, race, class, and sexuality. While these politics must be foregrounded, Lilith Fair was more than just its failures.

The focus of this chapter is the Lilith Fairs of 1997, 1998, and 1999. Poor ticket sales plagued the 2010 festival and many of the dates were cancelled. Pinpointing a reason the festival could not be revived with more financial success is difficult. Perhaps it was a reflection of changing times, including an economic recession that stalled sales for North American concert tours in 2009 and 2010.[9] The festival was also founded during a decade when a range of feminist perspectives circulated in the music industry, including the Riot Grrrl movement and The Spice Girls' brand of 'girl power'. Lilith Fair emerged during a cultural moment that celebrated feminist consciousness and women working in popular music, a climate that was not mirrored in 2010. The result was the cancellation of thirteen of the thirty-six scheduled dates. Many artists were forced to withdraw, and therefore the 2010 revival poses too many questions and problems to be considered here.

This chapter will expound upon the problems of representation the Lilith Fairs of 1997, 1998, and 1999 reproduced in order to scrutinise the festival's definition of women; it must be made pervious so as not to cement hegemonic understandings of 'women'. It is only in this context that the scope of the conversation can be broadened to address the following questions. How do criticisms that Lilith Fair privileged singer-songwriters over rock musicians ignore how gender and race intersect with genre in popular music? White female singer-songwriters dominated Lilith Fair, but what does this mean musically? As the first opportunity female musicians had to tour together in a festival setting, how did Lilith Fair engage with 'women's music' and community? Women (specifically white women) have historically been well represented as singer-songwriters, but are often talked about in ways that enlist the notion of 'women's music' and render musical differences irrelevant. Given the visibility of singer-songwriters within Lilith Fair, it may be useful to rethink the festival's musical and extra-musical activities in a way that politicises a tradition often sutured to introspection and confession, deemed appropriate for women, and ghettoised as 'women's music'.

Scrutinising Lilith Fair

Festival organisers were quick to respond to criticisms that highlighted the issue of diversity in the 1997 Lilith Fair lineup. Organisers of the festival released this statement on the Lilith Fair 1998 website: 'In addition to the Main Stage, Lilith Fair will again incorporate Second and Village Stages for both established and emerging artists, with an emphasis being placed on offering an even broader range of musicianship to this year's audience.'[10] While the 1997 Main Stage included only singer-songwriters, a survey of the women who performed on the Main Stage in 1998 shows that while white female singer-songwriters were still present, so too were rappers Missy Elliott and Queen Latifah, rock band Luscious Jackson, and soul singers Me'shell Ndegeocello, and Erykah Badu.

Notably, eighteen of the twenty-four Main Stage performers in 1998 were white and six were African American.[11] This dualism also functioned in Lilith Fair 1999, as twelve of the seventeen Main Stage acts were white, five African American.[12] Although Lilith Fair diversified the music heard on its Main Stage, overall white female singer-songwriters still comprised approximately two-thirds of the lineup, and rock bands were scarce.

Lilith Fair's predominance of singer-songwriters and relative invisibility of rock musicians is not a situation unique to the festival, but a disparity that exists in popular music generally. The reasons behind this have as much to do with rock's hegemonic masculinity as they do with

Table 19.1 *Lilith Fair Main Stage 1998 performers.*

Me'Shell Ndegeocello
Erykah Badu
Missy Elliott
Queen Latifah
Des'Ree
Luscious Jackson
N'Dea Davenport
Diana Krall
Cowboy Junkies
Mary Chapin Carpenter
Emmylou Harris
Indigo Girls
Sarah McLachlan
Meredith Brooks
Natalie Merchant
Shawn Colvin
Liz Phair
Bonnie Raitt
Tracy Bonham
Suzanne Vega
Paula Cole
Chantal Kreviazuk
Joan Osborne
Lisa Loeb

the relationship between singer-songwriters and gender. Since the 1950s, rock has been a male-dominated space that typically only makes room for women as the lyrical objects of desire or resentment, or as devoted fans and groupies.[13] The reasons for this are numerous, and include such issues as performance aesthetics, rock criticism, the electric guitar as phallic symbol, the masculinisation of technology, and gendered barriers to knowledge acquisition and gear. As a result, women tend to be far less visible in rock music than their male counterparts.[14]

In contrast, women have prospered and been heard as singer-songwriters. Gillian Mitchell contends the singer-songwriter tradition was the most visible outcome of the folk revival from the 1960s onwards.[15] By the end of the 1960s, many folk revival performers began drifting towards the mainstream, in large part due to a shift in the cultural climate. The eclecticism and optimism that characterised the revival movement chafed against the conflict, protest, and rallies of the 1960s. As revival-style folk music began mingling with the sounds of mainstream popular music, lyrics gravitated towards introspection and personal experience, and women such as Joan Baez, Joni Mitchell, and Judy Collins, who were prominent in the folk scene, continued to be at the forefront.

Women's visibility as singer-songwriters has much to do with the introspection and confession that characterised the music of singer-songwriters during the 1970s. The image of a lone, self-accompanied female musician with an acoustic instrument, stoically delivering confessional lyrics does not challenge traditional representations of femininity informed by white, middle-class respectability. Because of these associations, women are better-represented as singer-songwriters than rock musicians – at least some women are better-represented.[16] The visibility of Joni Mitchell, Joan Baez, and Judy Collins during the 1960s and 1970s leads Gillian Mitchell to suggest the folk revival's ideals of inclusiveness were actively materialised. A closer look at the women Mitchell cites, however, reveals a different picture. Thirteen of the fifteen women she cites as active in the Greenwich Village and Yorkville folk/singer-songwriter scenes in the 1950s and 1960s are white.[17] Lilith Fair clearly demonstrates white women have continued to thrive as singer-songwriters, while women of other ethnicities are less visible as singer-songwriters in the mainstream, commercial market. Ellie Hisama and bell hooks suggest this is in large part due to the pressure many black female singers experience to cultivate an image of sexual availability, a direct consequence of ideologies that situate black sexuality as more free and liberated than white sexuality. As a result, black women do not always figure into either the racially marked women's music scene or singer-songwriter category, where whiteness and respectability run deep.[18]

Lilith Fair did not create a space in which an equitable representation of female musicians in popular music was materialised, but in this respect the festival is not unique. While the women's music scene was largely comprised of white, lesbian women, the first Ladyfest focused on indie rock, privileging white female musicians.[19] As subsequent Ladyfests were organised internationally, each struggled to create inclusive lineups that acknowledged, 'the contributions of women of colour as fellow organisers, musicians, and volunteers without rendering them as either token participants or invisible.'[20] Arguably, this is where Lilith Fair struggled most. Because the Main Stage remained predominantly white, the majority of women who were not Caucasian were included on the Second and Village Stages.

Lilith Fair concerts were primarily held in amphitheatres, where a single stage was already in place and utilised as the festival's Main Stage. Seating consisted of rows of seats in front of the Main Stage, grass seating behind them. The secondary stages were necessary because the eleven to twelve acts included on each concert bill performed consecutively. While one musician performed on the Village Stage, another could set up on the Second Stage, minimising the time spent setting up and removing equipment. Typically, the only delay between performances occurred during the evening when the Main Stage acts performed. Although a necessity in terms of production, the way in which these stages were positioned established hierarchies. The Second Stage was commonly situated amongst the grass seating, leaving those in the permanent seating with their backs to the Second Stage performers. The Village Stage was often located in the Village, an area not usually visible from the permanent or grass seating, and which included the distractions of booths and vendors. One might argue the musicians included on the secondary stages were lesser known and did not have a large enough audience to warrant billing on the Main Stage. Such thinking only reiterates the hegemony at play in Lilith Fair, and overlooks the choices made that favoured commercially successful white women.

Lilith Fair, genre, and 'women's music'

Lilith Fair's definition of women musicians was narrow and physically inscribed on the festival's landscape. Highlighting these issues is imperative in order not to perpetuate the recuperation of white female musicians as all 'women in music'. To abandon the conversation at this juncture obscures the practices that prompted the founding of Lilith Fair, and implies female singer-songwriters have circumvented resistance in the popular music industry. Male singer-songwriters of the 1970s were intellectually appreciated for their views on politics and cultural events, and artistically revered for sensitive and autobiographical lyrics that ruminated on sex, love, and relationships.[21] Descriptions of singer-songwriters as confessional and introspective proved thorny for female singer-songwriters. When applied to women, these adjectives become sutured to cultural representations of women as emotional and irrational. Joni Mitchell, Carole King, and Carly Simon produced a wealth of music during the 1970s that reflected a changing social climate. As they contemplated sex, relationships, politics, family, and work, female singer-songwriters questioned traditional ideals and considered new perspectives, particularly as they related to white, middle-class women benefiting from the women's liberation movement.[22]

Socially and politically conscious lyrics did not necessarily ensure a serious reception. Stuart Henderson has examined the critical discourse surrounding Joni Mitchell's musical output and found over the course of her first three albums, Mitchell was described using language that evoked youthfulness and naïveté. As her work became increasingly biographical and reflected the complexities of relationships and sex, the discourse was condescending and patronising. In 1970, *Rolling Stone* labelled her the 'Queen of el-Lay' and later published a list of her alleged lovers. Her record label Reprise published advertisements such as 'Joni Mitchell is

90% Virgin' and 'Joni Mitchell Takes Forever'.[23] (See also Chapter 18 in this volume) Mitchell's personal disclosures and reflections were co-opted and used to depoliticise a body of work that clearly reflected the influence of both the sexual revolution and women's liberation movement.[24] Despite this, many female listeners saw themselves in the songs of Mitchell, Simon, and King and became a large market willing to purchase music that spoke to their experiences. By the early 1970s, the percentage of top-selling albums recorded by female artists reached double digits, and in 1974, *Time* magazine concluded 'women's music sells'.[25]

Twenty years later and these issues persisted. Singer-songwriter Fiona Apple gave voice to her personal story of rape in 'Sullen Girl', but a 1997 performance of the song was described as a 'precocious teen-age girl becoming sure of herself' by the *New York Times*.[26] Various incarnations of 'women's music' and 'women in music' also appeared as headlines during the 1990s, touting the success of such singer-songwriters as Jewel, Alanis Morissette, Tracy Chapman, Sarah McLachlan, Fiona Apple, and Liz Phair.[27] In the wake of their commercial success, Warner Elektra Atlantic released five volumes of the compilation album *Women & Songs* between 1997 and 2000.

These headlines and compilation albums perpetuate the notion that music performed by female singer-songwriters is 'women's music'; that music made by female singer-songwriters constitutes a genre simply by virtue of their sex. 'Women's music' is not imbued with musicological meaning, and in fact subsumes musical differences. Female singer-songwriters have been labelled 'women's music' because they are women who write and perform their own music, not because of shared musical characteristics. The assumption that these women constitute a genre on the basis of their sex is what informed the music industry's practice of not billing multiple women on a single concert tour; such a bill would be too similar. 'Women's music' is also frequently conflated with the women's music scene of the 1970s, a lesbian feminist project with the goal of transforming the mainstream music industry through women's music recording and distribution companies, and enacting lesbian feminist politics through women-only events such as the Michigan Womyn's Festival.[28] A distinction between the marginalising label 'women's music' and the women's music scene is often lost, and therefore 'women's music' invokes intimations of queerness whether they are real or imagined.

Lilith Fair provides an opportunity to further a critical dialogue around the relationship between female singer-songwriters and 'women's music'. Norma Coates' discussion of 'women in rock' provides a useful starting point as she argues 'women in rock' separates rock and women; women are only related to rock by being allowed in. The label 'women in music' functions similarly by positioning women only in relation to music, not as a natural part. Coates proposes that rather than rejecting these gendered labels, 'women in rock' may be a politically useful term because it designates rock as contested ground: 'By latching on to the label, women involved with rock can problematise the very practices and conditions which necessitate the use of that term within popular rock discourse'.[29] Whether prohibited from touring with other women or excluded from rock festivals such as Lollapalooza, the need for Lilith Fair was clear. Lilith Fair's 'celebration of women in music' designated music as contested ground and problematised the conditions that prompted the festival by deploying a roster comprised primarily of singer-songwriters to interrupt sexist music industry practices. The favouring of white female singer-songwriters highlighted inequities between female musicians and clearly situated the singer-songwriter tradition as a racially marked category that remains contested ground for those women who are not Caucasian.

The commercial success of Lilith Fair did not simply defy faulty industry logic, but also placed so-called 'women's music' in a highly visible position. From this position, the festival confronted the tendency to depoliticise female singer-songwriters by creating a socially and politically engaged environment. Forming corporate sponsorships with Bioré, Nine West, and Borders Books and Music, Lilith Fair and its sponsors made donations both to local charities and to organisations identified as official Lilith Fair charities, such as RAINN (Rape, Abuse and Incest National Network), Planned Parenthood, and Artists Against Racism.[30] These organisations addressed social, political, and economic issues with particular relevance to women, and were represented in the Lilith Fair Village in the form of booths providing information and education for audience members. Many of the topics and issues that were visible in the Lilith Fair Village were also voiced during festival performances. Alongside introspective performances contemplating love, such as in Jewel's 'Foolish Games', Tracy Chapman spoke to cyclical poverty and unemployment in 'Fast Car', while Suzanne Vega commented on domestic violence in 'Luka'.

Foregrounding a range of sounds and musicians would also problematise the tendency to group female singer-songwriters as 'women's music', and those industry practices that rested on the same notion.[31] In 1997, for instance, Emmylou Harris' folk, country, rock, and bluegrass-inspired material was featured alongside Yungchen Lhamo's unaccompanied vocals that drew on traditional and world music influences. Meredith Brooks' guitar-based, rock-influenced performances also stood in stark contrast to Sarah McLachlan's adult contemporary, piano-accompanied soprano. Singer-songwriters dominated the landscape of Lilith Fair, but the music they performed was varied and diverse and reflected the myriad of musical influences shaping the output of singer-songwriters. As Lilith Fair toured in subsequent years, female singer-songwriters performed alongside the pop vocals of Christina Aguilera, Cibo Matto's indie rock and trip hop sounds, the soul, R&B, funk, and hip-hop-inspired repertoire of Me'shell Ndegeocello, the country sounds of the Dixie Chicks, and the rock, trip hop, down-tempo material of Morcheeba, broadening the festival's definition of 'women in music'.

At the end of each evening, the performers gathered onstage for an all-artist finale reminiscent of the folk revival's emphasis on community and participation. The socially and politically conscious lyrics of Joni Mitchell's 'Big Yellow Taxi' and Marvin Gaye's 'What's Going On' were the preferred choices and provided an audible example of community. Lilith Fair artists assembled informally and shared lead and backing vocal duties. The all-artist finales signalled a collective while defying the traditionally solitary nature of the singer-songwriter and the notion that female musicians should not share concert billing. Both factors have hindered a sense of community and belonging for female musicians in the popular music industry, something Sarah McLachlan hoped Lilith Fair could counter: 'Lilith Fair was created for many reasons … the desire to create a sense of community that I felt was lacking in our industry'.[32]

Community did not refer to a fixed location or group of performers, but was imagined in the sense proposed by Benedict Anderson. As geographical exploration and the evolution of the printing press destabilised religious universalism and exposed the pluralistic nature of the world, people found new ways to define their place in the world, imagining this new place and their relationship to other people. The community Lilith Fair cultivated extended to only a small segment of female musicians working in popular music, but as Hayes argues, the women's music scene did not change the music industry in the ways the scene had hoped, but it did play a valuable role in 'buoying women's spirits in the process of community formation'.[33] Lilith Fair addressed only a handful of issues that some women in popular music face, but it did foster a sense of community that was lacking. Lilith Fair participants shared billing, attended press conferences together, and gathered in spontaneous musical moments backstage. As the festival stopped in various cities across the continent, local female musicians were invited to compete in the Village Stage Talent Search for the opportunity to perform on the Village Stage. Lilith Fair created a space that had not previously existed, even if that space had its limitations.

Conclusion

Lilith Fair's version of 'women in music' was clearly flawed, foregrounding gender and clouding the way in which race, class, and sexuality informs the participation of female musicians in popular music. Lilith Fair signified a cultural moment when some women in popular music were able to openly problematise gendered practices that had existed in the popular music industry for decades. Expanding the conversation beyond Lilith Fair's shortcomings to include a survey of the women and musics that Lilith Fair featured makes it clear it is necessary to interrogate both who was included and what music was heard. To dismiss the festival for its privileging of white singer-songwriters both obscures the racialised history of the singer-songwriter tradition, and overlooks the problematic ways 'women's music' informs the reception of female singer-songwriters. Female singer-songwriters do not constitute a genre of music. Lilith Fair confronted the tendency to depoliticise and ghettoise female singer-songwriters as 'women's music' by highlighting the range of musical traditions informing the output of singer-songwriters in an environment that emphasised social and political awareness. Lilith Fair's landscape was far from the paradise Joni Mitchell laments in 'Big Yellow Taxi', but it should be considered anew as a space from which to explore the intersection of female singer-songwriters, genre, and 'women's music'.

Notes

1 Buffy Childerhose, *From Lilith to Lilith Fair* (Vancouver: Madrigal Press, 1998), p. xi. Similarly, radio programmers have been reluctant to play singles by women back to back, and in the 1960s and 1970s major labels were often unwilling to sign more than one all-female band. For more on this see Mary A. Bufwack and Robert K. Oermann, *Finding Her Voice: Women in Country Music 1800–2000* (Nashville: Vanderbilt University Press/Country Music Foundation Press, 2003); and Gillian G. Gaar, *She's a Rebel: The History of Women in Rock & Roll, Expanded Second Edition* (New York: Seal Press, 2002).
2 McLachlan founded Lilith Fair with the help of Nettwerk Music Group's Dan Fraser and Terry McBride, as well as New York Talent agent Marty Diamond.
3 Alongside Chapman, Tibetan singer-songwriter Yungchen Lhamo and Mexican American singer-songwriter Lhasa were included. African American jazz vocalist Cassandra Wilson was the only other non-white performer included that year.
4 Neva Chonin, 'Lilith Fair', *Rolling Stone* (6 August 1998), p. 34.
5 Gayle Wald, 'Just a Girl? Rock Music, Feminism, and the Cultural Construction of Female Youth', *Signs* 23/3 (Spring 1998), p. 589.
6 For more on this criticism of Lilith Fair see Monique Bourdage, 'A Young Girl's Dream: Examining the Barriers Facing Female

Electric Guitarists', *Journal of the International Association for the Study of Popular Music* 1/1 (2010), available at www.iaspmjournal.net (accessed 5 July 2014); Theodore Gracyk, *I Wanna Be Me: Rock Music and the Politics of Identity* (Philadelphia: Temple University Press, 2001); and Jennifer Witt, 'Feminism Across Generations: The Importance of Youth Culture Lyrics and Performances' *MP: A Feminist Journal Online* 1/6 (June 2007), available at academinist.org/wp-content/uploads/2010/07/witt.pdf (accessed 17 July 2014).
7 The annual Michigan Womyn's Festival was founded in 1976 as an exclusively female festival.
8 Robin D.G. Kelley, *Freedom Dreams*, cited in Eileen M. Hayes, *Songs in Black and Lavender: Race, Sexual Politics, and Women's Music* (Champaign: University of Illinois Press, 2010), p. 5.
9 Ray Waddell, 'The Year in Touring 2013: Beyond the Numbers', *Billboard Magazine*, 13 December 2013, available at: www.billboard.com/articles/columns/chart-beat/5827394/the-year-in-touring-2013-beyond-the-numbers (accessed 24 November 2014).
10 'Plans for Lilith Fair 1998 near completion', formerly at: www.lilithfair.com/lilith98/pressrelease.com (accessed 24 May 2004).
11 'Artists', formerly at: www.lilithfair.com/lilith98/docs/artists/ (accessed 17 May 2004).
12 'Artists', formerly at: www.lilithfair.com/artists/99.html (accessed 8 June 2004).

13 Joanne Gottlieb and Gayle Wald, 'Smells Like Teen Spirit: Riot Grrrls, Revolution and Women in Independent Rock', in Andrew Ross and Tricia Rose (eds.), *Microphone Fiends: Youth Music and Youth Culture* (New York: Routledge, 1994), p. 257.

14 See Mavis Bayton, 'Women and the Electric Guitar', in Sheila Whiteley (ed.), *Sexing the Groove: Popular Music and Gender* (London: Routledge, 1997), pp. 37–49; Mary Ann Clawson, 'When Women Play the Bass: Instrument Specialisation and Gender Interpretation in Alternative Rock Music', *Gender and Society* 13/2 (April 1999), pp. 193–210; Norma Coates, '(R)evolution Now?', in Whiteley, *Sexing the Groove*, pp. 50–64; Gottlieb and Wald, 'Smells Like Teen Spirit', pp. 250–74; Marion Leonard, *Gender in the Music Industry: Rock, Discourse and Girl Power* (Aldershot: Ashgate Publishing, 2007); and Bourdage, 'A Young Girl's Dream'.

15 Gillian Mitchell, *The North American Folk Music Revival: Nation and Identity in the United States and Canada, 1945–1980* (Aldershot: Ashgate, 2007), p. 124.

16 See Sherrie A. Inness, *Disco Divas: Women and Popular Culture in the 1970s* (London: Routledge, 2003); Mitchell, *The North American Folk Music Revival*; and Sheila Whiteley, *Women and Popular Music: Sexuality, Identity, and Subjectivity* (London: Routledge, 2000).

17 Mitchell, *The North American Folk Revival*, p. 124. African American folk singer Odetta and Native American folk singer-songwriter Buffy Sainte-Marie are the only women mentioned who are not Caucasian.

18 See Ellie Hisama, 'Voice, Race, and Sexuality in the music of Joan Armatrading', in Elaine Barkin and Lydia Hamessley (eds.), *Audible Traces: Gender, Identity, and Music* (Zurich: Carciofoli Verlagshaus, 1999), pp. 115–32; and bell hooks, 'Selling Hot Pussy: Representations of Black Female Sexuality in the Cultural Marketplace', in Katie Conboy, Nadia Medina, and Sarah Stanbury (eds.), *Writing on the Body: Female Embodiment and Feminist Theory* (New York: Columbia University Press, 1997), pp. 113–28. The situation for African American women in rock music is not much different. For more on this see Maureen Mahon, *Right to Rock: The Black Rock Coalition and the Cultural Politics of Race* (North Carolina: Duke University Press, 2004).

19 See Hayes, *Songs in Black and Lavender*; and Elizabeth K. Keenan and Sarah Dougher, 'Riot Grrrl, Ladyfest and Rock Camps for Girls', in Julia Downes (ed.), *Women Make Noise: Girl Bands from Motown to the Modern* (Twickenham: Supernova Books, 2012), pp. 259–91. Ladyfests are community-based music and arts festivals. The first Ladyfest was held in Olympia, Washington in 2000.

20 Keenan and Dougher, 'Riot Grrrl, Ladyfest and Rock Camps for Girls', p. 273.

21 Judy Kutulas, '"You Probably Think this Song is About You": 1970s Women's Music from Carole King to the Disco Divas', in *Disco Divas: Women and Popular Culture in the 1970s* (Philadelphia: University of Pennsylvania Press, 2003), pp. 173–4.

22 For more on female singer-songwriters in the 1970s, see Inness, *Disco Divas*; and Whiteley, *Women and Popular Music*.

23 Stuart Henderson, 'All Pink and Clean and Full of Wonder? Gendering "Joni Mitchell" 1966–74', *Left History* 10/2 (Fall 2005), p. 95.

24 For more on this see Judy Kutulas, '"That's the Way I've Always Heard it Should Be": Baby Boomers, 1970s Singer-Songwriters, and Romantic Relationships', *Journal of American History* 97/3 (December 2010), pp. 682–702.

25 Kutulas, 'That's the Way I've Always Heard it Should Be', p. 690.

26 Ann Powers, 'Fiona Apple: Trying Something New, Trying Something Mellow', *New York Times* 25 October 1997. For further examples see Anna Feigenbaum, '"Some Guy Designed this Room I'm Standing In": Marking Gender in Press Coverage of Ani DiFranco', *Popular Music* 25/1 (January 2005), pp. 37–56; and Brenda Johnson-Grau, 'Sweet Nothings: Presentation of Women Musicians in Pop Journalism', in Steve Jones (ed.), *Pop Music and the Press* (Philadelphia: Temple University Press, 2002), pp. 202–18.

27 For example, *Rolling Stone* published several 'Women in Rock' feature articles between 1994 and 1997, *Spin* splashed the headline 'The Girl Issue' across the November 1994 issue, and *Time* magazine proclaimed 'The Gals Take Over' on 21 July 1997.

28 Hayes, *Songs in Black and Lavender*, p. 1.

29 Coates, '(R)evolution Now', p. 62.

30 Singer-songwriter Tori Amos was RAINN's first national spokesperson.

31 Use of the term 'musicians' over 'women' is meant to distinguish between the music made and performed by Lilith Fair participants and the ethnicity of participants.

32 Sarah McLachlan cited in Childerhose, *From Lilith to Lilith Fair*, pp. xiv–xv.

33 Hayes, *Songs in Black and Lavender*, p. 47.

20 Changing openness and tolerance towards LGBTQ singer-songwriters

KATHERINE WILLIAMS

A characteristic feature of the singer-songwriter idiom is the perceived confessional and personal nature of communication from musician to listener. The most commercially successful singer-songwriters use lyrics to describe personal experiences in ways heard by the listener as shared, universal experiences (falling in love, breaking up with a partner, and so on).[1] Allan Moore concurs, describing this validation of listener's life experiences as 'second-person authenticity'.[2] In most cases in the Anglophone pop mainstream, these assumed shared life experiences between creator and receiver reinforce the expected norm of the heterosexual, usually white, Western adult.[3]

Lesbian, gay, bisexual, transgender and queer (LGBTQ) perspectives complicate this universality.[4] In this chapter, I consider how three LGBTQ singer-songwriters have used musical styles, lyrics, and extramusical actions and activities to effect and respond to changing social attitudes and tolerance over the last fifty years.[5]

Elton John

Reginald Kenneth Dwight was born in Pinner, Middlesex (UK) on 25 March 1947. He began playing the piano aged three, and was awarded a Junior Scholarship to the Royal Academy of Music aged eleven. In 1962, he began performing in a local pub, playing the piano to accompany himself singing cover versions of contemporary hits as well as his own songs. Two years later he joined his first band, The Corvettes, which later reformed as Bluesology. Dwight took his stage name from the Bluesology saxophonist Elton Dean and their lead singer Long John Baldry, and legally changed his name to Elton Hercules John in 1967.

In 1967, Elton John answered a 'Talent Wanted' advert in the *New Musical Express*. Ray Williams of the *NME* put him in touch with lyricist Bernie Taupin, and thus began the longstanding songwriting collaboration that persists to this day. (For more biographical detail, and issues of authorship and performance, see Chapter 11.)

The collaboration began remotely, with Taupin sending John completed lyrics to set to music. This can be seen as a modern-day counterpart to the 'Lied singer-songwriters' of the nineteenth-century (see Hamilton and Loges in Chapter 2) – although a distinction may be drawn between the latters' tradition of setting established poetry to music, and John setting lyrics that Taupin had written for the purpose. Despite changing environments – the pair shared bunk beds at John's mother's Pinner home in the 1970s and later flat-shared – they have continued working in series to this day (2015).[6] Due to their longstanding working relationship, the popular persona known as 'Elton John' embodies Taupin's lyrics and John's musical and performing input. Elton John has continued to record prolifically, and at the time of writing has recorded and released over thirty studio albums and four live albums.

In Britain, centuries of intolerance meant that that, by the 1950s, the official mood towards homosexuality was hostile. In 1952, the commissioner of Scotland Yard Sir John Nott-Bower, began to eliminate suspected homosexuals from the British Government.[7] (At the same time in the United States, Senator Joseph McCarthy carried out a federally endorsed witch-hunt against Communists and, on a lesser scale, homosexuals.) In the late 1960s, Elton John became engaged to secretary Linda Woodrow (who is mentioned in the song 'Someone Saved My Life Tonight'), publicly showing his involvement in a relationship that was socially acceptable.[8]

'Your Song' (1970)

One of John and Taupin's best-known collaborations was 'Your Song', released on John's self-titled second album (1970). 'Your Song' was released in the United States in October 1970, as the B-side to 'Take Me to the Pilot', eventually replacing the latter as the A-side due to its popularity; it reached Number 8 in the US charts, and Number 7 in the UK.

'Your Song' has a contrasting verse-chorus structure, where each chorus is preceded by two iterations of a four-line verse with changing text.[9] The song has an acoustic soundworld that builds throughout. The lyrics of the chorus are self-referential, as John sings about writing the song for his loved one.

> And you can tell everybody this is your song
> It may be quite simple but now that it's done
> I hope you don't mind
> I hope you don't mind that I put down in words …
> How wonderful life is while you're in the world

The lyrics are gender neutral; the addressee is always referred to in the second person ('you', 'your'). The ambiguity allowed by these terms enables listeners to create their own interpretation: heterosexual listeners will interpret this as a straight relationship, while LGBTQ listeners will hear representations of their own sexual preference. John's use of unmarked gender terminology leaves room for listener interpretations.[10] However, given the societal and officially encouraged norm of heterosexuality in 1970s Britain, 'Your Song' can be assumed to be documenting such a relationship – ambiguously creating Moore's second-person authenticity by validating the emotions and experience of mainstream culture as understood by the listener. The ongoing resonances of these emotions are reinforced by the song's popularity, and the numerous cover versions by singers of both sexes over the decades.[11]

Despite the fact that at this point John's biography was carefully managed to keep his sexuality ambiguous, the low and expressive vocal quality and unobtrusive recording techniques used in 'Your Song' begin to subvert traditional notions of masculinity. In subsequent decades, traditional notions of masculinity as labour were reversed by vocal and recording qualities that suggest directness and intimacy, as Ian Biddle notes.[12]

Homosexual acts between men (two consenting adults, in private) were decriminalised in England and Wales in 1967. In 1976, Elton John publicly came out as bisexual in an article in the music magazine *Rolling Stone*, claiming that he had not felt the need to acknowledge it openly before.[13]

In the same interview, Elton John explained that his first sexual relationships were with women. He was married to record producer Renate Blauel from 1984–8 – a relationship that could be seen publicly as conforming to the socially accepted heterosexual norm, but privately reinforced his bisexuality. However, by 1992 John informed *Rolling Stone* that he was 'comfortable being gay', explaining that he had settled with a male partner and felt happy and optimistic about the future.[14]

In October 1993, John entered a relationship with Canadian/British film producer David Furnish. The couple was one of the first in the UK to form a civil partnership when the Civil Partnership Act came into force on 21 December 2005. They have since adopted two children, Zachary Jackson Furnish-John (b. 25 December 2010) and Elijah Joseph Daniel Furnish-John (b. 11 January 2013). Furnish has since stated their intention to marry, since same-sex marriage was legalised in the UK on 29 March 2014:

> Elton and I will marry … When it was announced that gay couples were able to obtain a civil partnership, Elton and I did so on the day it came into law. As something of a showman, [Elton] is aware that whatever he says and does, people will sit up and take notice. So what better way to celebrate that historic moment in time. Our big day made the news, it was all over the Internet within minutes of happening and front page news the next day.[15]

A significant change can be seen in societal attitudes towards homosexuality in the forty-eight years since John's public career began. In the 1970s, he was reticent about his private life, but by 2015, he and Furnish felt able to use their fame to bring general attention to some of the social and civil restrictions faced by same-sex partners.

k. d. lang

Kathryn Dawn Lang was born in Edmonton, Alberta, Canada on 2 November 1961. She started singing at the age of five, and became fascinated with the life and music of country singer Patsy Cline while attending the Red Deer Community College. At the same time, Lang expressed her creativity in a series of performance art shows. She also formed a tribute band (the reclines), and adopted the stage name k. d. lang.

Their debut album, *A Truly Western Experience*, received positive reviews and national attention on its release in 1984. k. d. lang and the reclines released two further albums in the country style, *Absolute Torch and Twang* (1987) and *Angel with a Lariat* (1989). Richard Middleton comments on the rigid conventional gender politics of the country music scene, suggesting that lang's complex gender identity began with *Absolute Torch and Twang*:

> Here is some form of female masculinity … applied to country (including covers of songs 'belonging' to men), yet also performing torch songs (a genre traditionally associated with submissive, suffering femininity) … Her bluesy articulations come from torch song, but are smoothly integrated into a full range of country vocal conventions (growl, falsetto, catch in the throat) so that the overall impression, particularly in light of her powerful, gleaming timbres produced through a wide range of registers, is one of (phallic?) control.[16]

lang released her first solo album in 1988. As well as overt stylistic traits such as yodelling, steel guitars and the lush strings of the Nashville sound, *Shadowland* was linked to country and western music through producer Owen Bradley (who had produced *Patsy Cline*, 1957; *Patsy Cline Showcase*, 1961; and *Sentimentally Yours*, 1962). The performing persona that she developed was androgynous and grungy: she favoured short haircuts, and low-maintenance outfits such as jeans, check shirts, and dungarees. Again, lang used the strictures of country music and the associated cowboy scene to develop and nuance her gender identity: as Corey Johnson explains, at that time sartorial decisions based on cowboys were used by the LGBTQ community to satirise aggressive heteronormative masculinity, and to inform drag costumes.[17]

In 1990, lang recorded Cole Porter's 'So in Love' for *Red Hot & Blue*, a compilation album to benefit AIDS research and relief.[18] Themes of non-heteronormative sexualities pervade her cover version: although he married Linda in 1919, Porter is described variously as bisexual and homosexual.[19] In the accompanying music video lang wears androgynous dungarees while doing a woman's laundry. She buries her face in a negligee, lending weight to the rumours that were circulating of her lesbianism.

Her next solo album, *Ingénue*, was released in March 1992, and represented a change in musical direction from her previous work. Lang and her musical collaborator Ben Mink drew influences from many styles, including '1940s movie musicals, spiritual hymns, Russian folk music, American jazz, Joni Mitchell-like tunings and harmonies, Indian folk music and more'.[20]

'Constant Craving' (1992)

'Constant Craving', featured last on *Ingénue*, is lang's most famous song. It was the first single released from the album, and charted at number 38 on the Billboard 100 and number 2 on the Adult Contemporary Chart. The following year, k. d. lang won multiple awards with the song, including Grammy Award for Best Female Pop Vocal, and the MTV award for Best Female Video.

The soundworld is established with a gentle rock beat, strummed acoustic guitar and melancholy harmonica, and is later enriched by a vibraphone counter melody. The minimal lyrical content depicts the relentless yearning of the song title. lang sings two verses, alternating with a chorus, with further repetitions of the chorus to finish. Her solo vocal is supported by a backing choir that echos her lyrics.

In contrast to 'Your Song', the lyrics of 'Constant Craving' do not refer to a loved one. Instead, they document and reflect upon the emotion of yearning. lang's biographer Victoria Starr states that this 'tormented splendor' applies to the whole album, and refers to an unrequited love experience – exhibiting second-person authenticity.[21] However, as explained below, in combination with lang's biography, the lyrics create something more akin to *first*-person authenticity – where the listener believes that the musician is expressing their own lived experiences, in a direct and unmediated format.[22]

lang publicly came out as lesbian in a June 1992 issue of LGBTQ magazine *The Advocate*, and has actively championed gay rights causes since.[23] Taken in combination with her personal life, the gender-neutral pronouns of the songs and the lyrical descriptions of love, yearning, and loss, take on a different meaning.

lang's plea in the fourth song on the same album, 'Save Me', can be understood as an appeal to either gender, as she sings to an unnamed addressee: 'Save me from you … Pave me/The way to you'. However, a closer reading of the album shows playfulness with gender construction and ambiguity. The song's video depicts lang in an exaggeratedly feminine manner, surrounded by bright colours and bubbles. This stands in contrast to the persona that lang has chosen to adopt: a brief glance at her album covers, media presence, and performances show that she prefers androgynous hairstyles and clothing. The caricatured account of femininity lang creates on the 'Save Me' video perhaps satirises the fact that the English-language Canadian magazine *Chatelaine* once chose her as its 'Woman of the Year'.

The following year, lang famously appeared in a cover photo and photo spread in the mainstream magazine *Vanity Fair*. The cover of the August 1993 issue featured a seated lang being shaved by supermodel Cindy Crawford. In contrast to the singer's stereotypically masculine pinstripe suit and waistcoat, Crawford is dressed in a revealing swimsuit and high heels. As anthropologist Joyce D. Hammond explains, the photo shoot (conceived by lang, photographed by Herb Ritts, and willingly participated in by Crawford), challenges typical gender constructions by subverting both expected power dynamics in heterosexual relationships and those of lesbian and homosexual couples.[24] The photo caricatured the stereotypical lesbian combination of butch and femme, by placing lang (dressed as a man, complete with shaving foam and the masculine stance of a crossed leg balanced on the opposite knee) in the submissive role of being tended to by an overly feminised and hypersexualised female supermodel in a dominant standing position, complete with careful makeup and hair. Although she claims that she came out publicly for personal, rather than political reasons, lang's public profile, her 1992 article in *The Advocate*, and her photo shoot for *Vanity Fair* all contributed to a mainstreaming of lesbianism. Neil Miller concludes: 'Nineteen ninety-three was the year of the lesbian. The print media discovered lesbians … Television discovered lesbians'.[25]

A subversion of traditional gender roles can also be seen in lang's 1997 album *Drag*. The album is a covers album, with songs (such as 'Don't Smoke in Bed', and 'My Last Cigarette', 'The Old Addiction', and 'Love is Like a Cigarette') supporting the album's ostensible theme of smoking. However, the term 'drag' has been used in British slang since the late 1800s to refer to clothing associated with one gender but worn by the other. The term 'drag queen' is used to identify (often homosexual) men in women's clothing, while 'drag kings' refers to women in mens' garb. The album art for *Drag* features a close-up portrait of a carefully made-up lang in a mens' formal black suit, with a white shirt and burgundy cravat, thereby reinforcing the gender ambiguity of the album but reversing the expected gender roles of drag queens.

On 11 November 2009, lang entered into a domestic partnership with Jamie Price, who she had met in 2003. They separated in September 2012, and lang filed for a dissolution of the marriage. Since coming out in 1992, lang has used her position as a famous musician to raise public awareness of lesbians.

Rufus Wainwright

Rufus Wainwright was born on 22 July 1973 in Rhinebeck, New York, to parents Kate McGarrigle and Loudon Wainwright III, both of whom were successful and well-known folk singers. They divorced when he was three, and he spent much of his childhood in Kate's home town of Montreal, Canada.

Societal tolerance of non-heteronormative sexualities was growing: in June 1969 police raids on the Stonewall Inn in Greenwich Village, New York City had prompted members of the gay community to violent demonstrations, physically showing their dissatisfaction with the status quo; while in the year of Wainwright's birth, the American Psychological Association removed homosexuality from its diagnostic manual (suggesting it had been considered an illness until that point). This social tolerance was tempered by a fear and lack of knowledge about the growing AIDS epidemic at the time, which public misconception frequently linked to homosexual activity.

Wainwright accepted his own homosexuality early on, stating in a 2009 documentary: 'I knew when I was very young, when I was about fourteen, that I was gay.'[26] As a teen, he spent many of his evenings sneaking out to gay bars, where he was 'a Lolita-esque character, a fourteen-year-old boy who looked no older than his years, leaning at the bar, craving attention from older men'.[27] In the summer of 1988, he engaged in similar behaviour while visiting Loudon in London, and suffered a violent sexual assault while walking in Hyde Park with a man he met at a bar. He subsequently entered a period of reclusivity and sexual abstinence. At around this time, Loudon and Kate sent him to finish his high school education at Millbrook, a private boarding school in upstate New York. Wainwright therefore went through initial experiences of his sexuality without the support of his family and friends, choosing to come out to his parents a few years later.

After beginning and dropping out of a music degree at McGill University in Canada, Wainwright returned to Montreal in 1991 and began building a repertoire of original material, performing frequently on the cabaret and club circuit. Like Elton John, his instrument of choice was the piano – but Wainwright differed in that he wrote the music and lyrics to his songs.[28] Wainwright has an enormous vocal range, which he utilised more in performance and recordings as his career progressed. He is able to slide smoothly through a warm tenor, chest alto voice, head voice into falsetto, and a true falsetto, enabling a range of vocalised gendered personas.[29] Wainwright has candidly displayed a queerness in his performance and recordings, which is supported by his developing performing person, his lyrical content, and his vocal qualities.[30]

The second song on *Rufus Wainwright*, his 1998 debut album, 'Danny Boy', describes his infatuation with a straight man named Danny. Apart from the fact that the lyrics are sung by a man, they could refer to a heterosexual relationship. Unlike either John or lang before him, though, Wainwright names his addressee, singing: 'You broke my heart, Danny Boy/Not your fault, Danny Boy'. Other songs on the album deal with his sexuality more implicitly: 'Every kind of love, or at least my kind of love/Must be an imaginary love to start with' (from the closing song 'Imaginary Love').

The early 1990s saw a wave of critical and cultural theory that explored queerness as an alternative to binaries apparent in previous society and scholarship. Rufus Wainwright associates his awareness of his homosexuality with discovering opera in his teens, a connection also drawn by influential literary figures such as Wayne Koestenbaum and Sam Abel.[31] 'New musicology' echoed conventions of literary criticism by introducing interdisciplinary approaches, focusing on the cultural study and criticism of music. In *Queering the Pitch: The New Lesbian and Gay Musicology* (1994), a collection of 'mostly gay and lesbian scholars' aimed to challenge binary tactics and positivistic approaches to previous musicological scholarship, claiming that they found it less interesting to 'out' composers and musicians (such as Franz Schubert, explained in more detail below and on accompanying website) than to reveal the homophobia present in previous scholarship and readings.[32] By the mid-1990s, cultural awareness of LGBTQ music-making and appreciation went outside the media 'year of the lesbian' cited by Miller: it had become an academic discipline.

'Pretty Things' (2003)

In 'Pretty Things', the fifth song on Wainwright's 2003 album *Want One*, he subtly expresses his sexuality. The assumed autobiography of his songs means that Moore's authenticity is reinforced, but rather than validating listeners' experiences (second-person authenticity), here the listener is encouraged to believe that Wainwright is sharing his own experiences (first-person authenticity).[33] In line with the singer-songwriter idiom, his songs are perceived as more truthful because they appear unmediated.

From a compositional/songwriting perspective, the song pays homage to the nineteenth-century Austrian composer Franz Schubert (to whom Wainwright had already paid tribute to with the line 'Schubert bust my brain' in the aforementioned 'Imaginary Love'). Wainwright scored 'Pretty Things' for solo piano and voice, and marketed the song as a twenty-first century Lied (piano and vocal song, usually written for pre-existing text in the German vernacular, made famous by Schubert).[34]

The lines 'Pretty Things, so what if I like pretty things/Pretty lies, so what if I like pretty lies' give an insight into the tastes that Wainwright chooses to share. He continues by lamenting his alienation from society and his loved one: 'From where you are/To where I am now'. It is but a small step to unite the two lyrical features: a man who is attracted to the typically feminine 'pretty things' may be ostracised and alienated from society. In his 2010 analysis of 'Pretty Things', Kevin C. Schwandt makes a connection between the isolating and ostracising device of Wainwright's (assumed autobiographical) protagonist's taste for pretty things (going against the masculine norm), and the standard Western musicological reading of Schubert as Beethoven's feminine Other. Schwandt suggests that by associating himself and his music with Schubert, Wainwright implicitly aligns himself with these domestic and feminine readings.[35] Schwandt implies that Wainwright was aware of the academic controversy that surrounded Maynard Solomon's 'outing' of Schubert in 1989, and the longstanding tradition of homosexual oppression associated with Schubert's life and music, and deliberately associated himself with it, in order to align himself with historic homosexuals.[36] The lyrics are gender neutral, but Wainwright's male voice and evocation of 'pretty things' make his subject position clear.

Wainwright maintained and developed his autobiographical subject matter and flamboyant performing persona, and made his sexuality more explicit in later songs and performances. While touring the *Want* albums, Wainwright routinely performed the overtly political 'Gay Messiah' (*Want Two*, 2004) dressed in heavenly garb, descending from the sky on a crucifix. The lyrics evoke a Gay Messiah, sent to save homosexuals the world around, and entangle religious stories with themes of salvation and sexual practices.

The song opens with a suggestion that listeners pray for salvation, before announcing that the gay messiah is coming (as in arriving). This final word is transformed at the end of the second stanza, when Wainwright claims to be 'baptised in cum' (the lyrics in the *Want Two* liner booklet use the spelling commonly associated with the male ejaculate). Wainwright continues twisting and conjoining sexual and biblical imagery, referencing the story of John the Baptist by suggesting that 'someone will demand my head'. Again, he turns it back to a sexual metaphor, with a word play on 'giving head', a common expression for oral sex. 'I will kneel down', he sings, 'and give it to them looking down'.

The lyrics to 'Gay Messiah' are an extreme example of sexual openness from a member of the LGBTQ community. Lake remarks upon Wainwright's 'gleeful' smile at some of the more sexually explicit lines, when he first performed it on the national talk show *Jimmy Kimmel Live* in March 2004, and explains how the song also served as an expression of Wainwright's opposition to the increasingly right-wing, conservative and intolerant government under George W. Bush in the post-9/11 years. By intertwining lyrical references to biblical stories, Wainwright implicitly shows his dissatisfaction with the intolerance shown by fundamentalist Christians.[37]

In 2007, Wainwright moved to Berlin to work on and record *Release the Stars*. During this period Rufus Wainwright met Jörn Weisbrodt, who at the time was working as Head of Special Projects at the Berlin Opera. The couple got engaged in late 2010, and Lorca Cohen (daughter of Leonard) gave birth to a daughter fathered by Rufus, in February 2011. Wainwright explains that when he met Weisbrodt, he began openly campaigning for legalised gay marriage in the United States. He explicitly connects this to the social climate in North America in the 2010s:

> I am very aware of living in the US, of the conundrum that you can't marry your gay partner and give him citizenship. He has to apply for a green card and he may or may not get accepted, which is annoying when you're in a committed relationship. If we were straight, we could get married and he'd get his American passport and it would make a lot of sense.[38]

Until recently, in the United States of America, the legality of marriage regulation was enforced by state legislature. New York legalised same-sex marriage in November 2011, before the 2012 election. On 24 July 2012, Rufus and Jörn married at their family home in Long Island, New York State. On the 26 June 2015, the US Supreme Court ruled that same-sex marriage be legalised in all fifty states.

Conclusion

The life and work of selected LGBTQ singer-songwriters has provided a useful lens through which to view the increasing social tolerance of sexualities and perspectives outside the heterosexual norm. A major upswing in social awareness occurred in the early 1990s, and since then John, lang and Wainwright have actively used their fame to promote LGBTQ causes and same-sex marriage. In addition, each of the case studies under consideration has supported activism in other areas: in 1992 Elton John founded an eponymous AIDS foundation to support research and work into HIV and related illnesses, and in 1997 reworked and reissued the 1973 tribute to Marilyn Monroe 'Candle in the Wind' in memory of Princess Diana, which raised millions of pounds for the Diana, Princess of Wales Memorial Fund to support humanitarian causes in the UK and worldwide. k d. lang's popstar persona lent heft to the PETA 'Meat Stinks' campaign in 1990, and Rufus Wainwright began promoting the environmentally conscious Blackoutsabbath in 2008.[39]

LGBTQ singer-songwriters have become more open in expressing their subject position, both as cause and effect of changing attitudes and increasing social tolerance. As a result, more perspectives on life and love are heard and understood by fans.

Notes

1 Sheila Davis, *The Craft of Lyric Writing* (London/New York/Sydney, Omnibus Press, 1985), p. 3.

2 Allan F. Moore, 'Authenticity as Authentication', *Popular Music* 21/2 (2002), p. 220. He extends his listener-centric perspective on popular song in his monograph *Song Means: Analysing and Interpreting Recorded Popular Song* (Farnham: Ashgate, 2012).

3 Here I must acknowledge my own position as a white British heterosexual woman. I have attempted to maintain neutrality in the issues and laws I discuss, but my cultural position is undoubtedly affected by the environment in which I grew up.

4 Although many of these terms (LGBTQ) historically carried stigma and negative social connotations, since the 1980s they have been reclaimed as unifying and empowering terminology for people who do not feel part of the heterosexual norm.

5 These case studies are drawn from the white Anglophone world. I acknowledge that the issue of ethnicity when exploring otherness in pop is a complex and multilayered one. Space prevents me from expanding my discussion to include it here, but Kevin Fellezs' Joni Mitchell chapter in this volume offers one racial reading to nuance the white female singer-songwriter trope (in Chapter 18).

6 Rumours abounded about John's close relationship with Bernie Taupin, but he always strenuously denied any romantic involvement, and has been keen to emphasise the fact that it was a close *working* relationship. Cliff Jahr, 'It's Lonely at the Top', *Rolling Stone* 223 (1976), p. 17.

7 The British mistrust of homosexuals at this era is portrayed in the 2014 film *The Imitation Game* (dir. Morten Tyldum), where homosexual computer scientist Alan Turing is lauded for his codebreaking efforts in WWII, but lambasted by the government in the years that follow for his personal life. In 1952 police arrested him for gross indecency. Turing accepted oestregen 'treatment' for his homosexuality, but died from self-inflicted cyanide poisoning in 1954.

8 The relationship ended in the summer of 1970, just months before the planned nuptials.

9 John Covach and Andy Flory provide a taxonomy of popular song forms in *What's That Sound: An Introduction to Rock and Its History*, 3rd Edition (New York/London: W. W. Norton and Company, 2012), pp. 10–16.

10 Bethany Lowe deconstructs the use of 'marked' and 'unmarked' gender terminology affecting listener assumptions in 'On the Relationship Between Analysis and Performance', *Indiana Theory Review* vol. 24 (Spring–Fall 2003): p. 82. Her use of the term adopts and manipulates Douglas Hofstadter's theory in 'Changes in Default Words and Images, Engendered by Rising Consciousness' in *Metamagical Themas: Questing for the Essence of Mind and Pattern* (London: Penguin, 1986).

11 A demo version of 'Your Song' was included in John's 1990 box set *To Be Continued…*, and it was inducted into the Grammy Hall of Fame in 1998. Duet performances include Billy Joel in 2001, Alessandro Safina for Comic Relief in 2002, and Lady Gaga in 2010, and there are cover versions by artists such as Al Jarreau in 1976, Rod Steward in 1991, Ewan MacGregor in the 2001 film *Moulin Rouge*, Celine Dion in 2008, Harry Connick, Jr in 2009, and Ellie Goulding in 2010.

12 Ian Biddle, 'The Singsong of "Undead Labour": Gender, Nostalgia, and the Vocal

Fantasy of Intimacy in the "New" Male Singer-Songwriter', in Freya Jarman-Ivens (ed.), *Oh Boy!: Masculinities and Popular Music* (New York: Routledge, 2007), p. 126.

13 Cliff Jahr. 'The Rebirth of Elton John', *Rolling Stone* 626 (1992), p. 17.

14 Philip Norman, *Rolling Stone* no. 626 (19 March 1992), p. 23.

15 David Furnish, quoted in Nick Levine 'Elton John and David Furnish reveal plans to marry', *Attitude* (2014). Available at attitude.co.uk/elton-john-david-furnish-reveal-plans-marry/ (accessed 9 December 2014). The couple converted their civil partnership to marriage on 21 December 2014: www.bbc.co.uk/news/entertainment-arts-30568634 (accessed 10 February 2015).

16 Richard Middleton, 'Mum's the Word: Men's Singing and Maternal Law', in *Oh Boy!*, pp. 116–17.

17 Corey Johnson, '"Don't Call Him A Cowboy": Masculinity, Cowboy Drag, and a Costume Change', *Journal of Leisure Research* 40/3 (2008), pp. 385–403.

18 This cover of 'So in Love' is also included on her 2010 greatest hits album *Recollection*. In 1999 she recorded 'Fada Hilario' (sung in Portuguese) for the Red Hot AIDS benefit album *Ondo Sonora: Red Hot & Lisbon*.

19 J. X. Bell, 'Cole Porter Biography', available at: www.coleporter.org/bio.html (accessed 3 July 2015); Stephen Citron, *Noel &Cole: the Sophisticates* (Milwaukee: Hal Leonard Corporation, 2005), 142.

20 Paul Zollo, *Songwriters on Songwriting* (New York: Da Capo, 1997), p. 605.

21 Victoria Starr, *k. d. lang: All You Get Is Me* (Toronto: Random House, 1994), p. 191; Moore, 'Authenticity as Authentication', p. 220.

22 Ibid., p. 213.

23 Brendon Lemon, 'k. d. lang: a quiet life', *The Advocate* (16 June 1992).

24 Joyce D. Hammond, 'Making a Spectacle of Herself: Lesbian Visibility and k. d. lang on Vanity Fair's Cover', *Journal of Lesbian Studies* 1/3–4 (1997), p. 11.

25 Neil Miller, *Out of the Past: Gay and Lesbian History from 1869 to the Present* (New York: Alyson, 1995), p. 551. The first lesbian kiss on US national television had aired in 1991, between the characters Abby Perkins and C. J. Lamb in an episode of *LA Law*.

26 *Prima Donna: The Story of an Opera* (dir. George Scott, 2009), at 10:08.

27 Kirk Lake, *There Will Be Rainbows: A Biography of Rufus Wainwright* (London: Orion Books, 2009), p. 52.

28 Kevin C. Schwandt makes a compelling case for the 'queerness' of the piano in Chapter 4 of his PhD dissertation '"Schubert Bust My Brain": Musical Cyborgs and Wainwright's Queering of Art Song', in '"Oh What A World": Queer Masculinities, the Musical Construction of a Reparative Cultural Historiography, and the Music of Rufus Wainwright' (PhD Thesis: University of Minnesota, 2010), pp. 151–204.

29 Shana Goldin-Perschbacher comments on a similar vocal ability in Wainwright's contemporary Jeff Buckley, explaining that Buckley could shift between 'multiple and changing gender identifications'. While Wainwright almost always sings his own songs in the first person, occasional pronoun shifts ('I was just a girl then' in *Want Two's* 'The Art Teacher') enable some play between genders. Buckley exploited this still further by singing both male and female covers in their original ranges, with their original pronouns. '"Not With You But of You": "Unbearable Intimacy" and Jeff Buckley's Transgendered Vocality', in Jarman-Ivens, *Oh Boy!*, p. 214.

30 Stan Hawkins locates Wainwright's voice as a knowing musical representation of camp in 'Chapter 5: Talking Blah Blah Blah: Camp into Queer', in Stan Hawkins, *Queerness in Pop Music: Aesthetics, Gender Norms, and Temporality* (New York: Routledge: 2015).

31 Wayne Koestenbaum, *The Queen's Throat: Opera, Homosexuality and the Mystery of Desire* (London: Penguin Books, 1993), and Sam Abel, *Opera in the Flesh: Sexuality in Operatic Performance* (Boulder: Colorado, 1996).

32 Philip Brett, Elizabeth Wood, Gary C. Thomas, 'Preface', *Queering the Pitch* (New York: Routledge, 1994), p. x.

33 Moore, 'Authenticity as Authentication', p. 213.

34 Anon., *Want One* Press Materials, DreamWorks Records, 2003.

35 Schwandt, '"Oh What a World", p. 170.

36 Ibid., pp. 159–70.

37 Lake, *There Will Be Rainbows*, pp. 192–3.

38 Rufus Wainwright, quoted in 'Rufus Wainwright Wants to Marry His Partner', available at: www.starpulse.com/news/index.php/2010/04/02/rufus_wainwright_wants_to_marry_his_pa (accessed 28 November 2014).

39 See www.rufuswainwright.com/blackoutsabbath-2009/.

21 Tori Amos as shaman

CHRIS MCDONALD

Tori Amos appeared in the early 1990s as a prototypical confessional singer-songwriter. She sang candidly about the intimate details of a troubled, yet vividly lived life. Her recordings were marked by closely miked vocals and minimal arrangements which sometimes featured only her voice and piano. Both in terms of music and lyrics, it takes great courage to perform in such an exposed and revealing way, and it is difficult to come away from Amos' performances or recordings without feeling like one has had an up-close and personal encounter with the musician. This effect is the stock-in-trade of the confessional singer-songwriter, and this is one key reason why mass audiences connect so strongly with artists like Amos. Her songs about her strict religious upbringing, her struggles to reconcile her budding sexuality with it, her recounting of rape and recovery, and her later miscarriage have called in a large audience who, in many cases, do more than relate to her experiences; in the manner of a 'talking cure', Amos' songs have a healing effect for some by opening up topics, experiences and feelings that are often kept repressed or hidden.

In the analysis below, I consider how Amos' songs of personal confession and mythology are framed by her cultivation of an image of an almost mystical 'healer'. Indeed, Amos' songs cohere around the notion of revelation: Amos reveals personal, spiritual, and symbolic 'truths' as a way to heal. Recalling the songs she wrote leading up to her 1991 debut album, *Little Earthquakes*, Amos said:

> I think I'm working on that place in me that was terrorised and really afraid. Now when I sing it, it gives me a lot of strength because I'm not running. At a certain point, there does become a place where the heart opens up and people express their fears and pain. That's when the healing really takes place.[1]

Elsewhere, Amos characterises healing through performance as an existential journey into the underworld of the self: 'I'm very interested in chasing a shadow and chasing the dark side. This is what I do … To heal the wound, you have to go into the dark night of the soul'.[2] The healing journey Amos describes here is self-consciously drawn from shamanism, a form of ritual and mystical healing. This chapter explores the idea of the popular performer as a kind of modern-day 'shaman', with singer-songwriters like

Amos using the archetype of the spiritual healer as an important authenticating frame and a means to connect with her audience.

Shamanism in popular culture

The term 'shaman' is believed to have come from the Tungusic languages found in Siberia and Mongolia, referring to a medicinal and spiritual healer. Though applied initially to the ancient religions of Turks and Mongols, the term was later used by anthropologists to describe a variety of tribal spiritual practices, including those of the natives of the Americas. What most 'shamanic' religions share are practices involving chant, trance, spirit possession or contact, and the evoking of powerful symbolism, all of which are brought about by a shaman through charismatic ritual performances. Despite similarities among reputedly shamanic religions, by the 1960s, some anthropologists criticised the universal usage of the term by Western scholars for religious practices in almost any tribal society, which sometimes glossed over the significant differences between them.[3] Nevertheless, renewed interest in shamanism among academics and the general public arose in the 1980s, as reflected in the appearance of popular books on the topic.[4]

Tori Amos performs a shamanic persona onstage and on recordings, and there is a long history of entertainers enacting such roles. Rogan Taylor, in his book *The Death and Resurrection Show: From Shaman to Superstar* (1985), makes a provocative argument that contemporary popular performers *are* the shamans of the modern West. Taylor states that:

> the power that entertainers wield over their audiences cannot be explained [merely] by the advent of mass media. Performers have been surrounded by a highly potent aura for an extremely long time ... It may be a long way from the shamans of the ancient past to the pop idols of today, but between them there stretches an unbroken line of descent. The 'magic' of show business is *real* magic. It draws its power from an immensely well-stocked religious bank, which contains the deposited riches of perhaps a million years of human genius.[5]

Taylor argues that there is a human spiritual need for extraordinary and ecstatic experience. Expression of this need may be found in every human culture, even though, like language, the variations on this expression are as diverse as human cultures themselves. Many traditions of ecstatic religion, for Taylor, share a common feature – the presence of a mediator between the material and spirit worlds, which is the basis of shamanism. In late capitalist culture, this mediator can be a superstar of the mass media, and he tracks the careers of artists like Houdini, Bessie Smith, Bob

Dylan, Jimi Hendrix, and John Lennon as mass media 'shamans' whose power over audiences had almost mystical overtones.

Taylor defines the shaman as a 'transformed' individual, one 'who *must* change in order to survive'.[6] Archetypally, an individual is initiated into shamanhood through an extreme, existential experience, a brush with death, or a traumatic ordeal. Through this experience, the shaman gains access to the 'other-world', with the powers and insights that such access brings. Once initiated, the shaman can call up intuitive sources of knowledge, and navigate the imaginary worlds of myth, and channel the spirit world for purposes of physical and emotional healing. This role is *ambivalent*: a shaman may possess uncanny talents or insights which may benefit society, but they can also be outcasts.

Amos' biography manifests such 'differences' quite early. Born Myra Ellen Amos in 1963 in North Carolina to a Methodist minister and his wife, who was part native Cherokee, Amos showed prodigious talent on the piano as early as age two, and was sent to study at the Peabody Conservatory of Music in Baltimore at age five. However, she left the school at eleven, as her intuitive musicality and rebellious streak fit poorly with the highly prescribed and structured curriculum of the conservatory. Meanwhile, the conservative religious environment in which Amos grew up left an impression that impacted her creatively throughout her career. At fourteen, she performed professionally in gay bars and lounges, and by twenty-one, she moved to Los Angeles and fronted a glam rock group called Y Kant Tori Read. Despite releasing an album in 1988, the group was a commercial failure. Moreover, during her time in LA, she was raped by an acquaintance to whom she had offered a ride home after a gig. Part of her recovery involved returning to her roots as a singer-pianist, and crafting the songs that would appear on her solo debut, *Little Earthquakes*. The album, including its *a cappella* rape narrative in the song 'Me and a Gun', did much to establish Amos as a performer of 'healing' songs, and it was here that the trope of Amos as a shaman gained traction.

Such descriptions abound in representations of Amos in the press: journalist Lucy O'Brien introduces Amos in her *History of Women in Rock* as America's 'shamanic piano-playing answer to Kate Bush';[7] John Patrick Gatta refers to Amos' music as 'techno-shamanic music for a new millennium';[8] an MTV news feature speculated that 'the relationship that Tori Amos shares with her fans may well be studied by misguided religious historians centuries from now', and says of Amos and her fans, 'she is more than a musician to them; she is a mother, a healer, a saint and a shaman'.[9] Even a *People* magazine interviewer felt compelled to describe Amos' appeal in exotic spiritual terms: 'There is an other-worldly quality about her – the moment I saw her I was entranced', he says, speculating that 'her brand of sorcery is rooted in her part-Cherokee ancestry'.[10]

Amos herself is aware of the power of the shaman archetype, and has referred at various times to shamanic spirituality as a source of creative inspiration and therapeutic restoration. She described to Tom Doyle in *Q Magazine* a period in the late 1980s when, in an attempt to heal herself, she experimented with a neo-shamanic spiritual movement in Los Angeles, which included taking Ayahuasca, a hallucinogen associated with native Amazonian medicine.[11] With respect to her effort to discover her dark, angry side on the album *Boys for Pele* (1996), she told Ann Powers that she found 'a woman, a shaman, who was reputed to know how to take you on a spiritual journey by uncovering things that you were avoiding in your view of yourself'; she described the journey she took with this woman as a kind of 'initiation'.[12] Her 2005 album, *The Beekeeper* was partly inspired by Simon Buxton's book, *The Shamanic Way of the Bee* (2004), which, in part, probed pre-Christian spiritual ideas about female sexuality as nourishing and restorative, rather than sinful.[13]

Shamanism, healing, and song

Admittedly, the backstories of Amos' life which provide so much topical material, gravitas, and truth-value to so many of her songs could be viewed simply as part of a larger singer-songwriter pattern. As Donald Brackett concluded, the work of singer-songwriters can be viewed as a 'dark mirror', a reflection of the pathology that the artists see in themselves, yet 'speak[s] for all of us in a way that connects with what we all feel'.[14] For Brackett, singer-songwriters trade on expressions of 'dis-*ease*', 'travers[ing] an immensely huge landscape in a way that provides a haunting kind of coherence and continuity ... [and] a discovery of a shared melancholy of alarming proportions'.[15] It is striking how Rogan Taylor makes very similar remarks about the role of shaman with regard to pathology and healing: 'The shaman's sickness is, in reality, *everybody's* sickness'.[16] Even more broadly, the idea of musicians or poets speaking 'divinely inspired' and 'universal' truths is ingrained historically, and can be witnessed in, for example, the 'cult of virtuosity' in nineteenth-century European concert music, or in the 'bodhisattva' role ascribed to black bebop jazz musicians in twentieth-century American beat culture. The need to authenticate such music, or to explain experiences of 'depth' and profundity in its reception, may be the reason why the performers are sometimes given spiritual titles. For singer-songwriters, the terms 'visionary' or 'prophet' have been used in connection with artists like Bob Dylan and Leonard Cohen, so the term shaman is not an unprecedented means through which the potency of singer-songwriters may be described.

The songs which have been most closely associated with Amos as a healer are those which confess both trauma and feelings of isolation. Many commentators on Amos make 'Me and a Gun', where she narrates her experience of rape, a central part of this side of her repertoire, and with good reason.[17] Amos sings the song unaccompanied, underscoring how alone and vulnerable the victim was during the attack. The melody is spare and narrow in range, and the vocal is delivered in a reserved and deadpan manner, not with overt emotionalism and pathos. If anything, the minimal delivery adds to the bleakness of her account. The lyrics intersperse details from the rape – being attacked with a weapon inside a car – with surprisingly trivial thoughts that went through her head at the time, which were actually part of her survival strategy. 'I've never seen Barbados', she sings, 'so I must get out of this'. She also rehearses her response to the inevitable question levelled at the victim ('was she asking for it'?) by insisting that her right to wear tight clothing does not mean she has a 'right to be on [her] stomach' and be attacked in a car.

In her study of Tori Amos fans, Adrienne Trier-Bieniek quotes a number of women for whom 'Me and a Gun' was experienced as an important source of healing from their own experiences of sexual assault.[18] For one respondent, the song 'triggered a flood of emotion, I guess, and I felt incredibly overwhelmed but also incredibly grateful because it felt like … I wasn't so isolated … Tori is responsible for the first time I started healing from when I was raped. It's her music that led me there.'[19] Another respondent notes that Amos' song led her to start talking about her own rape for the first time, which began her own 'bridge from being a victim … to being a survivor'.[20]

While 'Me and a Gun' is perhaps the most high-profile example, a number of other songs work towards the same sort of healing through the breaking of silence. In the song 'Silent All These Years' (1991), Amos narrates the thoughts of a woman bravely rebuking an abuser after years of feeling voiceless. 'Precious Things' (1991) describes the ways in which Amos felt belittled and inadequate, and offers angry retorts against each of them. For example, an audience member says, 'You're really an ugly girl/ But I like the way you play', and Amos, to her own disbelief, thanks him for the backhanded compliment, and then curses him under her breath. Then Amos shouts down the sexual double-standards of the 'those Christian boys', and the 'fascist' backdrop to the world of the 'pretty' and 'nice' girls. The refrain of the song uses the image of a bloodletting ritual as a way of cleansing herself of these feelings: 'Let them bleed', she sings of these 'precious things' to which we hold on, 'Let them break their hold on me'. As Reynolds and Press note, this rich image of haemorrhage as cleansing and release 'offers physical and mental relief, gives vent to the festering negativity that's pent up inside the body that's been silenced for so long'.[21]

The song 'Spark' (1998) is another example of a deeply personal confession of trauma, in this case Amos' miscarriage, in which she narrates the doubts ('Doubting if there's a woman in there somewhere'), the denial ('You say you don't want it/Again and again'), and the shaking of her faith ('If the divine master plan is perfection/Maybe next I'll give Judas a try'). While the song offers no resolution or answer to what happened, it is the intimate nature of her revelations that give songs like this their power to connect.

Problems and issues with pop-culture 'shamans'

While it is clear that Amos has self-consciously cultivated shamanism as a frame surrounding many aspects of her songwriting and public image, problematic elements do surface. The image of the shaman or 'medicine man' carries historical connotations of primitive exoticism in Western entertainment. To appropriate shamanistic elements in song, concert, and video is, in part to take them out of their original contexts and into a sphere where their meanings and effects are unpredictable. Moreover, it places Amos' work in a similar category with popular writing about shamanism targeted at general audiences, such as that of Carlos Castaneda, Michael Harner and Rogan Taylor,[22] which some anthropologists suspect tell us more about what modern, Western urbanites want to believe about shamanism than about any actual shamanistic traditions.[23]

While Amos seems to genuinely respect the myths and spiritualities she explores, her own descriptions of participating in shamanistic rituals in Los Angeles and taking hallucinogenic plants like Ayahuasca are difficult not to see as embedded in the recent popularisation of shamanism which, for Atkinson, was 'spawned by the drug culture of the 1960s and 1970s, the human potential movement, environmentalism, interest in non-Western religions, and by popular anthropology, especially the Castaneda books'.[24] Like New Age spirituality and the self-actualisation movements of which it is a part, such 'neo-shamanism' may be critiqued as a sign of the privilege of white Americans, who can freely and eclectically sample the spiritually exotic as they search for meaning and identity.

Amos abets her spiritual experiments by publicly acknowledging her part-Cherokee ancestry, seemingly suggesting that the fraction of 'non-Western other' she carries within her provides a passport to authentic participation in alternative spirituality. Through this, she seems to use a kind of essentialism to add authenticity to her shamanic persona, and this is significant because none of the other rock musicians that have tried to tout a shaman-like performing persona – including her own influences in Led Zeppelin (who suggestively courted the Faustian myth of Robert Johnson), but also Jim Morrison (who believed himself to be haunted by the spirit of a Navajo shaman) and Bob Dylan, who was received as a countercultural prophet – could claim the kind of ethnic or biographical backstory that made Amos' shamanic image seem so plausible.

In light of this, I believe that conferring some kind of authority and authenticity on Amos (and similar performers) is partly what is at stake with the rather loaded, complex shamanic label. Insofar as the term 'shaman' can denote a venerable spiritual tradition to some people, and is regarded as a universal human phenomenon by writers such as Rogan Taylor and Joseph Campbell,[25] the label might be used to construct a sense of legitimacy when applied to a performer. The constructed relationship between shamanism and Western entertainment is discussed by Richard Schechner, who notes, like Taylor, that myth, ritual, and entertainment (theatre, especially) are more related than is commonly thought. Authenticity, in particular, is at stake. Schechner describes 'attempts at ritualizing performance, of finding in the theatre itself authenticating acts. In a period when authenticity is increasingly rare in public life, the performer has been asked ... [not just to] mirror his [or her] times ... but to remedy them'. Intriguingly, Schechner discusses shamanism as an appropriate metaphor for this process: 'The professions taken as models for the theatre are medicine and the church. No wonder shamanism is popular among theatre people: shamanism is that branch of doctoring that is religious, and that kind of religion that is full of ironies and tricks.'[26] This gives us a good lens with which to contextualise the shaman image surrounding Tori Amos as a cumulative effect of her confessional, mythical and symbolic lyrical narratives, her career biography, and her reception in the press. This image is tied to discourses of authenticity, but also provides an example of an artist's persona symbolising redemptive acts of ritual or theatre, as suggested by the theories of Taylor and Schechner. It places the theme of personal and psychological healing, common within the confessional singer-songwriter genre, in a compelling, if exotic, frame. With this in mind, one could regard 'shamanism' as a convenient and appropriate, if contestable, term for the functions and pleasures that Amos' music serves.

Notes

1 Quoted in Kevin C. Johnson, 'Healing Through Song: Singing About a Painful Experience Gives Tori Amos Strength', *Akron Beacon Journal* (1996). www.yessaid.com/interviews/96-09-12AkronBeaconJournal.html, Accessed 13 May 2014.
2 Quoted in Elizabeth Vargas, 'Chase Away the Darkness', *20/20* (1999). Available at: www.youtube.com/watch?v=UXKK2JeC_tY (accessed 27 May 2014).

3 Jane Monnig Atkinson, 'Shamanisms Today', *Annual Review of Anthropology* 21 (1992), p. 307.
4 Ibid., pp. 307–8.
5 Rogan Taylor, *The Death and Resurrection Show: From Shaman to Superstar* (London: Anthony Blond, 1985), pp. 12–13.
6 Ibid., p. 19.
7 Lucy O'Brien, *She-Bop: The Definitive History of Women in Rock, Pop and Soul.* (London: Continuum, 2002), p. 205.

8 John Patrick Gatta, 'It's a Free Will Planet: An Interview with Tori Amos'. *Magical Blend* 63 (1998).

9 MTV News Feature. 'Tori Amos Brings the Noise'. Available at: www.angelfire.com/mi2/ starchild/toriart10a.html (originally sourced at www.mtv.com/news/gallery/a/torifeature.html (1999), accessed 19 February 2000).

10 Kevin Aucoin, 'The 50 Most Beautiful People of the Year', *People*, vol. 45, no. 18 (May 1996), p. 154.

11 Tom Doyle, 'Tori Amos: Ready, Steady, Kook!', *Q Magazine* (1998), 80–8. thedent.com/ q0598.html (accessed 29 May 2014).

12 Tori Amos and Anne Powers, *Tori Amos: Piece by Piece*. (New York: Broadway Books, 2005), p. 85.

13 Aaron Alper, 'A Chat with Tori Amos', *Tampa Bay Times* (2005). Available at: aaronalper.com/interviews/tori.html (accessed 27 May 2014).

14 Donald Brackett, *Dark Mirror: The Pathology of the Singer-Songwriter* (Westport, CT: Greenwood Publishing Group, 2008), p. xii.

15 Ibid., p. xv.

16 Taylor, *The Death and Resurrection Show*, p. 40.

17 For analyses of 'Me and a Gun' see Simon Reynolds and Joy Press. *The Sex Revolts: Gender, Rebellion and Rock 'n Roll.* (Cambridge, MA: Harvard University Press, 1995),

pp. 267–8; Adrienne Trier-Bieniek, *Sing Us a Song, Piano Woman: Female Fans and the Music of Tori Amos* (Lanham, MD: Scarecrow Press, 2013), pp. 267–70; Sheila Whiteley, *Women and Popular Music: Sexuality, Identity and Subjectivity* (London and New York: Routledge, 2013), pp. 197–8.

18 Trier-Bieniek, *Sing us a Song, Piano Woman*, pp. 267–70.

19 Ibid., p. 69.

20 Ibid., p. 70.

21 Reynolds and Press, *The Sex Revolts*, p. 269.

22 See, for example, Carlos Castaneda, *The Teachings of Don Juan: A Yaqui Way of Knowledge* (New York: The Viking Press, 1968) and *Tales of Power* (New York: Washington Square Press, 1974); Michael Harner, *The Way of the Shaman* (San Francisco: Harperone, 1980); Taylor, *The Death and Resurrection Show*.

23 Atkinson, 'Shamanisms Today', p. 307; Roy Willis, 'New Shamanism', *Anthropology Today* 10.6 (1993), pp. 16–17.

24 Atkinson, 'Shamanisms Today', p. 322.

25 See Joseph Campbell, *The Masks of God: Creative Mythology* (New York: The Viking Press, 1968).

26 Richard Schechner, *Essays on Performance Theory 1970–1976* (New York: Drama Book Specialists, 1977), p. 76.

22 Gender identity, the queer gaze, and female singer-songwriters

MEGAN BERRY

The construction and representation of the gender identities of singer-songwriters KT Tunstall (UK), Missy Higgins (Australia), and Bic Runga (New Zealand), artists who destabilise typical binary notions of gender in their media output (specifically their music videos), will be analysed in order to argue that female masculinity is a means for singer-songwriters to negotiate a dichotomously gendered mainstream, constructed to appeal to the 'male gaze'.[1] I contend that blurring the lines of 'cultural differentiation of females from males'[2] allows for multidimensional readings that appeal to a queer gaze. The effect of this is arguably a wider mainstream appeal, inclusive of heterosexual and queer female spectators, increasing cultural and economic capital and artistic credibility.

The key issue underpinning the discussion of gender identity in this chapter is the difficulty female musicians in the popular music industry have traditionally had attaining commercial success whilst gaining or maintaining artistic credibility, potentially caused by the heteropatriarchal and sexist hegemonies that have existed in mainstream Western music since its inception. The 'mainstream cultural industries'[3] of rock and pop are closely linked with gender and 'perceived as masculine or feminine'.[4] While rock music has connotations of authenticity, autonomy and seriousness, pop music faces negative bias as a 'feminized form of mass culture'[5] that is superficial, formulaic, and commercialised. Bannister points out that the difficulty women have in gaining artistic credibility exists because 'female performers are identified with genres viewed as having less cultural capital'[6] in contrast to their male peers.

As the notion of gender identity is so critical to this chapter, it will be useful to clarify my usage of the expression before continuing to the case studies. My ideas around gender identity are heavily influenced by the work of Judith Butler, who argues that 'there is no gender identity behind the expressions of gender; that identity is performatively constituted by the "expressions" that are said to be its results'.[7] In other words, gender is a set of acts and rituals that we perform constantly.[8] As such, masculinity and femininity as attached to male and female bodies are simply a cultural construct. When discussing the gender identity of a particular artist,

I am referring to the set of acts or representations that connote either masculinity or femininity, regardless of sex. Lucy Green provides a helpful summary of indicators of masculinity and femininity in her book *Gender, Music and Education* (1997). She states, 'masculinity tends to be defined as active, rational, inventive, experimental, scientific, unified, as a catalyst to culture and an emblem of the controlling powers of mind; femininity tends to be defined as passive, reproductive, caring, emotional, contrary, as part of nature, controlled by the body'.[9]

Hence, female masculinity is simply a displacement of performances of masculinity from male to female bodies. Judith Halberstam in her influential work *Female Masculinity* (1998) argues that masculinity exists across both male and female bodies, that masculinity does not need male bodies to exist within, in order to explore queer subject positions that can subvert or displace heteronormative gender identities.[10] According to Halberstam, female masculinity is performed in a variety of ways, from the drag king, to the butch dyke through to the subtle performative masculinity of the tomboy.[11] She notes that 'tomboyism tends to be associated with a "natural" desire for the greater freedoms and mobilities enjoyed by boys. Very often it is read as a sign of independence and self-motivation'.[12] This is appropriate to female singer-songwriters who wish to free themselves from the sexualised representations of femininity that occur in mainstream pop music. It also opens opportunities for greater displays of musicianship that are usually associated with men in popular music, but conflict with signifiers of femininity.

Representations of gender in popular music performance predominantly focus on women's bodies, either as sexual objects, or the source of their voices.[13] This is due in part to the male gaze – a term coined by Laura Mulvey,[14] developed from the work of John Berger in the 1970s to describe the way art (particularly the nude) was constructed to offer pleasure to an ideally male spectator. 'Men look at women. Women watch themselves being looked at.'[15] Green expounds on this as she argues that in Western culture, 'display' is coded as feminine, whereas spectatorship is coded as masculine.[16] She posits that singing reaffirms patriarchal definitions of femininity.[17]

The queer gaze is preferable to the concept of a lesbian gaze or female gaze because it refers to a gaze that is uncertain of its gender and sexuality.[18] A female gaze predominantly refers to the way women look at men, or how women look at other woman in view of their desirability towards men, and is thus heterosexual in nature.[19] Tamsin Wilton states 'the lesbian desiring gaze simultaneously *of* and *at* a woman contradicts utterly the heterosexual master narrative',[20] which although useful, is not as flexible as a queer gaze because it requires sexual desire. Although a queer gaze may be attributed to a male viewer, it is appropriate to hetero- and homosexual female spectatorship because it acknowledges the complex set of identifications that can take place in order for viewing pleasure or identification to occur when women are both subject and object. For the queer female viewer (primarily lesbian and bisexual women), there are a number of possible spectator positions that can be taken up. Depending on the representation of a popular musician's gender identity, a 'queer viewer finds that … desire is mobile here and may take up butch, femme, masculine, or feminine spectator positions'.[21]

The role of singer-songwriter in the folk or neo-folk tradition provides a vehicle for female (or male, for that matter) musicians to construct less dichotomous gender identities than would be possible in pop and rock genres. Female singer-songwriters can negotiate the male gaze without creating overt sexual feminine gender identities. Jodie Taylor makes a critical point when discussing the folk movement of the 1970s. She states, 'folk was … less bound to the rigid gender roles ascribed to rock and pop'.[22] As such, folk and its successor neo-folk enable women musicians to create queer gender identities that invite a multiplicity of readings and offer various viewing pleasures to a variety of spectators, particularly heterosexual and queer *female* spectators.

Female singer-songwriters have a certain flexibility to perform different roles – this is suggested in the very title of the role. The singer-songwriter performs two roles – both singer (reaffirming femininity) and songwriter (linked to authorship and thus connoting masculinity), thus destabilising heteronormative gender binaries. This enables a queer gaze, arguably widening appeal, and increasing artistic credibility and cultural capital. The following case studies will examine how each artist destabilises heteronormative binary gender identities in their media output, primarily their music videos, and how this enables a queer gaze and increases artistic credibility.

It is important to note that the videos in which these singer-songwriters play with gender identities and female masculinity seem to be targeted to audiences outside of the United States. There are a few possible reasons for this, the most logical relating to the harshness of the American mainstream popular music market, which is 'a hostile environment for lesbian and bisexual women, with marketability requiring certain compromises at the political level',[23] namely, their gender identity. It is possible Missy Higgins and Bic Runga have attempted to negotiate this struggle by feminising their gender identity in order to appeal to the male gaze in the US versions of their videos, supposedly in an attempt to break into the mainstream market. However at the very least, the different versions of each song, or duality within the videos (as in the case of KT Tunstall) allow us to uncover ways female singer-songwriters can displace or play with gender identity in their media output.

KT Tunstall

For Scottish singer-songwriter KT Tunstall, whose debut album *Eye to the Telescope* (2005) was an international success,[24] gender identity is a site of conflict. Tunstall has garnered a large lesbian following arguably due to her tomboy, ergo masculine gender identity that invites the queer gaze.[25] Her music videos for 'Suddenly I See'[26] from *Eye to the Telescope* and '(Still a) Weirdo'[27] from her 2010 album *Tiger Suit* show two versions of Tunstall – an authentic, strong-minded, tomboy version, and a constructed feminine or muted and suppressed version. The lyrical themes of both videos suggest an internal struggle between how Tunstall perceives herself (a weirdo), and how the world expects her to be represented. These videos emphasise Tunstall's apparent struggle with herself and mask, as Lucy Green points out: 'the mask has the effect of splitting the displayer in two. From the point of view of the onlooker, the displayer takes on a double form, as both 'other' and 'mask'; from the point of view of the displayer, the self is doubled into 'self' and 'mask'.[28]

KT Tunstall demonstrates this struggle, and in doing so, the flexibility accorded to female singer-songwriters in a number of ways. Firstly, she is represented as both an authentic self and a constructed mask. In 'Suddenly I See', the establishing shots of Tunstall lit in blue, performing in a live set up with an electric arch-top guitar in an industrial warehouse establishes a tomboy gender identity as Tunstall's true and authentic self. Tunstall's performance on electric guitar is significant, because as Green notes, 'women singers … who make use of technology as part of the inherent meanings of their music … threaten in some ways to break out of definitions of femininity, by challenging women's alienation from technology'.[29] This representation of Tunstall is juxtaposed with a sexualised, red-lit doppelgänger who enters about a third of the way through the video. This juxtaposition establishes the second Tunstall as the mask – a realisation of patriarchal expectations of femininity. She is sexualised, not playing an instrument, and the camera focuses on her body more than her face. This establishes her as an inferior musician, as according to Green, 'the more she goes in for displaying her body, the less likely it is that she is a "good" musician'.[30] However, this video, rather than confirming patriarchal definitions of femininity, destabilises or queers them.

Although the doppelgänger Tunstall is represented primarily as in competition to the first Tunstall (emphasising the self vs. mask), Tunstall interacts with the doppelgänger by singing with her, either in call and response, or chorus. This demonstrates Tunstall's representation as both self *and* mask – further queering gender binaries through the connotations linked to how both Tunstalls are represented. Additionally, both Tunstalls stand opposite each other, reminiscent of a mirror. Tunstall thus reveals her position as both subject and object of her own gaze. As such, she is able to play with her mask because 'display is not so much a single act by a displayer as a relationship, an exchange which is mutually constructed by both displayer and onlooker'[31] and as an onlooker to her own display, 'since … s/he participates in the active construction of the mask, so s/he can "play with the mask" conceptually'.[32]

Representations of Tunstall in the music video for '(Still a) Weirdo'[33] reaffirm her tomboy gender identity. In the lyric of the song, Tunstall describes herself as 'eloquent', but 'never quite elegant', and the video reflects this struggle. It employs the use of a masculine geography – a local pub, as the setting. Tunstall is seen in isolation either a bare rustic room or by an empty pool table, or walking empty streets. The video is saturated with natural light contrasted with the dark interior of the bar. She is presented finger-picking an acoustic guitar, wearing ripped jeans, a t-shirt and stereotypical 'dyke boots'. At one stage in the video, Tunstall is seen at the bar, drinking a beer (a masculine coded drink), when she sees herself as the bar tender in a mirror. This doppelgänger Tunstall is represented as suppressed, as the viewer only snatches glimpses of her at the bar, or passing the original Tunstall in a car driven by an aggressive-looking man. Her face is constantly in the shadows. Whereas the original Tunstall is represented as autonomous, free to roam the streets and visit pubs, the 'suppressed' Tunstall is always confined to a particular space.

As mentioned earlier, Green argues that in the West, display is coded as feminine, whereas the position of spectator is masculine.[34] What effect does this have when the object is both displayer and spectator as in the case of '(Still a) Weirdo'? Tunstall is the displayer (ergo feminine) in that she is the object of the video. However, there are a number of devices used to destabilise typical femininity and construct a masculine gender identity. Primarily, that she is the spectator of her doppelgänger – this is the only interaction she has in the video: she is otherwise represented as an outsider and loner.

Through being the displayer and the spectator simultaneously, Tunstall is coded as both masculine and feminine at the same time. Thus, gender binaries are destabilised, and lines are blurred between her masculinity and femininity. This enables the queer gaze because, through gazing at her doppelgänger, Tunstall invites a gaze directed at her doppelgänger from the perspective of a female (here read queer gaze, as the gaze is both of and at a woman). This reveals an apparent suppression and passivity of her doppelgänger who is placed within the confines of patriarchal definitions of feminine gender identity, juxtaposed with Tunstall's masculinity, which provides a sort of freedom. This enables a mode of identification for the queer viewer due to the freedom afforded Tunstall's tomboy persona, in contrast with the suppressed, passive, thus feminine, Tunstall. However, this freedom that

Tunstall enjoys in the video comes at a cost – she is portrayed as a social outsider, a weirdo, who does not interact with any other characters in the video, walking along the street by herself, drinking by herself, and playing her music in isolation. Again, this provides a site for queer identification as it aligns with narratives of homosexuality in the Western heteropatriarchal world. Up until very recently, homosexuals have been viewed as outsiders – always in a heterosexually permeated society, but never quite part of it.

Missy Higgins

Singer-songwriter Missy Higgins is an openly bisexual artist, whose catchy tunes and down-to-earth tomboy persona have made her an Australian super-star.[35] The original music video for 'Where I Stood'[36] from her 2007 album *On a Clear Night* is exemplary in its emphasis of Missy Higgins' tomboy gender identity. The lyrical content of the song is ambiguous in regards to the gender of the object, which creates an opportunity for a queer reading. The break-up narrative is addressed to an ambiguous 'you' but there are hints that the object could be female. There are two lines in particular that invite this reading. The first line in the second verse; 'I thought love was black and white, that it was wrong or it was right', offers the possibility of an internal struggle between a supposed heterosexual right and white and homosexual wrong and black, which to the queer listener may suggest that Higgins was taken off guard by homosexual desire, forcing her to reassess traditional views on romantic relationships. Indeed there is a strong theme of discovery throughout the song, with the first two lines of the chorus containing themes of internal conflict and then addressing her former lover saying 'you taught me how to trust myself'. These themes are typical of a coming-out narrative – a journey of self-discovery. The hook line of the song 'cos she will love you more than I could, she who dares to stand where I stood' emphasises this gender ambiguity, as the woman who dares to stand where Higgins stood could either be homo- or heterosexual.[37]

The original version of Higgins' 'Where I Stood' music video places her firmly within a masculine geography and away from the feminine domestic interior. The video is set in an urban subway, in a photo booth, and on city streets. The colour palette of the video consists of masculine-coded colours, mainly blues and greys and faded greens. The film is edited with a dark filter, emphasising the darker colours. Overall, the effect is a gritty urban look, typically used in male rock videos that destabilises Higgins' gender identity. This can be juxtaposed with the domestic interior that the US version of 'Where I Stood'[38] is set in. Higgins plays the piano in a studio apartment filled with seemingly natural light, emphasising nature and domesticity, two of the signifiers that, according to Green, reaffirm femininity. She states, 'first, the woman singer continues to appear masked and enclosed in her body; secondly, this helps to affirm her closeness to nature and her alienation from technology; thirdly, public singing calls into question her sexual life; fourthly, she is contrarily counterposed as an image of maternal perfection in the domestic setting'.[39] Through affirming her femininity by a connection to nature and a domestic setting in the US version, Higgins promotes a heterosexual viewing and invites a male gaze. However, through destabilising these indicators of femininity in the original version of the video, Higgins creates a tomboy gender identity and opens up opportunities for queer readings of both the lyric and video.

Additionally, Higgins' drab costume in the original video, consisting of a woolly beanie and a big coat and scarf with her greasy hair, downplays her sexuality and emphasise her tomboyish carelessness. Higgins is also represented as a solitary figure throughout the video, firstly through her isolation in the photo booth, and then by her walking towards the camera in the opposite direction to the extras, who are always walking away from the camera. This invites a queer reading of the video and the lyric as it constructs a loner narrative tied to Higgins' queer gender identity. In contrast, through the US version, she is shown wearing a short pink dress, playing piano and painting boxes which she eventually arranges into a makeshift projection surface that plays images of polaroid photographs superimposed with lyrics from the song. There are multiple shots of Higgins' face, but the camera focus is soft, ergo, feminine. There are lingering shots of her hands, legs and body as she sings. Although the image of Higgins is not highly sexualised, there is a noticeable difference in the construction of her gender identity between the two videos. The US version invites the male gaze by emphasising Higgins' femininity through its use of colour, costume, lighting and camera techniques. There are not many opportunities for queer subversive readings as there are little or no indications of female masculinity, and the narrative of the video does not support queer narratives, in fact, it has little to do with the lyrical narrative.

The same can be said about the two different versions of Higgins music videos for 'Steer', also from *On a Clear Night*. The US version's representations of Higgins are feminine, but not highly sexualised.[40] She is shown in a passive role, lying under an autumn tree, standing on a mountain, silhouetted against a bright moon, occasionally playing an acoustic guitar. There is no particular narrative permeating this video – its sole purpose seems to be to present Higgins in a variety of natural settings, emphasising her femininity. Shots of Higgins' face have a soft focus, which in combination with the natural yellow lighting serves to construct a feminine gender identity. The many shots of Higgins' body invite 'thoughts about sex and sexuality rather than intellect and character'.[41] While this video serves the male gaze, it detracts from Higgins' authenticity and artistic credibility as a songwriter leaving her in a murky no-man's-land, away from the highly sexualised, yet commercially viable representations of women in pop, but without anything to compensate for its lack.

The Australian version of 'Steer'[42] offers more options for queer readings. The video has a strong narrative – aligning with the lyrical themes of autonomy and 'taking control of the wheel'. Somewhat literal in its interpretation, Higgins is portrayed as a car-crash test driver by day, driving cars at speed into walls. It shows Higgins stuck in her routine, with little activity outside of her work. Towards the end of the video, Higgins appears to realise she doesn't have to keep hitting a brick wall and escapes into the Australian outback. The video primarily, again, has an urban setting, switching between an industrial warehouse where Higgins works, and a high-rise rooftop. The colour palette of the video consists of mainly greys and blues, as with the Australian version of 'Where I Stood', emphasising Higgins' masculine gender identity.

The occupation in which Higgins is depicted is a gendered one. Typically most occupations dealing with mechanics and cars are coded as masculine. This connection destabilises Higgins' gender identity as it connects her with technology.[43] It is also interesting to note that Higgins is the only female character in the video. There are two male doctors, and two male technicians dressed in the same blue overalls that Higgins is dressed in, but it is she who performing the active role of driving the car. This suggests that, not only is Higgins one of the boys (the matching blue overalls suggests this), she is actually at the top of the boys' game, being the driver instead of a passive observer.

The most obvious, yet crucial point here is that, when taken as a body of work, the two different versions for each of Higgins' videos destabilise her gender identity. This flexibility aligns with the role of the singer-songwriter, which is can be seen as both a masculine and feminine role. The US versions for each song seem to construct a more feminine gender identity for Higgins, but it becomes obvious that this is only a part of Higgins' mask of display when compared to the original videos for each song, which demonstrate her ability to play with this mask by constructing a masculine gender identity. I am suggesting that, like Tunstall, Higgins indicates an awareness of different representations and their effect, and her female masculinity offers the queer spectator multiple sites for identification.

Bic Runga

Bic Runga is an iconic New Zealand singer-songwriter who became securely ensconced in the Kiwi rock canon early on in her career through representing herself as a working, touring musician who is one of the boys.[44] She has maintained a mostly feminine gender identity, with only subtle indications of female masculinity, however I posit that this has been instrumental to her success in the New Zealand popular music industry.[45] In the New Zealand version of her music video 'Get Some Sleep',[46] Runga is represented in an active and stereotypically masculine role as a travelling DJ. The narrative centres on her operating a mobile radio station out of an old Bedford van that is travelling around the New Zealand countryside to remote towns. In addition to this, snippets of old 8mm handheld footage supposedly shot by Runga whilst travelling in the van add connotations of authenticity attached to documentary modes of signification. More traditional devices that invite the male gaze, such as the soft focus on Runga's face when she is shown operating the DJ equipment, have toned down these masculine aspects of Runga's representation. However, Runga's mastery over electronic equipment (the sound desk and 8mm camera), as well as her isolation in the DJ booth is essentially disruptive to the male gaze and elicits identification from queer viewers because it places her firmly within a discourse of female masculinity.

A comparison of this video with the international version of 'Get Some Sleep'[47] will reveal the full effect of the masculine aspects of Runga's gender identity. This version shows Runga in a heteronormative passive role – being driven around in the back of a car, and rolling around on a bed. She gazes into the camera alluringly, inviting the male gaze. There are many body shots of Runga, with shots lingering on her legs and at one point, flirtatious movements of her hand whilst she is talking on the phone, inciting connotations of her feminine sexuality, appealing to the male gaze. At one stage, she is shown deciding which outfit to wear out. A series of shots show her trying on different outfits- mainly different variations of jeans and a shirt – a decidedly tomboy outfit – before settling on a little black dress – the epitome of feminine sexuality.

There are two important devices used to destabilise Runga's gender identity in the videos for this song. Firstly, although she is coded as feminine through her position as the object of the video, in the original video, she refuses to engage the spectator by avoiding eye contact with the camera, whereas in the international version, she actively invites masculine spectatorship by gazing seductively into the camera throughout the video. Secondly, the narrative of the lyric unveils Runga's life as a working musician, and this reveals her awareness of the mask of display when she sings 'putting on my daytime eyes, a good enough disguise until I get some sleep'. As with Tunstall and Higgins, this awareness is emphasised by the fact that there are two different videos for the same song, hence two different representations of Runga, indicating her willingness to play with her mask, destabilising her gender identity.

Conclusion

A queer gaze finds many opportunities for identification and desire within these videos, whether through a potentially queer video narrative, as in the case of '(Still a) Weirdo' and 'Steer', lyric narrative ('Where I Stood'), or the destabilising of typical feminine gender identities throughout these case studies. The heterosexual female viewer may either identify with the artist's representations of strong-mindedness and independence often associated with masculinity, or temporarily desire the facets of masculinity as portrayed by them. This chapter has attempted to add to discourses on women in popular music by defining a role – the singer-songwriter in the folk tradition – that enables female musicians to construct masculine gender identities, destabilising heteropatriarchal gender binaries and appealing to a queer gaze.

Acknowledgements

My heartfelt thanks go to Matthew Bannister for his input and encouragement in the development of this chapter.

Notes

1 Laura Mulvey, 'Visual Pleasure in Narrative Cinema', *Screen*, vol. 16, no.3 (1975), pp. 6–18.

2 Roy Shuker, *Key Concepts in Popular Music* (Oxon: Routledge, 1998), p. 142.

3 Jodie Taylor, 'Lesbian Musicalities, Queer Strains and Celesbian Pop' in Sarah Baker, Andy Bennett, and Jodie Taylor (eds.), *Redefining Mainstream Popular Music* (New York: Routledge, 2013), p. 41.

4 Shuker, *Key Concepts in Popular Music*, p. 143.

5 Matthew Bannister 'Going out to Everyone? Bic Runga as a New Zealand Artist' in Henry Johnston (ed.), *Many Voices: Music and National Identity in Aotearoa/New Zealand* (Newcastle: Cambridge Scholars Publishing, 2010), p. 86.

6 Ibid. Cultural capital is distinguished from economic capital in that it is a symbolic form of capital, and 'operates as signs of their addresser's position in a social space'. For example, 'to prefer beer to wine is a sign that may say "working-class"'. Tony Thwaites, Lloyd David & Warwick Mules, *Introducing Cultural and Media Studies: A Semiotic Approach* (Hampshire: Palgrave, 2002), p. 196.

7 Judith Butler, *Gender Trouble: Feminism and the Subversion of Identity*, 2nd edition (London and New York: Routledge, 1999), p. 33.

8 Niall Richardson, Clarissa Smith, & Angela Werndly, *Studying Sexualities; Theories, Representations, Cultures* (Hampshire: Palgrave Macmillan, 2013), p. 41.

9 Lucy Green, *Gender, Music and Education* (Cambridge University Press, 1997), p. 27.

10 Judith Halberstam, *Female Masculinity* (Durham: Duke University Press, 1998), p. 9.

11 Ibid.

12 Ibid., p. 6.

13 Bannister, 'Going out to Everyone?', p. 86.

14 Mulvey, 'Visual Pleasure in Narrative Cinema', pp. 6–18.

15 John Berger, *Ways of Seeing* (London: Penguin, 1972), p. 47.

16 Green, *Gender, Music and Education*, p. 25.

17 Ibid, p. 27.

18 Halberstam, *Female Masculinity*, p. 179.

19 See Lorraine Gamman & Margaret Marshement (eds.), *The Female Gaze: Women as Viewers of Popular Culture* (London: The Women's Press Limited, 1988).

20 Tamsin Wilton, *Lesbian Studies; Setting an Agenda* (London & New York: Routledge, 1995), p. 154.

21 Halberstam, *Female Masculinity*, p. 176.

22 Taylor, 'Lesbian Musicalities, Queer Strains and Celesbian Pop', p. 41.

23 Ibid, p. 42.

24 KT Tunstall released her debut *Eye to the Telescope* in the UK in 2005, and in the US in 2006. In 2006 she won Best British Female Solo Artist at the Brit Awards. She has since released three studio albums (*Drastic Fantastic*, *Tiger Suit* and *Invisible Empire// Crescent Moon*) and an EP entitled the *Scarlet Tulip*. Corey Apar, 'KT Tunstall', *Billboard*, n.d., available at: www.billboard.com/artist/276661/kt-tunstall/biography (accessed 30 January 2015).

25 'KT Tunstall: I'm Proud of my Lesbian Following', *Pinknews*, 8 February 2006, available at: www.pinknews.co.uk/2006/02/08/kt-tunstall-im-proud-of-my-lesbian-following/ (accessed 30 January 2015).

26 'KT Tunstall – Suddenly I See', available at www.youtube.com/watch?v=Wh2AEwOtFHA (accessed on 30 January 2015).

27 'KT Tunstall – (Still A) Weirdo', 2010, available at www.youtube.com/watch?v=zqADjtAPi1Y (accessed on 30 January 2015).

28 Green, *Gender, Music and Education*, p. 21.

29 Ibid, p. 38.

30 Ibid, p. 39.

31 Ibid, p. 21.

32 Ibid, p. 39.

33 KT Tunstall, '(Still A) Weirdo'.

34 Green, *Gender, Music and Education*, p. 25.

35 Three of Higgins' albums, *The Sound of White* (2005), *On A Clear Night* (2007), and *The Ol' Razzle Dazzle* (2012), reached number one on the Australian charts, sold over a million copies, and have won ARIA (Australian Recording Industry Association) awards. www.missyhiggins.com/about/ (accessed on 25 September 2014).

36 'Missy Higgins – Where I Stood (Official Video)', available at www.youtube.com/watch?v=c9QNRvXH1HI (accessed on 30 January 2015).

37 For more on this, see Chapter 20 by Katherine Williams in this volume.

38 'Missy Higgins – Where I Stood – US Version (Official video)', available at https://www.youtube.com/watch?v=ADV4Orr9r-o (accessed on 15 September 2015).

39 Green, *Gender, Music and Education*, p. 36

40 'Missy Higgins – Steer [US Version]', available at www.youtube.com/watch?v=XL0LkP94Il0 (accessed on 30 January 2015).

41 Kristen J. Lieb, *Gender, Branding and the Modern Music Industry* (New York: Routledge, 2013), p. 143.

42 'Missy Higgins – Steer (Video)', available at www.youtube.com/watch?v=gf0qu3EAfTY (accessed on 30 January 2015).

43 Green, *Gender, Music and Education*, p. 38. Green is primarily referring to the connection between technology and femininity in the context of the construction of inherent musical meaning. She cites Laurie Anderson as an example. However, I think this notion is flexible enough to include a visual connection between women and technology as in the case of Higgins.

44 Bannister 'Going out to Everyone?', p. 84.

45 Runga's debut album *Drive* (1997) established her firmly in the New Zealand popular music scene, going platinum seven times, followed by her eleven times platinum sophomore effort *Beautiful Collision* (2002), and triple platinum third album *Birds* (2005). She has won multiple awards and in 2006 was made a member of the New Zealand Order of Merit. Available at: www.bicrunga.com/about/ (accessed 1 September 2014).

46 'Bic Runga – Get Some Sleep', available at www.youtube.com/watch?v=qzTUSR3fbfU (accessed on 30 January 2015).

47 'Bic Runga Get Some Sleep', available at: www.youtube.com/watch?v=EfSp_YeYMYI (accessed on 30 January 2015).

23 The female singer-songwriter in the 1990s

SARAH BOAK

Introduction

In May 1994 the cover of *Q* magazine featured three female singer-songwriters, PJ Harvey, Björk, and Tori Amos, with the strapline 'Hips. Lips. Tits. Power.' These three women were hugely popular artists, all riding high with five commercially successful albums between them at that point in time. The 1990s saw a new kind of female artist emerge, writing songs that focused on intimate topics of sexuality, gender and the body in an explicit, direct way. The artists pictured on the *Q* cover represented varying expressions from this new wave of singer-songwriters. They explored how everyday life is experienced *through* the body and at the centre of their songwriting was a specifically female experience, drawing on female agency and power, all experienced through an embodied self. The strapline of the *Q* cover neatly draws out these themes in its punchy four-word phrase. These artists also drew on the confessional history of singer-songwriters, drawing in their audiences with a closeness and intimacy, through their bodily experiences. Other singer-songwriters in this group included Fiona Apple, Liz Phair, Alanis Morissette, and Ani DiFranco.[1] This chapter will explore these themes of embodiment in the work of this wider group of singer-songwriters, whilst locating their work in a broader cultural and musical context.

As songwriters, these women had creative control over their output and a high level of agency. All of the artists in this group wrote their own material, predominantly with sole writing credit, and most played an instrument as well as providing lead vocals. They often worked with independent labels, whose ethos allowed for more experimentation and more artist control. For example, Björk has released all her work on One Little Indian, Harvey's debut was on Too Pure, and DiFranco has her own label, Righteous Babe Records. These singer-songwriters drew on a number of stylistic approaches, with their music straddling multiple genres; Björk's jazz and dance music influences, Harvey's distorted punk guitar, DiFranco's acoustic folk, and Amos' classical piano technique painted varied sonic worlds.

It could be argued that, despite being contemporaries, pulling together these women into one coherent grouping is rather arbitrary, given their stylistic diversity. In the 1994 *Q* interview, Björk, Polly Harvey, and Tori Amos are asked if they feel in competition with each other. All answer in the negative, and Amos goes on to say: 'If you think about Jimi Hendrix, Jimmy Page and Eric Clapton they were all much more similar to each other than we are. We have tits. We have three holes. That's what we have in common. We don't even play the same instruments.'[2] This answer, in response to a question phrased rather negatively about a competitive mode – which be seen as a misogynistic strategy to undermine female power or positivity, as Amos notes in the interview – draws a reactive response, and therefore does not allow the question of commonality to be fully discussed in a more nuanced way. There are, in fact, many similarities in these singer-songwriters' approaches, the thematic content in their work, their reception (both in terms of media and fan responses), and the social context of their music. However, Amos' response does highlight the need for a simultaneous awareness of difference, fissures and discontinuity, particularly in terms of the artists' self-definitions.

Alternative and mainstream

The 1990s saw the increase in popularity of what was described as 'alternative' music, and singer-songwriters such as Harvey, Björk, Morissette, et al., highlight the problems of the terms 'alternative' and 'mainstream'. On the one hand, many of these artists had significant mainstream commercial success. Alanis Morissette's 1995 album *Jagged Little Pill* reached number 1 in the Billboard charts. Björk had significant sales with *Debut* in 1993, and was certified double platinum (two million units sold) by BPI (British Phonographic Industry) by mid-1994.[3] Yet on the other hand, the material they were releasing was, in parts, experimental and genre-bending, with subject matter that differed hugely from what had been heard in the mainstream pop charts. At this point in the late 1980s and early 1990s, the term 'alternative' shifted in terms of its connotations. Music that had come from an underground or niche scene – and had specific sonic or lyrical qualities that were previously considered to be too abrasive or challenging for mainstream listeners – was now achieving mainstream commercial success. With the popularity of grunge – indeed the industry's invention of the term and capitalisation on all things grunge-related – the music industry had realised that 'alternative' music was a lucrative and untapped market.[4] As Catherine Strong argues, grunge can be described as a mainstream music despite it having 'oppositional qualities'.[5] The female singer-songwriters that also found mainstream success had been partly enabled to do so by this mainstreaming of the alternative that began in the late 1980s and, though they occupied a mainstream position, could simultaneously exercise a dissenting and oppositional voice.

Embodying femininity and female power

Grappling with societal expectations around female sexuality, bodies and behaviours is expounded in multiple ways across the output of these singer-songwriters. In particular, expressions of embodied selves are at the centre of their work, and an oppositional voice is spoken through the body. Fiona Apple's direct statement of 'This mind, this body, and this voice cannot be stifled' in 'Sleep to Dream' (1996 from *Tidal*) rings true for many of these artists, who express strong views about their experience of 'bodily being-in-the-world', and in particular their experience as sexual and gendered individuals.[6] PJ Harvey's 'Dress' (1992 from *Dry*) explicitly explores the paradoxes of trying to fit within gendered corporeal norms of femininity.[7] Harvey presents a stark picture of the impossibility of trying to please a man, under stereotypical societal expectations. Lyrically, the individual woman tries to achieve feminine status through manipulating her body into a prescribed template of what a woman should be. However, because she does not fit the template, and cannot fulfil what is expected, she becomes a 'fallen woman', by breaking taboos both around femininity and appropriate sexual behaviour. By the last verse she is described as 'it', as though becoming ungendered through the very act of failing to live up to these expectations. Harvey's sonic world becomes louder, more distorted and dissonant as the track progresses, and gives an aural representation of the anger and discomfort felt at the impossibility of task at hand.

Having a sense of a strong individual voice and expressing forthright opinions also set apart this cohort of women. The *Q* cover identified these women with 'power' and a common media characterisation was one of 'angry young women' or, in the case of Harvey in the *Q* interview, the 'mad bitch woman from hell'.[8] In particular, Alanis Morissette's 'You Oughta Know' (1995) was an anthem for female rage. Morissette's track is commonly believed to be autobiographical and documents an explosive, sarcastic anger against a former lover, and his new partner. Part of the definition of power in the output of these singer-songwriters is tied to an unashamed sexuality which characterises much of this work. In 'You Oughta Know' Morissette's question 'Is she perverted like me? Would she go down on you in a theatre?' puts the narrator's sexuality front and centre. From Björk's 'Big Time Sensuality' (1993) to Liz Phair's 'Fuck and Run' (1993), these artists were not afraid of censorship, or expressing their sexual nature. And the sexuality expressed was about their own pleasure, rather than an expression of expected female desire. Tori Amos' 'Icicle' (1994 from *Under the Pink*) is about masturbating whilst her father, a minister, is downstairs conducting a prayer group. There is no sense of guilt or shame, as might be traditionally expected from a self-orientated expression of female desire.[9] Amos also expresses a sense of pointed indifference about male sexual power over the female body in 'Precious Things' (1991) when she sings 'So you can make me come, it doesn't make you Jesus'.

Other embodied topics in the work of the singer-songwriters related to more taboo issues around sexual violence, miscarriage, and abortion. Tori Amos' 1998 album *From the Choirgirl Hotel* was written 'from a place of grief' after a series of miscarriages.[10] Fiona Apple's 'Sullen Girl', from her debut 1996 album *Tidal*, is an autobiographical and intensely emotional track, dealing with her experience of rape at the age of twelve.[11] Tori Amos' debut album *Little Earthquakes* also features the striking *a capella* song 'Me and a Gun' which is a bold narrative retelling of her experience of rape. Both women have spoken about their aims to connect with other rape survivors and provide support, with Amos going on to become spokesperson and patron for the charity RAINN (Rape, Abuse and Incest National Network).[12] Ani DiFranco's 'Lost Woman Song' from her 1990 self-titled debut album deals with the complex political issues around abortion, through her own personal experience of abortion as an eighteen-year-old. DiFranco says: 'On my first record, I wrote about my own abortion when I was 18. I wasn't just trying to "get away" with something, but connect with people, and not just those in my own tribe, but maybe people with different opinions.'[13] This sense of connection with others, in a range of different ways and settings, marks out the work of these singer-songwriters, and connects them with concepts of authenticity and truthfulness.

In the sonic world drawn out by female singer-songwriters in the 1990s, there are numerous sounds where the artists are drawing attention to bodily expressions, through the use of paralanguage; non-lexical communication.[14] In these instances, bodily experience can be heard through the voice, through various screams, whispers, murmurs, and whimpers.

Paralanguage allows artists to draw attention to the body, and gives a more embodied listening experience. Instead of removing sounds to disembody the voice, such as breath and the moistening of lips, these sounds are retained, in order to become a part of the timbral palette of the song. Furthermore, including paralinguistic features actively focuses attention on to the bodily source of the sound, from Amos' shriek after the first chorus of 'Precious Things' (1991) to Harvey's guttural and sexual word elongations in 'The Dancer' (1995).

Social context in the 1990s

In order to fully understand the work of these singer-songwriters, it is critical to analyse what was happening culturally in the early 1990s that allowed for women singer-songwriters to begin writing more freely about bodily experiences. Through the 1990s we see parallels in other movements and fields, where the body was becoming of more interest. In academia, feminist writers were exploring bodies in culture. Judith Butler began to write complex and involved theoretical work that engaged much more transparently with culturally situated bodies.[15] She evidenced the performativity of not only gender, but also of sex, and how the two relate to bodily practices and norms. The range of bodies analysed and philosophised was being broadened, and writers such as Elizabeth Grosz engaged with what she termed 'volatile bodies' – bodies that shifted and were dependent on cultural prescription; the naturalness of the body and of sex was being heavily challenged. A new playfulness was also becoming apparent in the academic literature; if sex and sexualities could be performed, then they could be moulded, played with, shaped, and reorientated, in new and exciting ways.

This playfulness was also paralleled in the musical experiences and cultures of the late 1980s and early 1990s. The music saw not only a revelation of taboo and explicit bodily experiences, but also showed a playful and humorous approach to gender, sex, sexuality, and bodies. Madonna's output during the early 1990s evidenced this clearly. Her book *Sex* (1992) and her tracks such as 'Erotica' (1992) and 'Hanky Panky' (1990) showcased a new openness about sexuality and bodies. Madonna could be said to have laid the ground for future musical explorations of the body and of sexualities. However, where Madonna's work was camp, theatrical and played on notions of drag and performativity, the women singer-songwriters that came to prominence in the early 1990s took their cue from a more confessional style of singing. Their work followed on from artists such as Joni Mitchell, who were writing songs with an autobiographical and deeply personal approach. This emotional and truthful style of songwriting, which reveals flaws in the narrator and a complexity of character, became the vocabulary of the 1990s singer-songwriters. Building upon this emotionality and confessional style of singing, the 1990s scene of female writers spoke more explicitly of bodily experiences and traumas. Whereas many of the singer-songwriters from the 1960s and 1970s had spoken of war and broader societal trauma, these artists in the 1990s initially at least, looked at more individualised traumas, and with a focus on personal bodily traumas such as rape and sexual abuse.[16]

It is important to note that a number of cultural shifts had taken place that resulted in more frank discussions about bodies and sexuality. In the

1980s the AIDS epidemic, and the media representations thereof, had spawned a culture of fear and caution around both bodies in general, and sexual bodies in particular. The AIDS advertising campaigns of the 1980s in the United Kingdom featured graphic images of tombstones, and there was significant anxiety about how widespread the epidemic could be. Towards the end of the 1980s, however, it became apparent that the AIDS threat had lessened somewhat but its cultural impact had not. The AIDS crisis had engendered a culture where more open and frank discussions about bodies and sexualities took place, both in the private and public sphere. This, combined with a more liberal approach to homosexuality, meant that once-taboo subjects were now being discussed openly in a range of settings. Within this changing context, a third wave of feminism was developing that broke down some of the second-wave concepts of a singularly defined 'woman' and drew attention to difference, often through a more embodied notion of the self.[17]

Riot Grrrl

The Riot Grrrl movement was important culturally and musically as an expression of these changing cultural circumstances. Riot Grrrl shared similar characteristics to female singer-songwriters in the 1990s, with a lyrical focus on bodies, the challenging of gender norms, and explicit content about taboo bodily subjects such as rape, menstruation, abortion, and masturbation. In contrast, however, Riot Grrrl bands (e.g. Huggy Bear, Bikini Kill, Bratmobile, Heavens to Betsy) focused on a collective and DIY approach to music, levelling the musical field as punk had done before it. Being part of a group, and part of a community, was central to the Riot Grrrl ethos.[18] Musicians such as Amos and DiFranco raised themselves into a more singular and iconic position. Rather than being part of a community of women, they became role models and representatives, expressing the emotions, feelings and experiences of young women but from an iconic and individualised standpoint. Most importantly, they became idolised by audiences who felt they spoke the truth about their own experiences.[19]

Riot Grrrls drew directly from feminist heritage, and were explicitly part of the third wave movement. There was anger around women's position in society, about the regulation and control of female bodies, and about the silencing of women's voices. This same anger translated into the work of the female singer-songwriters but perhaps in a more subtle way, for example in Tori Amos' 'Crucify' or 'Silent All These Years' (1991).[20] The feminist label was hugely applicable to the Riot Grrrls and many were vocal about their feminist sensibilities. The singer-songwriters, however, had a more troubled relationship with the term 'feminist'. Whilst the content of the singer-songwriters' music explicitly referenced frustration around the expectations placed on women, and discussed ways in which women could gain more power and more agency in their lives, the label itself was rejected by some of these women. Ani DiFranco explicitly owned her feminism, arguing that 'all decent people, male and female, are feminists. The only people who are not feminists are those who believe that women are inherently inferior or undeserving of the respect and opportunity afforded men. Either you are a feminist or you are a sexist/misogynist. There is no box marked "other"'.[21] Tori Amos has also been very vocal about her feminism, arguing 'I was born a feminist'.[22] However, others were much more reluctant to align themselves with feminist principles. PJ Harvey in particular disavowed the label, saying 'I don't ever think about [feminism] … I don't see that there's any need to be aware of being a woman in this business. It just seems a waste of time.'[23] Despite her protestations, the content of her work clearly spoke of feminist issues and many felt aligned well with the concerns of third wave feminists.

Female singer-songwriters in the 1990s were diverse in many ways, yet came together through a shared exploration of embodied femininity, sexuality and female power. Through vocal and lyrical strategies they connected with female listeners, and became icons for a new expressivity and for female agency.

Notes

1 I am discussing a group of women who were popular in the UK and US during the 1990s. Their own heritage varies slightly – most of the artists are US, though Alanis Morissette is Canadian, Polly Harvey is from the UK and Björk is Icelandic – but it is important to note that the discussion here is in terms of the music's circulation and reception in the Anglophone world. There is also much to be said about race – specifically whiteness – in relation to this cohort of singer-songwriters, but this is outside the scope of this chapter.

2 *Q Magazine*, May 1994, no. 92.

3 See www.bpi.co.uk/certified-awards.aspx (Accessed 21 October 2014).

4 See Doug Pray's 1996 documentary film *Hype!* for a discussion of the media's role in the grunge scene.

5 Catherine Strong, *Grunge: Music and Memory* (Farnham; Ashgate, 2011), p. 12.

6 Thomas Csordas in *Perspectives on Embodiment* by Gail Weiss and Honi Fern Haber (eds.). (New York; Routledge, 1999).

7 For a detailed analysis see Nicola Dibben 'Representations of Femininity in Popular Music' *Popular Music* vol. 18/3 (1999), pp. 331–55.

8 *Q Magazine*, May 1994.

9 See Sheila Whiteley, *Women and Popular Music: Sexuality, Identity and Subjectivity* (New York: Routledge, 2000) for an analysis of 'Icicle'.

10 Tori Amos and Ann Powers, *Piece by Piece* (USA: Broadway Books, 2005), p. 163.

11 See www.rollingstone.com/music/news/fiona-the-caged-bird-sings-19980122 (accessed 15 October 2014).

12 See Deborah Finding, 'Unlocking the Silence: Tori Amos, Sexual Violence and Affect' in Peddie, Ian (ed.), *Popular Music and Human Rights* (Farnham: Ashgate, 2011) for a discussion of how Amos' work connects with rape survivors. See also Chapter 21 in this volume.

13 See innerviews.org/inner/difranco.html where DiFranco discusses her 2012 track. 'Amendment' which also takes an explicit political stance on abortion.

14 See Serge Lacasse, 'The Phonographic Voice: Paralinguistic Features and Phonographic Staging in Popular Music Singing', in Amanda Bayley (ed.), *Recorded*

Music: Performance, Culture and Technology (Cambridge University Press, 2010).

15 Judith Butler, *Gender Trouble* (New York: Routledge, 1990) and Judith Butler, *Bodies that Matter* (New York: Routledge, 1993).

16 Both Tori Amos and PJ Harvey's later work engages with more political topics, particularly post-9/11. It could be argued that Ani DiFranco has always engaged more overtly with politics in its broader sense, embodying the feminist maxim 'the personal is political'.

17 Feminism is broadly defined into 'waves', with the first wave of activism around women's right to vote in the late nineteenth and early twentieth centuries. The second wave of feminism occurred in the late 1960s and early 1970s, with feminists campaigning across a range of issues around equality, including in education and the workplace. The idea of a third wave of feminism is more contested, with its precise historical location also debated, though the early 1990s seems to be most widely accepted. Whilst defining the third wave is complex, it is almost always described as a critical response to the second wave. See Stanford Encyclopedia of Philosophy 'Topics in Feminism' for further detail plato.stanford.edu/entries/feminism-topics/ (accessed 15 October 2014).

18 Whiteley (2000) notes that Riot Grrrl stressed 'the importance of female address and identification' and was all about 'process and interaction' (p. 209).

19 This is not to say that Riot Grrrl did not have its icons but iconic status was avoided and discouraged, in favour of a more collective approach (see Meltzer, Marisa *Girl Power: The Nineties Revolution in Music* (New York: Faber and Faber, 2010) on Kathleen Hanna).

20 In her 2003 article "A Little Too Ironic': The Appropriation and Packaging of Riot Grrrl Politics by Mainstream Female Musicians', Kristen Schilt discusses how mainstream female musicians repackage the riot grrrl ethos, in a commercial setting. She groups women musicians such as Morissette and Meredith Brooks, that came post-1995, without acknowledging that this music had an earlier grouping in Amos, Björk and Harvey, who could also be seen as part of this cohort: Kristen Schilt, "A Little Too Ironic': The Appropriation and Packaging of Riot Grrrl Politics by Mainstream Female Musicians' in *Popular Music and Society* (2003)26:1, 5–16.

21 Ani DiFranco. 'Ani DiFranco Chats With the Iconic Joni Mitchell' *Los Angeles Times*, 20 September 1998, available at: jonimitchell.com/library/view.cfm?id=150 (accessed 15 October 2014).

22 Tori Amos and Ann Powers, *Piece by Piece* (USA: Broadway Books, 2005) p. 12.

23 *Bust* magazine, Fall 2004.

PART IV

Frameworks and methods

24 Reconciling theory with practice in the teaching of songwriting

MARK MARRINGTON

My aim in this chapter is to isolate certain key threads that have emerged from the substantial body of literature on songwriting that has been produced over the last few decades – threads that constitute those theoretical perspectives that might usefully inform the development of practical pedagogical frameworks for the teaching of songwriting.[1] In particular this will involve a consideration of the nature of the songwriter's social environment (or 'domain') and the apparent tensions between this and the educational context, as well as a discussion of the range of factors that determine the means by which songwriters come to understand the practice of songwriting in technical terms. My principal objective is to demonstrate that approaching the study of songwriting from this vantage point can provide useful insight into the creative process and engender constructive self-reflection on an activity that is often engaged in intuitively. It will be useful, as a starting point, to provide an overview of the literature in question as a means of highlighting the kinds of sources that have a bearing on the discussion.

An overview of the literature on songwriting

Songwriting is today well established as an area of formal musical study and is widely taught within academic courses at universities and colleges. A survey on the teaching and assessment of songwriting in the UK (Isherwood 2014), for example, represented data drawn from over forty programmes, across twenty-two institutions in which songwriting tuition was available in one form or another.[2] Discussions of songwriting pedagogy have emerged naturally in response to a need on the part of tutors to find effective ways to formalise their teaching, resulting in two particular avenues of enquiry. The first is concerned with getting to the heart of the songwriter's creative process itself, while the second aims to clarify the nature of the text that is actually being taught, in other words, what constitutes a song? Investigations into the creative process have typically been concerned with the conditions (or environment) that produce the songwriter, as well as finding a means of judging what constitutes a valuable creative contribution to the discipline. Questions of the nature of the songwriting text direct attention towards the songwriter's medium, be it, for example, the handwritten score, the musical instrument, or the Digital Audio Workstation, as well as the form in which the song is realised, such as the live performance, the sound recording and so on. Current thinking with regard to both areas owes something to the climate created by educational theorists whose focus has been on exploring the differences of approach to learning in musical contexts that have been considered outside of the Western educational mainstream. This can be recognised, for example, in the work of Lucy Green where a distinction is made between those musicians who learn formally (using notation on manuscript paper for example) and those who adopt informal approaches (such as learning by ear from records or teaching themselves an instrument).[3]

Alongside the academic commentary there is an extant body of literature on songwriting, which represents, for all intents and purposes, the practitioner perspective. While such material varies widely in terms of its analytical rigour and mode of expression, it nonetheless contains much that can be considered pedagogically useful. Typically, such texts are designed as instruction manuals (or 'how to' guides), covering in a step-by-step fashion the technical principles of musical composition and lyric writing, or alternatively, autobiographical accounts that combine technical discussion with anecdotal observation designed to convey industry know-how. An early example, which may have provided the original template, is Charles K. Harris' *How to Write a Popular Song* (1906), written at the point of the song's emergence as a mass-consumed sheet music commodity. The bulk of Harris' discussion is devoted to the techniques of lyric writing, melodic construction, and arranging piano accompaniments, but also contains advice on self-publishing and distribution, copyright, and earning royalties. This model has persisted through to more recent times, for example, Stephen Citron's *Songwriting: A Complete Guide to the Craft* (first published in 1985) bears a close affinity to Harris' book in its structure and approach. The practitioner literature is particularly useful because it provides an informative document of the ways in which perspectives on songwriting technique have changed over the decades, along with musical style, and technological developments which have impacted upon the songwriter's medium. Harris and Citron, for example, situate their approaches in the piano-led Tin Pan Alley/Great American Songbook tradition, while later texts, such as Rikky Rooksby's *Writing Songs on Guitar* (2000), or Jeffrey Rodgers' *Songwriting and the Guitar* (2000), offer useful discussions of the guitar-focused songwriting styles of the 1960s and beyond. Another important source for the practitioner viewpoint is the now substantial body of published interviews with songwriters, of which the most substantial compilations are those by

Bill Flanagan (1986), Paul Zollo (2003), and more recently, Daniel Rachel (2013). Academic discussions of songwriting have tended to downplay the value of such literature on account of the overly subjective terms in which practitioners couch their discussions of their own approach. However, given that the vast majority of successful songwriters of the last century have not felt the need to commit their advice on songwriting to paper, these documents are highly valuable. Aside from the legacy of the songs themselves, the documented interview often stands as the sole formalised representation of the ideas of songwriters, and in the hands of an incisive interviewer, coupled with a certain amount of reading between the lines, much insight can be gleaned from what is said.[4]

Creativity and the environment of the songwriter

One of the most significant lines of enquiry to have emerged from the recent academic literature has focused on the question of what constitutes 'creativity', with a view both to developing a means of cultivating it in songwriters and measuring (or assessing) it effectively. Discussions here have typically been informed by terms derived from the 'psychology of creativity' literature, drawing from such writers as Arthur Koestler (1964), Margaret Boden (2005), and in particular Mihaly Csikszentmihalyi (1988 and 1996).[5] Among the more notable contributors in this regard have been Philip McIntyre and Joe Bennett, both of whom are university academics with backgrounds as professional songwriters, and whose writing has been influenced by Csikszentmihalyi's 'systems theory'.[6] Summarised broadly, Csikszentmihalyi's theory considers creativity relative to the particular environment within which the individual operates. The terms he employs to articulate the structure of this environment are 'domain' and 'field'. 'Domain' refers to an existing context of practice from which one assimilates patterns of creative approach (the rules of the game as it were) while 'field' refers to the social factors (namely people and institutions) which determine those creative contributions that are most likely to be accepted into the domain – in other words, there are gatekeepers who judge the success with which the rules have been observed.[7] Creativity is thus not an objective quality but rather something that is determined at a given stage of the domain's evolution by its dominant practitioners, who are highly responsive to changes in the environment. Domain immersion – in other words being thoroughly conversant with the domain's 'memes and systems of notation', having an ability to evaluate past and present knowledge of practice, as well as discern potential future directions – is essential if the songwriter is to make a valid contribution. If a songwriter's work bears no relationship to the domain then the field will be unlikely to recognise it (in McIntyre's words, 'without the knowledge of the songs being in place, the person cannot act in the field').[8]

Given that the domain is essentially the prime determinant of the songwriter's knowledge-base, the approach taken by a teacher (a representative of the field) to defining it will obviously have significant implications for the ways in which his/her ideas about songwriting are articulated to students. Before addressing the educational context specifically, it is useful to consider how the domain/field relationship may be more generally understood in relation to the social environment of the songwriter. Peter Etzkorn, in a pioneering early study of American songwriters in the 1960s, offers the following account of the social constitution of the songwriter's domain:

> The system as such is not the creation of any single individual but represents the *conscience collective* of those who are socially participating in it. No single interest group within society can radically alter its form and content. Changes in the system will occur at a slow pace and will always be traceable to some social development which affects the total social awareness.[9]

It is the factors that condition this social awareness that are of interest here, and their role in shaping the specific resources that a given environment provides to the songwriter about what songwriting actually is. Some of the most notable contexts in which songwriting has evolved have been socially and geographically situated phenomena, existing in forms ranging from business and educational institutions to studio facilities, performance venues and arbitrarily constructed musical scenes. Among the more familiar examples are Tin Pan Alley and the Brill Building in New York, Motown in Detroit, the Liverpool scene and Laurel Canyon in the 1960s, and, more recently, the UK's BRIT School and Xenomania, all environments in which communities of songwriters have drawn from a shared pool of ideas that have contributed towards an era's songwriting zeitgeist. A precisely situated notion of the domain is only convenient to a certain degree however, given that the songs produced in these environments were/are ultimately mass-disseminated, either as sheet music or recordings, implying a considerably broader social scope. Once the song is outside the orbit of the tight-knit collective that produced it, its structural components may be subject to considerable reinterpretation. A songwriter's knowledge of the domain might result from autonomously instigated contact with recordings of songs whose elements bear little relationship to what is happening in their own locale, as occurred, for instance, when British teenagers gained access to blues and rock 'n' roll recordings during the late 1950s/early 1960s. Assimilation of the vocabulary of songwriting might also take place in rather less formalised circumstances: many of these same teenagers learned to write songs on the guitar at a time when the instrument's use in songwriting was not well documented in the literature. Instead, songwriter literacy was evolved through exchange among peers of knowledge about particular guitar chords, or guitar riffs, learned by ear from records rather than from (often unreliable) sheet music transcriptions.[10] As recent ethnographic studies of songwriters have indicated (see for example, DeVries 2005; Burnard 2012), to understand the songwriter's domain in terms of a micro-social context is unrealistic: instead educators should expect to encounter a multiplicity of creative perspectives, deriving from a broad range of cultural contexts, operating within a single individual.[11] With the now seemingly limitless possibilities afforded by the worldwide web for access on a global scale to past and present modes of creative practice, the domain appears more difficult than ever to pin down in social terms.

An alternative approach, which may be more reliable for the teacher, is to view the songwriter's domain as an essentially marketplace-driven phenomenon, whose parameters correspond to the expectations of a field group comprised of consumers and industry personnel. A defining trait of the marketplace domain is that new practice approaches are always emerging at speed to assimilate or eclipse earlier ones, something that the commercially inclined 'how to' literature has naturally drawn attention to over the years. Harris, for example, in *How to Write a Popular Song*, quaintly remarks that 'Styles in songs change as quickly as ladies' millinery. Each seems to have a cycle which comes and goes, whose length of life is only increased occasionally by the introduction of some new idea which is merely wedged into the original style or mode.'[12] Decades later in *Tunesmith*, Webb observes that 'Songwriting styles since the early 1970s have incorporated more and more frequently what has come to be called a *conversational tone* … an almost off-hand "this is the way people talk" minimalism … which has eroded to some extent the cut-and-dried, formulaic techniques of our predecessors.'[13] In this instance, domain immersion is motivated by a commercial imperative, with the dual purpose of acquiring the most up-to-date contextual knowledge in order to emulate the success of one's competitors, while anticipating or spearheading changes in taste that will enable one to retain the field's approval.

Turning to the pedagogical context, a principal challenge for the songwriting teacher is to translate the songwriter's domain, as it exists in the world of practice, into terms that can be handled by educational constructs. The obvious strategy is to reflect the movement of the marketplace, although this brings the particular difficulty of reconciling the rapidly changing commercial landscape with the need to provide stable curricula. Educators, if they are to communicate their ideas effectively, need to acquire a certain amount of perspective on what has taken place in the domain over a particular time period and those more comfortable with the practices of their own era may either not wish to incorporate current trends into their teaching or may find it difficult to articulate these in terms of well-digested curriculum content. One way to address this issue is to involve commercially proven songwriters in the teaching team, who will be able to make students aware of what is happening on the ground as well as effectively judge what is produced relative to the marketplace. If this is not the case, then it follows that programmes at least ought be to be designed to be responsive to a range of marketplace positions, which could be facilitated for example, by incorporating student-led contributions.

There is of course no obligation in the educational context to gear the teaching of songwriting exclusively towards what is happening in the commercial arena. In this author's experience of teaching at a UK Higher Education establishment, for example, songwriting tuition was delivered in the context of a Popular Music Studies degree curriculum. While by no means eschewing current trends, the course placed emphasis on historical and musicological approaches (mirroring to a certain extent the older Western art music curriculum model), which students were expected to acknowledge in their creative practice. The point was to develop a broad appreciation of the discipline and a critical approach to evaluating one's own work. Students, having acquired such a perspective, were often inclined to take a more exploratory attitude in their songwriting and question the value of simply reproducing the latest commercially proven tropes.

It is apparent in the recent pedagogical literature that academics have sought a middle ground enabling them to encompass a wide range of perspectives on the songwriting discipline within the curriculum, while at the same time retaining secure criteria for valuing an individual contribution. Bennett, for example, argues that students' creative work should be judged in relation to what he calls the 'constraints' of a recognisable popular song domain (Csikszentmihalyi is implied). The student is required to demonstrate domain immersion, with the success of the song being considered with reference to how well certain constraints have been observed. To facilitate this, song analysis aids the student in determining the 'statistical norms' of the chosen domain – in other words, those elements that are commonly found within it at a given moment (for example, a particular song structure, a regularly used chord progression, the recurrence of certain genre-specific lyrical subject matter and so on).[14] Such an approach, which is akin to pastiche-work, certainly has value as a means of building a strong technical foundation, as well as facilitating the assessment of songs due to the clear criteria involved. It leaves the important question, however, of how far the songwriter may be allowed to progress beyond such constraints in the service of originality or individuality. Csikszentmihalyi's ideas again have a bearing on the debate here, and in particular his assertion that genuine creativity involves introducing 'variations' into the domain which are 'instrumental in revising and the enlarging' it, as opposed to 'simply reproducing existing forms'.[15] If the songwriter's aim is to reflect the marketplace-driven domain, then the scope of the creativity in these terms might arguably be somewhat akin to Adorno-esque pseudo-individualisation, in other words, minor adaptations that do not undermine the stability of the template from an audience perspective. In the educational context it should be possible for the student to go further than this, given that the commercial field need not be the final arbiter, but this leaves the question of what, therefore, ought the work be measured against? Allan F. Moore (2004), in a bid to resolve this issue, has employed the term 'idiolect', derived from linguistics, to express what the student might realistically aspire to in these circumstances. Idiolect refers to that which is unique about an individual's creative approach when considered within an established stylistic context – 'their personal fingerprints … by which we identify what they do, and how they differ from others'. A range of attributes could be implied here, from particular harmonic or melodic quirks and lyrical turns-of-phrase to unique performance gestures or certain recurrent timbral properties.[16] Expertise and experience will obviously play a large part in enabling a tutor to decide when, and in what ways, idiolect is apparent in student work, as well as in providing pointers as to when the borders of the containing stylistic framework are being breached. On the whole, Moore's comments reflect a position which is broadly congruent with discussions of songwriting found throughout the literature: namely that subtle adjustments to existing frameworks, rather than radical paradigm shifts, are the norm where this particular field is concerned.

Defining the contemporary song text

Aside from discussions of the nature of creativity in songwriting, it is also apparent that there is a need for clarification of what precisely is being studied in the name of 'song'. Isherwood's aforementioned survey highlights the current inconsistencies where educational institutions are concerned, noting that there is 'little consensus as to what a song is'.[17] A particular concern is to establish the terms in which songs are articulated, entailing consideration of, for example, the particular 'memes and systems of notation' (modes of representation) used by songwriters both in apprehending their craft and communicating what they do. In essence we are dealing here with questions of what constitutes songwriter literacy, as well as debates with regard to what constitutes the song as a material entity. Clearly the various ways in which the song has been mediated over the last century – from a sheet music form, comprising melody, harmony, and lyric, to the fully arranged and produced sonic artefact consumed today – have had a key role to play in determining how a song is viewed by songwriters. McIntyre, who has written extensively on this question of the song text, has pointed out that in spite of such changes of mediation, the melodic and lyrical elements of the song remain as a fundamental underlying structure.[18] This is a significant observation because it implies a certain consistency in the domain that teachers can potentially rely upon when articulating ideas about songs.

A perusal of much of the 'how to' literature suggests that a melodic/ harmonic conception remains central to thinking on the compositional aspects of songwriting technique (see for example, Citron 1985; Webb 1998; Perricone 2000; Rooksby 2000; Cope 2009), much of it assuming a familiarity with musical notation and a willingness on the part of the reader to engage with the complexities of music theory. Webb's account, in reference to the earlier discussion of progressiveness, is particularly notable for its advocating experimentation within the melodic/harmonic domain in chapters discussing the use of chord substitutions and alternate basses as a means of breaking out of tried and tested formulae, and constructing melodies that do not necessarily neatly fit with vocal range or singing style. He sounds a cautionary note, however, with regard to the acceptance of a predominantly melodic element within the songwriting tradition, pointing out that words and music since the 1950s have become increasingly 'subordinate to the rhythms evolved from blues, Latin, and Caribbean music … reaching its zenith in the 90s with the advent of rap and hip-hop', raising the question of whether 'the next decade would see the complete demise of melody'.[19] This insight serves as a reminder of the dangers of limiting technical discussions of songwriting to one or two established theoretical perspectives, as these may not be able to account for fundamental changes that take place within the domain. To this end, the academic literature has acknowledged that the definition of the song needs to be broadened to include a more comprehensive range of parameters. Moore (2010), in an influential essay where pedagogical theory is concerned, has argued convincingly for the focus to shift from 'song' to 'track' to highlight the distinction between the song as a blueprint for potential performance, and the track 'which is already its own per-formance' (i.e. the recording).[20] This has also been reflected in the writ-ings of commentators such as McIntyre and Bennett whose individual discussions point towards a consideration of idea of the song in terms of the specific production strategies that have contributed to its actualised recorded form.[21] For educators this entails rethinking (where necessary) the songwriting curriculum to incorporate elements of arranging, session musicianship, recording techniques, signal processing, mixing etc., all of which, it can be argued, are integral to both the conception of the song and its communication to an audience.[22]

A final point, related to this discussion of modes of song conception, is that there has to date been relatively little attention given to the effect of the songwriter's tools (or technologies) on the creative outcome. This might imply, for example, studies of the roles of particular musical instruments in the creative process (to ascertain, say, the difference of approach in writing songs on the guitar, compared to the piano), or a consideration of the impact of the software interfaces (Digital Audio Workstations, or DAWs), which are now employed with increasing frequency in both the conception of the 'song' and its realisation as the 'track'. It is apparent that in certain quarters there is something of a chasm between older and more recent perspectives on songwriting where the recent digital technologies are concerned, as demonstrated in the following statement by Citron (in the 2008 revision of his book):

> It is so easy to sit at a computer, toy with a MIDI input device such as a digital keyboard, play in a tune, and have the computer print it out, making a hard copy of the song or if desired, have the computer burn a CD or create an mp3 of the song. But this is, in my estimation, not songwriting.[23]

Citron's remarks reflect the position of the songwriter whose working methods are deeply rooted in the earlier sheet music tradition, relative to which the computer is an unwelcome imposition on the craft with no particular properties of its own to contribute to the creative process.[24] However, as a number of recent commentaries have illustrated (for example, Brown 2007; Mooney 2010; Marrington 2011), the computer, like any other tool, is a mediating structure which has the potential to impact upon the character of the songwriter's materials as well as their organisation.[25] The usefulness of studying the role of tools may be briefly illustrated by considering the example of the guitar, a technology which has revolutionised popular music and become embedded in the culture of modern songwriting. From the blues and folk musicians of the early twentieth century through to the most recent singer-songwriters, there has been a tradition of exploring the instrument's possibilities, ranging from the invention of unique playing approaches with the left and right hands to devising radical modifications of the guitar's standard tunings (as discussed in Chapter 13 on Nick Drake). In effect this has enabled the musical vocabularies employed by guitarist-songwriters to be repeatedly renewed and enriched.[26] Hence, when songwriters do develop a consciousness of the role such tools play in their writing, they potentially gain access to a means of engendering transformations within the domain that go much further than self-conscious experimentation within the boundaries of a particular stylistic framework.

Conclusion

As this chapter has shown, a particular use of theory is to provoke important epistemological questions relating to practice, specifically regarding those processes by which songwriters come to understand the nature of songwriting. It is accepted by both academics and practitioners that proficiency in songwriting requires mastery of a domain: in other words one needs to become fully conversant with the creative products that are most highly valued in one's field. A central problem for teachers is to establish the terms in which the domain is discussed, particularly given the wide range of individual perspectives that they are now likely to encounter in their students. While the most obvious position from which to view the songwriter's domain is the commercial market place and its over-coded products, this may not suit all teachers, and a preferred approach may be to teach in terms of a broad stylistic knowledge of the songwriting discipline, providing historical insight through the study of examples that highlight certain norms that can be emulated. There remains the question of what role experimentation ought to play in the songwriter's creative approach and the extent to which students can be permitted to break out of established domain constraints without alienating themselves from the tutor-defined field. Clearly it is in those educational environments freed from the expectations of the marketplace that debates concerning experimentation with the parameters of the songwriter's domain might most usefully flourish. An area that educators also ought to take into account, when considering the structure of the domain, is the role of the technological medium in shaping a songwriter's creative approach, as this may offer useful insight into additional processes by which variations within the domain are made possible.

Notes

1 I approach this discussion from the perspective of an academic who has taught songwriting and other forms of popular music composition for a number of years at Higher Education level in the UK.

2 Martin Isherwood, *Sounding Out Songwriting: An Investigation into the Teaching and Assessment of Songwriting in Higher Education*; Higher Education Academy Report (York: Higher Education Academy, January 2014). Isherwood's research was questionnaire-based and commissioned by the UK's Higher Education Academy (HEA) and he acknowledges that the study is not completely representative of the UK scene.

3 See in particular, Lucy Green, *Music on Deaf Ears: Musical Meaning, Ideology and Education* (Manchester: Manchester University Press, 1988) and *How Popular Musicians Learn* (London: Ashgate, 2001).

4 See Bill Flanagan, *Written in My Soul* (Chicago: Contemporary Books, 1986); Paul Zollo, *Songwriters on Songwriting* (Cambridge, MA: Da Capo, 2003) and Daniel Rachel, *Isle of Noises: Conversations with Great British Songwriters* (London: Picador, 2013). Examples of discussions that shed useful light on songwriter practice are Zollo's interviews with Jimmy Webb and Carole King and Rachel's interviews with Andy Partridge, Ray Davies and Sting.

5 Key texts here include Arthur Koestler, *The Act of Creation* (London: Hutchinson and Co., 1964); Margaret Boden, *The Creative Mind: Myths and Mechanisms* (London: Routledge, 2005); Mihalyi Csikszentmihalyi, 'Society, Culture and Person: A Systems View of Creativity', in Robert J. Sternberg (ed.), *The Nature of Creativity: Contemporary Psychological Perspectives* (Cambridge University Press, 1988), pp. 325–39; and Mihaly

Csikszentmihalyi, *Creativity, Flow and the Psychology of Discovery and Invention* (New York: Harper Collins, 1996).

6 See for example Joe Bennett, 'Creativities in Popular Songwriting Curricula: Teaching or Learning?', in Pamela Burnard and Elizabeth Haddon (eds.), *Activating Diverse Musical Creativities: Teaching and Learning in Higher Education* (London: Bloomsbury, 2015), pp. 37–56; Philip McIntyre, 'Creativity and Cultural Production: A Study of Contemporary Western Popular Music Songwriting', *Creativity Research Journal*, 20/1 (2008), pp. 40–52.

7 McIntyre has also pointed out the connection between Csikszentmihalyi's terms and those employed by Pierre Bourdieu's educational theory, specifically 'habitus' and 'field'.

8 McIntyre, 'Creativity and Cultural Production', p. 49.

9 Peter Etzkorn, 'The Relationship Between Musical and Social Patterns in American Popular Music', *Journal of Research in Music Education*, 12/4 (1964), p. 284. See also, 'Social Context of Songwriting in the United States', *Ethnomusicology*, 7/2 (1963), pp. 96–106; 'On Esthetic Standards and Reference Groups of Popular Songwriters', *Sociological Enquiry*, 36/1 (1966), pp. 39–47.

10 For an informative discussion of the role of the guitar in shaping British musicians during this period, see Mo Foster, *Play Like Elvis: How British Musicians Bought the American Dream* (London: Sanctuary 1997).

11 See Peter DeVries, 'The Rise and Fall of a Songwriting Partnership', *The Qualitative Report*, 10/1 (2005) pp. 39–54; Pamela Burnard, *Musical Creativities in Practice* (Oxford: Oxford University Press, 2012), pp. 72–99.

12 Charles K. Harris, *How to Write a Popular Song* (New York: Charles K. Harris, 1906), p. 11.

13 Jimmy Webb, *Tunesmith* (New York: Hyperion, 1998), p. 91.

14 Cullen has proposed a similar strategy in the context of teaching songwriting to L2 (English as a second language) students, using the expression, 'English song norms'. See Brian Cullen, 'Exploring Second Language Creativity: Understanding and Helping L2 Songwriters', unpublished PhD thesis, Leeds Metropolitan University (2009).

15 Csikszentmihalyi, 'Society, Culture and Person', p. 326.

16 See Allan F. Moore, 'Principles for Teaching and Assessing Songwriting in Higher Education', Palatine Papers (2004), formerly at www.lancs.ac.uk/palatine/reports/ allanmoore .htm (accessed 7 August 2014). For further contextualisation of the use of the term idiolect, see Richard Middleton, *Studying Popular Music* (Buckingham: Open University Press, 1990), p. 174.

17 Isherwood, 'Sounding Out Songwriting', p. 2.

18 Philip McIntyre, 'The Domain of Songwriters: Towards Defining the Term "Song"', *Perfect Beat*, 5/3 (2001), p. 109.

19 Webb, *Tunesmith*, p. 156.

20 For further discussion Allan F. Moore, 'The Track', in Amanda Bayley (ed.), *Recorded Music: Performance, Culture and Technology* (Cambridge University Press, 2010), pp. 252–67; Allan F. Moore, *Song Means: Analysing and Interpreting Recorded Popular Song* (Farnham: Ashgate, 2012).

21 McIntyre has made some useful observations on this in 'The Domain of Songwriters', pp. 105–8. Bennett (see 'Creativities in Popular Songwriting Curricula'), has built his own framework for song analysis on Moore's model, coining the term 'Track Imperatives' to encompass the various aspects that should be studied.

22 Useful texts providing tools for the analysis of song production include Simon Frith and Simon Zagorski-Thomas (eds.), *The Art of Record Production: An introductory Reader for a New Academic Field* (Aldershot: Ashgate, 2012); Robert Toft, *Hits and Misses: Crafting Top 40 Singles, 1963–71* (London: Continuum, 2011).

23 Stephen Citron, *Songwriting: A Complete Guide to the Craft* (New York: Limelight Editions, 2008). p. 284.

24 It is interesting to note that some of the more recent 'how to' guides have attempted to fuse old and new perspectives in their presentation. Cope, for example, shows melodic notation alongside snapshots from the DAW key editor. See Danny Cope, *Righting Wrongs in Writing Songs* (Boston, MA: Couse Technology, 2009).

25 For useful further discussion of the effects of digital interfaces on the creative process see: Andrew Brown, *Computers in Music Education: Amplifying Musicality* (New York, Routledge, 2007); James Mooney, 'Frameworks and Affordances: Understanding the Tools of Music-making', *Journal of Music, Technology and Education* 3/2&3 (2010), pp. 141–54; Mark Marrington, 'Experiencing Musical Composition in the DAW: The Software Interface as Mediator of the Musical Idea', *Journal on the Art of Record Production (online)*, 5 (2011); Lauri Väkevä, 'Garage Band or Garage Band ®? Remixing Musical Futures', *British Journal of Music Education*, 27/1 (2010), pp. 59–70;

26 Approaches to exploring the creative possibilities of the guitar as a songwriting tool are particularly well documented in the interview literature – see for example, Jeffrey Pepper Rodgers (ed.), *Songwriting and the Guitar (Acoustic Guitar Guides)* (San Anselmo, CA: String Letter Publishing, 2000).

25 Singer-songwriters and open mics

MARCUS ALDREDGE

The Western motif of musician as a creative but lonely journeyman harkens back to the medieval days of the European troubadour.[1] Singer-songwriters are one version of a modern-day musical troubadour.[2] Many of today's singer-songwriters are closely connected with the increasingly widespread musical event called an 'open mic'. The development of the musical open mic, where many musicians perform short sets back-to-back, exemplifies the growth of hybridised performance forums (e.g. karaoke)[3] and changing practices and rituals of public performance. A contemporary discussion about the genesis of the (post-)modern singer-songwriter would be remiss if a historical and organisational component linking singer-songwriters' biographies and pathways is absent. This chapter explores the open mic event as one historical, organisational, and biographical linkage.

Open mics ushered in a new organisational, intermediate place for artists' performing styles and genres to expand and hone their skills in music-making. These burgeoning activities help musicians practise and improve the playing of instrument(s) and the techniques of musical composition and public performance within a quasi-public setting. These recurring events provide an interstitial place revealing malleable biographical and murkier performance boundaries. A further examination of singer-songwriters and open mics illuminates a rich social and symbolic fabric underlying the lonely and seemingly polished forms on the surface.

While today's connection between singer-songwriters and open mics began in the late 1970s, academic literature investigating this cultural sphere remains lean. As of now, Behr[4] and I[5] have published the only academic investigations of these specific intersections between singer-songwriters and open mic settings and scenes. Much of this section's specific ethnographic examples, social regularities or patterns, and biographical experiences derive from these few research projects. This includes qualitative data such as quotations taken directly from singer-songwriters interviewed in these noted research projects. Nevertheless, this research topic remains extraordinarily ripe for future research.

An open mic is a group activity comprised of many shortened musical performances by different singer-songwriters, folk and popular musicians. This activity is a recurring performance setting and meeting place that also represents intersections of different musical genres and performance practices. The contemporary but dynamic musical open mic was birthed from different performance and musical activities of the past, some connected to the precursors of the twentieth-century singer-songwriter.

A discussion of the historical groundwork and cultural development of the open mic is followed by a description of its common characteristics and state today. The analysis segues into a genealogy and the merits of Arnold van Gennep's concept of liminality connecting open mics and singer-songwriters. Liminality denotes a cultural or personal state of ambiguity, in-between-ness or incompleteness. We will explore how this imbues the experiences and connections between singer-songwriters and open mic activities. The conclusion focuses on discussing two related concepts, *communitas* and the pilgrim, and how these ideas enhance a scholarly understanding of this worthy topic.

A historical evolution

The term 'open mike' (for open microphone) was coined in the early twentieth century. Open mikes began as a radio format on the quickly proliferating stations across the USA in the 1920s. These open mikes were forums airing live music or public discourse about civic matters. Open mikes were heavily censored by the government during World War II out of the fear of giving a public forum for oppositional voices, but they eventually returned with loosened restrictions by the 1950s. By the 1960s these public radio formats expanded, exposing more political commentary and beliefs in call-in radio open mikes. Even though it slowly disappeared from common media vernacular by the early 1970s, the open mike's persistence symbolised a nascent democratisation of voices and ideas through changing media forms.

Other precursors to the musical open mic were group activities involving some soloist musical improvisation. Three particularly influential events in America were the hoedown, the jazz jam session, and the folk music hootenanny. Hoedowns were community festivities focusing on musical performance and dancing. They trace back to the nineteenth century in Anglo-American groups in the southern and Appalachian regions of the USA. During the hoedown activity, many people would perform over a long period, alternating in and out, over the course of the event. The compositions would rely on folk traditionals, but would sometimes allow for musical improvisation.[6]

Jam sessions blossomed within the largely African American jazz communities of the mid-twentieth century. This format was typically a group of different musicians coming together to play, most frequently with an improvisational style, in bars in jazz meccas like New York City.

The group's common aesthetic was oriented towards the musician's preferences, not necessarily the audience's.[7] Balancing unique contributions and individual virtuosity with group directions and norms was important.

The closest predecessor to the modern open mic was the folk hootenanny, or hoot. Cultural and organisational similarities with the jazz jam session were even recognised and discussed in the early 1960s.[8] This musical activity arose from the folk music revival in the 1950s–60s and is accredited at least partially to Pete Seeger and Woody Guthrie.[9] Held often on college campuses, cafes, or coffee houses by mostly young people, hootenannies were ensembles of musicians playing with a frequent turnover in participating musicians. The music was largely folk and blues played with guitars and other string instruments.[10]

The inevitable collision of these different cultural and musical activities occurred in the late 1970s when the first located record of open mic appears in popular media with its current descriptive meaning. Critical to the inception was a Do-it-Yourself (DIY) ethos in the burgeoning youth culture since the punk rock scene of the 1970s and a recent surge in musical amateurism. Open mikes for folk, jazz, and rock music, comedy, and eventually poetry appear in newspaper listings for bars and coffee houses in Toronto, Washington DC, Boston, and New York City. In 1980, a few *New York Times* articles describe the resurgence of folk music and the rise of singer-songwriters in Greenwich Village and Washington Square Park. Gerdes Folk City (also referred to just as 'Folk City'), which had hosted some of Bob Dylan's first gigs in 1961, had an increasingly popular Monday night 'open-mike hootenanny' event for musicians, singer-songwriters, and performers.[11]

The abbreviated 'open *mike*' transformed into 'open *mic*' as the creative format slowly sprouted in urban areas in the USA during the 1980s. The spelling change was likely made to distance the new event from the former radio format. One iconoclastic open mic erupted in the mid-1980s in the East Village of New York City called the Antihoot. This became the weekly event most young, budding but especially quirky, alternative folk and rock-inspired singer-songwriters and musicians journeyed to play at least once. Eventually housed at the Sidewalk Café every Monday, it is said the antihoot birthed the anti-folk songwriting movement.[12] The anti-folk genre was a foundation for future stylistic variations such as freak, indie, and urban folk music. Well-known singer-songwriters, such as Beck, Michelle Shocked, and Regina Spektor, all made significant stops emerging as alumni of this locale's event.[13]

Today, a wide variety of songwriting styles, musical traditions and genres are performed at open mics by singer-songwriters and popular musicians around the world. This event is utilised by resourceful and adaptable singer-songwriters in many ways. For example, it provides novice singer-songwriters with their first stage time, or a means of acquiring a booking or gig. Amateurs and professionals also use these opportunities to have side-projects, practise new songs, find potential collaborators, or to play in front of others after a hiatus from public performances. At minimum, it provides an avenue of bringing songs to some perceivably objective, albeit potentially temporary, apex in the presence of others.

As to that particular point, a commonality across open mics is in how they allow the breaking of modern boundaries defining the processes and phases towards a finality of a song. Such 'upstream' processes or phases geared towards an artistic work's completion include the social practices of musical writing, composition, practising, and eventually performing.[14] As 'upstream' suggests, the activity of practising is done prior to a finalising performance. Practising is commonly held in removed or isolated places (e.g. garages, warehouses, or bedrooms) lacking certain qualities like designated audiences, performance rituals, and stricter norms governing fashion and speech.[15] Today's open mic displays the relativeness of these distinctions, representing a blurry middle ground as clarified with the concept of liminality, which is discussed later.

Open mics and singer-songwriters

The emergence of the Western singer-songwriter since the 1960s parallels the development of open mics. Today, open mics for popular and folk musicians are produced in abundance across cities in North America where the event originated. It has expanded into other Western and non-Western cultures via the expansion and access of the Internet at the turn of the millennium.[16] Internet-based open mics have appeared recently and spread with greater technological and communicational advancements.[17] As the local open mics have accomplished on a smaller scale, these new virtual formats have helped traverse different spatial, symbolic, and social boundaries. As a forum inspiring greater access for public expressions of creativity, they have also ostensibly democratised opportunities for artistic expression. Unlike open mics for distinctively different genres and performance styles,[18] a paralleled growth of singer-songwriters and open mics has fostered a more direct association in recent decades.

Briefly, an open mic is a weekly, bimonthly or monthly musical, artistic or expressive event for people across different levels of creative expertise and performance prowess, from novices to professionals. They are typically held at a sociable 'third place',[19] such as a public bar, club, coffee house, or café. Most open mics are geared either for comedians, poets, other spoken-word artists, or musicians. For the current discussion, the focus is open mics for popular, folk musicians and singer-songwriters who voluntarily show up, guitar in hand, to perform without a booking. The musicians sign up (in person or through email) in some type of sequential order (or they select a number in a lottery) and eventually either perform a limited number of songs or for an allotted amount of time (e.g. 8 minutes), as monitored by the host.

The host, or leader, is appointed by the establishment to regulate the sequence of performances. The number of musicians and singer-songwriters can range considerably from five to well over fifty and the entire event generally lasts between three and five hours. After all signed-up participants have performed, and given any remaining time in the establishment's evening, a jam among remaining musicians is common. In terms of how the musicians perform, the majority are soloists who also comprise the audience throughout the night's many performances. Outsiders to the performers, who often constitute an audience in public musical performances, are usually absent at open mics.

Open mics are accessible to the public and to any singer-songwriter, although often few outsiders attend. The open mic provides and represents greater accessibility to previously restricted, 'back stage'[20] locations erected to protect and elevate the prestige of particular musical and performance professions and genres in the twentieth century.[21] Transforming the production process into a more public and open context adds a new level of involvement and tension between solidarity and competition for singer-songwriters. This intermediate place and activity allows for different phases of songwriting within the songwriter's biographical processes of becoming.[22] Thus, as a symbolic island, the open mic provides a means for singer-songwriters to engage themselves in either tenuous or pivotal points in their careers or musical journeys for creative and developmental growth. These are the characteristics of liminality.

Liminality, *communitas*, and pilgrims

Contemporary open mics represent diffuse cultural changes in the social rituals and practices defining public and group musical performances. This shift embodies greater access and involvement in the upstream and production practices formerly protected by a select few in the culture industry. This is a critical theme to the intersections of singer-songwriters and open mics as they relate to the concepts of liminality, *communitas*, and pilgrims. In 1909 van Gennep proposed liminality as a middle phase within a three-phased ritual he termed rites of passage.[23] This concept was expanded by British cultural anthropologists Victor and Edith Turner, beginning in the late 1960s as they also added the term, liminoid and its relation to cultural pilgrims.

The rites of passage were cultural rituals marking and helping a transition between two fairly defined and fixed statuses or states for a person or group. Such processes for young singer-songwriters include transitioning into a new and often isolated amateur status. The process has three phases: separation, the limen, and aggregation or incorporation. Separation signifies an act of detachment or separation of an individual, group or society from a fixed point or cultural state. The limen is an intervening phase where the passenger or occupant experiences ambiguity, confusion, contradiction, or a paradoxical state – potentially containing aspects of the previous and forthcoming states. Aggregation, the final step, is when the passage is finalised or consummated with the person or group reentering a stable order.[24]

Most pertinent for this analysis is this middle, transitional or liminal phase. For van Gennep, life's transitions are essential to giving life coherence and experiential progression. These dramatic moments of unfolding transition often produce tremendous creativity as Victor Turner eventually recognised, an aspect important to framing the relationship between singer-songwriters and open mics. These periods and moments are usually embedded within social and daily dramas of life.[25] Turner recognised that these periods of liminality produce what he identified as *communitas*. *Communitas*, a general state of solidarity, equality, and openness, is discussed as it pertains to singer-songwriters and open mics. These concepts relate to the framing of singer-songwriters as pilgrims pursuing personal journeys in search of a finalising state, or particular musical shrines for performances.

Liminality: singer-songwriters and open mics

According to the African American singer-songwriter below, interviewed in 2007 as a part of a New York City-based study, open mics are commonly viewed and used thus: '[Open mics are where] singer-songwriters mostly play … almost an amateur night to expose your songs with an audience. [With] an open mic and without a gig it can provide a good thing for musicians. [Open mics] can be a gig for some people, but not for others.'[26] According to Jeffrey Pepper Rodgers' *The Complete Singer-Songwriter: A Troubadour's Guide to Writing, Performing, Recording and Business*,[27] open mics provide forums for musicians and singer-songwriters to get some stage time, and meet and talk shop with other musicians in the local community. They also provide a time-sensitive motivation for musicians to write and compose songs to perform in front of peers.[28]

Depending upon each singer-songwriter's developmental progress, open mics help musicians with different performance and musical objectives over time. Such changes partially reflect the variation of the somewhat nebulous positions of musical novice, amateur or professional all represented in varying magnitudes at open mics. It is in this way a crucial concept in understanding open-mics, in that liminality is, 'a world of contingency where events and ideas, and reality itself, can be carried in different directions … it serves to conceptualise moments where the relationship between structure and agency is not easily resolved or even understood'.[29] The transitional and contingent qualities of open mics are evidenced in a few notable dimensions.

Singer-songwriters use the open mic to perform unfinished musical compositions seeking various responses and input into their continued composition. This includes an audience's verbal and non-verbal forms of expression and possible discussions with other singer-songwriters after-ward. A harmonica player who frequently plays an open mic in Greenwich Village, New York highlights this theme:

> It's a place where anyone can get up and play anything they want and workshop material and try to get confidence and network with people. Get into a scene of likeminded people and to get gigs. Sure, it's a good interme-diary between performing on your own and warming up yourself and get [sic]comfortable in front of people.[30]

Individual performances show a wide range of stage techniques and pro-jected confidence or stage presence.

The verbal and non-verbal forms of performance communication are predicated on learning the techniques and scripts in the presentation of self onstage. Part and parcel to this is fine-tuning the processes of impres-sion management, or the ways in which one interprets and attempts to manage how an audience views one's actions.[31] On the other hand, just completing a song can be a monumental achievement for a novice and the stage time provides a helpful means in these incremental steps towards learning and gaining confidence. Stage talk, or talking with the audience, is one non-musical form of communication that is refined as performers become comfortable interacting in new, different and challenging per-formance situations and settings.[32] Possible difficulties for performances onstage may include breaking a string, forgetting the lyrics of a song, or simply playing a wrong chord or note. How a performer responds to and repairs these potentially discrediting moments is important and learned through more stage time. Learning and refining how to introduce songs and tell relevant stories are also essential scripts and skills learned in play-ing open mics.

These individual performances fall on a continuum between musical performance and practise; it is worth noting that different musical genres are often differentiated by distinctive performance routines, conventions and rituals. The open mic is typically a more practise-like atmosphere lacking outsiders, and lacking the process of prior booking, advertising, payment, and fashion norms for the performers. Each performance's brevity and contingent nature at the open mic, as someone who is absent can be bypassed, contributes to the more practise-like ambiance and vibe. Yet, these musicians often perform on the same stage, using the same staging equipment as used for normal gigs. Performers also typically have some degree of prior preparation for the open mic performance, which give it some performance-like qualities.[33]

A blending of different musical compositional practices appears at open mics. One technique composes music prior to the performance, another is a more improvisational and situational form of composition and a final type is some degree of collective decision-making prior and during the performance. The latter applies only to the few performances that are not soloists, making up a minority of the performances.[34] This variety of techniques is evident. A performer having written the song two hours prior reading the lyrics from a crumbled sheet of paper and trying to recall chord progressions is one such hybridity. The rare band in these events using the third, and more rock-like, technique of composition, or a novice who has worked on two songs for weeks leading up to the performance for the first time, represent common forms of composition at open mics.[35]

Adding to this dynamic is the tension between the sequential series of singer-songwriters switching places from the role of soloist performer to audience member. This presents a murky set of role relations recognising an audience as an important force in any performance. The historical audience-performer divide has varied, depending upon genre of music (e.g. folk, blues, rock, or pop), but these differences mostly vary across open mics.[36] Such indefinite, in-between-like qualities of performance rituals exemplify the liminality of these activities and settings.

My study in New York City suggests the aggregate population of singer-songwriters performing in open mics is a moderately diverse population in terms of class, education, and ethnicity, but a sizable plurality are white and college-educated. A significant majority of the performers are also male.[37] Most singer-songwriters begin musical careers in their adolescence and youth. Those regularly performing in open mics are often in their twenties or thirties, an age which scholars in Western societies associate today with a more ambiguous and confusing period of life.[38] Most of these musicians hold occupations or jobs to pay bills so they can pursue this perceived calling and avocation in writing and performing music.

Liminality is exemplified by singer-songwriters and how they use open mics for different purposes at different times of their career. These transitions are apparent across this malleable and multidimensional activity. Some singer-songwriters prefer playing exclusively by themselves as preparation for other gigs while others try to obtain gigs by playing open mics. Other musicians seek out potential collaborators or attempt to forge other beneficial connections. Trying new music which a singer-songwriter hopes to perform in a band elsewhere is another possible impetus for attending. Open mics can also serve as platforms to segue back into performing solo after a hiatus or a band's demise.

Most seasoned singer-songwriters are multi-instrumentalists but usually perform solo with an acoustic guitar. Other commonly played stand-alone instruments include the piano, electric guitar, and more esoteric instruments such as ukuleles, banjos, and dulcimers. These more marginal instruments often correspond to established musical genres, like folk, blues, and bluegrass, from which they usually draw multiple influences. The music performed at open mics often embodies diverse, hybrid or eclectic qualities indicative of inclusive musical tastes.[39]

Today's youthful singer-songwriters often traverse boundaries of taste, having been exposed to a variety of musical styles in their lifetime. They may incorporate a wide variety of traditions and genres into the writing of their original music.[40] The broad canopy of musical and performance influences contributes to the more fluid and unfinished state of musical discovery, biography, and identity. The term singer-songwriter increasingly represents more than a musical identity but also a musical style structures, set of practices, and genre.

Communitas at the open mics

These indeterminate, ambiguous yet creatively oriented qualities represent a liminal convergence for singer-songwriters. Victor Turner asserts liminality and liminoid, the latter associated with leisurely pursuits and activities in post-industrial societies, lead to an achieved state of *communitas*. *Communitas* is conducive to creative expression, community, equality, and sociability, closely idealised with the open mic activity. Singer-songwriters often metaphorically and spatially refer to this activity as an opportunity to leave the 'bedroom', one middle-aged male singer-songwriter who plays open mics in New York City stated; yet, the open mic does not quite constitute a gig. Thus, the open mic resides in-between a place for practising and a place for performing, where songs achieve some level of temporary completion consecrated with an audience and applause, only to likely go through further revision.[41]

This interstitial quality of the open mic acts as a proverbial way station in musician's journeys and pathways.[42] To extend the metaphor, these open mics more often act as a *chain of islands* or an archipelago for singer-songwriters to explore and find new lands, people, and cultures.

Open mics help musicians refuel, retool, and reaffirm the social identity as singer-songwriter that is often in isolation from the time working in the 'woodshed', as Robert Faulkner calls it.[43] Singer-songwriters discover more about themselves by encountering others on concurrent pilgrimages. These events function to bring together divergent musical pathways in a means of convergence and creative dialogue, not a final port of destination. The liminal place accommodates these musical pilgrims as they attempt to access the shrine of musical performance and sought-after success.

In this theoretically open, spontaneous, and receptive state of mind and relations, occupants forge social bonds helping diminish the cultural emphasis on class, ethnic, or rank divisions. Open mics are events embodied by transition and ambiguity; thus, *communitas* has the potential to ensue. According to Turner, this state brings together marginalised outsiders, newcomers, and other types of inferiors.[44] Forms of *communitas* appear in leisurely activities Turner identifies in industrial and likely post-industrial societies, called liminoid. This includes poets, novelists, painters, and musicians who commune to playfully subvert standards, emulated by the singer-songwriters at open mics.[45]

The degree of *communitas* persisting across these activities parallels the spectrum of social and cultural diversity, hybridity, and ambiguity. Although open mics are an important performance place in music scenes, they vary in terms of who attends and what type of local culture is created. Some are consistently more homogeneous than others in terms of the level of performance, musical prowess, and experience. Although diverse on an aggregate, specific open mics often attract singer-songwriters with similar genre influences, such as rock, blues, and traditional folk or urban folk music. Open mics vary depending upon preferred instrumentations, age groups, frequency of collaboration with other singer-songwriters and how each one is organised. Therefore, these different patterns and variations lead to a spectrum of openness, equality, acceptance, and joy among the participants.[46]

Edith Turner discusses the specific processes of 'agreeing to help one another' in a jam session, identifying *communitas* as it manifests in musical collaborations. This, however, does not completely address singer-songwriters; alternatively, soloists often get caught up in the flow, or zone of experience she approximates with *communitas* as very similar to, but in isolation from, others.[47] Flow is a state of mental concentration and loss of self-consciousness for a person absorbed in the experience of an activity.[48] This self-contained affect entices singer-songwriters to perform open mics, too.

Flow is individualised in its inception compared with *communitas* which is more externally contingent.[49] Achieving a unifying experience of *communitas* within open mic settings is more tentative and relative, but is replaceable with individualised experiences of flow within performances. As a greater feeling of acceptance and equality between singer-songwriters, *communitas* may persist where flow is not as consistent, such as with novices and beginners. In either case, these emotional and social changes drive singer-songwriters to use open mics through their journey and pilgrimage across the musical landscape.

Conclusion: singer-songwriters as pilgrims

The journey and transition from amateur to professional is not a new trope, as evidenced in J.A. Fuller Maitland's *The Musician's Pilgrimage: A Study in Artistic Development* published in 1898.[50] Today's biographical journey to different open mics expands performance experiences, and different forms of exchangeable resources such as expanded networks, greater knowledge, and refined performance techniques; however, there are distinguishing patterns and sequences taken in and across singer-songwriters' pathways. Some singer-songwriters only attend one open mic while others perform multiple events each week. Some singer-songwriters use one event as a home, so to speak, but slowly venture out exploring others. A less geographically stable but less common route is pursued by singer-songwriters who tour regions or a country performing at these events. Nevertheless, there are different pathways but most share a common desire to continue a pilgrimage to new places. This is one salient tie that binds these activities and participants.

Victor Turner identifies pilgrimages, most commonly associated with religion, to have liminality and qualities of *communitas*. Within the ritual journey, although norms often persist to some degree, a more simple and levelled co-presence persists among those collectively seeking a sacred site or finality. This shared journey reflects greater openness, universalism, and community of feeling by the participants.[51] Within the pilgrimage, the liminal state can become fixed or permanent for the travellers.[52]

It has been argued that singer-songwriters are authentic islands juggling issues of loneliness and critical self-examination.[53] One commonly referenced historical figure in describing modern singer-songwriters is the troubadour. The troubadour was a wandering performer of creative inspiration and musical and poetic expression in medieval Europe. This term today is used romantically to symbolise similar characteristics in a creatively inspired but solitary and troubled musical pilgrim – a singer-songwriter.

Many troubadours of the past were in liminal positions in the areas of economic class, artistic mediums, and court positions, retiring to a monastery eventually.[54] The troubadour bridged the medieval period and the Renaissance when creative expression transitioned from a place of anonymity to individuality.[55] A similar transition in time, place, and practice is evidential with the (post-)modern singer-songwriting troubadours as they encounter each other over their personal journeys at various open mics.

The latter half of the twentieth century represents to many scholars a period of significant transition and uprooting. The singer-songwriter's pilgrimage for creative and musical meaning represents a larger cultural transition in the Western world. The encounters, open mic performances and biographical searches persist across these events, imbued with degrees of liminality and *communitas*. In an ostensibly chaotic musical landscape, open mics perform as essential islands providing structure and support to musicians' developmental pathways. As soloists, singer-songwriters know as well as anyone that isolation may be romantic and creatively productive, but it is ideal if not necessary to converge for moments of sociability and performance.

Notes

1 Adam Gussow, *Journeyman's Road: Modern Blues Lives from Faulkner's Mississippi to Post 9/11 New York* (Knoxville: University of Tennessee Press, 2007).

2 Donald Brackett, *Dark Mirror: The Pathology of the Singer-Songwriter* (Westport: Praeger, 2008), p. XVIII.

3 Rob Drew, *Karaoke Nights: An Ethnographic Rhapsody* (New York: Altamira, 2001).

4 Adam Behr, 'The Real "Crossroads" of Live Music – the Conventions of Performance at Open Mic Nights in Edinburgh', *Social Semiotics*, 22/5 (2012), pp. 559–73.

5 Marcus Aldredge, *Singer-Songwriters and Musical Open Mics* (Farnham: Ashgate, 2013); Marcus Aldredge, 'Negotiating and Practicing Performance: An Ethnographic Study of a Musical Open Mic in Brooklyn, New York', *Symbolic Interaction*, 29/1 (2006), pp. 109–17.

6 Roger Abrahams and George Foss, *Anglo-American Folksong Style* (Englewood Cliffs: Prentice Hall, 1968).

7 William Bruce Cameron, 'Sociological Notes on the Jam Session', *Social Forces* 33/2 (1954), pp. 177–82.

8 *Time Magazine*, 'Folk-singing: Sibyl with Guitar', 23 November 1962, pp. 54–60.

9 David King Dunaway. *How Can I Keep From Singing: The Ballad of Pete Seeger* (New York: Random House, 2009).

10 S.L. Forcucci, *A Folk Song History of America* (Englewood Cliffs: Prentice Hall, 1984).

11 Gilbert Millstein, 'Making the Village Scene', *The New York Times*, 12 February 1961, p. 28; Robert Shelton, 'Bob Dylan: A Distinctive Folk Song Stylist', *The New York Times*, 29 September 1961, p. 31.

12 Amanda Petrusich, *It Still Moves: Lost Songs, Lost Highways and the Search for the Next American Music* (New York: Faber & Faber, 2008), pp. 233–60.

13 SideWalk Café History, Available at: www.sidewalkny.com/history/ (accessed 1 September 2014).

14 Howard S. Becker, Robert R. Faulkner and Barbara Kirshenblatt-Gimblett, 'Editors' Introduction: Art from Start to Finish', in *Art from Start to Finish: Jazz, Painting, Writing, and Other Improvisations* (Chicago: University of Chicago Press, 2006), pp. 3–13.

15 Ruth Finnegan, *The Hidden Musicians: Music Making in an English Town* (Middletown: Wesleyan University Press, 2007), pp. 266–8.

16 This is one of multiple online listings of open mics around the world: 'Welcome to BadSlava.com, the World's Largest Open Mic Website'. Available at: www.badslava.com/ (accessed 1 July 2014).

17 There are world-wide virtual open mics. Available at: www.virtualopenmic.org/ (accessed 1 July 2014).

18 See the following study on a hip-hop/rap open mic: Jooyoung Lee, 'Open Mic: Professionalizing the Rap Career', *Ethnography* 10/4 (2009), pp. 475–95; See the following study on a spoken word and poetry open mic:

Maisha Fisher, 'Open Mics and Open Minds: Spoken Word Poetry in African Diaspora Participatory Literacy Communities', *Harvard Educational Review* 73/3 (2003), pp. 362–89.

19 Ray Oldenburg, *The Great, Good Place: Coffee Shops, Bookstores, Bars, Hair Salons, and Other Hangouts at the Heart of a Community* (New York: Marlowe & Co, 1999).

20 Erving Goffman, *The Presentation of Self in Everyday Life* (New York: Anchor, 1959), p. 112.

21 Lawrence W. Levine, *Highbrow/Lowbrow: The Emergence of Cultural Hierarchy in America* (Cambridge: Harvard University Press, 1988); Steven J. Tepper, 'The Next Great Transformation: Leveraging Policy and Research to Advance Cultural Vitality', in Steven J. Tepper and B. Ivey (eds.), *Engaging Art: The Next Great Transformation of America's Cultural Life* (New York: Routledge, 2008).

22 Becker, Faulkner and Kirshenblatt-Gimblett, *Art from Start to Finish*, pp. 3–5.

23 Arnold van Gennep, 'Netting Without a Knot', in *Man* 9 (1909), pp. 38–9.

24 Victor Turner, *The Forest of Symbols: Aspects of Ndembu Ritual* (London: Cornell University Press, 1967), pp. 93–111; Victor Turner, *The Ritual Process: Structure and Anti-structure* (Ithaca: Cornell University Press, 1969), pp. 94–166.

25 Bjorn Thomassen, 'The Uses and Meanings of Liminality', *International Political Anthropology*, 2/1 (2009), pp. 5–27.

26 Aldredge, *Singer-Songwriters and Musical Open Mics*, p. 19.

27 Jeffrey Pepper Rodgers, *The Complete Singer-Songwriter: A Troubadour's Guide to Writing, Performing, Recording and Business* (San Francisco: Backbeat Books, 2003), pp. 93–5.

28 Ibid., p. 36.

29 Thomassen, 'The Uses and Meanings of Liminality', p. 5.

30 Aldredge, *Singer-Songwriters and Musical Open Mics*, p. 126.

31 Goffman, *The Presentation of Self in Everyday Life*, pp. 208–37.

32 John Bealle, 'Self-Involvement in Musical Performance: Stage Talk and Interpretive Control at a Bluegrass Festival', *Ethnomusicology*, 37/1 (1993), pp. 63–86.

33 Finnegan, *The Hidden Musicians*, pp. 143–59.

34 Aldredge, Negotiating and Practicing Performance, p. 114; Aldredge, *Singer-Songwriters and Musical Open Mics*, pp. 77–9.

35 Finnegan, *The Hidden Musicians*, pp. 160–79.

36 Aldredge, *Singer-Songwriters and Musical Open Mics*, pp. 123–59.

37 Ibid., pp. 78–9.

38 Jeffrey Jensen Arnett, *Adolescence and Emerging Adulthood: A Cultural Approach* (Upper Saddle River: Prentice Hall, 2001).

39 Adam Behr, 'The Real "Crossroads" of Live Music', p. 563; Aldredge, *Singer-Songwriters and Musical Open Mics*, pp. 78–9.

40 Younger, well-educated people today have a very expansive set of musical tastes and influences. See Richard Peterson, 'Changing Highbrow Taste: From Snob to Omnivore', *American Sociological Review*, 61/5 (1996), pp. 900–7.

41 Marcus D. Aldredge, 'Profiles in Courage: Practicing and Performing at Musical Open Mics and Scenes', PhD thesis, Texas A&M University (2009), p. 202. Available at: oaktrust. library.tamu.edu/bitstream/handle/1969.1/ ETD-TAMU-2009-08-7193/ALDREDGE-DISSERTATION.pdf (accessed 20 September 2015).

42 Behr, 'The Real "Crossroads" of Live Music', p. 565.

43 Robert Faulkner, 'Shedding Culture', in Becker, Faulkner and Kirshenblatt-Gimblett, *Art from Start to Finish*, pp. 91–117.

44 Turner, *The Ritual Process*, pp. 110–11.

45 Victor Turner, *Dramas, Fields and Metaphors: Symbolic Action in Human Society* (Ithaca: Cornell University Press, 1974), pp. 14–17.

46 Aldredge, *Singer-Songwriters and Musical Open Mics*, p. 45.

47 Edith Turner, *Communitas: The Anthropology of Collective Joy* (New York: Palgrave-Macmillan, 2011), pp. 47–50.

48 Mihaly Csikszentmihalyi, *Flow: The Psychology of Optimal Experience* (New York: Harper and Row, 1990).

49 Lee Phillip McGinnis, James W. Gentry and Tao Gao, 'The Impact of Flow and *Communitas* on Enduring Involvement in Extended Service Encounters', *Journal of Service Research*, 11 (2008), pp. 74–90.

50 J.A. Fuller Maitland's *The Musician's Pilgrimage: A Study in Artistic Development* (London: Smith, Elder & Co., 1898).

51 Turner, *Dramas, Fields and Metaphors*, p. 201.

52 Thomassen, 'The Uses and Meanings of Liminality', p. 15.

53 Brackett, *Dark Mirror*, pp. 1–9.

54 H.J. Chaytor, *The Troubadours* (Port Washington: Kennikat Press, 1912).

55 Gregory Stone, *The Death of the Troubadour: The Late Medieval Resistance to the Renaissance* (Philadelphia: University of Pennsylvania Press, 1994).

26 Singer-songwriter authenticity, the unconscious and emotions (feat. Adele's 'Someone Like You')

RUPERT TILL

This study addresses how singer-songwriters engage with emotion, unconscious processes, and effect, and therefore embodiment, feelings, and experiences. It also considers reception and various forms of mediation. This involves a discussion of authenticity of various types, of inscribing and ascribing authentication. It questions the use of the term singer-songwriter, what it means to use this term to refer to popular music composition, and whether it relates to a set of practices or a genre. Adele's song 'Someone Like You'[1] is used as a case study that illustrates these issues. Additionally, this chapter will also draw upon interviews with successful musicians in order to answer these questions. While such an approach raises the issue of authorial intent as valuable to the study of texts,[2] popular music, as a highly performative text, requires a differing approach. Even if one cannot be certain of the veracity of the opinions expressed by musicians in interviews, these reported opinions, as well as the other ways musicians present themselves to audiences, form an important element of their performativity, and greatly affect its reception. Whether or not addressing authorial intent is thought of as problematic or useful, it is in this situation certainly relevant, as it forms part of the artist's field[3] of activity, the artist acting as or constructing a frame[4] around the music.

Defining the singer-songwriter

The term singer-songwriter implies three key activities, singing, writing songs, and performing one's own material. Singer-songwriters are usually thought of as singing songs they have composed themselves, so some would argue that one would think of Paul Simon's solo work, rather than his work with Art Garfunkel, and exclude a songwriting team such as Burt Bacharach and Hal David; some identifiable singer-songwriters, however, are also associated with more overt collaborative work. One thinks of singer-songwriters as writing both the music and the lyrics, such as Bob Dylan rather than Elton John, as the latter seldom writes lyrics. They are usually solo artists, rather than performing in a band or writing collaboratively, so one might suggest John Lennon in his solo career, but not with

The Beatles. They tend to use simple arrangements, with a focus on the voice, thus perhaps Suzanne Vega, but not Frank Zappa.

There is a focus on songs that appear stripped-down and on their own rather than that are wrapped up in complex layers of recording and production, for example, Leonard Cohen rather than Danger Mouse. They usually play instruments, most typically playing guitar (Bob Dylan or Joni Mitchell) or piano (Carole King, Tom Waits, or Tori Amos), rather than only singing and writing songs. They are usually able to accompany themselves and perform on their own if required, so one thinks of Norah Jones rather than Jessie J. Finally, they often are perceived as writing principally about themselves, their experiences and their emotions, or at least as presenting themselves as if their songs are about themselves, for example Johnny Cash or Joni Mitchell. Most important perhaps is the idea of individually writing original material for performance, rather than performing compositions written by someone else, thus Elvis Costello rather than Elvis Presley.

There are a number of difficulties with this use of the term singer-songwriter to define a (usually single) popular music performer. Singing and songwriting are often quite separate and collaborative processes, not a merged holistic activity. The term 'song' itself is problematic in this context, for example Cone suggests it implies a number of creators, pointing out that the processes related to singing and accompaniment, and composition of both, are all to some extent separate and separated.[5] Even the use of 'writer' within songwriter is questionable, implying a paper-and-pen-based approach to composition. Singer-songwriter conventions draw from and rely on oral traditions and methods, whereas writing songs scored on paper is an approach more commonly associated with the commercial, professional songwriting teams that dominated popular music writing before the 1950s, or with art music composition.

A further issue is that many popular musicians call themselves composers rather than singer-songwriters. Joni Mitchell for example is often presented as an archetypal singer-songwriter, associated with similar artists such as Bob Dylan and David Crosby. However Mitchell's website avoids the term singer-songwriter, calling her a poet and songwriter, and 'singer, composer and lyricist';[6] she separates these activities.

It was in the 1950s and 1960s that writing original material began to become the dominant mode of creation for popular music performers. Buddy Holly and Chuck Berry were two prominent US popular musicians who became well known writing and singing their own original material. They both influenced The Beach Boys and The Beatles,[7] these latter groups firmly establishing the practice of singing of original compositions within popular music. From 1965, The Beach Boys' main songwriter Brian Wilson began to increasingly write specifically and overtly about his own emotions, and to deal with issues he considered had gravitas, to begin to consciously focus on authenticity of experience. This is reflected in writings about the album: 'Early Beach Boys lyrics about surfing and cars were celebrations of youthful hedonism. However such simple ideas, expressed in straightforward forms, though commercially desirable, no longer satisfied Brian … he rejected hot dogging and hot rodding in favour of writing about his own emotional experience.'[8] 'Brian's *Pet Sounds*[9] songs were different. They preserve the innocence of youth, speaking eloquently of love gained and love lost and all the emotional nuances in between. The message was personal rather than social, prodding us to analyze and reassess the way we interacted with each other, not how we interacted with the outside world.'[10] Although The Beatles and The Beach Boys certainly influenced one another, in *The Beatles Anthology* DVD, Paul McCartney tells us that he was inspired to compose by Buddy Holly and Chuck Berry, describing the latter as someone

> who was in the tradition of the great blues artists but he really wrote his own stuff … One of the main things about The Beatles is that we started out writing our own material. People these days take it for granted that you do, but nobody used to then. John and I started to write because of Buddy Holly. It was like, 'Wow! He writes and is a musician'.[11]

Both groups wrote their own songs and started to focus the subjects of their songs on their own experiences, on expressions of their own feelings, about their emotions (a subject we will return to later in this chapter). The most successful popular music stars before this time, such as Frank Sinatra, Bing Crosby, or Elvis Presley, sang other people's material. The Beatles became the most successful recording act of all time in the UK as well as the USA, and played a key role in making the singer-songwriter a dominant model within popular music.

The singer-songwriter has developed significantly from this 1960s model, from the individual activity of a solo-performing guitar and voice performer, to something that is often and increasingly a team activity. Singer-songwriters often collaborate with producers, band members, co-writers and an army of backroom music industry staff. There are many other layers of process involved, all of which are linked and related. Sting tells us 'I'm committed to that goal, that lifetime search. I still study music, I still want to be a better composer, a better songwriter, better singer, better performer'.[12] He separates out composition, songwriting and performance as disparate but coordinated activities. For Gary Barlow, the main songwriter of the band Take That, 'it's more than just the composition, I have to see it right through the whole recording procedure'.[13] Robin Gibb of The Bee Gees states that (his brother) 'Barry and myself, we always see it that way, composers first, recording artists second, and performers third. We've always loved the studio too, as it's like a painter's studio. You walk in, it's completely empty, it's like a clean canvas, or an altar'.[14] Composing the music may be the primary activity, but this is mediated through arrangement in the recording studio, and performance live to an audience.

Gibb, Barlow and Sting describe themselves as composers. For Gibb there are clear reasons why this might be. Although known in particular for writing songs he performed, he also wrote songs for others, including Diana Ross, Tina Turner, Barbara Streisand, Dionne Warwick, Celine Dion, and Frankie Valli. Thus his songwriting is not wedded to his singing. Like Gibb, Nattiez[15] neatly divides music into three areas, the poietic (creation of the music/songwriting), the neutral (immanent final product/ recording), and the aesthetic (audience reception/performing). Including the poietic affords[16] the opportunity to discuss what Tagg and others see as an under-represented subject in the field, the "'music' in "popular music studies'".[17] For the singer-songwriter these three fields form an interactive, enmeshed triangular frame (see Figure 26.1).

Unlike the term composer, the singer-songwriter is not defined solely by creative practices, such as singing and songwriting, but by a range of conventions. The singer-songwriter might be more usefully thought of as framing/forming a musical genre, rather than as a description of a type of music-maker, bearing in mind Fabbri's definition of a genre as the 'set of music events regulated by conventions accepted by a community'.[18] A singer-songwriter is an accepted and descriptive popular cultural term for a composer/performer working within a specific genre. Its definition as a genre is in part what allows it to contain and integrate a range of conflicting elements. Within this frame, binary opposites such as lyrics/ music, composer/performer, black/white or recording/live become negotiations[19] between interacting fields (such as poietic/neutral/esthetic or

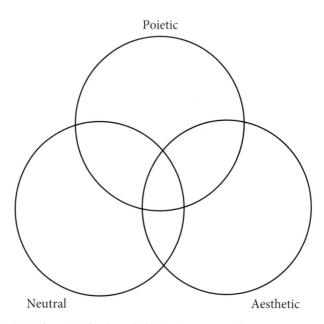

Figure 26.1. Nattiez's semiotic levels, applied to the singer-songwriter.

recording/composition/oral) that interact across the singer-songwriter spectrum within its range of conventions. This conception falls into the category of a non-representational theory (NRT),[20] avoiding binary oppositions using a fusion of discrete methodologies; NRTs are useful for addressing embodied cultures involving physical activities and direct experience, and have the potential for increasing inclusivity by eroding barriers that may lead to discrimination.

Jacques Attali discusses four codes or stages of music, of ritual (oral traditions),[21] representation (scored music), repetition (recordings), and composition. The contemporary singer-songwriter has roots in performative oral traditions of folk and African American music, but its texts exist primarily today as recordings. Performing original compositions places the singer-songwriter in this most recent stage, although only after popular music was defined as a recorded form. Integration of the folk singer-songwriter into an institutionally controlled music recording industry has seen it adopt hegemonic characteristics, and perhaps as a result, the relationships of the singer-songwriter tradition to issues of race has become somewhat problematic, the term usually referring to white musicians. African American musicians such as BB King, Chuck Berry, Ray Charles, Muddy Waters, Otis Redding, Stevie Wonder, James Brown, or Nina Simone are usually described as within a genre, such as soul, funk, rhythm'n' blues or jazz, rather than as singer-songwriters. The term singer-songwriter, if conceptualised as a genre rather than activity, is a frame readily able to bridge such complex issues and interactions. In addition its use can be political, by avoiding the use of existing terminology, taking pride in a language that is specific to a popular music context. The singer-songwriter frames many roles together within what Gelbart calls the composer-singer-instrumentalist-protagonist persona,[22] a number of participants often being embodied and represented by a publicly facing focus.

Popular music and authenticity

The term singer-songwriter separates those who sing their own songs from the professionalised approach of having a separate music composer, lyricist, performer and producer. The latter approach is received as more commercial, as somehow inauthentic, exemplified by commercially focused acts performing within talent shows such as *X Factor* or *American Idol*, in which performing original music is seen as in some way exceptional, rather than the norm. Popular music fandom generates an 'intensely felt desire for authenticity as compensation for the feeling that nothing escapes commerce'.[23] Allan Moore states that such authenticity is 'ascribed, not inscribed',[24] that it is principally given to a work by an audience, rather than being built in to the music. He suggests that 'the term has frequently been used to define a style of writing or performing, particularly anything associated with the practices of the singer-songwriter, where attributes of intimacy (just Joni Mitchell and her zither) and immediacy (in the sense of unmediated forms of sound production) tend to connote authenticity'.[25] The singer-songwriter genre, or style, is in particular defined by an ability to convince the audience that such self-authenticity is itself authentic. Authenticity is a defining aesthetic of the singer-songwriter genre.

Moore delineates three types of authenticity: first-person authenticity, or expressive authenticity, which arises when a composer or performer succeeds in conveying the impression that their work has integrity, and that it represents an attempt to communicate in an unmediated form with an audience;[26] second-person authenticity, or authenticity of experience, which occurs when a performance succeeds in conveying the impression to a listener that the listener's own experience of life is being validated;[27] and third-person authenticity, authenticity of execution, when an authentic mode of expression is acquired from another individual or community, arising 'when a performer successfully conveys the impression of accurately representing the ideas of another, embedded within a tradition of performance'.[28] The creation of first-person authenticity, suggesting the performance is unmediated, is a key aim of singer-songwriters, presenting their experiences through song, or giving that impression. Gelbart suggests that 'the musical qualities of "sincerity" or "directness" (as opposed to "mediation" or "artifice") were … valorized for their ability to create a "communal" experience'.[29]

Elvis Presley was ascribed third-person authenticity by audiences, as a result of his use of African American blues and rhythm 'n' blues music, but also through his abilities as a performer to connect with audiences and generate second-person authenticity. His lack of first-person authenticity to some extent undermined his overall authenticity and credibility, becoming regarded as someone who profited from African American culture.[30] In comparison, Adele, another white musician singing music of black origin, has the advantage of writing her own music, being thus ascribed greater first-person authenticity by fans and critics alike, through (re)presenting feelings and problems from her life in her songs.

Popular music and the unconscious transmission of emotion

One of the primary requirements of a song, especially for young people, is the need to listen to lyrics dealing with 'feelings and problems'.[31] Emotion and feelings, and their relations to music, are subjects that are much debated with little consensus. Juslin and Laukka conclude that there is now overwhelming evidence that music is primarily listened to for emotional reward, it is valued because it expresses and induces emotions.[32] Both Prinz[33] and Laird[34] describe emotions as unconscious processes. Further, 'Music is a sensory phenomena that elicits perceptual and emotional responses'[35] and 'appropriately structured music acts on the nervous system like a key on a lock, activating brain processes with corresponding emotional reactions'.[36] As Nettleton puts it, 'at the level of the id it (music) puts us in touch with primitive affective states'.[37] Music is able to express and induce emotion in an unconscious fashion.

In interviews, many singer-songwriters discuss presenting their unconscious emotions through their music. John Lennon tells us 'I'd struggled for days and hours, trying to write clever lyrics. Then I gave up, and "In My Life"[38] came to me – letting it go is the whole game'.[39] Lennon described this song as his first serious piece of work.[40] Ehrlich interviews a number of artists who address a similar approach, one of letting go, engaging with unconscious processes. Mick Jagger states songs 'rise to the surface if you give them the right atmosphere to come out'.[41] Billy Bragg says, 'you are trying to create a common bond with the listener … If you can reach inside yourself and find a metaphor to conjure up these deep human feelings, you will strike a common chord with a lot of listeners. Of course, you don't do this consciously'.[42] Perry Farrell: 'I might have written a particular song, but it might have been automatic writing done on behalf of all of us. That's what I kind of hope when I write a song'.[43]

Zollo interviews a number of songwriters who discuss this subject. Songwriter Hal David tells us 'it's in the subconscious somewhere',[44] and Lamont Dozier suggests, 'when I'm at the piano coming up with melodies and ideas, I'm somewhat in a trance … you learn to just shut out everything around you. I focus in on what I'm doing and nothing else can really penetrate my psyche at that particular time'.[45] Harry Nilsson states 'It happens so quickly it happens without you being aware of it, that's why it seems like it's coming from a different place … It's just that you're not that conscious of it all the time. You start studying it or analyzing it, it goes away. So I don't spend much time doing that'.[46] Randy Newman: 'When you get something going, that's what I love. When I don't know what time it is. When I know that time is going. When you got something, it's a great feeling'.[47] Neil Young: 'I don't force it. If it's not there, it's not there and there's nothing you can do about it … It's a subconscious thing'.[48] David Crosby: 'My songs emerge from my life or whatever they do unbidden and unplanned and completely on a schedule of their own'.[49] Jackson Browne: 'It almost feels like I'm not there when it happens, so it's hard to talk about it. Yeah, there's sort of a descent into a place below your conscious mind, a place where words have resonances and they have meaning and they don't necessarily make a kind of conscious sense'.[50] Todd Rundgren: 'I have this tendency sometimes to dream songs completely written'.[51] Madonna: 'I don't remember the name of my first song, but I do remember the feeling that I had when I wrote it. And it just came out of me. I don't know how. It was like somebody possessed me'.[52] David Byrne comments:

> I tend to believe that it comes from something within myself. But it comes from the collective unconscious, from a part of myself that's also very similar to other people, so it becomes a part of myself that's no longer me. It's not I any longer. It doesn't reflect my petty concerns or desires or problems, It's tapping into something universal.[53]

KT Tunstall says that 'I kind of feel that they're done already and they're just waiting … it was very automatic writing … it's a bit of a lightning bolt and it'll just go and go and it will come very quickly'.[54]

All discuss trying to remove as much mediation as possible in the songwriting process, by tapping into unconscious processes. This affords the expression of internal emotions when singing, further affording a direct connection with the emotions of the audience and a resultant ascription of first- and second-person authenticity. These comments are from interviews, and are in part performances, and one must be cautious not to uncritically accept such assertions as 'truth'. However numerous other examples could be given, and this evidence strongly suggests that both dealing with emotions and accessing unconscious processes are important areas of the work of the singer-songwriter, whether one believes this to be part of the culture surrounding the genre, or a fundamental part of the creative process.

The singer-songwriter model of popular music-making is able to address and afford ascription of all three types of authenticity, which is one of the factors that marks out the singer-songwriter from other types of popular music creation. This authenticity is enhanced through and framed by association and interaction with unconscious emotional processes. Adele provides an interesting example of this type of singer-songwriter.

'Someone Like You'

In the UK, Adele performed the song 'Someone Like You'[55] at the 2011 Brit Awards. She was introduced by host James Corden.

> There's nothing quite like the feeling when you're listening to a song written by someone you don't know, who you've never met, who somehow manages to describe exactly how you felt at a particular moment in your life. This next artist is able to do this time after time. For that reason she is currently number one in an astonishing seventeen countries. If you've ever had a broken heart, you are about to remember it now.[56]

This exemplifies what Cone[57] would call Adele's persona, the image presented of her, of being someone like you, where you is the listener (See Chapter 16 for more on Adele). Following this performance the song went to the top of the UK charts, going on to sell over a million copies. In a

Billboard magazine interview Colombia records chairman Steve Barnett says that the '"long tail" sales theory fundamentally shaped the label's *21* campaign'.[58] Adele's manager James Dickins explains:

> When she won the BRIT Award and the BBC poll, what came with that [in England] was a tremendous amount of hype … But no one cares about the BRIT awards in the US, so Columbia was brilliant in thinking, 'Right, OK, let's build this record at a grass-roots level.' It wasn't about flying the record out and going for the jugular. It was a slower process, looking for the right TV looks, building at triple A and hot AC,[59] generally snowballing through multiple platforms. Consequently people bought into her, not into a song.[60]

The appearance of marketing was minimised, though carefully planned, in order not to create an appearance of commercial focus and inauthenticity. Adele's team suggests: 'the key to great singers is believing every single word they sing … And I think you believe every word that comes out of Adele's mouth'.[61]

I saw Adele's song 'Someone Like You' (from the album *21*), performed at the O2 Academy in Leeds, UK (14 April 2011). It is an interesting example of emotionality in popular music. She preceded the performance by discussing the subject material of the song, describing how difficult it was to travel around Europe singing songs about a relationship break-up that was still fresh in her mind. As the song progressed, Adele paused, seemingly overcome in the moment, and invited the audience to take over singing for a few lines. The audience's emotional response and empathy for her had a corresponding emotional response in the singer. Tears rolled down her cheeks onstage, as well as throughout the audience, as a thousand voices sang the lyrics of her song. Still in tears Adele told the crowd, 'I think that might have been the best moment of my life, ever, thank you'.

In *The Independent* newspaper, reviewer Enjli Liston writes of the performance,

> Fists clench, voices crack, hairs stand on end and tears stream down cheeks as Adele weaves hopelessness, fragility, desperation and defiance into her timeless tale of the pain of unrequited love – recent No 1 single 'Someone Like You'. The notes come easily, underlined with the gentle rise and fall of simple keys, but she strives to hit them with every ounce of her strength before, as with her Brit awards performance, she is overcome by emotion.[62]

Audience members also posted reviews online:

> She gave you goosebumps when she sang 'Make You Feel My Love' and 'Someone Like You'. I don't think there was one person in the audience who didn't have a tear in their eye.
>
> The best bit was when the audience made Adele cry!! It was a very emotional gig. When she got upset and the audience took over, Was a spine tingling moment.[63]

The emotional response of the crowd was set up by the frame placed around the song by Adele, the audience members themselves, and by the music industry activities of her marketing team.

Adele began 'Somebody Like You' in Leeds playing the guitar, she then stopped after the first section, and was accompanied for the rest of the song by a keyboard player, as on the recording (the electronic keyboard onstage was clad in wood to make it look like a piano, to make it look authentic). The pianist in both cases was professional songwriter Dan Wilson, who also co-wrote the song:

> I was dead set on making the song sound great but very natural, very vulnerable, very devastated … For the next many months, I would hear sporadic reports from people who heard it, and everybody would tell me that it made them cry. It's kind of funny, it seems like a very common response to the recording. At first, I thought people were crying because they know Adele and they felt the pain of her break-up and were being empathetic. But then after a while, I kept hearing the same report from people who heard the song but don't know Adele personally. They were crying too.[64]

It seems that the song brings feeling to the fore for many listeners, and that they respond unconsciously, crying perhaps on remembering their own experiences of heartbreak, in response to Adele's evocation of her own feelings.

In DVD concert footage from the Royal Albert Hall, as in Leeds, Adele also sings 'Someone Like You' as her first encore. She tells the audience:

> When I was writing it … I didn't have that one song that I believed myself on, and that one song that moved me, and it's important that I do feel like that about at least one of my songs … I was a bit scared that I wasn't going to have that song, which just would have made the album not very believeable I think, because I would not have had that much conviction when I was talking about it, and singing about it.[65]

At the end of the song she is again crying. The DVD shows her wipe away tears, then cuts to a shot of a member of the audience also wiping away a tear. What was inscribed in this piece of music by Adele and the music industry machinations behind her, was sign after sign to encourage the audience to believe that this was a song that was true to life, was authentic. For the singer-songwriter, that music is considered authentic is an important part of the set of accepted conventions[66] that establish it as a genre.

The singer-songwriter in the twenty-first century

Moore is correct that artists cannot ensure that an audience will choose to ascribe music with authenticity, but something has to be created to be authenticated, the process of authentication is a negotiation between audiences and performers. The music industry can choose to present an artist as authentic, and this is usually the approach within the genre of the singer-songwriter. Music industry professionals, as well as audiences, encourage singer-songwriters to develop characteristics that will lead to ascription of authenticity, and to resultant sales. The conventions of the singer-songwriter genre also afford the development of these attributes. Inspiring people to consider you authentic is a skill performers develop, in part through learning not to become too caught up in processes of mediation, and to trust instincts, emotions, and unconscious processes. It is my contention, and the experience of the many artists I have referenced in this chapter, that a performer is able to make it more likely that an audience will ascribe music with authenticity using this approach. The musician has a choice whether to attempt to be opaque, true to what they consider to be themselves, whether or not it is possible for the audience to know whether the musician is being honest. Just as we unconsciously perceive untruths or untrustworthiness in other situations, such 'keeping it real' can contribute greatly to a performer's success, but more importantly perhaps, to their own happiness, to how they feel about themselves in the moment of performance. When musicians embrace this choice they comply with the conventions of the singer-songwriter genre.

The term singer-songwriter is useful as it addresses not just a type of popular musician, but a genre, an attitude, an ethos. A singer-songwriter is a subset of a term like composer or composer/performer. Artists are framed by the persona of the singer-songwriter, drawing down its authority. Individually framed moments of performance are empowered and ascribed with authenticity by audiences, affording a moment of community, releasing unconscious emotional responses in performer and audience alike. Frith describes such moments:

> Clearly one of the effects of all music, not just pop, is to intensify our experience of the present. One measure of good music, to put it another way, is, precisely, its 'presence', its ability to 'stop' time, to make us feel we are living within a moment, with no memory or anxiety about what has come before, what will come after.[67]

In such moments we are entrained to what the Greeks called *kairos*, qualitative time, rather than *chronos*, quantitative time. Musicians are well aware of the power of such emotional moments: 'Basically I think if you sort of put them all in one bag, I think my songs are all under the label emotion, you know, it's emotional feeling, I write songs that a lot of people have written before, it's all to do with love and emotion' (Freddie Mercury).[68] 'As composers, Barry and myself and Maurice, it's a labour of love. It's about emotional values, about human relationships, it's not a fashion thing. There will always be the mainstay of popular music songs about human relationships, and the human condition lasts forever' (Robin Gibb).[69] Gary Barlow describes the subject particularly effectively:

> Just touch them, give them a message no matter how complex it is or how simple it is as long as you touch people with it that's the job done right there … that's beautiful that is, that's changing the world right there. That's the power we've got. Work at it, be serious about it, put time in, because the more time and more effort, the more of your heart and soul you get into there, the more chance you've got of touching people. I think that's my opinion, that's the one I live by.[70]

The aesthetic priorities of singer-songwriters include issues of emotion, the unconscious and authenticity. The term also provides an alternative to the professionalised model of separation of the roles of producer, composer, lyricist and performer that is more common within other musical genres. The term singer-songwriter provides a frame for a popular music cultural field of activity that is both specific and highly developed. It is a frame that is unique to popular music, has its own history, power, and authority, and differentiates from the conventional aesthetic and tradition of the composer.

The singer-songwriter tradition draws upon folk and blues histories, suggesting a definition of popular music in terms of music of the populace, and connecting it with orality and issues of authenticity. In an era of composition[71] where computer music technology and online distribution have made more accessible the creation, performance and distribution of popular music, the singer-songwriter model of popular music creation is gaining attention from those who recognise its increasing relevance and importance within musical culture. It is also being reinvented and revived, from bedroom electronic music producers to new folk musicians, and continues to be highly relevant within contemporary musical culture. For these latter examples, its conventions of authenticity keep it untainted by the greatest extremes of music industry control and manipulation, framing, negotiating, and balancing a range of conflicting priorities, and allowing this tradition to maintain a spirit (or appearance depending on one's perspective) of unmediated emotional transmission born of oral traditions and unconscious processes.

Acknowledgements

Thanks to Aaron Cassidy, Lisa Colton, Rachel Cowgill, Lucy Harper and Catherine Haworth for advice and encouragement.

Notes

1 Adele. 'Someone Like You', *21*. XL Recordings XLS533D, 2011.

2 William K. Wimsatt and Monroe C. Beardsley, 'The Intentional Fallacy', *Sewanee Review*, 54 (1946), pp. 468–88. Revised and republished in William K. Wimsatt, *The Verbal Icon: Studies in the Meaning of Poetry* (Louisville, KY: University of Kentucky Press, 1954), pp. 3–18.

3 Rupert Sheldrake, *Morphic Resonance: The Nature of Formative Causation* (Rochester, VT: Park Street Press, 2009).

4 Jim A. Kuypers, *Rhetorical Criticism: Perspectives in Action* (Lanham, MD: Lexington Press, 2009).

5 Edward Cone, *The Composer's Voice* (Berkeley and Los Angeles: University of California Press, 1974), pp. 16–21.

6 *Joni Mitchell.com – Official Site*. Available at jonimitchell.com/music/ (accessed 25 February 2015).

7 Rupert Till, 'The Blues Blueprint: The Blues in the Music of The Beatles, The Rolling Stones, and Led Zeppelin', in Neil Wynn (ed.), *Cross the Water Blues: African American Music in Europe* (Jackson, MS: University Press of Mississippi, 2007) pp. 183–202.

8 Kingsley Abbott, *The Beach Boys' Pet Sounds: The Greatest Album of the Twentieth Century* (Helter Skelter: Bath, 2001), p. 38.

9 The Beach Boys. *Pet Sounds*. Capitol Records. T2458. 1966.

10 Charles Granata, *I Just Wasn't Made for These Times: Brian Wilson and the Making of Pet Sounds* (Unanimous: London, 2003), p. 14.

11 *The Beatles Anthology* (DVD). 1995. EMI. Dir. Bob Smeaton.

12 Sting discusses the craft of songwriting in this clip from 'Established in the Soul', an episode of the Australian ABC TV series 'Access All Areas' from 1997 (2009). Available at youtube/P5C7d8DM9Pc (accessed 25 February 2015).

13 *Show Me How To Play – Interview by Gary Barlow* (2009). Available at youtube/Tc44Ttxb2_Y (accessed 25 February 2015).

14 Robin Gibb, *The Art of Songwriting* (2012). Available at youtube/aeqGCUoVAsE (accessed 25 February 2015).

15 Jean-Jacques Nattiez, *Music and Discourse: Toward a Semiology of Music*. trans. Carolyn Abbate. (Princeton, NJ: Princeton University Press, 1990), p. 92.

16 For discussion of affordance see James, J. Gibson, *The Ecological Approach to Visual Perception* (Stanford, CA: Stanford University Press, 1979); Eric Clarke, *Ways of Listening: An Ecological Approach to the Perception of Musical Meaning* (Oxford: Oxford University Press, 2005).

17 Philip Tagg, 'Caught on the Back Foot: Epistemic Inertia and Visible Music', *IASPM Journal* 2/1–2 (2011), p. 12.

18 Franco Fabbri, 'How Genres are Born, Change, Die: Conventions, Communities and Diachronic Processes', in Stan Hawkins (ed.), *Critical Musicological Reflections* (Aldershot: Ashgate, 2012), p. 188.

19 For a discussion of Gramsci's concept of negotiation in reference to popular music, see Brian Longhurst, *Popular Music and Society* (Cambridge: Polity, 1995), pp. 20–1.

20 See Nigel Thrift, *Non-representational Theory: Space, Politics, Affect* (London: Routledge, 2007); John-David Dewsbury, 'Witnessing Space: "Knowledge Without Contemplation"', *Environment and Planning*, 35, pp. 1907–32.

21 Jacques Attali, *Noise: The Political Economy of Music* (University of Minnesota Press: Minneapolis, 1985); originally published in 1977 in French, updated as Jacques Attali, *Bruits: Essai sur l'Économie Politique de la Musique* (Paris: Presses Universitaires de France, 2001).

22 Matthew Gelbart, 'Persona and Voice in the Kinks' Songs of the Late 1960s', *Journal of the Royal Musical Association*, 128/2 (2003), p. 204; see also Rupert Till, 'We Could Be Heroes: Personality Cults of the Sacred Popular', in *Pop Cult: Religion and Popular Music* (London: Continuum, 2010), pp. 46–73.

23 Robert Walser, 'Popular Music Analysis: Ten Apothegms and Four Instances' in Allan F. Moore (ed.), *Analyzing Popular Music* (Cambridge University Press, 2003), p. 18.

24 Allan F. Moore, 'Authenticity as Authentication', *Popular Music* 21/2 (2002), p. 10.

25 Ibid., pp. 211–2.

26 Ibid., p. 6.

27 Ibid., p. 12.

28 Ibid., p. 10.

29 Gelbart, 'Persona and Voice in the Kinks' Songs of the Late 1960s', p. 206.

30 See Nelson George, *The Death of Rhythm and Blues* (New York: Penguin, 2003) and Reebee Garofalo, 'Crossing Over: From Black Rhythm &Blues to White Rock 'n' Roll' in Norman Kelley (ed.), *R'n'B (Rhythm and Business): The Political Economy of Black Music* (New York: Akashic, 2002): pp. 112–37.

31 Umberto Eco, *Apocalittici e integrati. Communicazioni di massa e teorie della cultura di massa* (Milan: Bompiani, 1964), p. 290; Luca Marconi, 'Canzoni Diverse: A Semiotic Approach to Luigi Tenco's Songs', in Franco Fabbri and Goffredo Plastino (eds.), *Made in Italy: Studies in Popular Music* (New York: Routledge, 2013), p. 109.

32 Patrik Juslin and Petri Laukka, 'Expression, Perception, and Induction of Musical Emotions. A Review and a Questionnaire Study of Everyday Listening' *Journal of New Music Research*, 33 (2004), p. 223.

33 Jesse Prinz, *Gut Reactions: A Perceptual Theory of Emotion* (New York: OUP, 2004).

34 James Laird, *Feelings: The Perception of Self* (Oxford: Oxford University Press, 2007).

35 Petr Janata and Scott Grafton, 'Swinging in the Brain: Shared Neural Substrates for

Behaviours Related to Sequencing and Music', *Nature Neuroscience* 6/7 (2003), p. 682.

36 Gordon Bruner II, 'Music, Mood and Marketing', *Journal of Marketing* 54/4 (2010), p. 94.

37 Sarah Nettleton, *Music and internal experience*. Available at www.limbus.org.uk/Music_and_internal_experience.doc (accessed 25 February 2015).

38 The Beatles, 'In My Life', *Rubber Soul*, Parlophone, PCS1375, 1965.

39 *The Beatles' Anthology* [DVD].

40 David Sheff, *All We Are Saying: The Last Major Interview with John Lennon and Yoko Ono* (New York: St. Martin's, 2000).

41 Dimitri Ehrlich, *Inside the Music: Conversations with Contemporary Musicians about Spirituality, Creativity and Consciousness* (Boston, MA: Shambhala Publications, 1997), pp. 65–6.

42 Ibid., 189.

43 Ibid., pp. 65–6.

44 Paul Zollo, *Songwriters on Songwriting* (New York: Da Capo, 1997), p. 212.

45 Ibid., p. 150.

46 Ibid., p. 241.

47 Ibid., p. 274.

48 Ibid., pp. 354–5.

49 Ibid., p. 373.

50 Ibid., p. 409.

51 Ibid., pp. 420–1.

52 Ibid., p. 616.

53 Ibid., pp. 496–7.

54 *KT Tunstall Talks About Songwriting Process* (2008). Available at youtube/70EL5Un0q5M (accessed 25 February 2015).

55 See n. 1.

56 Brit Awards, *Brit Awards 2011 Adele Performing Live* (2011). Available at www.youtube.com/watch?v=qemWRToNYJY (accessed 25 February 2015).

57 Cone, *The Composer's Voice*.

58 Mikael Wood, 'Adele: The Billboard Cover Story', *Billboard*. Prometheus Global Media (2011). Available at www.billboard.com/#/features/adele-the-billboard-cover-story-1005015182.story?page=2 (accessed 25 February 2015).

59 Triple A means sales platforms Apple (itunes), Android and Amazon; hot AC means 'Hot Adult Contemporary' radio stations, which mostly play classic hits and contemporary mainstream music, mainstream pop and alternative rock. The 'right TV looks' are carefully selected television programmes. Media coverage was targeted, rather than as wide as possible.

60 Ibid.

61 Ibid.

62 Enjoli Liston, 'Tears Fall as Records Tumble', *The Independent* (18 April 2011). Available at www.independent.co.uk/arts-entertainment/music/reviews/adele-02-academy-leeds-2269192.html (accessed 25 February 2015).

63 Ticketmaster, *Adele Fan Reviews* (2011). Available at reviews.ticketmaster.co.uk/7171-en_gb/1159272/adele-reviews/reviews.htm?page=6 (accessed 25 February 2015).

64 Doug Waterman, 'The Story Behind The Song: Adele, "Someone Like You". *American Songwriter, The Craft of Music* (2012). Available at www.americansongwriter.com/2012/01/the-story-behind-the-song-adele-someone-like-you/ (accessed 25 February 2015).

65 *Adele. Live at the Royal Albert Hall* [DVD]. 2011. XL Recordings. Dir. Paul Dugdale.

66 Fabbri, 'How Genres are Born, Change, Die', p. 188.

67 Simon Frith, 'Towards an Aesthetic of Popular Music', in Richard Leppert and Susan McClary (eds.), *Music and Society: The Politics of Composition, Performance and Reception* (Cambridge University Press, 1989), p. 142.

68 *Queen: Classic Albums. A Night at the Opera*. 2005. Eagle Rock Entertainment. Dir. Matthew Longfellow.

69 Gibb, *The Art of Songwriting*.

70 *Show Me How To Play – Interview by Gary Barlow*.

71 Attali, *Noise*.

PART V

Global perspectives

27 Don McGlashan and local authenticity

NICK BRAAE

Authenticity and singer-songwriters

Singer-songwriters have traditionally fared well in authenticity debates.[1] Those of a particularly style (acoustic and minimal instrumentation) have been considered to 'convey their own truth' by giving the impression of unmediated expression.[2] Further, the singer-songwriter's status rises in popular music discourse, by virtue of his or her fluency in multiple musical areas (i.e. singing and songwriting). This can be viewed in terms of Allan Moore's 'third-person authenticity' ('that they speak the truth of their own culture, thereby representing (present) others'),[3] insofar as the singer-songwriter is true to the values of their popular music culture.[4] Moore's third category also acts as the springboard for the current chapter, which addresses New Zealand singer-songwriter Don McGlashan. One of the prominent themes in New Zealand music discourse is what may be termed 'local authenticity'.[5] A number of authors have focused their work on artists who demonstrate a relationship, explicitly or implicitly, with their 'local' geographical and socio-cultural settings.[6] Zuberi argues that the nationalist strands of this idea are borne out of a 'postcolonial and oedipal reaction' to British influences and a 'backlash' against American cultural imperialism.[7] Authenticity, in this context, can thus be understood as presenting a distinct New Zealand voice in the face of global musical forces. McGlashan has been an important figure within this discourse; as per the ideas above, the aim of this chapter is to develop a greater understanding of McGlashan's status as an 'authentic' New Zealand singer-songwriter.

Don McGlashan's local authenticity

Firstly, however, some background material may be useful.[8] McGlashan has been the singer and songwriter for several New Zealand bands since the 1980s, including Blam Blam Blam, the Front Lawn, and the Muttonbirds, as well as forging a successful solo career. He plays multiple instruments, including the guitar, drums, and French horn, and has developed a stylistically plural approach to songwriting courtesy of a diverse musical upbringing: in his words, 'while my friends were listening to the Clash, I was listening to the Clash and Mahler'.[9] Critics and academics have held McGlashan's output in high esteem, with many highlighting the local connections in his songs. Tony Mitchell is particularly praiseworthy: 'McGlashan and the Muttonbirds [McGlashan's early 1990s band] have specialized most outstandingly in eerie divinings of the terrestrial spirits of the North Island';[10] McGlashan 'expresses one of the most profound relations to place' in New Zealand popular music,[11] and is 'the country's most profound sonic "psychogeographer"'.[12] Critic Russell Baillie has noted the geographical aspects that run through the singer-songwriter's work.[13] McGlashan himself has encouraged these views, arguing that New Zealand's environment has a profound impact on local musicians and, subsequently, local music.[14] He has further commented that, having spent time abroad in the 1990s, New Zealand settings resonated with him and inspired his songwriting in a way that English settings did not.

McGlashan's place in this discourse invariably rests on the fact that he writes song lyrics that address the people, places, attitudes, and culture of New Zealand. In this regard, he exemplifies notions of local authenticity as invoked in the work of the aforementioned New Zealand academics and critics. The problem, however, in accounts of his work is that they are limited, for the most part, to discussions of the lyrical content. Mitchell provides some general musical descriptions, such as the 'jaunty, uptempo' nature of 'Queen Street' or the 'very Pākehā-styled musical setting' of 'Andy', with the latter description referring to the folk elements of the song;[15] but elsewhere, he refers only to the words of songs.[16] Bannister's analysis of McGlashan is nuanced and ties the singer-songwriter into New Zealand cultural tropes and identity themes, but does not cover specifically the musical components of his output.[17] Accordingly, there is a disconnect between Mitchell's claim that McGlashan is 'surely the most important New Zealand singer-songwriter after Neil Finn',[18] and the writing that both enhances and seeks to explain his importance. In other words, how do McGlashan's singing and the musical aspects of his songwriting contribute to appraisals of local authenticity? An immediate problem is that there are few, if any, stylistic traits of his songs that are distinct to New Zealand: as McGlashan puts it, 'most New Zealand songs and instrumental pieces don't come with their birthplace clearly stamped on them for the listener's convenience'.[19] What this points to is a need for a different means of engaging McGlashan's singing and songwriting techniques.

'Andy' and the persona–environment model

I propose that Moore's 'persona–environment' framework provides a useful lens through which one can evaluate McGlashan's songwriting in relation to the notions of local authenticity. This is not to suggest that it is the only means of understanding McGlashan's authenticity, as individual listeners will make such assessments based on their unique interpretations of the song. Nonetheless, the persona–environment model allows for coverage of the full compass of McGlashan's singing and songwriting techniques. Moore's analytical method considers how the environment of a song, consisting initially of the musical accompaniment, shapes the listener's interpretation of the song's persona, primarily articulated through the lyrics, the voice, and the vocal melody.[20] There are a number of components to Moore's model: the relationship between the persona, performer and protagonist; the role and place of the persona within the narrative; how the listener relates to the persona; and, finally, how the environment relates to the persona.[21]

I will draw on Moore's approach with respect to only one of McGlashan's songs, 'Andy'. The song was written by McGlashan in the second half of the 1980s. It was recorded with his band at the time, the Front Lawn (a collaboration with Harry Sinclair), with additional support from the musical group, Six Volts. The song featured on the Front Lawn's debut album *Songs from the Front Lawn* (1989).[22] What one finds in 'Andy' is a rich tapestry of details, concerning the persona, the environment, and their interrelationships, all of which combine to amplify the autobiographical story of losing a family member, and of losing one's home town. Although Moore's model admits the interpretation of myriad details, I will limit the discussion and analysis to the text of the song (what the persona conveys), McGlashan's vocal tone and stylings (how the words are conveyed), and several rhythmic, harmonic and textural features (how the environment frames the persona).[23]

To start, the persona's words in 'Andy' are plain.[24] The song begins midscene with the narrator proposing a walk along the beach; he lightly scolds his companion for missing a party last night. Initially, the first-person plural ('Let's take a walk') and the second-person ('You sure missed one hell of a party last night') voices raise questions as to whom the narrator is addressing – another person? The audience? The ambiguity is resolved shortly thereafter with the short refrain – 'Andy, don't keep your distance from me'.

As the song progresses, we learn that the titular character is the narrator's brother; the narrator starts to recall elements of their childhood, such as roaming on the beach, watching sailing races up at 'North Head'. The nostalgic tone is clear. From the mid-point of the song, however, the nostalgia gives way to anger, as the persona relates the gross urbanisation that has taken place in his home town. Where there was once a beach, there are now 'buildings [made] of glass'. Where the children used to explore and roam, there are now vapid teenagers who are concerned only about their looks. The third and final verse further highlights two important pieces of information:

> On Takapuna Beach I can still see you,
> I can let myself pretend you're still around.
> I turned 28 last night.
> If you were still alive you'd be just short of 33.
> If only you could see your home town now.

Firstly, the song is set in Takapuna, a suburb located on the North Shore of Auckland. Secondly, we learn the reason Andy was not at the party, and the reason he cannot see the transformation of his home town is simple: he is dead. The persona's words thus deal with the pain of loss, and perhaps, a type of unnecessary loss – the places for childhood adventures have been replaced by buildings; Andy has died at a young age. While these broad themes may be applicable to varied locations, the important detail in this context is the specific reference to 'Takapuna Beach'. 'Andy' and McGlashan acquire their authentic status because the song is situated in the metropolitan heart of New Zealand. Accordingly, by telling a story in a local setting, McGlashan 'validates' the 'experience of life' of other New Zealanders.[25]

What of the persona's voice? McGlashan's singing is resonant and firm in tone, but also unstylised. His voice has little vibrato, pitches are attacked more or less directly, and there is little in the way of added rasps, gravel, or breathiness. These traits minimise any sense of vocal strain. The primary change occurs in the bridge sections, as the melody extends out of his comfortable register, to G above middle C. At this point, there is a slight crack in McGlashan's voice, and the resulting tone is thinner. The combination of these singing traits is important because it connotes a sense of normality and ordinariness in the persona of the song. McGlashan's singing voice is tuneful, pleasant, and lacking in any demonstrative flair. The fact that his upper register thins out in tone supports this reading, giving the impression of a voice that is, if not untrained, then lacking in overt finesse and polish.[26] Thus the persona of the song does not necessarily strike one as being unique or exceptional; he could be a friend or a relative singing to the listener, an observation borne out in the very opening lines of the song. What we have is McGlashan engaging with, to a certain extent, Moore's second category of authenticity, in terms of 'conveying the impression of accurately representing the ideas of another'.[27] The 'everyman' singing style gives the impression that the persona is not just relating his experiences, but relating, on their behalf, the views and experiences of others who have suffered similar losses.

On the persona side of the equation, then, McGlashan's words authenticate a specific aspect of New Zealand life; his singing does not necessarily concern the local narrative, but it authenticates his listeners who have shared cultural experiences. The environment side of the equation is notable for the way it strengthens the conviction of the persona's story. To begin with, McGlashan has set the song in a folk-derived style: the song can be heard as in a fast triple or slow compound metre and the refrain sections conclude with plagal cadences. With the inclusion of the gamelan, the instrumental connotations are complicated somewhat, but the presence of acoustic instruments including an accordion

Example 27.1. The Front Lawn, 'Andy', Introduction, 0'00"–0'17".

and tambura have immediate folk connotations.[28] This stylistic setting supports the persona's general attitudes of nostalgia and anti-urbanisation; further, the rural connotations of the folk style support the song's setting, New Zealand being a traditionally rural-oriented country.

Beyond these general characteristics, there are passages and details that frame the narrator and offer insight into his emotional state. Example 27.1 reproduces the opening instrumental section and first vocal phrase.[29] Several details stand out. Firstly, there are the contrasting surface rhythms provided by the triangle and gamelan (a 3/4-like pattern) and the lap steel guitar (a 6/8-like pattern). The drone of the double bass does little to confirm a dominant metre. Secondly, the harmonic orientation of the introduction is equally unsettled. The double bass and lap steel guitar outline an open fifth chord on F. The fragments of gamelan melody complete an F major triad, but with no other melodic or harmonic material initially, there are few clues as to the tonal context of this chord. Thirdly, the texture of the introduction is striking, partly because of the unusual instrumental combination, but mostly because of the spatial arrangement of sounds: the double bass sustains an F three octaves below middle C; the steel guitar oscillates between F and C directly above middle C; the gamelan plays a short melodic fragment an octave higher. There are holes in the texture; the instrumental combination spans four and a half octaves, but each instrument occupies a narrow region of the pitch spectrum, resulting in a hollow and empty sound.

This environment is important for several reasons. As with the style settings mentioned above, the meandering quality of the accompaniment sets the laid-back and casual tone for the narrator; when McGlashan starts singing, his delivery is marked by rhythmic fluidity, with words falling around, rather than on the beats. Equally, the environment hints at the persona's emotional state-of-being, details of which are made clearer as the song progresses. The accompaniment that goes nowhere, rhythmically or harmonically, enacts the narrator's inability to move forward in his life. The environment's sparse and hollow sonic qualities further speak to the emotional emptiness of the persona. When he starts talking to 'Andy', there is a suggestion that the narrator's casual outwards demeanour is masking a sense of inner uncertainty and uneasiness.

The environment of the bridge section contributes further to one's understanding of the persona; Example 27.2 presents the bridge vocal melody and the harmonic outline. Through the initial lines, one can observe a turn away from the tonic, insofar as the harmonies hover predominantly between C major and B♭ major, IV and V, without resolving

Example 27.2. The Front Lawn, 'Andy', Bridge, 1'55"–2'41".

(Continued)

Example 27.2. (*Continued*)

They're ma - king buil - dings   out of   glass___   Their kids___ look like they've

stepped   out of fash - ion   ma-ga - zines___   and

none of it's   gon - na   last   A man___ gets   an - gry___

But what   can___   you do___   Don't know why I'm tell - ling all___ this to

you___   On   Ta - ka - pu - na Beach

back to F. This harmonic tension is made more explicit after sixteen bars, with the appearance of oscillating D and D^{sus4} chords, the lack of a tonic now giving way to repeated chromatic chords. This increasingly pent-up harmonic energy mirrors the tension riddling the narrator – for much of the song, he appears to express only mild frustration and disappointment at the various events; as the harmonies move further away from the tonic, it appears more likely that a change in his sentiments is forthcoming.

This is indeed the case. As the D^{sus4} chord resolves to G (a local V^{sus4}–I movement), the persona's emotional wall cracks and he delivers his bluntest and most pointed words. And yet, it is not the case that the narrator's anger represents the final point of resolution. In the subsequent passage, his words become somewhat more tired, as he wonders, 'Don't know why I'm telling all this to you' and repeats the line 'On Takapuna Beach'. The supporting harmonies at this point are G major and D minor; with the vocal melody falling to D in each phrase, there is a strong suggestion of a modal turn to D Dorian. Moore has observed that the Dorian mode evokes an 'illusory possibility of escape'.[30] The environment therefore potentially provides a more nuanced view of the narrator's emotional scope. His words suggest anger at the events that have happened around him; the environment suggests to the listener that the narrator wants, but cannot escape from this situation. He is weary from the conflicting feelings over the death of 'Andy' and the loss of his home town. Earlier in the song, the narrator told his brother that the 'rest of the family don't even mention his name'; while the family may have moved on from Andy's early death, the narrator, it appears, remains caught between reliving his past with people and places no longer present, and moving forward in his life.

Conclusion

Two final remarks are necessary. Firstly, the analysis above was couched within a singer-songwriter framework. Although McGlashan was primarily responsible for many aspects of the song that create meaning (the lyrics, the voice, the melodic shape, the harmonic language), other elements, namely textural design, lay outside McGlashan's immediate control. Indeed, he has been effusive in his praise for other musicians with whom he has worked during his career; in particular, he has noted their ability to provide colour and shape to a song. This raises interesting issues of perceived authorship, issues which are touched on in a number of chapters in this volume (e.g. Chapters 3, 11, 14, and 26).

Secondly, one can draw several conclusions regarding McGlashan's local authenticity with respect to his singing and songwriting. Through the lyrical components of his songs, McGlashan connects his narratives directly with New Zealand places and people, thus validating the lives of other New Zealanders. His 'ordinary' singing gives the impression that his narratives are representative of others, thus validating the experiences of those who cannot tell their stories. His song environments support and amplify the narratives being told; this reflects another of Moore's poles of authenticity, in that McGlashan 'succeeds in conveying the impression that his/her utterance is one of integrity'.[31] To varying extents, these ideas hold for other McGlashan songs that are informed by local contexts ('A Thing Well Made', 'There is No Depression in New Zealand', 'Dominion Road', for example). Accordingly, one can conclude that it is through McGlashan's lyrical writing that he engages notions of local authenticity; his singing and musical components do not directly connect with New Zealand contexts, but they engage other forms of authenticity, and thus they are equally responsible for strengthening McGlashan's standing as an authentic New Zealand singer-songwriter.

Acknowledgements

I am grateful to Matthew Bannister and Jeff Wragg who critiqued drafts of this chapter. I wish to thank Don McGlashan also for sharing his thoughts on songwriting processes and 'Andy'.

Notes

1 See, for example, Mark Butler, 'Taking It Seriously: Intertextuality and Authenticity in Two Covers by the Pet Shop Boys', *Popular Music* 22/1 (2003); Emily I. Dolan, '"… This Little Ukulele Tells the Truth": Indie Pop and Kitsch Authenticity', *Popular Music* 29/3 (2010).

2 Allan F. Moore, 'Authenticity as Authentication', *Popular Music* 21/2 (2002), pp. 210–11.; Other valuable studies of authenticity include Allan F. Moore, 'U2 and the Myth of Authenticity in Rock', *Popular Musicology* 3 (1998); Edward G. Armstrong, 'Eminem's Construction of Authenticity', *Popular Music and Society* 27/3 (2004); Henry Adam Svec, '"Who Don't Care If The Money's No Good?": Authenticity and The Band', *Popular Music and Society* 35/3 (2012); Elizabeth Eva Leach, 'Vicars of "Wannabe": Authenticity and The Spice Girls', *Popular Music* 20/2 (2001); Jessica L. Wood, 'Pained Expression: Metaphors of Sickness and Signs of "Authenticity" in Kurt Cobain's Journals', *Popular Music* 30/3 (2011).

3 Moore, 'Authenticity', p. 209.

4 See Motti Regev, 'Producing Artistic Value: The Case of Rock Music', *The Sociological Quarterly* 35/1 (1994), pp. 91–2. Also relevant in this regard are Michèle Ollivier, 'Snobs and Quétaines: Prestige and Boundaries in Popular Music in Quebec', *Popular Music* 25/1 (2006), p. 98ff; and, Don Cusic, 'In Defense of Cover Songs', *Popular Music and Society* 28/2 (2005).

5 The term is drawn from Regev's study of Israeli popular music; he is similarly concerned with how international popular styles become accepted as 'authentic' in a local social and cultural context. Motti Regev, 'Israeli Rock, or a Study in the Politics of "Local Authenticity"', *Popular Music* 11/1 (1992), p. 1ff.

6 See, for example, the chapters in Glenda Keam and Tony Mitchell (eds.), *Home, Land and Sea: Situating Music in Aotearoa/New Zealand* (Auckland: Pearson, 2011); Henry Johnson (ed.), *Many Voices: Music and National*

Identity in Aotearoa/New Zealand (Newcastle: Cambridge Scholars Publishing, 2010).

7 Nabeel Zuberi, 'Sounds Like Us: Popular Music and Cultural Nationalism in Aotearoa/ New Zealand', *Perfect Beat* 8/3 (2007), p. 9.

8 For extra material on McGlashan's biography and songwriting, see Matthew Bannister, 'A Thing Well Made? NZ Settler Identity and Pakeha Masculinity in the Work of Don McGlashan', *Perfect Beat* 8/1 (2006).

9 Unless otherwise cited, material from McGlashan comes from an interview conducted with the author, 16 September 2011.

10 Tony Mitchell, 'Aotearoa Songlines', *Perfect Beat* 8 (2007), p. 70.

11 Tony Mitchell, 'Sonic Psychogeography: A Poetics of Place in Popular Music in Aotearoa/ New Zealand', *Perfect Beat* 10/2 (2009), p. 154.

12 Glenda Keam and Tony Mitchell, 'New Zealand Music and a Poetics of Place', in Keam and Mitchell, *Home, Land and Sea*, p. xvi.

13 Russell Baillie, 'Don McGlashan and the Seven Sisters – Marvellous Year', *New Zealand Herald*, 11 March 2009. www .nzherald.co.nz/music/news/article.cfm?c_ id=264&objectid=10561129 (accessed 17 July 2014); Russell Baillie, 'Concert Review: Kiwi Legends' Double Act is Heaven Sent', *New Zealand Herald*, 30 September 2013. www .nzherald.co.nz/music/news/article.cfm?c_ id=264&objectid=11131978 (accessed 17 July 2014).

14 Don McGlashan, 'Afterword', in Keam and Mitchell, *Home, Land and Sea*, pp. 280–1.

15 'Pakēhā' is a Māori term, which is understood, generally, as referring to New Zealanders of European descent, but may also be understood as referring to those who are not of Māori descent. Mitchell's appraisal appears to rest on the latter understanding, implying that 'Andy' is styled without reference to Māori musical traditions. The Māori are the indigenous population of New Zealand.

16 Mitchell, 'Sonic Psychogeography', p. 156.

17 Bannister, 'A Thing Well Made?'.

18 Mitchell, 'Aotearoa Songlines', p. 69.

19 McGlashan, 'Afterword', p. 281. An exception may be McGlashan's singing pronunciation. He does not revert to an overt British or American accent, in contrast to other New Zealand singers (consider, for instance, the faux-British accent on display in the Swingers' 'Counting the Beat', clearly derived from the likes of Johnny Rotten and Joe Strummer); likewise, he does not shy from singing in his New Zealand accent. For more on this issue, see Roy Shuker and Michael Pickering, 'Kiwi Rock: Popular Music and Cultural Identity in New Zealand', *Popular Music* 13/3 (1994), p. 272.

20 Allan F. Moore, 'The Persona–Environment Relation in Recorded Song', *Music Theory Online* 11.4 (2005), www.mtosmt.org/issues/ mto.05.11.4/mto.05.11.4.moore.html (accessed 23 June 2014); Allan F. Moore, *Song Means: Analysing and Interpreting Recorded Popular Song* (Farnham, Surrey: Ashgate, 2012), pp. 179–214. An analogous situation is when one interprets a person's words, in relation to his or her body language; see, Allan F. Moore, *Rock: The Primary Text*, 2nd edn (Aldershot: Ashgate, 2001), pp. 219, n. 5.

21 See, for the respective components, Moore, *Song Means*, pp. 181, 182, 184–8, 188–207.

22 'Andy' is credited jointly to McGlashan and Sinclair, although the former was primarily responsible for writing the song. In recent years, McGlashan has frequently performed the song during his solo shows.

23 Space here does not permit it, but further investigations into melodic contour and production techniques may be fruitful.

24 In this and other McGlashan songs, the term 'persona' can be considered synonymous with 'narrator'.

25 Moore, 'Authenticity', p. 220. Bannister notes that the themes of McGlashan's songs are tied predominantly to the identities of white, male New Zealanders. Thus, in positing a connection between McGlashan and local culture through 'Andy', there is the added question of whose culture and lives, exactly, are being validated? For reasons of space, I have not pursued this issue here. See Bannister, 'A Thing Well Made?', p. 22ff.

26 This is not to say that McGlashan's singing *is* ordinary or lacking in skill; other songs, such as 'Anchor Me', demonstrate an ability to maintain a full tone in his upper range. What is important is the impression made by his vocal traits in this specific context.

27 Moore, 'Authenticity', p. 218.

28 The tambura is a mandolin-like instrument originating from the Balkan Peninsula. The particular combination of instruments, metre, and cadence figures draw a basic stylistic line between 'Andy' and, for example, Bob Dylan's 'A Hard Rain's A-Gonna Fall'.

29 The double bass sounds an octave lower than written; in example 27.2, McGlashan's voice sounds an octave lower than written. For both transcriptions, I have attempted to strike a balance between clean presentation and accuracy in terms of the vocal rhythms.

30 Allan F. Moore, 'The So-Called 'Flattened Seventh' in Rock', *Popular Music* 14/2 (1995), p. 188.

31 Moore, 'Authenticity', p. 214.

28 Italian *canzone d'autore* and Greek *entechno tragoudi*: a comparative overview

FRANCO FABBRI AND IOANNIS TSIOULAKIS

Origins of *canzone d'autore*

Early attempts to renovate Italian popular song, freeing it from old-fashioned escapist lyrics and pre-WWII music styles took place in the late 1950s. Most lyricists and composers active then had started their careers in the 1920s and 30s, and their songs circulated thanks to the Sanremo Festival (established in 1951) and RAI's broadcasting monopoly.[1] No trend comparable to the renovation of cinema (neo-realism) or literature could be found in post-war (and post-Fascist) Italian popular music, until a group of composers, poets, and singers established 'Il Cantacronache' in Turin in 1958, with the aim to 'escape from escapism'.[2] Influenced by French *auteurs-compositeurs-interprètes* (ACI) and by Brecht's collaborations with Weill and Eisler, Cantacronache was a marginal group of *engagé* intellectuals (including writers like Italo Calvino, Franco Fortini, Umberto Eco), and their work left traces mostly in political song and folk revival.[3] In 1958, the winning song at Sanremo was Domenico Modugno's (and Franco Migliacci's) 'Nel blu dipinto di blu'. It was a huge international hit, composed by its performer: a rare feature in Italian popular music history. Modugno's success encouraged young recording industry executives to sign new lyricists and/or composers as performers (as they wouldn't find proper interpreters for their songs), or to persuade singers to write their own songs (rather than cover foreign material or interpret songs by old-fashioned professional authors). Between 1959 and 1961 some of these singer-songwriters (Umberto Bindi, Gino Paoli, Giorgio Gaber, Gianni Meccia) hit the charts. A new term, *cantautori*,[4] created by one of the first (and few) female representatives of the category, Maria Monti, was adopted to designate them: by 1961 it was firmly established in Italian language. Initially, it was intended almost as a joke – a lighter term compared to the cultural connotations of *chansonnier*.[5] However, during the 1960s *cantautori* became more and more involved in the debate on cultural and political commitment (versus commercialism) in popular music, also under the influence of foreign examples: from French ACI to Bob Dylan, and also Theodorakis (especially after the 1967 coup in Greece). When one of the best-known *cantautori*, Luigi Tenco, committed suicide during the Sanremo Festival in January 1967 (see p. 322 below),[6] amongst the reactions to this event emerged the perception of a need that a type of popular song be identified, which could be opposed to the commercial mainstream: after '*canzone diversa*',[7] and '*nuova canzone*',[8] the term '*canzone d'autore*' (author's song, obviously modelled after *cinéma d'auteur*, and coined in 1969)[9] was proposed. It was officially adopted in 1974 within the title of a festival ('Rassegna della canzone d'autore' – hereafter 'Rassegna' – organised since then annually by Club Tenco), and soon became a widely accepted concept.

Origins of *entechno*

The Greek term *entechno* [*tragoudi*], the literal translation of which is 'artful' [song], originally emerged as the first component of the paradoxical term *entechno-laïko tragoudi* ('art-folk song')[10] invented largely by leftist intellectuals in urban Greece, prominent among whom was Mikis Theodorakis. This artistic endeavour followed an effort to sanctify the previously repudiated *rebetiko* music, initiated by the composer Manos Hadjidakis with a groundbreaking speech in 1949.[11] *Rebetiko* song was an urban popular music genre, which emerged prominently during the relocation of refugees from Asia Minor to the Greek mainland, as a result of the Greek–Turkish war between 1919 and 1922. Influenced by genres prominent in the urban areas of Athens and Piraeus and folk musical elements from the refugees' home culture, *rebetiko* became connected in the Greek middle-class imagination with marginalised underclasses and perceived 'decadent' behaviours.

From the late 1950s onwards, both Theodorakis and Hadjidakis invested their creativity in the search for new genres that utilised the *rebetiko* style within more highbrow musical forms combined with contemporary poetry. The Greek popular music scene after the 1960s was dominated by the work of Theodorakis and Hadjidakis to the extent that, within international music circles, Greece was often referred to as 'the country of the two composers'.[12] Specifically the release of Theodorakis' album *Epitáfios* in 1960 epitomises the new *entechno-laïkó* genre by combining the leftist poetry of Yannis Ritsos with *laïko* compositions.[13] A dedicated Marxist and Western-educated composer,[14] Theodorakis aimed to create a genre that would familiarise the working class with contemporary poetry, while at the same time incorporating pan-Hellenic folk musical idioms, free of references to particular regions.[15] Manos Hadjidakis' role, even though less political, was equally important to the development of *entechno-laïko*. His incorporation of folk music was part of a wider search for compositional styles, less pompous and patriotic and more introverted than Theodorakis, thus closer to the *entechno* style that survives after the 1970s.

The transition from this period of *entechno-laïko* to the more eclectic (if less wordy) *entechno*, coincided with the emergence of the term *tragou-dopios* (literally, 'song-crafter'). Similarly to the Italian *cantautori*, Greek *tragoudopii* (pl.) used the term as a less charged offset to the 'composers' (*synthetes*) of the Theodorakis–Hadjidakis period. Epitomised by the versatile performer Dionysis Savvopoulos, this new caste of singers-song-writers emerged through the turbulent years of the Junta of the Colonels (1967–74), and achieved popular stardom after the restoration of democracy. The aesthetic foundations for this new trend were set by the artists of the so-called *neo kyma* (lit. 'new wave', a direct translation of the French *nouvelle vague* artistic movement), most prominent among whom was the composer Yiannis Spanos. Utilising some of the musical principles of intellectualism and left-leaning sensibility from Theodorakis along with the lyricism of Hadjidakis, *neo kyma* artists were decidedly more low-key and minimalistic, often their music comprising merely vocals with an accompanying guitar.

Entechno after the dictatorship: new directions

If *entechno-laiko* was created by Theodorakis with a clear political agenda, the musical production that came to be known plainly as *entechno* after the end of the Junta was characterised by a process of depoliticisation. The restoration of democracy (or *metapolitefsi* as it is often referred to in Greek) brought about a number of political developments with the clear intention of reconciling populations on the left and the right of the political spectrum who were in open or concealed conflict since the end of the Nazi occupation and the Civil War in the 1940s. The most important of those were the abolition of the monarchy with a referendum and the legalisation of the Greek Communist Party (KKE), both within months of the end of the dictatorship in 1974. These new developments cultivated a climate of acceptance, or even open celebration of leftist aesthetics and ideals, especially among urban intellectual circles. The electoral victory of the Social-Democrat party PASOK in 1981 sealed this transitional period and was accepted by many, even within the communist left, as the end of the national divide.

While Theodorakis was turning from a prosecuted communist (during the Junta) to a celebrated artist,[16] the need for his maximalist revolutionary music was diminishing. Ironically, the more Theodorakis' music was featured in state-sponsored festivals and performances, the less relevant it was becoming to current aesthetics. The new wave of *entechno* that developed from the 1980s onwards was less overtly political, more introvert, wider in its musical references, and more diverse and experimental. The aesthetic of the post-dicatorship *entechno* is defined by three fundamental features: eclecticism, intellectualism, and technophobia.

The effective abandonment of 'folk' (*laïko*) in the genre label from the late 1980s onwards is due to the fact that its artists began to expand well outside the realm of Greek urban-folk music in their pursuit of inspiration. The popularity of French chanson, as well as the Anglo-American folk revival and its singer-songwriters became catalytic in this new trend, but *entechno* artists of the Greek 1980s and 1990s utilised influences as diverse as jazz, fado, and Brazilian popular music (MPB).[17] While *entechno* expanded its musical influences, it similarly widened its lyrical themes from leftist activism to a range of other topics, most notably romantic, poeticised love. If this signalled an abandonment of Theodorakis' militant aesthetic, however, the emphasis on intellectualism remained intact. Singer-songwriters such as Dionysis Savvopoulos were celebrated as both musicians and poets, while a whole caste of professional poet-lyricists emerged, including Manos Eleftheriou, Manolis Rasoulis, and later Lina Nikolakopoulou.

Within the 1990s, *entechno* artists incorporated more forcefully two, until then clearly demarcated, music styles: rock and 'traditional' (*paradosiaka*). Greek rock music, which in its more subcultural form was already in the 1980s expressed forcefully by numerous bands, broke into the mainstream through the voice of Vassilis Papakonstantinou. His collaborations with *entechno* composers such as Manos Loizos and Thanos Mikroutsikos paved the way for the incorporation of rock idioms, and specifically the sound of the electric guitar, within *entechno* productions. In the 1990s this practice became prominent in the work of singer-songwriters Dionysis Tsaknis and Lavrentis Mahairitsas. If the electric sound of rock was a natural development within the cosmopolitan *entechno* aesthetic, the search for sounds from rural 'traditions' was more problematic, since rural folk music (*dimotiko*) was often perceived among urban middle classes as having nationalistic overtones, heavily connected in their imagination with cultural displays promoted by the Junta. The incorporation of traditional instruments from the Eastern Mediterranean, including rural Greek instruments like the *laouto* and the *lyra*, was eventually made possible through an engagement with an 'ethnic' aesthetic, in its essence utterly cosmopolitan.[18]

Technophobia is a less-discussed but equally important defining element of *entechno*. Although, as we saw, the electric sound eventually made it into mainstream *entechno* in the late 1980s and 1990s, the aversion towards anything electronic or programmed has been a consistent attitude. This, however, applies to the aesthetic rather than the practical dimension. For example, digital technology in the recording studios is widespread in *entechno* productions, and this is not seen as a breach as long as it remains inaudible.[19] To use Thomas Turino's celebrated terms, *entechno* has consistently produced 'high fidelity' rather than 'studio audio art' recordings.[20] This aesthetic choice should be understood within the increasing dipole between *entechno* and folk-pop (*laikopop*), with the latter genre availing of the opportunities of digital programming to an extent that is often perceived by *entechno* artists and fans as overly commercial and kitsch.

From *cantautori* to *canzone d'autore*

The choice of '*canzone d'autore*' as a label for Italy's singer-songwriter genre was a political one. Amongst the possible choices, it was the most neutral term: '*nuova canzone*' (a label that was used, anyway, for conferences held during Club Tenco's 'Rassegna') had its origins in the context of folk revival and political song, '*canzone diversa*' bore excessive connotations of otherness, and notwithstanding the prestige of its creator (semiotician Umberto Eco) had never become part of the community's common cultural awareness. In the *Sessantotto* – the years of Italy's political turmoil, which lasted from 1968 to the end of the 1970s – what was needed was the delimitation and distinction of a field of music activities, different both from conventional, market-oriented Italian popular music, identifiable with the Sanremo Festival, and from radical leftist political song, as well as from the Anglo-American pop-rock mainstream, then hegemonic in the record market. As a matter of fact, *cantautori*, before Tenco's suicide in 1967, had been sharing the same scenes and places with more traditional singers: they participated in the Sanremo Festival and had huge juke-box hits. The name *cantautore* itself had ambivalent meanings and connotations, suggesting the existence of two subcategories: 1. an artist who was at the same time a singer and a songwriter – often just a composer, as it soon became common in Italy for singer-songwriters to collaborate with professional lyricists; 2. an author of songs of a 'special kind', implying uncommon artistry or engagement, which deserved to be performed by the author himself. As the very figure of the singer-songwriter was new in Italy's late 1950s and early 1960s, the two meanings were blurred, although – as we shall see – the difference will emerge later as a substantial factor in the construction of *canzone d'autore*'s ideology. Technically, the list of *cantautori* in the early 1960s includes singer-songwriters who won or scored well at the Sanremo Festival, like Domenico Modugno,[21] Tony Renis,[22] Pino Donaggio,[23] Bobby Solo:[24] but with the exception of Modugno, for his role as a pioneer, these *cantautori* are very seldom included in accounts on the genre, and other best-selling early singer-songwriters, like Gianni Meccia, Nico Fidenco, or Edoardo Vianello, are similarly forgotten. It must also be said that other *cantautori*, like Gino Paoli, Umberto Bindi, Giorgio Gaber, Sergio Endrigo – generally ascribed to the second subcategory – took part in the Sanremo Festival in the early 1960s, and that some of their songs aimed at the mainstream market (not presented at the Festival) enjoyed great commercial success, like Paoli's 'Sapore di sale' of 1963.

Luigi Tenco's participation in the 1967 edition of Sanremo was not a novelty or a special compromise: it followed a wave of *cantautori* trying to use the Festival as a platform to reach a wider audience: Tenco himself had declared a few months earlier that he would 'use' media and commercial institutions (including Sanremo) like American singer-songwriters had been doing in the USA.[25] His models were Bob Dylan and Barry McGuire. His disillusion at the results (his song was immediately eliminated), his suicide, and especially the cold, embarrassed reaction of the industry, of the media, even of his colleagues (only one, Fabrizio De André, attended Tenco's funeral), moved a burgeoning community of fans and activists to see Sanremo as the paradigm of commercialism, lack of artistry and authenticity, the exact contrary of what lovers of 'quality songs' were looking for.[26] Journalists hailed Endrigo's victory at Sanremo in 1968 as Tenco's – or the *cantautori*'s – revenge, forgetting the continuing participation and success of *cantautori* in former editions, and possibly implying with that *lapsus memoriae* that the term *cantautore* was not apt to sustain an overt semantic and political opposition against the music industry. The *Sessantotto* had begun.

New *cantautori*, and a new genre.

While the term '*canzone d'autore*' was making its way from the columns of a local newspaper to the title of a festival celebrating Tenco's memory, provocatively based in Sanremo, new *cantautori* became popular: among them, Fabrizio De André,[27] Francesco Guccini, Lucio Battisti, Lucio Dalla, Francesco De Gregori, Antonello Venditti. With two notable exceptions, they were all authors of their own lyrics; they were also composers of their songs' music, but their craftsmanship as musicians (composers, or singers, or players) was bound to occupy a lower place in the new genre's ideological hierarchy compared to their ability and authenticity as poets. Exceptions were Lucio Dalla, who emerged from Italian beat[28] and participated in the Sanremo Festival, collaborating with lyricists and poets, as well as writing his own lyrics, and Lucio Battisti, who became one of the best-known artists in Italian popular music, collaborating with professional lyricist Mogol, and later with poet Pasquale Panella. The very existence of Dalla and Battisti is a challenge to *canzone d'autore*'s ideology: they were among the best-known *cantautori* for nearly three decades, but – especially Battisti – they failed to be acknowledged as 'proper' members of the genre. Battisti never took part in the 'Rassegna', Lucio Dalla partici-pated just once, in 1986. They were never awarded the Tenco Prize, which has been given since 1974 to almost every famous *cantautore* and to many singer-songwriters from other countries.[29] The obvious explanation for such an anomaly is that Battisti was not left-wing, and scorned the intel-lectualism and political commitment of most other *cantautori*.[30] But this cannot be applied to Dalla. It is also worth noting that until 2014, when Maria Farantouri (not a songwriter!) was awarded the prize for her role in the international success of *entechno*, no Greek author or singer had ever been invited to the 'Rassegna'. If we add that Battisti and Dalla are probably the only Italian *cantautori* known in Greece,[31] we are suggesting another possible explanation: that the top hierarchical criterion for authorship in *canzone d'autore* was attached to the image of the 'singing poet', and singer-songwriters who focused mainly on music (just like some forgot-ten early *cantautori*, or like some prominent figures in *entechno*) have been seen by the genre's communities as 'out of place'. In fact, the practice of setting to music existing (literary) poems, or lyrics written by known poets, which has been an important feature of French *chanson* (since at least Yvette Guilbert in the 1910s), and of Greek *entechno*, never took off in Italy, with very few exceptions related to lesser-known *cantautori*; on the contrary, the public debate about *canzone d'autore* has been focused for decades on the issue of whether *cantautori* should be considered as poets, or even as 'the *real* poets of the twentieth century'.[32]

Genre conventions ('norms') are often hierarchically ordered, and ideology can be seen as the hyper-code controlling such hierarchy.[33] The focus on the *cantautore* as a poet, articulated in various conven-tions (formal-technical, communicational, behavioural, proxemic, eco-nomic, etc.), also dictates the relevance of practices 'allowed' in the genre. Two striking examples, which emerge in the comparison between *can-zone d'autore* and *entechno*, are: 1. the relative scarcity of collaborations between authors/interpreters in Italy (regarded as notable exceptions, rather than almost a norm, like in Greece); 2. the acknowledgement of 'pure' performers as fully representative of the genre, which is again com-mon in Greece (including male interpreters, like Manolis Lidakis), while limited to a handful of 'classy' female singers in Italy (Ornella Vanoni, Fiorella Mannoia), who have been seen as, so to speak, 'guests' of the genre and corresponding scene. On the other hand, a number of *cantautrici* (female singer-songwriters) have appeared since the mid-1970s: Gianna Nannini, Alice, Carmen Consoli, Paola Turci, Elisa, Cristina Donà, Nada

Malanima,[34] and others. However, *cantautori* still outnumber *cantautrici* by at least an order of magnitude.

Any genre's hierarchical system of values (i.e. its ideology) is subject to continuous negotiations within the genre's interrelated communities: artists, producers, critics, fans, etc. In *canzone d'autore* a community of 'experts', formed by members of the Club Tenco, by the organisers of the 'Rassegna' and other festivals and prizes, by critics and organised fans, has been 'dictating the rules' for about forty years, slowly evolving from the early celebration of the French ACI model to the formulation of a more general 'quality principle', at least theoretically unbound from the figure of the singer-songwriter. In fact, groups have participated in the 'Rassegna' since the earliest editions, and, more recently, prizes for the interpreter or the record producer of the year were launched, opening to a collaborative model closer to the cinematic origins of the *canzone d'autore* concept. Although *canzone d'autore* originally implied an anti-rock stance, sooner or later its communities had to acknowledge the success of singer-songwriters whose styles were closer to those of British or US singer-songwriters: from Franco Battiato, who drew initially from Brian Eno's solo albums, to Ivano Fossati, who dedicated his first album (1983) to Randy Newman, from Vasco Rossi to Luciano Ligabue, both strongly indebted to Bruce Springsteen, to Vinicio Capossela, initially a Tom Waits epigone, later a *rebetiko* addict (he imitated or covered classics of the genre, even recording them with Greek instrumentalists from the *entechno* scene).

Nonetheless, some artists are still closer to the canon than others, and it isn't surprising to see that they are (or were) *cantautori* in the stricter sense: Paolo Conte (as a singer-songwriter, a creature of the 'Rassegna', as he had been a successful song composer earlier), Roberto Vecchioni, Fabrizio De André, Giorgio Gaber, and Enzo Jannacci. The last three in the list died recently (respectively in 1999, 2003, and 2013): their deaths, along with Battisti's (1998), were the origin of a flood of comments with ambivalent effects, on one hand allowing a deeper critical reflection on *canzone d'autore*, on the other consolidating some aspects of the genre's ideology, like the demiurgical image of the *auteur*/poet. The effect was especially notable in many accounts of Fabrizio De André, who excelled in collaborating with lyricists, composers, arrangers, and engineers, and could be best described as a 'singing producer', but was sanctified as the archetypal poet.[35] As a reaction, some of the new Italian singer-songwriters preferred to hide behind a fictional band's name, like Bologna violenta (Nicola Manzan, from 2005) or Luci della centrale elettrica (Vasco Brondi, from 2007). It is also true that, especially after the beginning of the recording industry's downfall, 'pure' performers became a rare species in Italy (like almost everywhere), as co-authoring a song is a way for singers to compensate for decreasing record sales and royalties.

Contemporary *entechno*: artists, roles, and gender conventions

As we have seen, after the dictatorship *entechno* emerged and developed with close reference to the image of the lone singer-songwriter. This image is compatible with all its origins: Theodorakis the pioneer, left-wing intellectual composer/activist, the influences from international artists (*chanson*, *cantautori*, folk-revivalists), and the low-key solo performers of *neo kyma* during the dictatorship. However, to assume that contemporary *entechno* is dominated by singer-songwriters is quite misleading. Instead, what should be noted is a change in the distribution of creative roles that happened around the early 1990s; the early period of the 1970s–80s was characterised by collaborations, while the latter period, from the 1990s onwards, becomes defined by a strictly gendered division of roles, focusing mainly on the singer.

In order to identify that change, it suffices to examine some of the key artists of the two periods. The collaboration between composer Manos Loizos and singer Haris Alexiou, or that of composer Apostolos Kaldaras and singer Yiorgos Dalaras, produced multiple albums in the 1970s. It is indicative that, in many of those albums, the names of singers, composers, and lyricists are written alongside each other on the cover, turning the collaborative procedure into a point of attraction for the audiences. Similarly, the collaboration between composer Nikos Ksydakis, lyricist Manolis Rasoulis, singer Nikos Papazoglou, and producer Alekos Patsifas for the albums *Ekdikisi tis Gyftias* ('Revenge of Gypsydom', 1978) and *Ta Dithen* ('The Pretentious', 1979), has been seen as catalytic for the musical production of the period. In fact, such collaborations have been heavily mythologised within the audience's imagination, with numerous stories of their internal conflicts surviving through the interviews of the artists until today.

During the period after the 1990s, however, the discography of *entechno* revolves around two types of artists: female solo singers, and male singer-songwriters. Female singers such as Eleftheria Arvanitaki, Alkistis Protopsalti, Melina Kana, and Eleni Tsaligopoulou perform songs written by male composers such as Nikos Ksydakis, Stamatis Kraounakis, or Thanos Mikroutsikos, and appear in live performances as solo singers with almost exclusively male backing orchestras. With the roles of the composer and lyricist diminishing in favour of the singer after the 1990s, albums often feature multiple, lesser-known songwriters who are commissioned to support the presence of a popular singer. Their contribution is rarely acknowledged on the album cover, thus altering the previous attitude of collaboration towards a division between main artists and supporting personnel.

At the same time, male representatives of contemporary *entechno* are more often than not the authors of the songs that they perform. Singer-songwriters Orfeas Peridis, Alkinoos Ioannidis, Sokratis Malamas, Christos Thivaios, and Thanassis Papakonstantinou are the most prominent exponents of the genre from the late 1990s until today. All of them are equally appreciated as composers, lyricists, and singers, and they usually appear onstage with an instrument (acoustic guitar or lute), a practice almost unheard-of among the female artists. In some notable collaborations between male and female *entechno* artists, such as Malamas with Kana or Ioannidis with Arvanitaki, the norm is for the male to take the role of song-writer and backing vocalist, while the female is promoted as the main singer.

This change in roles and production style from the 1970s to the 1990s, cannot be seen outside of the political circumstances explained earlier and the neoliberalisation of the Greek music market. While the leftist political imperative of *entechno* as represented by Theodorakis, Loizos, and the early Savvopoulos increasingly lost its aesthetic appeal, the industry switched to the more globally established norm of promoting vocalists. This coincided from the mid-1990s onwards with the economic decline of the label Lyra, the main production force of *entechno* from the 1960s, and the eventual dominance of multinational recording companies over the Greek popular music scenes.

Conclusion

Two genres that sound very little alike, *canzone d'autore* and *entechno* have remarkably parallel histories. The emergence of the terms *cantautore* and *tragoudopios*, and the scenes that followed, have similarly fluctuated between left-wing sensibilities and commercialism, often taking advantage of the converging interests of the political opposition and the music industry (like in the US: 'The Revolutionaries Are on Columbia!'). The intense debates of authenticity exercised by critics, artists, producers, and audiences have managed to turn these seemingly low-key performance styles into terrains of ideological–aesthetic conflict, through which national politics and transnational affinities are tried. The remarkable ways in which *canzone d'autore* and *entechno* artists managed to bring poetry and ideology into the everyday musicality of people of all social backgrounds seems to serve as a common thread between many singer-songwriter genres of the late twentieth century. Yet, the different political phases through which people in the two nations have related to each other, to Europe, and the international stage, have ensured that *canzone d'autore* and *entechno* are as deeply entwined in the particularities of their homelands as in their cosmopolitan influences.

Notes

1 Franco Fabbri, *Around the Clock. Una breve storia della popular music* (Turin: UTET Libreria, 2008), pp. 83–7.
2 Carlo Pestelli, 'An Escape from Escapism: The Short History of Cantacronache', in Franco Fabbri and Goffredo Plastino (eds.), *Made in Italy: Studies in Popular Music* (New York and London: Routledge, 2014), pp. 153–61.
3 Quite unlike Theodorakis' and Hadjidakis' vast popularity in Greece (see below).
4 *Cantautore* (plural *cantautori*) is a crasis between *cantante* (singer) and *autore* (author), resonant with the archaic term *cantatore* (singer, minstrel). Although a feminine version of the term, *cantautrice*, does exist, the vast majority of early singer-songwriters in Italy were male, and female singer-songwriters emerged only from the mid-1970s. Therefore, in this text *cantautore/cantautori* will be referred to mostly in the masculine.
5 The meaning of *chansonnier* as a performer who composes his/her own songs was abandoned in France in the early decades of the twentieth century. However, in many other cultures the term was (and still is) used to designate what the French now call ACI, like Trénet, Ferré, Brassens, Brel, etc.
6 Marco Santoro, 'The Tenco Effect. Suicide, San Remo, and the Social Construction of the Canzone D'autore', *Journal of Modern Italian Studies* 3 (2006), pp. 342–66.
7 Umberto Eco, 'Prefazione', in Michele L. Straniero, Sergio Liberovici, Emilio Jona, and Giorgio De Maria (eds.), *Le canzoni della cattiva coscienza* (Milan: Bompiani, 1964), pp. 5–28.
8 Roberto Leydi, 'Nuova canzone e rapporto città–campagna oggi', in Roberto Leydi (ed.), *Il folk music revival* (Palermo: Flaccovio, 1972), pp. 247–51; Jacopo Tomatis, 'A Portrait of the Author as an Artist. Ideology, Authenticity, and Stylization in the Canzone d'Autore', in Fabbri and Plastino, *Made in Italy*, p. 90.
9 It appeared as the title of a regular column, written by music critic Enrico De Angelis, in the daily *L'Arena di Verona*.
10 The translation of the term *laïko* is a thorny subject among musicologists. Even though the term linguistically translates as 'folk', *laïko* should analytically be regarded as popular music par excellence: it was created by named composers and lyricists and was made prominent through the national music industry. However, the term 'urban-folk' that we use to describe *laïko* in this chapter reflects its position as a genre within the aesthetic debates of the period. Rather than a music *of* the people, *laïko* was intended as a music *for* the

people. See Dafni Tragaki, '"Humanizing the Masses": Enlightened Intellectuals and the Music of the People', in David Cooper and Kevin Dawe (eds.), *The Mediterranean in Music: Critical Perspectives, Common Concerns, Cultural Differences.* (Lanham, MD: Scarecrow Press, 2005).
11 See Dafni Tragaki, *Rebetiko Worlds* (Newcastle: Cambridge Scholars, 2007), p. 52; Dimitris Papanikolaou, *Singing Poets. Literature and Popular Music in France and Greece* (Oxford: Legenda, 2007), p. 63; Andreas Andreopoulos, 'Imago Poetae: The Aesthetics of Manos Hadjidakis', *Journal of Modern Greek Studies* 19 (2001), pp. 256–7.
12 See Papanikolaou (*Singing Poets*), p. 61.
13 Gail Holst-Warhaft, 'Politics and Popular Music in Modern Greece'. *Journal of Political and Military Sociology*, 30: 2 (2002), pp. 313–17.
14 Gail Holst-Warhaft, *Theodorakis: Myth and Politics in Modern Greek Music* (Amsterdam: Hakkert, 1980).
15 See Jane K. Cowan, 'Politics, Identity and Popular Music in Contemporary Greece', Κάμπος: Cambridge Papers in Modern Greek 1 (1993), p. 5. Papanikolaou (*Singing Poets*, p. 87) regards the *entechno-laïkó* song as Theodorákis' answer to the Gramscian call for 'a modern humanism able to reach right to the simplest and most uneducated classes'.
16 Holst-Warhaft, *Theodorakis*.
17 Frederic Moehn describes the rise of Música Popular Brasileira (MPB) as a similar bricolage of cosmopolitan aspiration filtered through local/national political circumstances. See Fredecick Moehn, *Contemporary Carioca: Technologies of Mixing in a Brazilian Music Scene* (Durham: Duke University Press, 2012).
18 For a discussion of the ethnic aesthetic in Greek jazz music see Ioannis Tsioulakis 'Jazz in Athens: Frustrated Cosmopolitans in a Music Subculture'. *Ethnomusicology Forum* 20 (2) (2011), pp. 175–99. Also, for a discussion on the importation of instruments and styles from Turkey and other Eastern Mediterranean regions into Greek urban music-making, see Eleni Kallimopoulou, Paradosiaká: Music, Meaning and Identity in Modern Greece (London: Ashgate, 2009).
19 For a discussion of how *entechno* becomes produced in the studio, see Dimitris Varelopoulos, 'Producing Entechno: Amalgamation and Hybridization in a Controversial Musical Style', in Dafni Tragaki (ed.), *Made in Greece: Studies in Popular Music* (New York and London: Routledge, forthcoming).

20 Thomas Turino, *Music as Social Life: the Politics of Participation* (Chicago: The University of Chicago Press, 2008), pp. 66–92.

21 Modugno won at Sanremo in 1958, 1959, 1962, 1966, and was second in 1960.

22 Renis won in 1963; he was co-author and interpreter of 'Quando Quando Quando' – fourth in 1962 – and other international hits.

23 Donaggio scored sixth in 1961, third in 1963, fourth in 1966: his 'Io che non vivo', seventh in 1965, became a world hit as 'You Don't Have to Say You Love Me'; later, Donaggio became a well-known composer of film scores, especially for Brian De Palma.

24 Bobby Solo (Roberto Satti) enjoyed tremendous success at Sanremo in 1964 and won in 1965.

25 There was a clear mismatch between RAI, a state-owned broadcasting monopoly, controlled by the conservative Christian Democratic Party, and the cynical exploitation of 'revolutionary' music by CBS: but Tenco didn't acknowledge it.

26 There is a wide critical and academic consensus on the conservative function of the Sanremo Festival, especially in the 1950s and 1960s; see Franco Fabbri, 'Il Trentennio: "musica leggera" alla radio italiana, 1928–1958', in Angela Ida De Benedictis (ed.), *La musica alla radio: 1924–1954. Storia, effetti, contesti in prospettiva europea.* (Rome: Bulzoni Editore, 2014), pp. 225–43.

27 De André's first single was released in 1961, but he remained known just by a niche of students until 1968.

28 Referring to the genre ('beat', or 'bitt') that emerged in Italy in the mid-1960s, based on the imitation of British bands. See Franco Fabbri, 'And the Bitt Went On', in Fabbri and Plastino (eds.), *Made in Italy*, pp. 41–55.

29 See the full list in http://it.wikipedia.org/wiki/Premio_Tenco

30 There were rumours (never confirmed, of course) that Battisti was a supporter of neo-fascist movements. On Battisti as a musician, see Jacopo Conti, 'You Can Call Them, If You Like, Emotions. The (Un)Orthodox Songs of Lucio Battisti', in Fabbri and Plastino, *Made in Italy*, pp. 110–22.

31 Some of their songs were covered by Vassilis Papaconstantinou and Maria Farantouri.

32 See Tomatis, 'A Portrait of the Author as an Artist', *passim*; emphasis added.

33 See Franco Fabbri, 'How Genres Are Born, Change, Die: Conventions, Communities and Diachronic Processes', in Stan Hawkins (ed.), *Critical Musicological Reflections* (Aldershot: Ashgate, 2012), pp. 179–91 (n. 18).

34 Nada debuted very successfully at the Sanremo Festival in 1969, when she was fifteen years old, as a pop-rock singer. She almost disappeared from that scene soon, and slowly approached *canzone d'autore* in the 1970s, first by singing songs by known *cantautori*, then composing her own. Her acknowledgement as a distinguished *cantautrice* took place in the 1990s.

35 See Errico Pavese, 'Saved Souls. Locating Style in Fabrizio De André's and Ivano Fossati's Record Production', in Fabbri and Plastino, *Made in Italy*, pp. 123–35.

29 Singer-songwriters and fandom in the digital age

LUCY BENNETT

The arrival of social media platforms such as Twitter, Facebook and Instagram have permitted and fostered new avenues of communication between some singer-songwriters and their fans. As Nancy Baym discovered, in her 2012 study of the online interactions between fans and independent musicians,[1] social media are offering the possibility that 'through the eyes of musicians, [fans] are revealed in part as relational partners. They may be distant 'fans', relegated to interacting primarily with one another, but they may be people who become friends'.[2]

This chapter will explore how some singer-songwriters are using digital tools and social media to connect with their online fans and how understandings of participation and connection are being currently negotiated and formed. It will also unravel how the nature of the media, which can invoke feelings of close proximity and intimacy,[3] can be skilfully used in particular by musicians who write and perform their own material. Rather than focus specifically on one artist (though considering the online strategies and posts of musicians such as Amanda Palmer, Tori Amos, Suzanne Vega, Neil Tennant, James Arthur, and James Blunt), this chapter will give a wider overview of how some singer-songwriters are engaging with these social media platforms, the new opportunities for connection and participation with their fan bases that they offer, and the implications of these changing modes of interaction on relations with their fans and the creative process. I will argue that the confessional and personal nature fostered within the music of some singer-songwriters can compliment and lend itself well to communicative practices on social media platforms, with fans seemingly being offered striking and valued insights into everyday and 'intimate' moments of the musicians' lives that were previously unobtainable for many. In addition, I will argue that Twitter use by musical artists can sometimes reveal transgressive elements of the individual that had not been clearly visible as part of their public image, elements which can either enhance or shatter relations with fans and their wider online public.

Framing intimacy: singer-songwriters and their use of social media platforms

When examining the contemporary vista of engagement between musicians and their fans, use of social media platforms such as Twitter, Facebook, and Instagram has proffered a most startling and disruptive interjection. Prior to this, although fans have always been able to attempt to communicate in some form with their object of fandom, these communications would have had to be via a letter[4] or through a personal encounter, both forms of which may have been filtered by management or security. In addition, aside from the music itself, and any possible fan club magazines or official website posts, the majority of revelations and insights from the musicians would have been through media interviews, which are again possibly filtered by the press. Social media disrupts this and permits messages seemingly direct from the poster and the ability to reply and engage in conversation with fans. In this sense, it appears that musicians can use these platforms, whether strategically or not, to 'build camaraderie over distance through the dynamic and ongoing practice of disclosing the everyday'.[5] It is this 'everyday' that can be confessed most explicitly though Twitter, with it being determined as 'the most salient means of generating 'authentic' celebrity disclosure' in that it can offer the potential to 'simultaneously [counter] the efforts of the paparazzi, fan mags, and gossip blogs to complicate or rewrite the meaning of the star'.[6]

To give a snapshot of the possibilities of contemporary engagement with digital media, a musician that has dynamically embraced these platforms is American singer-songwriter Amanda Palmer. Utilising blogs, Twitter, Facebook, and Instagram, Palmer speaks directly to her audience, who are 'her contributors, co-conspirators, and supporters within a much larger do it yourself (DIY), participatory culture forming between artist and fan'.[7] This participatory culture has formed within a space where both parties work together to challenge traditional understandings and barriers within the music industry – Palmer successfully crowdfunded over $1million on Kickstarter in 2012 to fund a new record, art book, and tour[8] and also used crowdsourcing to locate fans who were willing to volunteer as musicians during her tour.[9] In this sense, Palmer's fans became active funders and contributors to her musical output and thereby somewhat integral to the music production process.

For other singer-songwriters, a transition from online communities and blogs into social media has also been apparent, in similarly explicit ways. For example, Suzanne Vega's official website maintained an online community/bulletin board named 'the Undertow' from the early 2000s, where members were informed that Suzanne read the messages posted to the community and made an effort to reply to them as often as she could.[10]

This openness to communicate with fans has been further cultivated by Vega within her use of Twitter, which she joined in February 2009. Since then, she has been replying directly to fans, retweeting their mentions of her music and engaging in conversations with listeners on the platform. Her official Facebook continues this momentum, as does her Instagram account, which features snapshots of her concerts and life on the road.

Most recently, use of social media is also being embraced by singer-songwriters that previously had not fully aligned themselves with these forms of communication. For example, up until 2014, American musician Tori Amos, who has a dedicated online fan base, had previously explicitly refrained from fully engaging with these platforms. She did have a Facebook and Twitter account which, very occasionally, featured messages seemingly from her (which were signed with her name to indicate this), but the majority of the messages were formed with news and updates from her management. Although Amos did not engage with this media as other singer-songwriters did, she maintained strong connections with fans at live concerts (for example, keeping eye contact with audience members and playing requests for fans) and the meet-and-greets that regularly precede them. However, in 2014, during the release of *Unrepentant Geraldines*, and coinciding with her world tour, this momentum changed, with an explicit adjustment to social media. Although Amos maintains connections with fans at concerts and public appearances, she began to embrace these platforms in a skilful way that gave rise to two key dynamics: (1) this strategy not only gave further insight into her off-stage life, but also (2) engaged fans further in the proceedings to make them a part of this process, that worked further to promote her music and tour. For instance, on Instagram, the 'Unrepentant Selfie Tour Instagram Photo Contest' was launched where fans were asked to take selfies[11] of themselves demonstrating that they were attending a concert (showing the venue or ticket)– using the hashtag #Unrepentantselfie and also a hashtag for the city they were seeing the show in. One winner in each 'tour market' could then win a signed tour programme. Amos also seemingly engaged in this initiative herself, taking selfies in different locations and submitting them via the hashtag. However, this was then taken further, with Amos taking two kinds of selfies surrounding each concert that were simultaneously posted on Twitter, Facebook, and Instagram: pictures of herself backstage preparing for the show and pictures afterwards of the set-list (complete with hand-written chords and last minute changes) adorned with a few items from her dressing room. This use of social media has been very effective for some fans – even if this process is constructed (with her management sometimes helping and posting the photos), it gives a key impression that Tori is trying to develop a stronger connection with her fan base through these channels – for those both physically present at the show and those following from afar.

These strategies also give insight into 'intimate' or everyday moments, that previously would have been unseen – the prospect that these pictures are 'selfies' taken by Tori herself also give further momentum to their seemingly intimate and revealing nature. This is a sense which, I would argue, is given further authenticity and credence by it coming from a singer-songwriter on social media – an individual who may have developed a fan base through connection to their personal and intimate lyrics and music and is now seemingly broadcasting their thoughts and photos to fans directly from their smart phones, without apparent management and media industry filter. In other words, the closeness that can sometimes be felt by listeners and fans towards singer-songwriters can also, on occasion, translate very well and skilfully to the terrain of social media. Thus, these are interesting examples of how social media use by these artists can deliver fans a sense of intimacy, so that it seems 'the long established, while historically variable, distance between [star] and interested enthusiast is eroded (although we can of course argue that this is illusory)'.[12]

In this sense, for some singer-songwriters, a developed and skilful use of social media platforms adds a further dimension to their engagement with their fans. However, for others, it is not viewed with this same positivity, or adjusted to in the same manner. For instance, Neil Tennant, half of British singer-songwriter duo The Pet Shop Boys, does not view these connections as valuable, due to social networks being 'fundamentally insincere', and working to foster a 'fake intimacy, which … results in frustration and ultimately makes people angry'.[13] This anger, he observes, results from unequal power and illusory connections between public figures and their fans: 'people tweet a celebrity and they get no response. It's a totally fake relationship'.[14] Tennant concludes that this situation is troubling, since 'everything turns into a row, and it's because it's presented as though they care what you think, but you realise they don't, and then it turns nasty'.[15] This tumultuous scene, then, and the realisation of falsity that he views fans as being confronted with, led to the musician refraining from using Twitter (aside from an official Pet Shop Boys account, run by their management), after experimenting with it for two years: 'it's a sort of fake democracy. And we prefer to be not fake'.[16] Instead, the band opt to communicate with followers through 'pet texts' which appear on their official website and feature photographs and messages from the musicians' smart phones – a practice which promotes a more one-way flow of communication, as fans can only read, but not comment on these updates. In this sense, for Tennant, 'pet texts' are a more realistic and less illusory form of communicating with The Pet Shop Boys' fan base, as they do not profess to offer replies and engage in conversation.

Both Amos and Tennant developed their careers in popular music before the inception of social media, and demonstrate how perception, approaches, and adjustment to social media use by musicians can differ between artists and fan cultures. Thus, while social media platform use can foster new trajectories in the contact and communications between fans and singer-songwriters – processes that can indeed be revelatory and highly pleasurable –they can also be complicated for both parties.

New trajectories, new implications: embracing and negotiating digital fandom

This section will consider more closely the areas and implications of these interactions and the questions that they can pose surrounding our contemporary uses and understandings of social and digital media. These include (1) crowd inspiration/involvement practices, (2) the negotiation of public/private selves, (3) music/fan expectations, and (4) exposure to anti-fandom and 'trolling', which will now be discussed in turn.

(1) Crowd inspiration/involvement practices:

The creative process of the singer-songwriter can now be charged by input from fans through digital media. For instance, this can take the form of funding, as evident in Amanda Palmer's aforementioned case. However, going beyond this, some music fans are now being invited and permitted through social media to engage in the creative process with the object of fandom. British independent musician Imogen Heap's strategy of allowing her fans to become active participants in the creation of her album *Ellipse (2010)* and ongoing project *Heapsongs* (2011–) through Twitter, YouTube, Soundcloud, and Facebook is a striking example of this practice. Permitting fans to send in snippet recordings of their everyday lives, known as 'sound seeds', alongside contributing their words to a 'word-cloud', Heap then uses these to form the basis of the music and lyrics to a new song. Working further with her fans as collaborators, they are then invited to submit images, record solos, suggest direction, and collectively develop each song together with the musician. As in Amanda Palmer's case, Heap also took her participatory efforts in a similar vein, by crowd-sourcing fans to volunteer to perform with her as part of her touring band. Although many fans take pleasure in being part of these processes, these practices have also raised questions and accusations by some such as Steve Albini being interviewed in 2013,[17] suggesting exploitation of these individuals by those more powerful and wealthy. In answer to this, I would argue that fans generally are not a passive mass, and can make a conscious decision to engage in these forms of labour, and are aware of their investments. As Bertha Chin argued when similar fan exploitation arguments were raised surrounding the *Veronica Mars* film crowdfunding campaign, 'fan agency always gets left out in arguments which purport concern that fans are being duped by studios and networks'.[18] In this sense, crowd inspiration and involvement practices cannot easily or simply be reduced to discourses of fan exploitation.

(2) Public/Private Selves:

The aforementioned circumvention of media and management filters, although often welcomed by fans and their wider audience of followers, can also have a detrimental impact. Exploring issues surrounding celebrities and their use of social media, P. David Marshall argues that 'what we are witnessing now is the staging of the self as both character and performance in on-line settings'.[19] By analysing how the private self is constructed for public presentation, he identifies the appearance of a transgressive intimate self, where public figures are motivated by strong temporary emotion that seemingly works to break through this performance and intensify the perception of proximity. In other words, in these moments, the individual posts or Tweets a message that appears to disrupt or break their public image. I would also here pose a question surrounding perceptions of objects of fandom (in this case, singer-songwriters) – how do fans respond when the musician may suddenly disrupt their online 'image', or appear completely different on these social media platforms to how they have appeared before? For example, British musician James Arthur had to leave Twitter in 2013 after posting a number of outbursts and content online that were perceived as displaying homophobia and an aggressive attitude.[20] Fans and fellow musicians took to Twitter to articulate their disappointment, which eventually led to his management taking over his Twitter account. On this occasion, Arthur's homophobia that had not been revealed during press interviews or his time during the X Factor (he won the programme in 2012) and may have otherwise been filtered by management, was transgressively made explicit to fans through his use of Twitter. Arthur lost considerable popularity due to his conduct on the social media platform, and during June 2014 was eventually dropped by his record label.

(3) Musician/fan expectations:

How artists manage their following on social media platforms is another area for consideration that can raise problematic issues regarding interactions and expectations. For example, as social media use becomes more widespread and proliferated, the numbers of followers of some artists may expand considerably and rapidly, with individual fans being placed as literally one amongst millions. When this occurs, and with some fans sending messages and hoping to be noticed, how can a 'direct' or reciprocal connection be fully maintained? With only some fans being replied to and noticed or followed, this situation could foster the problematic terrain alluded to by Neil Tennant. In these cases, some fans may make stronger attempts to get noticed, while others may experience frustration at being overlooked. Despite this though, in some cases, with music artists that have large followings, as is evident with Lady Gaga,[21] although an absolutely reciprocal relationship with fans is difficult to maintain, a skilful use of intimacy, in terms of tweets and photos that encompass revelations of everyday and personal activities, work to foster feelings of close proximity and directness within some fans, and between both parties.

In addition, there may be generally a strong pressure for artists to be on the media – both from record label management, and their fan bases. Although The Pet Shop Boys are outliers in the sense that they have shunned the platform and created their own preferred strategy of communicating with fans, new singer-songwriters who are establishing themselves in an effort to develop a large committed fan base may have little choice but to engage in social media platforms, to fulfil the expectations of others and develop a strong presence.

(4) Exposure to anti-fandom and 'trolling':

Another problematic aspect of Twitter use by singer-songwriters is exposure to declarations of hate online, and negotiating these outbursts. As outlined in the first section of this chapter, whereas during pre-social media times fans would have had to write a letter or meet their object of fandom in person to send a message (avenues that could be filtered by management or media), these processes have been disrupted by social media, offering new opportunities to seemingly connect directly with artists. However, this theory also applies to 'trolling', or what has been termed and theorised by Jonathan Gray as 'anti-fandom', individuals who 'strongly dislike a given text or genre, considering it inane, stupid, morally bankrupt and/or aesthetic drivel'.[22] A key element of Gray's analysis of anti-fans is his emphasis that they construct and form an image of the text that they can react against, with this process being 'as potentially powerful an emotion and reaction as is like'.[23] It is possible that this power within dislike also rests within, and is reinforced by, an element within much anti-fandom, of an 'interest, or even sense of responsibility, in sharing one's reading and, thus, encouraging an avoidance of the aesthetic text in others too'.[24] Anti-fandom translates strongly to Twitter, with not only anti-fans being able to bound and give strength to their hate-tinged messages through hashtags, but also, and most significantly, able to send these outpourings straight to the object of anti-fandom. In this sense, whereas before hate letters written by anti-fans to these individuals may have been filtered by management and not exposed to the artist, Twitter is a more direct form of communication that may give stronger possibilities for anti-fans to spread their dislike, and for the musicians to be exposed to, and possibly read, their hate mail.

This raises the question of how music artists, and their fans, negotiate anti-fandom online? An intriguing and successful example of how to navigate the terrain of hate online is British singer-songwriter James Blunt, who has 'been executing expertly judged smackdowns of people who tangle with him'[25] on Twitter, gaining him more followers and seemingly improving his public image. Building on this momentum, in 2013, Blunt was deemed by Buzzfeed as one of the necessary personalities to follow on Twitter.[26] For example, in response to one anti-fan who tweeted 'Jesus Christ, James Blunt's got a new album out. Is there anything else that can go wrong?' Blunt retweeted the tweet, prefixing it with 'Yes. He could start tweeting you' (20 October 2013, Figure 29.1). In response to another individual who tweeted 'I bet James Blunt is sitting in a dark room and crying somewhere', he did the same, prefixing it with, 'Crying with laughter, mate' (19 February 2012, Figure 29.2).

However, although these responses were humorous, they also had power and impact – they worked to expose the Twitter trolls and anti-fans,

Figure 29.1. James Blunt tweet, 9:08am, 20 October 2013.

Figure 29.2. James Blunt tweet, 12:35pm, 19 February 2012.

and publicly displayed the kinds of messages tinged with dislike and hate that he receives. As Blunt stated in an interview with the *Daily Mirror*: 'I'll read comments on Twitter which are often quite negative, but it seems to be this security in people's bedrooms where it's okay to write such aggressive things behind their computer screens'.[27] In this case, just as James Arthur's tweets displayed elements of his personality that did not previously form part of his public image, James Blunt's sense of humour and innovative method of dealing with hate and difficulty, positive elements of his character which had not previously been an evident part of his image were revealed in his tweets, thereby adding a further dimension to his engagement with his online public and fans.

Thus, overall, although social media use delivers both parties increased opportunities to interact and reveal elements of themselves and their thoughts that may have previously been filtered or blocked, it also raises some challenges and complications for both – many of which are not clear cut and evade easy solutions.

Concluding thoughts and suggestions

In this chapter I have argued that the personal and confessional framing of the musical output of some singer-songwriters can further charge their communicative practices on social media platforms, with fans given glimpses and previously unattained insights into the everyday, intimate lives of the musicians. As I have shown, these glimpses can often reveal elements of the artists that previously had not been explicitly forefronted or presented as part of their public image, as is the case with James Arthur and James Blunt. In addition, while use of social media has allowed new forms and methods of communication between singer-songwriters and their fans – processes that have been welcomed by some as revealing – they can also be complex and challenging.

From these arguments there are a number of related, and interconnecting, points to consider, that require further research, and may give rise to a multitude of further questions and implications. For example, how do fans negotiate any differences in the way that musicians approach and value these new forms of engagement and communication? For example, and as I have pondered elsewhere (see n. 21), while some singer-songwriters such as Amanda Palmer, and some of the musicians within Nancy Baym's 2012 study,[28] speak of robust, valued, and genuinely 'close' connections with their fans through social media, others such as Neil Tennant despair at the 'fake intimacy' that they view as conjured. When these differences of views occur, how do fans situate themselves? For example, how would a fan of both Amanda Palmer and Neil Tennant make sense of these differences in how the platform is valued and perceived in terms of communications between artist and fan? And to what extent would these perceptions impact on their connections with the music?

Further research that explores these issues and the questions and implications I have raised in this chapter will be vital, in order to move further towards understanding and making sense of contemporary forms of communication between singer-songwriters and fans. As technology develops further, and may possibly provide even more avenues for engagement and participation, we may witness even further trajectories and complications arise, as both parties continue to negotiate and attempt to situate themselves on digital and social media platforms.

Notes

1 Nancy Baym, 'Fans Or Friends? Seeing Social Media Audiences As Musicians Do'. *Participations* [online], 9/2 (2012), pp. 287–316. Available at: www.participations.org/Volume%209/Issue%202/17%20Baym.pdf (Accessed 17 August 2014).

2 Baym, 'Fans or Friends?', p. 313.

3 David Beer, 'Making Friends with Jarvis Cocker: Music Culture in the Context of Web 2.0'. Cultural Sociology, 2/2 (2008), pp. 222–41, and Alice Marwick and danah boyd, 'To See and Be Seen: Celebrity Practice on Twitter'. *Convergence*, 17 /2 (2011), pp. 139–58.

4 Courtney A. Bates, 'The Fan Letter Correspondence of Willa Cather: Challenging the Divide Between Professional and Common Reader'. *Transformative Works and Cultures* [online], 11 (2011). Available at: journal.transformativeworks.org/index.php/twc/article/view/221/214 (Accessed 5 January 2015). And Linda M. Grasso, '"You Are No Stranger To Me": Georgia O'Keeffe's Fan Mail'. *Reception: Texts, Readers, Audiences, History*, 5 (2013) pp. 24–40.

5 Kate Crawford, 'These Foolish Things: On Intimacy and Insignificance in Mobile Media', in Gerard Goggin and Larissa Hjorth, *Mobile Technologies: From Telecommunications to Media* (New York: Routledge, 2009), p. 254.

6 Nick Muntean and Anne Helen Peterson, 'Celebrity Twitter: Strategies of Intrusion and Disclosure in the Age of Technoculture', *M/C Journal*, 12/5 (2009). Available at: journal.media-culture.org.au/index.php/mcjournal/article/viewArticle/194 (Accessed 17 August 2014).

7 Liza Potts, 'Amanda Palmer and the #LOFNOTC: How Online Fan Participation is Rewriting Music Labels', *Participations*, 9/2 (2012), p. 361. Available at: www.participations.org/Volume%209/Issue%202/20%20Potts.pdf (Accessed 17 August 2014).

8 Amanda Palmer, 'Amanda Palmer: The new RECORD, ART BOOK, and TOUR', *Kickstarter*, 2012. Available at: www.kickstarter.com/projects/amandapalmer/amanda-palmer-the-new-record-art-book-and-tour (Accessed 17 August 2014).

9 Justin A. Williams and Ross Wilson, 'Music and Crowdfunded Websites: Digital Patronage and Fan–Artist Interactivity', in Sheila Whiteley and Shara Rambarran (eds.), *The Oxford Handbook of Music and Virtuality*. (New York: Oxford University Press, forthcoming).

10 Suzanne Vega personal website, formerly available at: www.suzannevega.com/suzanne/f-a-q/ (Accessed 17 August 2014).

11 Jill Walker Rettberg. *Seeing Ourselves Through Technology: How We Use Selfies, Blogs and Wearable Devices to See and Shape Ourselves* (Basingstoke: Palgrave Macmillan, 2014).

12 Beer, 'Making Friends with Jarvis Cocker'. pp. 232–3.

13 Danny Eccleston, 'Pet Shop Boys' Neil Tennant Slates Social Media', *Mojo*, 3 July 2013. Available at: www.mojo4music.com/642/pet-shop-boys-neil-tennant-slates-social-media/ (Accessed 17 August 2014).

14 Dorian Lynskey, 'Pet Shop Boys: Cab Drivers Ask Us If We've Retired', *The Guardian*, 13 September 2012. Available at: www.theguardian.com/music/2012/sep/13/pet-shop-boys (Accessed 17 August 2014).

15 Eccleston, 'Pet Shop Boys' Neil Tennant Slates Social Media'.

16 Ibid.

17 Alex Denney, 'Interview: Steve Albini', *The Stool Pigeon*, 6 February 2013. Available at: www.thestoolpigeon.co.uk/features/interview-steve-albini.html (Accessed 17 August 2014).

18 Bertha Chin, 'The Veronica Mars Movie: Crowdfunding – Or Fan-Funding – at Its Best?', *On/Off Screen*, 13 March 2013. Available at:

onoffscreen.wordpress.com/2013/03/13/the-veronica-mars-movie-crowdfunding-or-fan-funding-at-its-best/ (Accessed 17 August 2014).

19 P. David Marshall, 'The Promotion and Presentation of the Self: Celebrity as Marker of Presentational Media', *Celebrity Studies*, 1/1(2010), p. 40.

20 Pete Cashmore, 'James Arthur: Anatomy of a Twitter Disaster', *The Guardian*, 18 November 2013. Available at: www.theguardian.com/music/musicblog/2013/nov/18/james-arthur-anatomy-twitter-disaster (Accessed 17 August 2014).

21 Lucy Bennett, 'Fan-Celebrity Interactions and Social Media: Connectivity and Engagement in Lady Gaga Fandom' in Linda Duits, Koos Zwaan and Stijn Reijnders, S. (eds.), *The Ashgate Companion to Fan Cultures* (Ashgate Press, 2014), pp. 109–20.

22 Jonathan Gray, 'New Audiences, New Textualities: Anti-fans and Non-fans', *International Journal of Cultural Studies*, 6/1 (2003), p. 70.

23 Gray, 'New Audiences, new Textualities', p. 73.

24 Jonathan Gray, 'Antifandom and the Moral Text: Television Without Pity and Textual Dislike', *American Behavioral Scientist*, 48 (2005), p. 848.

25 Caroline Sullivan, 'James Blunt on Twitter: How the Most Hated Man in Pop is Fixing his Image', *The Guardian*, 29 October 2013. Available at: www.theguardian.com/music/shortcuts/2013/oct/29/james-blunt-twitter-most-hated-man-pop-fixing-image(Accessed 17 August 2014).

26 Ailbhe Malone, '17 Reasons You Should Be Following James Blunt On Twitter', *Buzzfeed*, 28 October 2013. Available at: www.buzzfeed.com/ailbhemalone/17-reasons-you-should-be-following-james-blunt-on-twitter (Accessed 17 August 2014).

27 Claire Carter, 'James Blunt Exposes Twitter Trolls', *The Telegraph*, 26 October 2013. Available at: www.telegraph.co.uk/culture/music/music-news/10406405/James-Blunt-exposes-Twitter-trolls.html (Accessed 17 August 2014).

28 Baym, 'Fans or Friends?'

Select Bibliography

Abel, Sam, *Opera in the Flesh: Sexuality in Operatic Performance* (Boulder: Colorado, 1996).

Adria, Marco, *Music of Our Times: Eight Canadian Singer-Songwriters* (Toronto: James Lorimer and Company, 1990).

Alberti, John, '"I Have Come Out to Play": Jonathan Richman and the Politics of the Faux Naif', in Kevin J. H. Dettmar and William Richey (eds.), *Reading Rock and Roll: Authenticity, Appropriation, Aesthetics* (New York: Columbia University Press, 1999), pp. 173–89.

Aldredge, Marcus, *Singer-Songwriters and Musical Open Mics* (Farnham, Ashgate, 2013).

Almén, Byron, *A Theory of Musical Narrative* (Bloomington: Indiana University Press, 2008).

Alper, Aaron, 'A Chat with Tori Amos', *Tampa Bay Times* (10 August 2005), available at: aaronalper.com/interviews/tori.html (accessed 27 May 2014).

Amos, Tori and Ann Powers, *Piece by Piece* (New York: Broadway Books, 2005).

Anderson, Benedict R., *Imagined Communities: Reflections on the Origins and Spread of Nationalism* (London: Verso, 1983).

Andreopoulos, Andreas, 'Imago Poetae: The Aesthetics of Manos Hadjidakis', *Journal of Modern Greek Studies*, 19 (2001), pp. 255–68.

Anon, 'Joanie Goes to Jail Again', Rolling Stone (23 November 1967), p. 7.

——— 'Wildflower, Judy Collins' New LP', Rolling Stone (23 November 1967), p. 7.

Armstrong, Edward G., 'Eminem's Construction of Authenticity'. *Popular Music and Society* 27/3 (2004), pp. 335–55.

Arthur, Dave, *Bert: the Life and Times of A. L. Lloyd* (London: Pluto, 2012).

Bacharach, Burt, *Anyone Who Had a Heart: My Life and Music* (London: Atlantic Books, 2013).

Baillie, Russell, 'Don McGlashan and the Seven Sisters – Marvellous Year'. *New Zealand Herald* (11 March 2009), available at: www.nzherald.co.nz/music/news/article.cfm?c_id=264&objectid=10561129 (accessed 17 July 2014).

——— 'Concert Review: Kiwi Legends' Double Act is Heaven Sent'. *New Zealand Herald* (30 September 2013), available at: www.nzherald.co.nz/music/news/article.cfm?c_id=264&objectid=11131978 (accessed 17 July 2014).

Banks, Mark, *The Politics of Cultural Work* (London: Palgrave, 2007).

Bannister, Matthew, 'A Thing Well Made? NZ Settler Identity and Pakeha Masculinity in the Work of Don McGlashan', *Perfect Beat* 8/1 (2006), pp. 22–49.

——— 'Going out to Everyone? Bic Runga as a New Zealand Artist', in Henry Johnston (ed.), *Many Voices: Music and National Identity in Aotearoa/New Zealand* (Newcastle: Cambridge Scholars Publishing, 2010), pp. 84–91.

Barretta, Scott (ed.), *The Conscience of the Folk Revival: The Writings of Israel 'Izzy' Young. American Folk Music and Musicians*, no. 18 (Lanham, MD: Scarecrow Press, 2013).

Bartlett, Andrew. 'Airshafts, Loudspeakers, and the Hip-Hop Sample', in Murray Forman and Mark Anthony Neal (eds.), *The Hip-Hop Studies Reader* (London: Routledge, 2012), pp. 565–79.

Bates, Courtney A., 'The Fan Letter Correspondence of Willa Cather: Challenging the Divide Between Professional and Common Reader'. *Transformative Works and Cultures [online]*, 11 (2011), available at: journal.transformativeworks.org/ index.php/twc/article/view/221/214 (Accessed 17 August 2014).

Baym, Nancy, 'Fans Or Friends? Seeing Social Media Audiences As Musicians Do'. *Participations: Journal of Audience & Reception Studies*, 9/2 (2012), pp. 287–316, available at: www.participations.org/Volume%209/Issue%20 2/17%20Baym.pdf (accessed 17 August 2014).

Bayton, Mavis, 'Women and the Electric Guitar', in Sheila Whiteley (ed.), *Sexing the Groove: Popular Music and Gender* (London: Routledge, 1997), pp. 37–49.

Beer, David, 'Making Friends with Jarvis Cocker: Music Culture in the Context of Web 2.0', *Cultural Sociology*, 2/2 (2008), pp. 222–41.

Behr, Adam. 'The Real "Crossroads" of Live Music – the Conventions of Performance at Open Mic Nights in Edinburgh', *Social Semiotics*, 22/5 (2012), pp. 559–73.

Bennett, Joe, 'Constraint, Collaboration and Creativity in Popular Songwriting Teams', in D. Collins (ed.), *The Act of Musical Composition: Studies in the Creative Process* (Aldershot: Ashgate, 2012), pp. 139–69.

——— 'You Can't Teach Songwriting', *Total Guitar* (September 2012), p. 34.

——— 'Creativities in Popular Songwriting Curricula', in Pamela Burnard and Elizabeth Haddon (eds.), *Activating Diverse Musical Creativities: Teaching and Learning in Higher Education* (London: Bloomsbury, 2015), pp. 37–56.

Bennett, Lucy, 'Fan-Celebrity Interactions and Social Media: Connectivity and Engagement in Lady Gaga Fandom' in Linda Duits, Koos Zwaan and Stijn Reijnders (eds.), *The Ashgate Companion to Fan Cultures* (Farnham: Ashgate Press, 2014), pp. 109–20.

Betrock, Alan, *Girl Groups: The Story of a Sound* (New York: Delilah, 1982).

Boden, Margaret, *The Creative Mind: Myths and Mechanisms* (London: Routledge, 2005).

Bogue, Ronald, *Deleuze on Music Painting and the Arts* (New York: Routledge, 2003).

Born, Georgina, and David Hesmondhalgh (eds.), *Western Music and Its Others: Difference,Representation and Appropriation in Music* (London: University of California Press, 2000).

Bourdage, Monique, 'A Young Girl's Dream: Examining the Barriers Facing Female Electric Guitarists', *Journal of the International Association for the Study of Popular Music* 1/1 (2010), available at www.iaspmjournal.net (accessed 5 July 2014).

Bourdieu, Pierre, and Richard Nice, 'The Production of Belief: Contribution to an Economy of Symbolic Goods', *Media, Culture & Society* 2/3 (1980), pp. 261–93.

Boyd, Joe, *White Bicycles: Making Music in the 1960s* (London: Serpent's Tail, 2006).

——— 'Bumpy, Bikers and the Story Behind "Leader of the Pack"', *Fresh Air*. NPR Radio (26 September 2013), available at www.npr.org/2013/09/26/200445875/

bumpy-bikers-and-the-story-behind-leader-of-the-pack (accessed 26 February 2015).

Brackett, Donald, *Dark Mirror: The Pathology of the Singer-Songwriter* (Westport, CT: Greenwood Publishing Group, 2008).

Bradley, Adam, *Book of Rhymes: The Poetics of Hip Hop* (New York: BasicCivitas, 2009).

Braudy, Susan, 'James Taylor, a New Troubadour', *New York Times Magazine* (21 February 1971), p. 28.

Breihan, Tom, 'Music: Post-Graduate Depression', *The Village Voice* 53/48 (2008), p. 64.

Breskin, David, 'Steely Dan Musician Interview' (1 March 1981), *The Steely Dan Reader: Four Decades of News and Interviews*, available at steelydanreader. com/1981/03/01/steely-dan-interview (accessed 27 February 2015).

Brett, Philip, Elizabeth Wood and Gary C. Thomas (eds.), *Queering the Pitch: The New Gay and Lesbian Musicology* (New York: Routledge, 1994. Second edn, 2006).

Brocken, Michael, *The British Folk Revival 1944–2002* (Aldershot, Hampshire: Ashgate, 2003).

Bromell, Nick, *Tomorrow Never Knows: Rock and Psychedelics in the 1960s.* (Chicago: University of Chicago Press, 2000).

Brooks, Daphne, '"This Voice Which is Not One": Amy Winehouse Sings the Ballad of Sonic Blue(s)face Culture', *Women & Performance: A Journal of Feminist Theory*, 20/1 (2010), pp. 37–60.

Brown, Andrew, *Computers in Music Education: Amplifying Musicality* (New York, Routledge, 2007).

Bryan Jr, Maurice L. , 'Good Morning Blues: Gordon Parks Imagines Leadbelly', in Tony Bolden (ed.), *The Funk Era and Beyond. New Perspectives on Black Popular Culture* (New York: Palgrave McMillan, 2008), pp. 125–42.

Buchanan, Brad, 'Am I So Dear? Do I Run Rare?: Affections and Affectations in Joanna Newsom's The Milk Eyed Mender', in Brad Buchanan (ed.), *Visions of Joanna Newsom* (Sacramento: Roan Press, 2010), pp. 37–56.

Burnard, Pamela, *Musical Creativities in Practice* (Oxford: Oxford University Press, 2012).

Büsser, Martin, 'Free Folk: Kollektive Improvisation. Kollektivimprovisation und Naturmystik', *De:Bug Magazin* (2007). Translated by Maximilian Georg Spiegel in 'Gender Construction', MPhil thesis, 2012.

Butler, Judith, *Gender Trouble: Feminism and the Subversion of Identity*, 2nd edn (London and New York: Routledge, 1999).

Butler, Mark, 'Taking It Seriously: Intertextuality and Authenticity in Two Covers by The Pet Shop Boys'. *Popular Music* 22/1 (2003), pp. 1–19.

Campbell, Laura, 'Joni Chic', *Sunday Telegraph* (London, 8 February 1998), available at: jonimitchell.com/library/print.cfm?id=367 (accessed 20 September 2015).

Cantwell, Robert, 'Smith's Memory Theatre: The Folkways Anthology of American Folk Music', *New England Review (1990–)* 13 (1991), pp. 364–97.

——— *When We Were Good: The Folk Revival* (Cambridge, MA: Harvard University Press, 1996).

——— *Bluegrass Breakdown: The Making of the Old Southern Sound* (Urbana and Chicago: University of Illinois Press, 2003).

Cardwell , Nancy, *The Words and Music of Dolly Parton: Getting to Know Country Music's 'Iron Butterfly'* (Santa Barbara: Praeger, 2011).

Carmichael, Emma, 'Kanye's 808s: How A Machine Brought Heartbreak to Hip Hop', *The Awl* (21 September 2011), available at: www.theawl.com/2011/09/kanye's-808s-how-a-machine-brought-heartbreak-to-hip-hop (accessed 27 February 2015).

Carroll, Hamilton. *Affirmative Reaction: New Formations of White Masculinity* (Durham & London: Duke University Press, 2011).

Carter, Claire, 'James Blunt Exposes Twitter Trolls', *The Telegraph* (26 October 2013). Available at: www.telegraph.co.uk/culture/music/music-news/10406405/James-Blunt-exposes-Twitter-trolls.html (accessed 17 August 2014).

Cashmore, Pete, 'James Arthur: Anatomy of a Twitter Disaster', *The Guardian* (18 November 2013). Available at: www.theguardian.com/music/musicblog/2013/nov/18/james-arthur-anatomy-twitter-disaster (accessed 17 August 2014).

Childerhose, Buffy, *From Lilith to Lilith Fair: The Authorized Story* (New York: St. Martin's Press, 1998).

Chin, Bertha, 'The Veronica Mars Movie: Crowdfunding – Or Fan-Funding – at Its Best?', *On/Off Screen* (13 March 2013), available at: onoffscreen.wordpress.com/2013/03/13/the-veronica-mars-movie-crowdfunding-or-fan-funding-at-its-best/. (accessed 25 February 2015).

Chonin, Neva, 'Lilith Fair', *Rolling Stone* (6 August 1998), p. 34.

Citron, Stephen, *Songwriting: A Complete Guide to the Craft (Revised and Updated Edition)* (New York: Limelight Editions, 2008).

Clawson, Mary Ann, 'When Women Play the Bass: Instrument Specialization and Gender Interpretation in Alternative Rock Music', *Gender and Society* 13/2 (April 1999), pp. 193–210.

Clifford, James, *Routes: Travel and Translation in the Late Twentieth Century* (Cambridge, MA: Harvard University Press, 1997).

Coates, Norma, 'Teenyboppers, Groupies, and Other Grotesques: Girls and Women and Rock Culture in the 1960s and early 1970s', *Journal of Popular Music Studies* 15/1 (2003), pp. 65–94.

Cohen, Ronald D. (ed.), *Rainbow Quest: The Folk Music Revival and American Society, 1940–1970* (Amherst, MA: University of Massachusetts Press, 2002).

Cohen, Ronald D. *Alan Lomax. Selected Writings 1934–1997* (New York: Routledge, 2003), p. 198.

Coleman, Vernon, 'Kanye West Says MBDTF was "Perfect", Yeezus is Advancing the Culture', *XXL.com* (3 September 2013). Available at: www.xxlmag.com/news/2013/09/kanye-west-says-mbdtf-perfect-yeezus-advancing-culture/ (accessed 27 February 2015).

Collinson Scott, Jo, 'Becoming Other: Only Skinlessness', in Brad Buchanan (ed.), *Visions of Joanna Newsom* (Sacramento: Roan Press, 2010), pp. 75–94.

Conti, Jacopo, 'You Can Call Them, If You Like, Emotions. The (Un)Orthodox Songs of Lucio Battisti', in Franco Fabbri and Goffredo Plastino (eds.), *Made in Italy: Studies in Popular Music* (New York and London: Routledge, 2014), pp. 110–22.

Cope, Danny, *Righting Wrongs in Writing Songs* (Boston, MA: Couse Technology, 2009).

Courrier, Kevin, *Randy Newman's American Dreams.* (Toronto: ECW Press, 2005).

Cowan, Jane K., 'Politics, Identity and Popular Music in Contemporary Greece', *Κάμπος: Cambridge Papers in Modern Greek*, 1 (1993), pp. 1–22.

Cragg, Gulliver, 'Ridiculous, Then Sublime', Review of Joanna Newsom, ICA, London. The Independent (9 November 2004). Available at: www.independent.co.uk/arts-entertainment/music/reviews/joanna-newsom-ica-london-19329.html (accessed 27 February 2015).

Crawford, Kate, 'These Foolish Things: On Intimacy and Insignificance in Mobile Media', in Gerard Goggin and Larissa Hjorth (eds.), *Mobile Technologies: From Telecommunications to Media* (New York:Routledge, 2009), pp. 252–65.

Crouse, Timothy. 'The First Family of the New Rock', *Rolling Stone* (18 February 1971), pp. 34–7.

——— 'Review of Blue', *Rolling Stone* (5 August 1971), 42.

Crowe, Cameron. 'A Child's Garden of Jackson Browne', *Rolling Stone* (23 May 1974), pp. 39–44.

——— 'Joni Mitchell', in Peter Herbst (ed.), *The Rolling Stone Interviews, 1967–1980: Talking with the Legends of Rock & Roll.* (New York: St. Martin's, 1981), pp. 376–91.

Csikszentmihalyi, Mihalyi, 'Society, Culture and Person: ASystems View of Creativity', in Robert J. Sternberg (ed.), *The Nature of Creativity: Contemporary Psychological Perspectives* (Cambridge: Cambridge University Press, 1988), pp. 325–39.

——— *Creativity, Flow and the Psychology of Discovery and Invention* (New York: Harper Collins, 1996).

Cullen, Brian, 'Exploring Second Language Creativity: Understanding and helping L2 Songwriters', unpublished PhD thesis, Leeds Metropolitan University (2009).

Cushing, Steve, *Pioneers of Blues Revival* (Champaign, IL: University of Illinois Press, 2014).

Cusic, Don. 'In Defense of Cover Songs'. *Popular Music and Society* 28/2 (2005), pp. 171–7.

Dann, Trevor, *Darker Than the Deepest Sea: The Search for Nick Drake* (Cambridge, MA: Da Capo Press, 2006).

Davis, Angela Y., *Blues Legacies and Black Feminism* (New York: Vintage Books, 1998), p. 67.

Davis, Eric, 'Nearer the Heart of Things', *Arthur Magazine*, 25 (Winter 2006). Available at: arthurmag.com/2006/12/23/nearer-the-heart-of-things-erik-davis-on-joanna-newsom-from-arthur-no-25winter-02006/ (accessed 27 February 2015).

Davis, Sheila, *The Craft of Lyric Writing* (New York/London/Sydney: Omnibus Press, 1985).

de Laat, Kim. '"Write a Word, Get a Third": Managing Conflict and Rewards in Professional Songwriting Teams', *Work and Occupations*, 42/2 (2015), pp. 225–56.

Deleuze, Gilles, and Felix Guattari, *What Is Philosophy?* (New York: Columbia University Press, 1994).

——— *A Thousand Plateaus: Capitalism and Schizophrenia* (London: Continuum, 2004).

Denney, Alex, 'Interview: Steve Albini', *The Stool Pigeon* (6 February 2013). Formerly available at: www.thestoolpigeon.co.uk/features/interview-steve-albini.html (accessed 17 August 2014).

DeVries, Peter, 'The Rise and Fall of a Songwriting Partnership', *The Qualitative Report*, 10/1 (2005) pp. 39–54.

Dibben, Nicola, 'Subjectivity and the Construction of Emotion in the Music of Björk', *Music Analysis* 25 (2007), pp. 171–97.

Diederichsen, Diedrich, 'Raus aus dem Kuscheluniversum', *Taz.de* (2007). Translated by Maximilian Georg Spiegel in, 'Gender Construction', MPhil thesis, 2012.

Dolan, Emily I. '"… This Little Ukulele Tells the Truth": Indie Pop and Kitsch Authenticity'. *Popular Music* 29/3 (2010): 457–69.

Douglas, Ann, *Terrible Honesty: Mongrel Manhattan in the 1920s* (New York: FSG, 1995).

Douglas, Susan J., *Where the Girls Are: Growing up Female with the Mass Media* (New York: Times, 1994).

Doyle, Tom, 'Tori Amos: Ready, Steady, Kook!', *Q Magazine* (12 April 1998), pp. 80–8. Available at: thedent.com/q0598.html (accessed 29 May 2014).

Driver, Susan. *Queer Girls and Popular Culture: Reading, Resisting, and Creating Media* (New York: Peter Lang, 2007).

Dukoff, Lauren, *Family* (San Francisco: Chronicle Books, 2009).

Dunlap, David W., 'Half Empty but Full of History, Brill Building Seeks Tenants', The New York Times (24 July 2013). Available at: www.nytimes.com/2013/07/25/nyregion/half-empty-but-full-of-history-brill-building-seeks-tenants.html (accessed 24 February 2015).

Dürr, Walther, *Das deutsche Sololied im 19. Jahrhundert: Untersuchungen zur Sprache und Musik* (Wilhelmshaven: Heinrichshofen, 1984).

Dyer, Richard, 'Heavenly Bodies' in Sean Redmond and Su Holmes (eds.), *Stardom and Celebrity: A Reader* (London: Sage 2007), pp. 85–9.

Eccleston, Danny, 'Pet Shop Boys' Neil Tennant Slates Social Media', Mojo (3 July 2013), available at: www.mojo4music.com/642/pet-shop-boys-neil-tennant-slates-social-media/ (accessed 17 August 2014).

Eco, Umberto, 'Prefazione', in Michele L. Straniero, Sergio Liberovici, Emilio Jona, and Giorgio De Maria (eds.), *Le canzoni della cattiva coscienza* (Milan: Bompiani, 1964), pp. 5–28.

Elton John website. Available at: www.eltonjohn.com/about/biography (accessed 24 February 2015).

Emerson, Ken, *Always Magic in the Air: The Bomp and Brilliance of the Brill Building Era* (London: Fourth Estate, 2006).

Encarnacao, John, *Punk Aesthetics and New Folk: Way Down the Old Plank Road* (Burlington: Ashgate, 2013).

Etzkorn, Peter, 'Social Context of Songwriting in the United States', *Ethnomusicology*, 7/2 (1963), pp. 96–106.

——— 'The Relationship Between Musical and Social Patterns in American Popular Music', *Journal of Research in Music Education*, 12/4 (1964), pp. 279–86.

——— 'On Esthetic Standards and Reference Groups of Popular Songwriters', *Sociological Enquiry*, 36/1 (1966), pp. 39–47.

Evans, David, 'Blues: Chronological Overview', in Melonee V. Burnim and Portia K. Maultsby (eds.), *African American Music: An Introduction* (New York: Routledge, 2006), pp. 79–96.

Evans, Liz, *Women, Sex and Rock 'n Roll in Their Own Words* (London: Pandora, 1994).

Everett, Walter, 'The Learned vs. The Vernacular in the Songs of Billy Joel', *Contemporary Music Review* 18/4 (2000), pp. 105–29.

Fabbri, Franco, *Around the Clock. Una breve storia della popular music* (Turin: UTET Libreria, 2008).

Fabbri, Franco 'How Genres Are Born, Change, Die: Conventions, Communities and Diachronic Processes', in Stan Hawkins (ed.), *Critical Musicological Reflections* (Aldershot: Ashgate, 2012), pp. 179–91.

——— 'Il Trentennio: "musica leggera" alla radio italiana, 1928–1958', in Angela Ida De Benedictis (ed.), *La musica alla radio: 1924–1954. Storia, effetti, contesti in prospettiva europea* (Rome: Bulzoni Editore, 2014), pp. 225–43.

Fabbri, Franco and Plastino, Goffredo (eds.), *Made in Italy: Studies in Popular Music* (New York and London: Routledge, 2014).

Fagen, Donald, *Eminent Hipsters* (New York: Viking, 2013).

Feigenbaum, Anna, '"Some Guy Designed this Room I'm Standing In": Marking Gender in Press Coverage of Ani DiFranco', *Popular Music* 25/1 (January 2005), pp. 37–56.

Fennessey, Sean, 'Pride (In the Name of Love)'. *Vibe Magazine* 17/2 (February 2009), p. 80.

Fenton, Natalie, 'Bridging the Mythical Divide: Political Economy and Cultural Studies Approaches to the Analysis of the Media', in Eoin Devereux (ed.), *Media Studies: Key Issues and Debates* (London: Sage, 2007), pp. 7–31.

Fitzgerald, Jon, 'When the Brill Building Met Lennon-McCartney: Continuity and Change in the Early Evolution of the Mainstream Pop Song', *Popular Music & Society* 19/1 (1995), pp. 59–77.

Flanagan, Bill, *Written in My Soul: Rock's Great Songwriters Talk About Creating Their Music* (Chicago, Contemporary Books, 1986).

Foster, Mo, *Play Like Elvis: How British Musicians Bought the American Dream* (London: Sanctuary 1997).

Fox, Aaron A., *Real Country: Music and Language in Working-Class Culture* (Durham: Duke University Press, 2004).

Frith, Simon, and Simon Zagorski-Thomas (eds.), *The Art of Record Production: An Introductory Reader for a New Academic Field* (Aldershot: Ashgate, 2012).

Gamman, Lorraine, and Margaret Marshement (eds.), *The Female Gaze: Women as Viewers of Popular Culture* (London: The Women's Press Limited, 1988).

Garbarini, Vic, 'Joni Mitchell Is A Nervy Broad'. *Musician* (January 1983), pp. 42–52.

George, Nelson, *Hip Hop America* (New York: Penguin Publishing, 1998).

Gilbert, Jeremy, 'More Than a Woman: Becoming-Woman on the Disco Floor', in Rosa Reitsamer and Rupert Weinzierl (eds.), *Female Consequences: Feminismus, Antirassimus, Popmusik* (Wien: Löcker, 2006), pp. 181–93.

Gill, John. *Queer Noises: Male and Female Homosexuality in 20th Century Music* (Minnesota: Minnesota University Press, 1995).

Golding, Peter, and Graham Murdock (eds.), *The Political Economy of the Media* (Cheltenham: Edward Elgar Publishing, 1997).

Goldman, Andrew, 'Billy Joel on Not Working and Not Giving Up Drinking.' *The New York Times* (24 May 2013). Available at www.nytimes.com/2013/05/26/magazine/billy-joel-on-not-working-and-not-giving-up-drinking.html (accessed 24 February 2015).

Goldsmith, Thomas (ed.), *The Bluegrass Reader* (Urbana and Chicago: University of Illinois Press, 2004).

Gorrell, Lorraine. *The Nineteenth-Century German Lied* (Portland: Amadeus Press, 1993).

Gottlieb, Joanne and Gayle Wald, 'Smells Like Teen Spirit: Riot Grrrls, Revolution and Women in Independent Rock', in Andrew Ross and Tricia Rose (eds.), *Microphone Fiends: Youth Music and Youth Culture* (New York: Routledge, 1994), pp. 250–74.

Govenar, Alan, *Texas Blues. The Rise of a Contemporary Sound* (College Station: Texas A&M University Press, 2008).

Gracyk, Theodore, *I Wanna Be Me: Rock Music and the Politics of Identity* (Philadelphia: Temple University Press, 2001).

Grasso, Linda M., '"You Are No Stranger to Me": Georgia O'Keeffe's Fan Mail', *Reception: Texts, Readers, Audienceses, History*, 5 (2013), pp. 24–40.

Gray, Jonathan, 'New Audiences, New Textualities: Anti-fans and Non-fans', *International Journal of Cultural Studies*, 6/1 (2003), pp. 64–81.

——— 'Antifandom and the Moral Text: Television Without Pity and Textual Dislike', *American Behavioral Scientist*, 48 (2005), pp. 840–58.

Grazian, David, 'The Production of Popular Music as a Confidence Game: The Case of the Chicago Blues', *Qualitative Sociology* 27 (2) (2004), pp. 137–158.

Green, Lucy, *Music on Deaf Ears: Musical Meaning, Ideology and Education* (Manchester: Manchester University Press, 1988).

——— *Gender, Music and Education* (Cambridge: Cambridge University Press, 1997).

——— *How Popular Musicians Learn* (Aldershot, Ashgate: 2001).

Grenfell, Michael and David James, *Bourdieu and Education* (London: Taylor and Francis, 1998).

Grier, Miles Park, 'The Only Black Man at the Party: Joni Mitchell Enters the Rock Canon'. *Genders* 56 (2012), pp. 1–44, available at: www.genders.org/g56/g56_grier.html (accessed 15 November 2012).

Halberstadt, Alex, *Lonely Avenue: The Unlikely Life and Times of Doc Pomus* (London: Jonathan Cape, 2007).

Halberstam, Judith, *Female Masculinity* (Durham: Duke University Press, 1998).

Hallmark, Rufus (ed.), *German Lieder in the Nineteenth Century*, 2nd edn (New York & London: Routledge, 2010).

Harker, Ben, *Class Act: the Cultural and Political Life of Ewan MacColl* (London: Pluto, 2007).

Harper, Colin, *Dazzling Stranger: Bert Jansch and the British Folk and Blues Revival* (London: Bloomsbury, 2000).

Harris, Charles K., *How to Write a Popular Song* (New York: Charles K. Harris, 1906.)

Hatten, Robert S., *Interpreting Musical Gestures, Topics, and Tropes: Mozart, Beethoven, Schubert* (Bloomington: Indiana University Press, 2004).

Hawkins, Stan, *Settling the Pop Score: Pop Texts and Identity Politics* (Aldershot: Ashgate, 2002).

——— *The British Pop Dandy: Masculinity, Popular Music and Culture* (Farnham, Surrey: Ashgate: 2009).

Hayes, Eileen M., *Songs in Black and Lavender: Race, Sexual Politics, and Women's Music* (Champaign: University of Illinois Press, 2010).

Heckman, Dan, 'Pop: Jim Morrison at the End; Joni Mitchell at a Crossroads', Review of Blue, by Joni Mitchell, *New York Times* (8 August 1971), p. D15.

Henderson, Stuart, '"All Pink and Clean and Full of Wonder?" Gendering "Joni Mitchell", 1966–1974', *New Left History* 10 (2) (2005), 83–109.

Hesmondhalgh, David and Sarah Baker, *Creative Labour: Media Work in Three Cultural Industries* (Basingstoke: Routledge, 2013).

Hirshey, Gerri, 'Women Who Rocked the World', *Rolling Stone* (13 November 1997): 64–80.

Hisama, Ellie, 'Voice, Race, and Sexuality in the music of Joan Armatrading', in Elaine Barkin and Lydia Hamessley (eds.), *Audible Traces: Gender, Identity, and Music* (Zurich: Carciofoli Verlagshaus, 1999), pp. 115–32.

Hodgkinson, Will, *The Ballad of Britain* (London: Portico, 2009).

Holden, Stephen. 'Tom Rush Does It Himself', *Rolling Stone* (2 October 1980), p. 22.

——— 'The Evolution of the Singer-Songwriter', in James Henke, Anthony DeCurtis, and Holly George-Warren (eds.), *The Rolling Stone Illustrated History of Rock & Roll* (New York: Random House, 1992), pp. 480–91.

——— 'The Ambivalent Hall of Famer', *New York Times* (1 December 1996), p. 36.

Holst-Warhaft, Gail, *Theodorakis: Myth and Politics in Modern Greek Music* (Amsterdam: Hakkert, 1980).

——— 'Politics and Popular Music in Modern Greece'. *Journal of Political and Military Sociology*, 30: 2 (2002), pp. 292–323.

hooks, bell, 'Selling Hot Pussy: Representations of Black Female Sexuality in the Cultural Marketplace', in Katie Conboy, Nadia Medina, and Sarah Stanbury (eds.), *Writing on the Body: Female Embodiment and Feminist Theory* (New York: Columbia University Press, 1997), pp. 113–28.

Hope, Clover, 'The 100 Problems of Kanye West', *The Village Voice* 54/4 (12–27 January 2009), p. 72.

Hoskyns, Barney, *Hotel California: The True-Life Adventures of Crosby, Stills, Nash, Young, Mitchell, Taylor, Browne, Ronstadt, Geffen, The Eagles, and Their Many Friends* (Hoboken, NJ: John Wiley & Sons, 2006).

Howe, Irving, 'The Plath Celebration: A Partial Dissent', In *The Critical Point: On Literature and Culture* (New York: Dell, 1973, pp. 158–69).

Hubbs, Nadine. *Rednecks, Queers, and Country Music* (Berkeley, CA: University of California Press, 2014).

Hunter, Tea, *To Joy My Freedom: Southern Black Women's Lives and Labors After the Civil War* (Cambridge, MA: Harvard University Press, 1997).

Hyland. William G, *The Song is Ended: Songwritersand American Music, 1900–1950*. (New York: Oxford University Press, 1995).

Inglis, Ian, '"Some Kind of Wonderful": The Creative Legacy of the Brill Building', *American Music* 21/2 (2003): pp. 214–35.

Inness, Sherrie A., *Disco Divas: Women and Popular Culture in the 1970s* (London: Routledge, 2003).

Isherwood, Martin, *Sounding Out Songwriting* (York: Higher Education AcademyReport, January 2014).

Jackson, Jerma A., *Singing in My Soul: Black Gospel Music in a Secular Age* (Chapel Hill: University of North Carolina Press, 2004).

Jacobs, Jay S. *Pretty Good Years: A Biography of Tori Amos* (Hal Leonard, 2006).

Jacobson, Marion, *Squeeze This!: A Cultural History of the Accordion in America* (Urbana, IL: University of Illinois Press, 2012).

Jahr, Cliff, 'Elton John: It's Lonely at the Top', *Rolling Stone*, 223 (1976), pp. 11, 16–17.

Jarman, Freya (ed.), *Oh Boy!: Masculinities and Popular Music Culture* (New York/London: Routledge, 2007).

Jasen, David, *Tin Pan Alley* (New York: Donald Fine, 1988).

Joel, Billy, Interview with Tom Hoving, *20/20*. ABC-TV. 1 May 1980, available at www.youtube.com/watch?v=i-gUgyf1-3w (accessed 24 February 2015).

Johnson-Grau, Brenda, 'Sweet Nothings: Presentation of Women Musicians in Pop Journalism', in Steve Jones (ed.), *Pop Music and the Press* (Philadelphia: Temple University Press, 2002), pp. 202–18.

Johnson, Corey W., '"Don't Call Him a Cowboy": Masculinity, Cowboy Drag, and a Costume Change', *Journal of Leisure Research*, 40/3 (2008), pp. 385–403.

Johnson, Henry, (ed.) *Many Voices: Music and National Identity in Aotearoa/New Zealand* (Newcastle: Cambridge Scholars Publishing, 2010).

Johnson, Kevin C., 'Healing Through Song: Singing About a Painful Experience Gives Tori Amos Strength', *Akron Beacon Journal* (12 September 1996). Available at: www.yessaid.com/interviews/96-09-12AkronBeaconJournal.html (accessed 13 May 2014).

Jones, Leroi Amiri Baraka, *Blues People. Negro Music in White America* (New York: Harper Perennial, 2002 [1963]).

Jones, A. Morgan, 'The Other Sides of Billy Joel: Six Case Studies Revealing the Sociologist, The Balladeer, and the Historian' (PhD dissertation, University of Western Ontario, 2011).

Kallimopoulou, Eleni, Paradosiaká: Music, *Meaning and Identity in Modern Greece* (London: Ashgate, 2009).

Keam, Glenda, and Tony Mitchell (eds.), *Home, Land and Sea: Situating Music in Aotearoa/New Zealand* (Auckland: Pearson, 2011).

Keenan, David, 'The Fire Down Below: Welcome to the New Weird America', *The Wire* 234 (2003), pp. 3–40.

Keenan, Elizabeth K., and Sarah Dougher, 'Riot Grrrl, Ladyfest, and Rock Camps for Girls', in Julia Downes (ed.), *Women Make Noise: Girl Bands from Motown to the Modern Twickenham* (UK: Supernova Books, 2012), pp. 259–91.

Keil, Charles, *Urban Blues* (Chicago: University of Chicago Press, 1991 [1966]).

Keil, Charles, and Angeliki V. Keil, *Polka Happiness* (Philadelphia: Temple University Press, 1992).

Kellman, Andy, 'My Beautiful Dark Twisted Fantasy Album Review', *AllMusic.com* (21 November 2010), available at: www.allmusic.com/album/my-beautiful-dark-twisted-fantasy-mw0002022752 (accessed 27 February 2015).

King, Carole, *A Natural Woman: A Memoir* (London: Virago, 2012).

Kirn, Peter, 'Data Moshing the Online Videos: My God, It's Full of Glitch', *Create Digital Motion* (18 February 2009). Formerly available at: createdigitalmotion. com/2009/02/data-moshing-the-online-videos-my-god-its-full-of-glitch/ (accessed 27 February 2015).

Klein, Michael, *Intertextuality in Western Art Music* (Bloomington: Indiana University Press, 2005).

Koestenbaum, Wayne, *The Queen's Throat: Opera, Homosexuality, and the Mystery of Desire* (London: Penguin Books, 1993).

Koestler, Arthur, *The Act of Creation* (London: Hutchinson and Co., 1964).

Koozin, Timothy, 'Guitar Voicing in Pop-Rock Music: A Performance-Based Analytical Approach', *Music Theory Online* 17/3 (2011). Available at: www .mtosmt.org/issues/mto.11.17.3/mto.11.17.3.koozin.html (accessed 27 February 2015).

Krims, Adam. *Rap Music and the Poetics of Identity* (New York: Cambridge University Press, 2001).

Kristeva, Julia, *La Révolution du Langage Poétique : L'avant-Garde à la Fin du XIXe Siècle, Lautréamont et Mallarmé* (Paris: Éditions du Seuil, 1974).

Kutulas, Judy, '"That's the Way I've Always Heard It Should Be": Baby Boomers, 1970s Singer-Songwriters, and Romantic Relationships', *Journal of American History* 97/3 (2010), pp. 682–702.

——— "You probably Think this Song is About You": 1970s Women's Music from Carole King to the Disco Divas', in Sherrie A. Inness(ed.), *Disco Divas: Women and Popular Culture in the 1970s* (Philadelphia: University of Pennsylvania Press, 2003), pp. 173–4.

Lake, Kirk, *There Will Be Rainbows: A Biography of Rufus Wainwright* (London: Orion Books, 2009).

LaMay, Thomasin and Robin Armstrong, 'The Navel, the Corporate, the Contradictory: Pop Sirens at the Twenty-first Century', in Linda Phyllis Austern and Irma Naroditskaya (eds.), *Music of the Sirens* (Bloomington: Indiana University Press, 2006), pp. 317–45.

Landau, Jon, Review of James Taylor. *Rolling Stone* (19 April 1969), p. 28.

Lankford, Ronald D., *Women Singer-Songwriters in Rock: A Populist Rebellion in the 1990s* (Plymouth: Scarecrow Press, 2010).

Larson, Steve, *Musical Forces: Motion, Metaphor, and Meaning in Music* (Bloomington: Indiana University Press, 2012).

Lawson, R. A., *Jim Crow's Counterculture. The Blues and Black Southerners 1890–1945* (Baton Rouge: Louisiana State University, 2013).

Leach, Elizabeth Eva, 'Vicars of "Wannabe": Authenticity and The Spice Girls'. *Popular Music* 20/2 (2001), pp. 143–67.

Leiber, Jerry, and Mike Stoller, *Hound Dog: The Leiber & Stoller Autobiography* (London: Omnibus Press, 2010).

Leibetseder, Doris, *Queer Tracks: Subversive Strategies in Rock and Pop Music* (Farnham: Ashgate, 2012).

Leonard, Marion, *Gender in the Music Industry: Rock, Discourse and Girl Power* (Aldershot: Ashgate Publishing, 2007).

Leydi, Roberto, 'Nuova canzone e rapporto città–campagna oggi', in Roberto Leydi (ed.), *Il folk music revival* (Palermo: Flaccovio, 1972), pp. 247–51.

Lidov, David, *Is Language a Music: Writings on Musical Form and Signification* (Bloomington: Indiana University Press, 2005).

Lipsitz, George, *Dangerous Crossroads: Popular Music, Postmodernism and the Poetics of Place* (New York: Verso, 1994).

Lister, Linda, 'Divafication: The Deification of Modern Female Pop Stars', *Popular Music & Society* 25/3–4 (2001), pp. 1–10.

Liszka, James Jakób, *The Semiotic of Myth: A Critical Study of the Symbol* (Bloomington: Indiana University Press, 1989).

Locke, Ralph P., *Musical Exoticism: Images and Reflections* (Cambridge: Cambridge University Press, 2009).

Lomax, Alan, 'Bluegrass Background: Folk Music with Overdrive', in Thomas Goldsmith (ed.), *The Bluegrass Reader* (Urbana and Chicago: University of Illinois Press, 2004), pp. 131–3.

Lott, Eric, *Love and Theft: Blackface Minstrelsy and the American Working Class* (New York: Oxford University Press, 1993).

Lowe, Zane. 'BBC Radio 1 Interview with Kanye West', *XXL* (23 September 2013). Available at: www.xxlmag.com/news/2013/09/kanye-west-says-mbdtf-perfect-yeezus-advancing-culture/ (accessed 27February 2015).

Lowell, Robert, *Life Studies* (New York: Farrar, Straus, 1959).

Luckett, Moya, 'Toxic: The Implosion of Britney Spears' Star Image', *The Velvet Light Trap* 65 (Spring 2010), pp. 39–41.

Luftig, Stacy (ed.), *The Joni Mitchell Companion: Four Decades of Commentary* (New York: Schirmer, 2000).

Lynskey, Dorian, 'Pet Shop Boys: Cab Drivers Ask Us if We've Retired', The Guardian (13 September 2012). Available at: www.theguardian.com/music/2012/sep/13/pet-shop-boys (accessed 17 August 2014).

Mahon, Maureen, *Right to Rock: The Black Rock Coalition and the Cultural Politics of Race* (North Carolina: Duke University Press, 2004).

Malone, Ailbhe, '17 Reasons You Should Be Following James Blunt On Twitter', Buzzfeed (28 October 2013), available at: www.buzzfeed.com/ailbhemalone/17-reasons-you-should-be-following-james-blunt-on-twitter (accessed 17 August 2014).

Manning, Kara, 'Lady Adele', *Jazziz* 25/6 (2008), p. 46.

Manuel, Peter, 'Composition, Authorship, and Ownership in Flamenco, Past and Present', *Ethnomusicology* 54/1 (2010), pp. 106–35.

Marcus, Greil, *Mystery Train: Images of America in Rock'n'Roll Music.* (New York: E.P. Dutton, 1975).

——— 'The Old, Weird America', in Various Artists, *Anthology of American Folk Music.* Smithsonian Folkways Recordings reissue, Sony SFW40090/A28750, 1997. Liner notes.

——— *Invisible Republic: Bob Dylan's Basement Tapes* (London: Picador, 1998).

Marom, Malka, *Joni Mitchell: In Her Own Words, Conversations with Malka Marom* (Toronto: ECW Press, 2014).

Marqusee, Mike, *Wicked Messenger: Bob Dylan and the 1960s* (New York: Seven Stories, 2005).

Marrington, Mark, 'Experiencing Musical Composition in the DAW: The Software Interface as Mediator of the Musical Idea', *Journal on the Art of Record Production* 5 (2011). Available at: www.academia.edu/6674629/Experiencing_Musical_Composition_In_The_DAW_The_Software_Interface_As_Mediator_Of_The_Musical_Idea (accessed 28 September 2015).

Marshall, P. David, *The Celebrity Culture Reader* (New York, London: Routledge, 2006).

———'The Promotion and Presentation of the Self: Celebrity as Marker of Presentational Media', *Celebrity Studies*, 1 (1) (2010), pp. 35–48.

Marwick, Alice and danah boyd, 'To See and Be Seen: Celebrity Practice on Twitter', *Convergence*, 17/2 (2011), pp. 139–58.

Maslin, Janet, 'Review of Merrimack County by Tom Rush', *Rolling Stone* (11 May 1972), p. 56.

Masters, Marc, 'Harp of Darkness', *The Wire*, 251 (2005), pp. 24–5

Mayer, Vicki, Miranda J. Banks, and John T. Caldwell (eds.), *Production Studies: Cultural Studies of Media Industries* (New York: Routledge, 2009).

McCarthy, Kate, 'Not Pretty Girls?: Sexuality, Spirituality, and Gender Construction in Women's Rock Music', *Journal of Popular Culture* 39/1 (2006), pp. 69–94.

McGlashan, Don, 'Afterword', in Glenda Keam and Tony Mitchell (eds.), *Home, Land and Sea: Situating Music in Aotearoa/New Zealand* (Auckland: Pearson, 2011), pp. 280–1.

McIntyre, Philip, 'The Domain of Songwriters: Towards Defining the Term "Song"', *Perfect Beat*, 5/3 (2001), pp. 100–11.

——— 'Paul McCartney and the Creation of "Yesterday": The Systems Model in Operation', *Popular Music*, 25/2 (2006), pp. 201–19.

——— 'Creativity and Cultural Production: A Study of Contemporary Western Popular Music Songwriting', *Creativity Research Journal*, 20/1 (2008), pp. 40–52.

McLeod, Kembrew, *Creative License: The Law and Culture of Digital Sampling* (Durham: Duke University Press, 2011).

Meltzer, Richard, 'Young Jackson Browne's Old Days', *Rolling Stone* (22 June 1972), pp. 14–16.

Middleton, Richard. *Studying Popular Music* (Buckingham: Open University Press, 1990).

Mitchell, Gillian, *The North American Folk Music Revival: Nation and Identity in the United States and Canada, 1945–1980* (Aldershot: Ashgate, 2007).

Mitchell, Tony, 'Aotearoa Songlines', *Perfect Beat* 8 (2007), pp. 68–75.

——— 'Sonic Psychogeography: A Poetics of Place in Popular Music in Aotearoa/New Zealand', *Perfect Beat* 10/2 (2009), pp. 145–75.

Moehn, Frederick, *Contemporary Carioca: Technologies of Mixing in a Brazilian Music Scene* (Durham: Duke University Press, 2012).

Monelle, Raymond, *The Sense of Music: Semiotic Essays* (Princeton, NJ: Princeton University Press, 2000).

Monk, Katherine, *Joni: The Creative Odyssey of Joni Mitchell* (Vancouver, Toronto, and Berkeley: Greystone Books, 2012).

Mooney, James, 'Frameworks and Affordances: Understanding the Tools of Music-making', *Journal of Music, Technology and Education* 3/2–3 (2010), pp. 141–54.

Moore, Allan F., 'The So-Called 'Flattened Seventh' in Rock'. *Popular Music* 14/2 (1995), pp. 185–201.

——— *Rock: The Primary Text*, 2nd edn (Aldershot: Ashgate, 2001).

——— 'Authenticity as Authentication', *Popular Music* 21/2 (2002): 209–23.

——— *The Cambridge Companion to Blues and Gospel Music* (Cambridge: Cambridge University Press, 2002).

——— 'Principles for Teaching and Assessing Songwriting in Higher Education', *Palatine Papers* (2004). Formerly available at www.lancs.ac.uk/palatine/reports/allanmoore.htm (accessed 7 August 2014).

——— 'The Track', in Amanda Bayley (ed.), *Recorded Music: Performance, Culture and Technology* (Cambridge: Cambridge University Press, 2010), pp. 252–67.

——— *Song Means: Analysing and Interpreting Recorded Popular Song* (Aldershot: Ashgate, 2012).

——— 'The Persona–Environment Relation in Recorded Song', *Music Theory Online* 11/4 (2005). Available at: mto.societymusictheory.org/issues/mto.05.11.4/toc.11.4.html (accessed 27 February 2015).

Moore, Allan and Giovanni Vacca (eds.), *The Legacies of Ewan MacColl* (Farnham, Surrey: Ashgate, 2014).

Morey, Justin and Phillip McIntyre, 'Working Out the Split': Creative Collaboration and the Assignation of Copyright Across Differing Musical Worlds', *Journal on the Art of Record Production* 5 (2011), available at arpjournal.com/ (accessed 24 June 2014).

Mosco, Vincent, *The Political Economy of Communication* (London: Sage, 1996).

——— *MTV News Feature*, 'Tori Amos Brings the Noise' (1999). Available at: www.angelfire.com/mi2/starchild/toriart10a.html (accessed 28 September 2015).

Mulvey, Laura, 'Visual Pleasure in Narrative Cinema', *Screen*, 16/3 (1975), pp. 6–18.

Muntean, Nick and Anne Helen Peterson, 'Celebrity Twitter: Strategies of Intrusion and Disclosure in the Age of Technoculture', *M/C Journal*, 12/5 (2009). Available at: journal.media-culture.org.au/index.php/mcjournal/article/viewArticle/194 (accessed 17 August 2014).

Nealon, Jeffrey T., 'Refraining, Becoming-Black: Repetition and Difference in Amiri Baraka's Blues People', *Sympoke* 61 (1998), pp. 83–95.

Negus, Keith, 'The Work of Cultural Intermediaries and the Enduring Distance Between Production and Consumption', *Cultural Studies* 16/4 (2002), pp. 501–15.

Newman, Meredith, 'Author discusses race, culture in relation to Joni Mitchell'. *The Daily Orange* (9 October 2011), available at: dailyorange.com/2011/10/author-discusses-race-culture-in-relation-to-joni-mitchell/ (accessed 1 May 2014).

Norman, Philip, 'The Rebirth of Elton John', *Rolling Stone* 626 (1992), pp. 43–9, 110.

O'Brien, Karen, *Joni Mitchell, Shadows and Light: The Definitive Biography* (London: Virgin Books, Ltd., 2002).

O'Brien, Lucy, *She-Bop: The Definitive History of Women in Rock, Pop and Soul* (London: Continuum, 2002).

Ollivier, Michèle. 'Snobs and Quétaines: Prestige and Boundaries in Popular Music in Quebec'. *Popular Music* 25/1 (2006), pp. 97–116.

Palmer, Amanda, 'Amanda Palmer: The new RECORD, ART BOOK, and TOUR', *Kickstarter* (2012). Available at: www.kickstarter.com/projects/amandapalmer/amanda-palmer-the-new-record-art-book-and-tour (accessed 17 August 2014).

Papanikolaou, Dimitris, *Singing Poets. Literature and Popular Music in France and Greece* (Oxford: Legenda, 2007).

Paphides, Peter, 'The Inner Life of Nick Drake', *The Observer* (24 April 2004).

Pareles, Jon, 'Songs for All Occasions, But Sparing Ground Zero'. The New York Times (14 June 2002), available at www.nytimes.com/2002/06/14/movies/pop-review-songs-for-all-occasions-but-sparing-ground-zero.html (accessed 24 February 2015).

Parsons, James (ed.), *The Cambridge Companion to the Lied* (Cambridge: Cambridge University Press, 2004).

Pavese, Errico, 'Saved Souls. Locating Style in Fabrizio De André's and Ivano Fossati's Record Production', in Franco Fabbri and Goffredo Plastino (eds.), *Made in Italy: Studies in Popular Music* (New York and London: Routledge, 2014), pp. 123–35.

Perricone, Jack, *Melody in Songwriting: Tools and Techniques for Writing Hit Songs* (Boston, MA: Berklee Press, 2000).

Perry, Imani, *Prophets of the Hood: Politics and Poetics in Hip Hop* (Durham: Duke University Press, 2004).

Pestelli, Carlo, 'An Escape from Escapism: The Short History of Cantacronache', in Franco Fabbri and Goffredo Plastino (eds.), *Made in Italy: Studies in Popular Music* (New York and London: Routledge, 2014), pp. 153–61.

Petrusich, Amanda, *Pink Moon* (New York: Continuum, 2007).

Podolsky, Rich, *Don Kirshner: The Man with the Golden Ear: How He Changed the Face of Rock and Roll* (Milwaukee: Hal Leonard Corporation, 2012).

——— *Neil Sedaka: Rock 'n' Roll Survivor: The Inside Story of His Incredible Comeback* (London: Jawbone Press, 2013).

Pollack, Bruce, 'Donald Fagen Interview'. *The Steely Dan Reader: Four Decades of News and Interviews* (7 November 2012). Available at: steelydanreader.com/2012/11/07/donald-fagen-interview/ (accessed 24 February 2015).

Postal, Matthew A., *The Brill Building (Designation Report)*, Landmarks Preservation Commission, List 427, LP-2387 (23 March 2010). Available at: www.nyc.gov/html/lpc/downloads/pdf/reports/brill.pdf (accessed 23 February 2015).

Potts, Liza, 'Amanda Palmer and the #LOFNOTC: How Online Fan Participation is Rewriting Music Labels', *Participations*, 9/2 (2012), pp. 360–82, available at: www.participations.org/Volume%209/Issue%202/20%20Potts.pdf (accessed 17 August 2014).

Powers, Ann, 'Fiona Apple: Trying Something New, Trying Something Mellow', *New York Times* (25 October 1997), p. B7.

Pullen, Christopher (ed.), *Queer Youth and Media Cultures* (New York: Palmgrave Macmillan, 2014).

Rachel, Daniel, *Isle of Noises: Conversations with Great British Songwriters* (London: Picador, 2013).

Rajchman, John, *The Deleuze Connections* (Athens: MIT Press, 2000).

Ratliff, Ben, 'Free Spirits in a Groove That's Folky and Tribal', *The New York Times* (5 February 2007). Available at: www.nytimes.com/2007/02/05/arts/music/05drea.html (accessed 27 February 2015).

Regev, Motti, 'Israeli Rock, or a Study in the Politics of "Local Authenticity"'. *Popular Music* 11/1 (1992), pp. 1–14.

——— 'Producing Artistic Value: The Case of Rock Music'. *The Sociological Quarterly* 35/1 (1994), pp. 85–102.

Reid, Vernon and Greg Tate, 'Steely Dan: Understood as the Redemption of the White Negro', in Greg Tate (ed.), *Nothing But the Burden* (New York: Broadway Books, 2003), pp. 110–15.

Reilly, Peter, Review of Blue, reprinted from Stereo Review, October 1971, in Stacy Luftig (ed.), *The Joni Mitchell Companion: Four Decades of Commentary* (New York: Schirmer, 2000), pp. 40–2.

Rettberg, Jill Walker, *Seeing Ourselves Through Technology: How We Use Selfies, Blogs and Wearable Devices to See and Shape Ourselves* (Basingstoke: Palgrave Macmillan, 2014).

Reynolds, Simon, *Retromania: Pop Culture's Addiction to its Own Past* (London: Faber and Faber, 2011).

——— *Energy Flash: A Journey Through Rave Music and Dance Culture* (Berkeley: Soft Skull Press, 2012)

Reynolds, Simon and Press, Joy. *The Sex Revolts: Gender, Rebellion and Rock 'n Roll.* (Cambridge, MA: Harvard University Press, 1995).

Rhiel, Mary and David Suchoff (eds.), *The Seductions of Biography* (New York: Routledge, 1996).

Richardson, Niall, Clarissa Smith, & Angela Werndly, *Studying Sexualities; Theories, Representations, Cultures* (Hampshire: Palgrave Macmillan, 2013)

Righi, Len, 'Billy Joel Revisits "Allentown"', *The Morning Call* (28 November 2007). Available at PopMatters, www.popmatters.com/article/billy-joel-revisits-allentown, on 15 May 2014).

Rodgers, Jeffrey Pepper (ed.), *Songwriting and the Guitar (Acoustic Guitar Guides)* (San Anselmo, CA: String Letter Publishing, 2000).

Rohlfing, Mary E., '"Don't say Nothin' Bad About My Baby": A Re-evaluation of Women's Roles in the Brill Building Era of Early Rock 'n' Roll', *Critical Studies in Media Communication* 13/2 (1996), pp. 93–114.

Rooksby, Rikky, *How to Write Songs on Guitar* (London: Balafon Books, 2000).

Rosand, Ellen, 'The Descending Tetrachord: An Emblem of Lament', *The Musical Quarterly* 65/3 (1979), pp. 346–59.

Rose, Tricia, *The Hip Hop Wars: What We Talk About When We Talk About Hip Hop – and Why It Matters* (New York: Basic Books, 2008).

Rosen, Jody, 'After a Hard Breakup, Kanye Writes His Own "Blood on the Tracks,"' *Rolling Stone* (11 December 2008), pp. 91–2.

Rosenberg, Neil V. and Charles K. Wolfe, *The Music of Bill Monroe* (Urbana and Chicago: University of Illinois Press, 2007).

Rosenthal, Elizabeth, *His Song: The Musical Journey of Elton John* (New York: Billboard Books, 2001).

Rosenthal, M. L., *The Modern Poets: A Critical Introduction* (New York: Oxford University Press, 1960).

Santoro, Marco, 'The Tenco Effect. Suicide, San Remo, and the Social Construction of the Canzone D'autore', *Journal of Modern Italian Studies*, 3 (2006), pp. 342–66.

Schechner, Richard, *Essays on Performance Theory 1970–1976* (New York City: Drama Book Specialists, 1977).

Scheurer, Timothy E., 'The Beatles, the Brill Building, and the Persistence of Tin Pan Alley in the Age of Rock', *Popular Music & Society* 20/4 (1996), pp. 89–102.

Schloss, Joseph G., *Making Beats: The Art of Sample-Based Hip-hop* (Middletown, CT: Wesleyan University Press, 2004).

Schmalfeldt, Janet, 'In Search of Dido', *The Journal of Musicology* 18/4 (2001), pp. 584–615.

Schultz, Robert D., 'Beethoven's Pop Legacy: Classical Structure in the Music of Billy Joel', in 'Three Analytical Essays in Twentieth-Century Music' (MA Thesis, University of Washington, 2005), pp. 26–54.

Schwartz, Tony, 'Billy the Kid', *Newsweek* (11 December 1978).

Scott, Richard, *Billy Joel: All About Soul* (New York: Vantage, 2000).

Selvin, Joel, *Here Comes the Night: The Dark Soul of Bert Berns and the Dirty Business of Rhythm and Blues* (Berkeley: Counterpoint Press, 2014).

Sheff, David and Victoria, 'Playboy Interview: Billy Joel', *Playboy* (May 1982), pp. 71–2.

Shuker, Roy, *Key Concepts in Popular Music* (New York: Routledge, 1998).

Shuker, Roy, and Michael Pickering, 'Kiwi Rock: Popular Music and Cultural Identity in New Zealand'. *Popular Music* 13/3 (1994), pp. 261–78.

Shumway, David R., *Rock Star: The Making of Cultural Icons from Elvis to Springsteen* (Baltimore: Johns Hopkins University Press, 2014).

Simonett, Helena, *The Accordion in the Americas: Klezmer, Polka, Zydeco, and More!* (Urbana, IL: University of Illinois Press, 2012).

Skinner, Katherine, '"Must Be Born Again": Resurrecting the Anthology of American Folk Music', *Popular Music* 25 (2006), pp. 57–75.

Smith, L. Mayne, 'An Introduction to Bluegrass', in Thomas Goldsmith (ed.), *The Bluegrass Reader* (Urbana and Chicago: University of Illinois Press, 2004), pp. 77–91.

Smith, Richard D., *Can't You Hear Me Callin': The Life of Bill Monroe, Father of Bluegrass* (Boston: Little, Brown and Company, 2000).

Solie, Ruth A., 'Introduction: On "Difference"'. *Musicology and Difference: Gender and Sexuality in Music Scholarship* (Berkeley: University of California Press, 1993).

Spiegel, Maximilian Georg, 'Gender Construction and American "Free Folk" Music(s)', MPhil thesis, University of Vienna (2012). Available at: othes.univie.ac.at/18384/1/2012-01-27_0348807.pdf.

Starr, Victoria, *k. d. lang: All You Get Is Me* (Toronto: Random House, 1994).

Sternberg, Robert J. (ed.), *The Nature of Creativity: Contemporary Psychological Perspectives* (Cambridge: Cambridge University Press, 1988).

Street, John, 'Invisible Republics and Secret Histories: A Politics of Music', *Cultural Values* 4 (2000), pp. 298–313.

Sullivan, Caroline, 'James Blunt on Twitter: how the most hated man in pop is fixing his image', *The Guardian* (29 October 2013). Available at: www.theguardian.com/music/shortcuts/2013/oct/29/james-blunt-twitter-most-hated-man-pop-fixing-image (accessed 17 August 2014).

Sullivan, Paul, *Remixology: Tracing the Dub Diaspora* (London: Reaktion Books, 2014).

Svec, Henry Adam, '"Who Don't Care If The Money's No Good?": Authenticity and
The Band'. *Popular Music and Society* 35/3 (2012), pp. 427–45.

Sweers, Britta, *Electric Folk: the Changing Face of English Traditional Music*
(Oxford: Oxford University Press, 2005).

Sweet, Brian. *Reelin' in the Years*, 3rd edn. (London: Ominbus, 2009).

Szwed, John, *Alan Lomax. The Man Who Recorded the World* (New York: Viking,
2010).

Taylor, Jodie, 'Lesbian Musicalities, Queer Strains and Celesbian Pop' in Sarah
Baker, Andy Bennet and Jodie Taylor (eds.), *Redefining Mainstream Popular
Music* (New York: Routledge, 2013), pp. 39–49.

Taylor, Timothy D., *Beyond Exoticism: Western Music and the World* (London:
Duke University Press, 2007).

Till, Rupert, *Pop Cult: Religion and Popular Music* (London: Continuum, 2010).

Toft, Robert, *Hits and Misses: Crafting Top 40 Singles, 1963–71* (London:
Continuum, 2011).

Tomatis, Jacopo, 'A Portrait of the Author as an Artist. Ideology, Authenticity,
and Stylization in the Canzone d'Autore', in Franco Fabbri and Goffredo
Plastino (eds.), *Made in Italy: Studies in Popular Music* (New York and London:
Routledge, 2014), pp. 87–99.

Toynbee, Jason, 'Musicians', in Simon Frith and Lee Marshall (eds.), *Music and
Copyright* (Edinburgh: Edinburgh University Press, 2004), pp. 123–38.

Tragaki, Dafni, '"Humanizing the Masses": Enlightened Intellectuals and the Music
of the People', in David Cooper and Kevin Dawe (eds.), *The Mediterranean in
Music: Critical Perspectives, Common Concerns, Cultural Differences* (Lanham,
MD: Scarecrow Press, 2005), pp. 49–76.

——— *Rebetiko Worlds* (Newcastle: Cambridge Scholars, 2007).

Trier-Bieniek, Adrienne, *Sing Us a Song, Piano Woman: Female Fans and the Music
of Tori Amos* (Lanham, MD: Scarecrow Press, 2013).

Tsioulakis, Ioannis, 'Jazz in Athens: Frustrated Cosmopolitans in a Music
Subculture', *Ethnomusicology Forum*, 20 (2) (2011), pp. 175–99.

Turner, Graeme, *Understanding Celebrity* (London: Sage, 2004).

Turino, Thomas, *Music as Social Life: the Politics of Participation* (Chicago: The
University of Chicago Press, 2008).

Tyrangiel, Josh, 'Why You Can't Ignore Kanye: More GQ than Gangsta, Kanye
West is Challenging the Way Rap Thinks About Race and Class – and Striking a
Chord with Fans of All Stripes', *TIME* 166/9 (29 August 2005), p. 54.

Väkevä, Lauri, 'Garage Band or Garage Band®? Remixing Musical Futures', *British
Journal of Music Education*, 27/1 (2010), pp. 59–70.

Varelopoulos, Dimitris, 'Producing Entechno: Amalgamation and Hybridization
in a Controversial Musical Style', in Dafni Tragaki (ed.), *Made in Greece: Studies
in Popular Music* (New York and London: Routledge, forthcoming).

Vargas, Elizabeth. 'Chase Away the Darkness', *20/20*, broadcast 15 February 1999.
Available at: www.youtube.com/watch?v=UXKK2JeC_tY (accessed 27 May 2014).

Veal, Michael Dub: *Soundscapes and Shattered Songs in Jamaican Reggae*
(Middletown: Wesleyan University Press, 2007).

Vega, Suzanne, Official Website, Frequently Asked Questions. Available at: www
.suzannevega.com/ (Accessed 23 September 2015).

Waksman, Steve, *This Ain't No Summer of Love: Conflict and Crossover in Heavy Metal and Punk* (Berkeley: University of California Press, 2009).

Wald, Gayle, 'Just a Girl? Rock Music, Feminism, and the Cultural Construction of Female Youth', *Signs*, 23/3 (Spring 1998), pp. 585–610.

Walker, Michael, *Laurel Canyon: The Inside Story of Rock and Roll's Legendary Neighborhood* (New York: Faber and Faber, 2006).

Warner, Jay, *American Singing Groups: A History from 1940s to Today* (New York: Hal Leonard, 1992).

Watson, Jada, 'The Dixie Chicks' "Lubbock or Leave it": Negotiating Identity and Place in Country Song', *Journal of the Society for American Music*, 8/1 (2014), pp. 49–75.

Webb, Jimmy, *Tunesmith* (New York: Hyperion, 1998).

Weisbard, Eric, 'Love, Lore, Celebrity, and Dead Babies: Dolly Parton's "Down from Dover"', in Sean Wilentz and Greil Marcus (eds.), *The Rose and the Briar: Death, Love and Liberty in the American Ballad* (New York: W.W. Norton & Company, 2004), pp. 287–304.

Weissman, Dick, *Which Side Are You On?: An Inside History of the Folk Music Revival in America* (New York: Continuum, 2005).

Weller, Sheila, *Girls Like Us: Carole King, Joni Mitchell, Carly Simon and the Journey of a Generation* (New York: Atria Books, 2008).

West, Andy, *Developing Pedagogical Tools for the Teaching of Songwriting at Postgraduate Level* (York: Higher Education Academy Report (2007). 78.158.56.101/archive/palatine/development-awards/297/index.html (accessed 7 August 2014).

West, Kanye, 'Singapore Press Conference' (3 November 2008). Available at: www.youtube.com/watch?v=VTNe5xcv3Y0&feature=player_embedded (accessed 27 February 2015).

——— 'New Zealand Press Conference' (1 December 2008) part 1, Available at: www.youtube.com/watch?v=fbzu8znDWoA (accessed 23 September 2015).

——— 'New Zealand Press Conference' (1 December 2008) part 2, Available at: www.youtube.com/watch?v=vtscn03scig (accessed 23 September 2015).

White, Timothy, 'A Portrait of the Artist', *Billboard* (9 December 1995), pp. 14–16.

Whiteley, Sheila (ed.), *Sexing the Groove: Popular Music and Gender* (London and New York: Routledge, 1997).

——— *Women and Popular Music: Sexuality, Identity and Subjectivity* (London and New York: Routledge, 2013 [2000]).

Whiteley, Sheila, Andy Bennett, and Stan Hawkins (eds.), *Music, Space and Place: Popular Music and Cultural Identity* (Aldershot: Ashgate, 2005).

Whiteley, Sheila, and Jennifer Rycenga (eds.), *Queering the Popular Pitch* (London and New York: Routledge, 2006).

Whitesell, Lloyd, *The Music of Joni Mitchell* (New York: Oxford University Press, 2008).

Wierzynski, Gregory, 'The Students: All Quiet on the Campus Front', *Time* (22 February 1971), 97/8, pp. 14–15.

Wilhardt, Mark, 'Available Rebels and Folk Authenticities: Michelle Shocked and Billy Bragg', in Iain Peddie (ed.), *The Resisting Muse: Popular Music and Social Protest* (Aldershot: Ashgate, 2006), pp. 30–48.

Williams, Justin and Wilson, Ross, 'Music and Crowdfunded Websites: Digital Patronage and Fan–Artist Interactivity', in Sheila Whiteley and Shara Rambarran (eds.), *The Oxford Handbook of Music and Virtuality*. (New York: Oxford University Press, forthcoming).

Williams, Katherine, 'Post-World War II Jazz in Britain: Venues and Values 1945–1970', *Jazz Research Journal*, 7/1 (2013), pp. 113–31.

——— *Rufus Wainwright* (London: Equinox, forthcoming).

Willis, Roy, 'New Shamanism', *Anthropology Today* 10/6 (1994), pp. 16–18.

Wilton, Tamsin, *Lesbian Studies; Setting an Agenda* (London & New York: Routledge, 1995).

Winsby, Meghan, 'Lady Sings The Blues: A Woman's Perspective on Authenticity', in Jesse R. Steinberg and Abrol Fairweather (eds.), *Blues-Philosophy for Everyone: Thinking Deep About Feeling Low* (Hoboken: Wiley-Blackwell, 2012), pp. 155–66.

Witt, Jennifer, 'Feminism Across Generations: The Importance of Youth Culture Lyrics and Performances', *MP: A Feminist Journal Online* 1/6 (2007). Available at academinist.org/wp-content/uploads/2010/07/witt.pdf (accessed 12 July 2014).

Wolfe, Charles and Lornell, Kip, *The Life and Legend of Leadbelly* (New York: Da Capo Press, 1992).

Wood, Jessica L., 'Pained Expression: Metaphors of Sickness and Signs of "Authenticity" in Kurt Cobain's Journals'. *Popular Music* 30/3 (2011), pp. 331–49.

Woods, Fred, *Folk Revival* (Poole, Dorset: Blandford, 1979).

Young, Rob, *Electric Eden: Unearthing Britain's Visionary Music* (London: Faber & Faber, 2010).

Zbikowski, Lawrence, *Conceptualizing Music: Cognitive Structure, Theory, and Analysis* (Oxford: Oxford University Press, 2002).

Zollo, Paul, *Songwriters on Songwriting* (New York: Da Capo Press, 1997).

Index

Cambridge Companions to Music

Topics

The Cambridge Companion to Ballet
Edited by Marion Kant

The Cambridge Companion to Blues and
Gospel Music
Edited by Allan Moore

The Cambridge Companion to Choral Music
Edited by André de Quadros

The Cambridge Companion to the Concerto
Edited by Simon P. Keefe

The Cambridge Companion to Conducting
Edited by José Antonio Bowen

The Cambridge Companion to Eighteenth-
Century Music
Edited by Anthony R. DelDonna and Pierpaolo
Polzonetti

The Cambridge Companion to Electronic
Music
Edited by Nick Collins and Julio D'Escriván

The Cambridge Companion to French Music
Edited by Simon Trezise

The Cambridge Companion to Grand Opera
Edited by David Charlton

The Cambridge Companion to Hip-Hop
Edited by Justin A. Williams

The Cambridge Companion to Jazz
Edited by Mervyn Cooke and David Horn

The Cambridge Companion to Jewish Music
Edited by Joshua S. Walden

The Cambridge Companion to the Lied
Edited by James Parsons

The Cambridge Companion to Medieval Music
Edited by Mark Everist

The Cambridge Companion to the Musical,
second edition
Edited by William Everett and Paul Laird

The Cambridge Companion to Opera Studies
Edited by Nicholas Till

The Cambridge Companion to the Orchestra
Edited by Colin Lawson

The Cambridge Companion to Pop and Rock
Edited by Simon Frith, Will Straw and John
Street

The Cambridge Companion to Recorded Music
Edited by Eric Clarke, Nicholas Cook, Daniel
Leech-Wilkinson and John Rink

The Cambridge Companion to the
Singer-Songwriter
Edited by Katherine Williams and Justin A.
Williams

The Cambridge Companion to the String
Quartet
Edited by Robin Stowell

The Cambridge Companion to Twentieth-
Century Opera
Edited by Mervyn Cooke

Composers

The Cambridge Companion to Bach
Edited by John Butt

The Cambridge Companion to Bartók
Edited by Amanda Bayley

The Cambridge Companion to The Beatles
Edited by Kenneth Womack

The Cambridge Companion to Beethoven
Edited by Glenn Stanley

The Cambridge Companion to Berg
Edited by Anthony Pople

The Cambridge Companion to Berlioz
Edited by Peter Bloom

The Cambridge Companion to Brahms
Edited by Michael Musgrave

The Cambridge Companion to Benjamin
Britten
Edited by Mervyn Cooke

The Cambridge Companion to Bruckner
Edited by John Williamson

The Cambridge Companion to John Cage
Edited by David Nicholls

The Cambridge Companion to Chopin
Edited by Jim Samson

The Cambridge Companion to Debussy
Edited by Simon Trezise

The Cambridge Companion to Elgar
Edited by Daniel M. Grimley and Julian
Rushton

The Cambridge Companion to Duke Ellington
Edited by Edward Green

The Cambridge Companion to Gilbert and
Sullivan
Edited by David Eden and Meinhard Saremba

The Cambridge Companion to Handel
Edited by Donald Burrows